WITHDRAWN

'A unique transnational take on the weaponisation of liberal values after the Paris attacks. *After Charlie Hebdo* takes Islamophobia apart and equips us for the fight back.'
Liz Fekete, Director, Institute of Race Relations

'An engaging contribution to our understanding of the 2015 attacks, examining the media framing of the event and the conflict of values it created in public debate.'
Romain Badouard, University of Cergy-Pontoise

'A bold, challenging and forthright collection that raises fundamental questions around issues of race and identity.'
Michael Cronin, Trinity College Dublin

'These essays offer stimulating perspectives on the violent paradoxes of French liberalism. For English speakers, they give valuable context to the political dynamics behind the Charlie episode.'
Nick Riemer, University of Sydney

'The attack on *Charlie Hebdo* has been a transformative event, one that presents particular challenges for freedom of speech. This insightful collection helps us to reflect on how we can develop an alternative narrative on violence, racism and freedom of expression.'
Donatella della Porta, Scuola Normale Superiore (Florence)

AFTER CHARLIE HEBDO

TERROR, RACISM AND FREE SPEECH

Edited by Gavan Titley, Des Freedman,
Gholam Khiabany and Aurélien Mondon

ZED

After Charlie Hebdo: Terror, Racism and Free Speech was first published in 2017 by Zed Books Ltd, The Foundry, 17 Oval Way, London SE11 5RR, UK.

www.zedbooks.net

Typeset in Plantin and Kievit by Swales & Willis Ltd, Exeter, Devon
Cover design by Andrew Brash

A catalogue record for this book is available from the British Library

ISBN 978-1-78360-939-0 hb
ISBN 978-1-78360-938-3 pb
ISBN 978-1-78360-940-6 pdf
ISBN 978-1-78360-941-3 epub
ISBN 978-1-78360-942-0 mobi

CONTENTS

PART III: MEDIA EVENTS AND MEDIA DYNAMICS

PART IV: THE POLITICS OF FREE SPEECH

PART V: RACISM AND ANTI-RACISM IN POST-RACIAL TIMES

ACKNOWLEDGEMENTS

The editors would like to thank Professor Bernard Mahon, the Research Development Office and the Department of Media Studies at Maynooth University for their support of the seminar from which this book was developed. Thanks also to Ken Barlow and all at Zed Books. This book is dedicated to our friend Sharam Alghasi.

INTRODUCTION

Becoming symbolic: from *Charlie Hebdo* to 'Charlie Hebdo'

Gavan Titley

Symbolic excess

It is rarely noted that a key dimension of 'symbolic violence' is the violence of being rendered symbolic. Speaking in advance of the publication of the 'Survivors' Issue', the first edition of *Charlie Hebdo* since the attacks of 7 January 2015, the cartoonist Renald Luzier – 'Luz' – remarked that: "This current symbolic weight is everything Charlie has always worked against: destroying symbols, knocking down taboos, setting fantasies straight." Freighted with projections and misunderstandings, the burden of symbolic weight compressed *Charlie Hebdo* into a singularity, one that could, inter alia, be made to stand for things that it was not. This *becoming symbolic* of *Charlie Hebdo* was a secondary tragedy, to be sure – a transnationally mediated, enfolding wave of emotion, reaction and dissent that began to take shape in the minutes and hours after Saïd and Chérif Kouachi crashed the newspaper's editorial meeting to enact a merciless exercise in *propagande par le fait*. But it was also an inevitable one, once the tragedy visited on the paper prompted its consecration as a symbol of innate Western values, as the spark for an authoritarian renewal of an idealised Republic, as the guarantee of a moral certitude no longer burdened by context and history, and as a licence for amplifying and extending the enthusiastic, multi-stranded anti-Muslim racism that has achieved a dangerous banality in the political rationalities and public cultures of 'the West'.

The attacks on *Charlie Hebdo* produced an event better understood as 'Charlie Hebdo': an intensive spectacle of identification and dis-identification, of ideological differentiation and moral antagonism, of political reaction and repression. A dense field of meaning-making and affect took shape around *Charlie Hebdo*, and positioned it as a mediating object for a knot of political tensions, competing imaginaries and interpretative conflicts that have been taking shape and gathering force in European public spheres for several decades. This field is the starting point for this book, as *After Charlie Hebdo* examines 'Charlie Hebdo', the political and communicative event. It explores the ways in which the attacks in Paris in 2015 acquired such accelerated and (unevenly) globalised symbolic weight, and examines their political and cultural generativity in France, and elsewhere, in terms of five key themes: the drive to use 'Charlie Hebdo' as a catalyst for renewing the French Republic, particularly through the remit of the nationalist state secularism of *laïcité*; the prolonged, shape-shifting 'war on terror' and the impact of securitarian and culturalist responses to attacks; the politics of freedom of expression in a context of abundant communication; the political generativity of accelerated and instantaneous networked media coverage; and the challenges for anti-racist thought and activism in the context of 'post-racial' politics.

What does it mean to approach the aftermath of the attacks on *Charlie Hebdo* as 'Charlie Hebdo', an event? The immediate aftermath was a moment of intense public emotion and anger in France, of mourning for the slaughter of well-known figures and ordinary workers, of solidarity expressed on the day of the attacks in spontaneous gatherings in places such as Place de la République – which became a 'living memorial' over the course of 2015, particularly after the 22 November attacks – and the charged spectacle of the enormous *marches républicaines* of 10 and 11 January. Condensed by the hashtag #JeSuisCharlie, and by the ubiquity of Joachim Roncin's sombre white-grey-black visualisation of the same message, 'Charlie Hebdo' rapidly came to encompass all of the attacks in the Île-de-France region between 7 and 9 January (nudging, from the start, those killed in the siege at the Hyper Cacher, and the policewoman Clarissa Jean-Philippe, murdered in Montrouge by Amedy Coulibaly, to the edges if not the margins of the story).

The aftermath was also a moment of relentless communicative output. The media industry quickly demonstrated material solidarity with *Charlie Hebdo*'s determination to keep publishing: the newspaper *Libération* hosted the survivors, the Guardian Media Group, among other supporters, donated £100,000, and individual and institutional subscriptions soared. Within the French public sphere it was taken as a transformative moment that prompted an immediate spike in writing about the 'state of the nation', with, as Amiraux and Fetiu note in their overview of the extraordinary explosion of writing about the attacks, 4.6 books a month being published between January 2015 and July 2016. It was an intensive media spectacle, commanding global headlines and in many contexts effectively blacking out all other news for days, as the live dynamic of the hunt for the Kouachi brothers and the visibility of the public response structured a 'real-time' media event of rolling coverage and constant reaction. As in large part an attack on media workers, it generated a particularly raw and invested response from journalists, and a debate as to how best to symbolically demonstrate solidarity with a publication whose political identity became an immediate focus of projection and contention.

In the wider networks of connective media, the demand, mediated by #JeSuisCharlie, to symbolically become Charlie was accepted, seized on, modified, questioned and resisted in torrents of statements, opinion pieces, blogs, cartoons, memes and social media threads. As it circulated transnationally, it took on varied significance in different national contexts; appropriated to established agendas and antagonisms, and filtered through latent debates and discursive formations. Yet it also created what Ingrid Volkmer has described as transnational 'public densities', bursts of 'connected discursive consciousness' that emerge from communicative actors "reproducing, delivering, accelerating and magnifying content within the chosen logics of subjective networks across a globalized scope" (2014: 3). Within this ever-expanding mass and mess of responses, narratives, explanations and predictions, particular lines of antagonism were quick to emerge. Citing the 'vigorous debate on issues' that the attacks precipitated among participants of different 'political positions and social backgrounds', a 'Charlie Archive' was established at Harvard University, aiming to gather not only the vast amount of comment produced, but also the ephemeral materials of sympathy and solidarity from a "peculiar moment in the early twenty-first century, when the word 'Charlie' all of a sudden took on a tragic significance, and became charged with conflicting emotions, opinions, and agendas".[1]

The question this book explores is how a 'peculiar moment' became a generative political event, one that fuelled predictable forms of repression and intensified existing modes of racialisation, while triggering unintended consequences across scales and contexts of action. In driving endless debates on seemingly fundamental questions, it cast a mesh of political antagonisms and interpretative frameworks into heightened relief by, as Markha Valenta argues, "enacting and channelling this fundamental question: what is to be our future?" This is a question haunted by the radically different visions of inclusion and belonging invoked by that plural pronoun, and also one that resonates far beyond the developments in France that provide it with such an acute focus. The contributors to this book approach the generativity of 'Charlie Hebdo' in a variety of ways, with some essays fully focused on France and others engaged in tracing comparative developments and transnational dynamics. Some offer detailed analyses of concrete developments while others respond to the thicket of normative and political questions thrown up by the attacks around the power of the state and the imagined futures of irreducibly multicultural societies, as well as their insistent indexing to the question of free speech. Before surveying their arguments, our approach to 'Charlie Hebdo' requires some discussion.

The 'event'

Unexpected and traumatic events enforce a temporality that is both seductive and unsettling for critical analysis. They are greeted as thresholds or ruptures, where the felt sense of the exceptional moment shapes understandings and demands interpretation. They can legitimate a suspension of the norm, creating spaces for struggle or reaction. At the same time, they instigate narratives of *before and after* that tend towards a refusal of historicity, and obscure continuities and structures. 'Charlie Hebdo' began to take shape in the immediate aftermath of the attacks in a foment of reaction as to why they happened, and what they must mean. Brian Klug writes of seeing a placard in a photograph of the Paris unity rally of 11 January with the message '*Je marche mais je suis conscient de la confusion et de l'hypocrisie de la situation*' ('I march but I am aware of the confusion and the hypocrisy of the situation'). While the question of hypocrisy informed much of the antagonism to the political staging of the marches, Klug is more interested in the question of confusion. Beyond the human suffering and cost of the murders, the question 'Fundamentally, what is the *Charlie Hebdo* affair about?' was everywhere being answered, and through a proliferating set of frames:

> Human rights? If so, *which* right: freedom of speech or the right to life? Or is it an expression of the ongoing international conflict between an American-led alliance and a certain kind of Islamic or Islamist

resistance in the Middle East, a conflict that has spilled over into the cities of Europe? Is the basic issue the use of violence to promote a political cause or religious idea? Or is it a perceived assault on the core identity of a minority? Are institutionalized social inequalities that run alongside ethno-religious lines in postcolonial France the crux of the matter? Or is it *laïcité*, the French version of separation of church and state, that is ultimately at stake? Nor are these the only possible ways of framing the issues raised by the Charlie Hebdo affair. To be sure, these different frames are not mutually exclusive. But in practice, when people focus on one frame they tend either to forget the others or to treat them as subordinate and incidental. (Klug 2016: 224)

This proliferation of frames is not surprising, as they encompass different dimensions of the attack, from possible explanations of its causes or motivations, to interpretations of its significance, to diagnoses of what responses it requires. But Klug's point is that these interpretative frames are politically located and mutually responsive; within the display of solidarity with *Charlie Hebdo*, 'Charlie Hebdo' was taking shape as a site of political investments, and as a conflict over what the attacks confirmed, constituted and demanded. Frames, in other words, are produced in response to the event but also constitutive of the event, or, as Ron Eyerman puts it, occurrences become events

[t]hrough a dialectic of actions and interpretation. Actions occur in time and space, events unfold and take shape. An event unfolds and takes shape in the interplay between protagonists, interpreters and audience, as sense and meaning is attributed and various interpretations compete with each other. As this meaning struggle proceeds various accounts stabilize, with perhaps one achieving some kind of hegemony, but counter interpretations or stories may continue to exist alongside. (Eyerman 2008: 22)

Events, as Annabelle Sreberny discusses, are not discrete moments, no matter how peculiar they may be. To artificially isolate a singular happening as an event is to ignore how the event is produced by the force of rival articulations working to establish their (preferred) historicity, and to establish the import of the event for future (re)actions. Each 'event', she argues, is in itself part of an immediate event chain and inducted to a "longer event chain, where historical narratives compete for explanation, motivation, rationalisation, justification" (p. 196). Thus, the frames Klug identifies are not frozen templates, but articulated to narratives of causality and significance. In the fraught aftermath of violent attacks, it is unsurprising that state actors will seek definitional power, to secure an *accepted version of events* designed to ground the inevitable reaction (which produces further events in the chain). The attack on a newspaper presented a particularly powerful political frame – an attack on freedom of expression, a foundational freedom embodied, the story goes, not only by *Charlie Hebdo*, but by the Republic itself, which was also deemed under attack. Yet, beyond this strategic response, this chain of identification clearly had wider resonance, for, as Didier Fassin has argued, the extent of the marches in Paris must be explained as "an affirmation of the importance of free speech and secularism for democracy", rather than a "strict allegiance to a magazine which was on the verge of insolvency, selling only 30,000 copies, and whose aggressiveness against all religions, with an obsession with Islam, they did not necessarily share" (2015: 4). And the sheer global diversity of locations in which solidarity rallies were held suggests that this was a broadly shared – and deeply contested – interpretation.

While a multiplicity of actors invested in a dominant narrative about free speech, it is this frame, Sadia Saeed argues, that was most successfully mobilised to enhance the disciplinary power of the state, particularly in France, but not only there, and not always in the same ways. That an event is hailed as being defined by a certain question does not mean that the question is being posed, never mind answered, in similar ways as it is integrated into the patterns of discourse and balance of forces within different polities. Saeed compares the punitive treatment of high school students in France who 'refused to be Charlie' with the reaction to the venerable Istanbul newspaper *Cumhuriyet* – 'The Republic' – including *Charlie Hebdo* images in a statement of solidarity on 14 January, which resulted in protests and ultimately a charge of 'provoking public sentiment'. That is, in one context it is 'Muslims' who are being disciplined by the *leitkultur* of the Republic, in the other, it is Republican secularists under fire; in Saaed's argument they structurally occupy the same position, as "disciplinary power is more readily exerted by a discourse when it claims the authority of tradition and enjoys the backing of the coercive and regulatory power of the state" (2015: 39). As she observes, "the globality of the *Charlie Hebdo* affair cannot escape the nationness of the spaces in which any stance, however global in orientation, is taken" (ibid.: 38; see for example, Gifford (2016) for a discussion of the affair's repercussions in Senegal).

The differentiation of 'Charlie Hebdo' from *Charlie Hebdo*, therefore, not only recognises the symbolic weight that came to freight the newspaper, but that much of what was invested in the event had little or nothing to do with *Charlie Hebdo*, or had anything meaningful to say about it. It is to examine how the 'global' spectacle the attacks prompted unfolded unevenly across time and space. 'Charlie Hebdo' provided a contingent space of political action, and therefore what is of interest is the different political dynamics in which it was integrated, the particular cultural politics it seemed to articulate, the contrasting scales at which it was deemed significant, the varying histories it seemed to confirm or be dislocated from, and the permissions for action it licensed.

The attack

The concept of a 'global war on terror', Grégoire Chamayou observes in *Drone Theory*, is an admission that "armed violence has lost its traditional limits: indefinite in time, it is also indefinite in space" (2015: 52). The attacks in Paris of January and November 2015 positioned France as a key site in an amorphous war that spills across territories and boundaries. In truth, France was already so positioned, involved in military intervention in the Middle East and Africa, allied to the Western military expansionism of the last fifteen years that created the conditions for the emergence of ISIS/Daesh. And, in keeping with what Stephen Graham terms the "new military urbanism" that connects spaces within "metropolitan cores and colonial peripheries" (2011), the state is fully invested in the militarised policing of 'the lost territories of the Republic', the *quartiers populaires* that circumscribe the centre of Paris and other cities. The result of the January and November attacks is the tightening of what Abdellali Hajjat, in his chapter, describes as a double bind situation, where "French people are murdered by takfiri fighters because they are supposedly complicit with the government's foreign policy, and, on the other hand, Islamophobic acts have dramatically increased since the January 2015 attacks and French Muslims are overtly targeted by law enforcement, mainstream politicians and far-right groups as the disloyal 'fifth column' of the Republic" (p. 79–80). (The widely circulated slogan after the November attacks, '*Leurs guerres, nos morts*' – 'Their wars, our dead' – sought to assert solidarity across this double bind.)

It is possible that it is precisely the tightening of this bind that the attack was designed to effect, combining the shock of calculated executions at coffee break in the heart of a global city with the symbolism of attacking a liberal-left paper, and one intimately associated with its cartoons of the Prophet Mohammed (and, internationally, not known for much else). The indefinite coordinates that Chamayou identifies ensure that killing in the name of democracy and killing in the name of Islam can be revitalised by ever-expanding ideological remits and spatial logics. As Benoit Challand argued in his response to the attacks, 'When the Far Enemy Becomes Near', the enemy for a 'new breed of jihadi extremists' can be a carrier not only of political or economic power, but also of the symbolic. And to target symbolic power is to transform it, in this instance, to channel it into a visceral, performative confirmation of the clash of civilisations. Tightening the bind and accelerating the contradictions, it is plausible to read the attacks as seeking to provoke an intensified reaction from those in France and Europe who view, through the overlapping aversions of a rich ideological kaleidoscope, Muslims *as in but not of Europe*, and, by inviting state repression and public suspicion upon them, "Muslims to act (violently) against a protean mythical enemy, one that can take many forms, be it the decadent moral order of the 'West' or even the vitriolic cartoons of Charlie Hebdo" (Challand 2015).

This is not to presume the motives for the attacks, but to interpret their form, to read their strategy back from the effects. However, as many contributions here point out, a more prevalent response has been to sublimate the political analysis of violence to a racial-religious-psychological nexus, to a motivation that can be read back from Islam, from an aversion to representations of the Prophet, from a blind desire for vengeance for blasphemy. In the *Charlie Hebdo* of 25 February 2015, for example, the first edition to discuss the attacks, several articles are given over to explaining the 'Muslim problem' with images of the Prophet. In an article entitled 'Jihadist and Muslim on the Sofa', the psychiatrist Gérard Bonnet explains in dialogue with Malek Chebel that a Muslim who objects to caricatures of the Prophet "remains in an infantile state that confuses the real and representation. It's like the primitive that believes that if one takes a photo of him, photography steals his soul. It's an enormous regression." This, as Anne Mulhall examines in her analysis of psychoanalytical responses to the attacks, is the Muslim as theological automaton, pre-modern and thus "'stuck'

in a more primitive stage of psychic and cultural development"
(p. 248). This presumptive interrogation of the 'Islamic disposition'
extends well beyond the domain of psychoanalysis to a public culture
that frequently depends on its terms to construct what David Theo
Goldberg describes as the 'Muslim image in contemporary Europe':
"overwhelmingly one of fanaticism, fundamentalism, female (women
and girls') suppression, subjugation and repression. The Muslim in
this view foments conflict ... He is a traditionalist, premodern, in the
tradition of racial historicism difficult if not impossible to modernize,
at least without ceasing to be 'the Muslim'" (2009: 165–6).

Goldberg's argument that the *idea* of the Muslim has "come to
represent the threat of death" may at first reading seem metaphorical,
but as Hajjat documents, it is literally this threat that 'Muslims' in
France were compelled to distance themselves from. A discourse of
the radicalised jihadist 'enemy within' (which forcefully pre-dates the
attacks, as Plenel makes clear (2016: 36–8)) provided the basis for calls
from politicians and 'intellectuals' for *désolidarisation*. This neologism
goes further than ritual Anglophone calls for 'moderate Muslims' to
distance themselves from 'extremists', because it presupposes a given,
determinist 'Muslim' solidarity that needs to be actively deconstructed.
It erases a hugely diverse population through a racialised imaginary of
the 'Muslim community', deprives French Muslims of their political
identity as French citizens, and ignores the active political engagement
of Muslim organisations against would-be warriors who have, as Hajjat
notes, consciously *désolidarised* themselves from their peers, families
and fellow worshippers:

> Every day, residents, activists and local politicians struggle almost
> unnoticed against the influences of these violent sub-groups without
> ever making front-page news. For example, the members of the Buttes
> de Chaumont Network, to which the Kouachi brothers belonged, were
> banned from pro-Palestine protests by immigration and antifascist
> activists in the early 2000s. The grand irony of the story is that the
> very people who used to fight on the ground against violent sub-
> groups are the same people who are now held responsible or complicit
> when they denounce Islamophobia. (p. 92)

The profile of the new wave of 'jihadi' attackers is of dispersed
and unevenly networked 'self-activated, entrepreneurial cells and
individuals', some with experience fighting in Syria and elsewhere,

often with petty criminal backgrounds, converts to Islam or late bloomers in their devotion or more than nonchalant about it, and often with hurried or tenuous links to Daesh or Al-Qaeda, even as they act, or have their acts claimed, in their name. As Arun Kundnani's analysis makes clear, the biographies of attackers, analysed after the facts of their actions, rarely map onto the modular understandings of 'extremism' and 'religious radicalisation' that have informed security operations and official narratives. For this reason, prominent scholars involved in the study of religious radicalisation have distanced themselves from the post-9/11 university/think tank/security apparatus 'radicalisation' industry, but, "because the power of the official narrative of extremism had not rested on the authority of scholarship, so developments in scholarship made little difference to the narrative's prominence" (p. 153).

Arguably, public debate on the causes and motivations of violence encoded as 'terrorism' is marked all too often by a clash of determinisms. There is certainly a form of left response to the elisions of (post)colonial amnesia that can only see such violence as, at some level, an expression of anti-imperialism, a reflex that grants no agency outside this relation, nor contingencies below the scale of the 'geopolitical'. In Valenta's argument, refusing the supposed centrality of the 'Islamic' identity of the attackers does not require pretending that they did not kill in the name of Islam, but rather understanding its status as a sign under which action is organised and history can be made, that is, as a characteristic of high modernity where "absolutist creedal political standpoints are not so much the mark of the religious, but of intensely politicised, polarised conflicts in which different sides are mobilised via arguments that their ways of life and existential futures are endangered" (p. 137).

Ultimately, an attempt to understand the attacks must return to the reconfiguration of geopolitical space intensified by the unintended consequences of the 'war on terror'. If postcolonial melancholia involves a mourning for, if not overtly the loss of territories, then a loss of prestige, it is also intertwined with an amnesia. As Nicholas De Genova argues, "France's desire to retreat into a sanitised narrative of national greatness, miraculously cleansed of the filth of its colonial legacy" is expressed through a withdrawal "into the narrow epistemic confines of its presumptive 'national' borders" (p. 98). Such amnesia is also a cultural conditionality of exploitative global relations and the imagined geographies of civilisation that see violence as an exception *here* and a (regrettable) norm *there*. The tensions of the extraordinary inequalities in power, wealth, resources and living conditions that characterise 'globalisation' are contained for the 'West' through "narratives, frameworks and sensibilities that obscure the extent and nature of global interdependence, naturalise global inequality, and regularly blame the world's poor for their poverty, wars and bad luck through culturalist explanations" (Valenta, p. 139).

The cacophony of liberal, conservative, integralist and supremacist nationalisms that are spliced together through articulating the *problem of migration* are united in extending this containment through the conceit that the global system, enfolded within the nation state through decades of postcolonial and globalised migration and settlement, can be undone, made over, or coerced into a sufficiently assimilationist replica of an imagined homogeneity or walled garden which was always, at best, a forgery. In this context, the *Charlie Hebdo* attack detonated a fragile web of fictions as to European exceptionalism, thus infusing the rally to an abstract freedom of speech with a forcefully recuperative affect. Its real symbolic potency, therefore, may lie in its gloating redistribution of the violence that permeates the global system, from its natural domains *there* to its baffling irruption *here*, through the claim of Al-Qaeda and Daesh to a parallel right to intervene violently anywhere in the world (the slaughter in the Bataclan, after all, was very different to the sudden evisceration of a suicide bomb attack; it marked a drastic amplification of the attack on *Charlie Hebdo*, with an organised armed group patiently and methodically slaughtering civilians over an extended period of time, as if they had taken a town in Syria). Valenta states:

> What has been disrupted instead has been the fundamental conceit that it is the West's right and might to make history; to write the geo-body; to judge the world's people and find them lacking; to go 'there' while restricting their right to come 'here'; to be wealthy and secure while they are doomed to poverty and precarity; to make use of the world – its resources, its labour, its hearts and minds – for our own ends but not to have them make use of us. (p. 142)

Within the double bind, therefore, a strange symmetry has emerged between state apparatuses "performing a largely symbolic politics of security with real repressive effects" and cellular, franchised and 'lone wolf' actors committing violence that performs a "largely symbolic politics of 'Islamic' identity with real violent effects" (p. 133).

The response

Events are not moments, but they can be hailed as such, and invested with transformative or reactionary possibility. Manuel Valls' declaration that "there will be a before and an after" positioned the attacks as a threshold of historical rupture. 'Le 11-Septembre Français', as *Le Monde*'s front page announced on 11 January, fixed the attacks in a particular genealogy of exceptional moments. Reflecting on the rapid adoption of the epithet '7/7' for the London bombings of 2005, Ben Pitcher noted how this immediate narrative identification with the New York and Washington attacks of 2001 made it "easy to neglect the social and historical specificity of either event, and to presuppose that both attacks were carried out by similar agents with common motives and objectives" (2009: 137). A similar drive was identified by Adam Shatz in the rush of some US intellectuals to declare 'Je Suis Charlie' and transmute its symbolism into a revitalising 'moral clarity' that

> [e]xpresses a peculiar nostalgia for 11 September, for the moment before the wars in Afghanistan and Iraq, before Abu Ghraib and extraordinary rendition, before all the things that did so much to tarnish America's image and to muddy the battle lines. In saying 'je suis Charlie', we can feel innocent again. Thanks to the massacre in Paris, we can forget the Senate torture report, and rally in defence of the West in good conscience. (Shatz 2015)

In Nicholas De Genova's analysis, this narrative insistence was not only hostile to inquiry, but also "served to institute a tragic rupture in time that severed the events from any prior history and ensnared the nation as unwitting witnesses in a spectacular present" (p. 99). For the state, the attacks produced an intensive symbolic effect that served to suture it explicitly to an event chain of previous atrocities. But in forging these connections, it also worked to refuse other histories and geopolitical relations, while simultaneously intensifying existing processes and creating a disjunctive space for exceptional action – nothing can be the same again, but everything that is done in the name of what went before is justified. If the question previously was 'Why do they hate our freedom?', the dominant answer now is because of *our values* – completely realised, polished and nestling in, to adapt

Karl Popper's phrase, a bucket theory of the nation state. As François Hollande declared immediately after the January attacks:

> The Republic equals freedom of expression; the Republic equals culture, creation, it equals pluralism and democracy. That is what the assassins were targeting. It equals the ideal of justice and peace that France promotes everywhere on the international stage, and the message of peace and tolerance that we defend – as do our soldiers – in the fight against terrorism and fundamentalism. (Hollande 2015)

Laurie Boussaguet and Florence Faucher's detailed research on official communication strategy after both sets of attacks demonstrates how there was a keen awareness that the government was involved in shaping the construction of the event, providing a 'Manichean and simple' message as to its meaning, and necessarily reflexive in the shifting mobilisation of symbols of national unity and identity to justify appropriate responses. The different targets in January were held to be symbolically charged in different ways, and in November, their significance was different still – an attack on a France that "loves life, culture, sport, partying, a France without distinction of colour, origin, path or religion. The France the assassins wanted to kill was the youth in its diversity ... a France opened to the world" (Faucher and Boussaguet 2017: 8). While in both instances it was France, above all, that was under attack, and from 'obscurantism', 'barbarism' and 'fundamentalism', the scale of difference in the death toll and nature of the attacks also influenced the valence of the Manichean and simple message. "In January, France was the victim but the enemy came from within: rebuilding unity was the solution ... the response of France after 13 November was to be 'merciless' and the objective was to 'retaliate' and 'eliminate' the 'barbarians' to 'destroy Daesh'" (ibid.: 9).

Discussing Valls' statement, days after the attacks, that 'France is at war with terrorism', and François Hollande's declaration, after the November attacks, that 'France is at war', Edwy Plenel, in a 2016 reissue of his 2014 tract *For the Muslims*, criticised this strategic foreclosure as "doubly blind: blind to causes, and thus to the past; blind to solutions, and thus future". In Plenel's assessment, the response of the French state was dangerously reminiscent of post-9/11 US administration attempts to imbue a violent political juncture with the drama of an existential threat:

Ignoring the contexts, genealogies and legacies that shaped this threat, this response is short-sighted and will soon fail. Beneath the determined appearance, it proceeds as though in a vacuum: not only disconnected from the international origins of the drama but also, what is more serious, oblivious to the national consequences of its stubbornness. (Plenel 2016: xv)

Of course, this foreclosure, the insistence that the event chain is nothing more than a barbarous necklace of attacks on freedom, was far from oblivious; it was an ideological choice. The forced genealogy with previous attacks on 'the West' was shaped by the immediate desire to shut down any analysis of the conditions of possibility for the attacks, either as political violence, or as acts that can be sociologically situated (Valls' maxim *"expliquer, c'est excuser"* achieved a pithiness that evaded George W. Bush and Tony Blair's similarly reductive post-9/11 injunctions). Invocations of war, however, are rarely just rhetorical manoeuvres, as Gholam Khiabany points out in his essay on the security state and the 'war on terror'; they are also mandates for exceptional action and the allocation of resources. The French military first launched attacks against 'Islamic State' in Iraq in September 2014, staging hundreds of strikes prior to a 'mission creep' extension to attack ISIS camps inside Syria a year later (Graham 2015). In the aftermath of the January attacks, the French state increased its military involvement in Syria, and immediately after the November attacks, following Hollande's promise to 'destroy Islamic state', launched bombing raids on Raqqa in northern Syria.

The 'internal' front of the war was pursued with equal vigour, with Republicanism, as Selim Nadi argues, the explicit 'war footing' from which the imagined community of the nation would be given "a certain coherence by excluding those who do not assume its values" (p. 300). Drawing on the 'apology for terrorism' provision from the 2014 anti-terrorism bill closely associated with the then Minister for the Interior Bernard Cazeneuve, scores of people – including children and people with learning difficulties – were investigated and frequently arrested for little more than isolated comments or jokes in school, work places and public settings (see the chapters by Marlière, De Genova and Hajjat). By July, the parliament and Constitutional Council had approved a surveillance bill that provided wide-ranging powers to intelligence services to monitor the communications of terrorism suspects and plant surveillance devices without legal oversight, and compel internet service providers to make data available to intelligence organisations (Toor 2015). Following the November attacks, a state of emergency was declared, and extended four times – the last bringing it up to after the presidential elections of 2017 – providing the government with the authority, again without judicial oversight, to order house arrests, police raids, bans on public assemblies and the activities of non-governmental organisations, and the closure of mosques.

In August 2016, the International Federation for Human Rights, supported by the *Ligue des droits de l'Homme*, issued a report on the impact of the state of emergency. *Quand l'exception devient la règle* ('When the Exception Becomes the Rule'; FIDH 2016) documents a significant scale of objective failure and predictable abuse; approximately 3,600 raids resulting in just six 'terrorism-related inquiries', with the majority of raids being conducted by narcotics police in 'terrorism-unrelated' operations, a pattern of misuse that extended to the use of summary house arrests to harass political activists in advance of the COP21 climate conference. Writing in *The New York Times* on the launch of the report, the participating legal expert Ramzi Kassem included a telling anecdote:

> Of our many interviews, one story stood out because it encapsulated how the state of emergency misses the mark. A Muslim man told us about a raid on his home near Paris. Armed, masked men burst in late at night without offering the occupants a chance to open the door, training their weapons on adults and children alike. The agents made the homeowner lie face down on the floor, cuffed him, then searched him in a needlessly harsh, humiliating way. All of a sudden, they hauled the homeowner to his feet and pointed to a picture of a bearded old man on his wall. 'Who is this bearded man?' barked a masked agent. 'Why sir', replied the homeowner, 'it's Victor Hugo'. (Kassem 2016)

Kassem's vignette is an almost perfect encapsulation of the repression being imposed on France's 'Muslim' urban underclass – if the picture had been of Émile Zola it would have been just too neat – and captures vividly the racialised valence of integration politics. It is this intensification of this state racism and the open, acceptable racism of much of the intellectual class that preoccupies many of the chapters in this book. The immediate political response of the deeply unpopular

Socialist government was to seek to channel what came to be called 'the Charlie Effect' of broadly felt togetherness into a 'national unity' predicated on framing the attacks as an assault on the Republic as the keeper of universal values, in particular of free speech and *laïcité*. This required a concerted political drive to defend and re-establish 'Republican values' as representing a fundamental bulwark against the 'war of religion' declared by the barbarous irrationality of the attackers, whose acts could be explained only in idealist terms to the exclusion of speculation on any concrete or political motivation (see Riemer 2015). As part of this, the 'iconoclastic' approach of *Charlie Hebdo*'s satire was elevated beyond the status of expressions that should unquestionably enjoy free speech to an iconic status as an expression of Republican virtue, and thus formed the basis for a demand: display the correct subject position, or face the consequences. The statement of the Minister of National Education Najat Vallaud-Belkacem in the National Assembly on 14 January has come to epitomise this repressive drive, when she assured parliamentarians that questions raised in high schools about the minute's silence by *those who are not Charlie* are "above all intolerable to us, when we hear them at school, which has the duty to teach our values".

In documenting the absurdist disciplining of children who 'disrespected' the minute's silence in schools and the subsequent drive to "mobilise schools around the values of the Republic", Philippe Marlière analyses the contemporary formation of state *laïcité* as a 'majority *communautarisme*', reversing the valence of the term in French, where it is negatively applied to any ethnic, cultural or religious difference that 'self-segregates' – while reading Victor Hugo – as a particular interest from the universality and unmediated citizen–state relationship of the Republic. The relentless scrutiny trained on those 'who would not be Charlie', Hajjat argues in a similar formulation, marks an intensification of the "*néo-laïcité* ... that since 1989 ... has strived to eliminate Islam from public view, framing the persistent belief in and practice of Islam by the children of postcolonial immigrants as a perceived threat to 'national identity'" (p. 89). Despite a narrative of *laïcité* as defining of public culture in France since the 1905 law of separation of church and state, Hajjat, Mondon and Winter and Marlière all provide accounts of its transformation, since the 1980s, from a law that sought to establish the neutrality of the state *and* freedom of expression and conscience for citizens, to one that, in a series of test cases brokered on the bodies and public subjectivities of women, demands 'neutrality' from the individual. But that neutrality, Marlière argues, is a majoritarian assimilationism, a threshold of integration that encodes "a kind of 'Frenchness', a set of unwritten rules of conduct and lifestyles which are compatible with 'being French' or simply with living in France" (p. 51). Republicanism, therefore, for all its fidelity to the idea of a general universal will, is a nationalism that has declared itself universal, and thus creates (another) double bind for those 'Muslims' obsessively fixed as its definitional Other – the demand to be Charlie as a Muslim, to *désolidariser* as a Muslim, is inseparable from the demand to not appear, or identify, as a Muslim in public. As Mayanthi L. Fernando summarises: "As in colonial Algeria, Muslims in France are consistently tethered to their embodied, communal, racial and religious difference" (2015: 29).

Thus, while 'religious accommodation' is clearly of importance to practising Muslims (see Bowen 2008), this tethering operates through relations of race and class, where the state and intellectual class obsession with religion, while not fully reducible to a screen for racism, is incorporated into the articulation of the 'culturalist' and 'differentialist' racism that has been hegemonic in Western Europe for decades (Lentin and Titley 2011). The political historian Jim Wolfreys (2015) identifies several key dimensions of this racism's operations and conditions of possibility: the realities of long-term structural unemployment, marginalisation and poverty; the burgeoning impact of the French New Right's project to rehabilitate racism through a putative emphasis on 'cultural' differentialism rather than 'racial' hierarchy; the complicities and affinities of the mainstream right and other political parties with this process; and the difficulty of an adequate anti-racist analysis and praxis on the left when "its most progressive elements [are] undermined by the affiliation to France's secular Republican tradition that pervades most significant left-of-centre organisations from the social liberal mainstream to the radical left" (a point explored by Selim Nadi in this book). Wolfreys' first point is examined in Christine Delphy's forceful delineation of what she terms a 'system of racial castes' in France, a term she uses to underline the implacable structuration of the social positioning of the descendants of ex-colonised Maghrebian (North African) immigrants. The development of 'castes', she argues, is a cumulative product of discrimination in housing, education, encounters with law enforcement and the judiciary, and also a socio-cultural stasis:

[I]t seems that the immigrant status of the parents of Maghrebians and Africans has been passed down across the generations, both materially and in terms of other people's perceptions. That is, they still imagine that these people are destined to one day leave French territory. And when people inherit exactly the same status that their parents had, with no probability or even possibility of social mobility, then what we're dealing with is a caste situation, not a class situation. That's what's now being created in France. We even see it in language: when we speak of 'second-' or even 'third-generation immigrants', we transform the immigrant condition – which is, by definition, temporary – into a hereditary and almost biological trait. (p. 290)

The constant cultural surveillance, recuperative public spectacles of prohibition and prescription and periodic hysteria as to the 'Muslim problem', Delphy argues, constitute a – particularly gendered – form of restoring control. In his chapter Hajjat discusses it as a 'politics of compensation', while De Genova examines it as a process of 'subordinate inclusion' that can mobilise loyalty and compatibility tests where, inter alia, 'free speech' acts as a modality of sifting and ranking 'good' and 'bad' Muslims (p. 107). This is why, for Selim Nadi, the critique of Republicanism cannot be limited to supposed hypocrisies or to the revelations of discourse analysis, because what is politically at stake is the material and institutional force of Republicanism's deployment by the state, and the centrality of Republicanism to the justification of state racism.

Both Nadi and Alana Lentin examine the weaknesses of left anti-racism noted by Wolfreys, but Lentin's critique, which engages extensively with the political thought of Houria Bouteldja, the spokesperson for the *Parti des Indigènes de la République*, explores how the Republican alignment of official anti-racism in France inevitably casts autonomous anti-racist groups as 'racist'. This is not the 'anti-white racism' that features in the rhetoric of *Les Républicaines*, or the network of integralist groups and movements inspired by the malleable 'new racism' of the *Nouvelle Droite*, or even the concern-trolling of the *nouveau philosophe* rear guard, but a charge of 'racist anti-racism' for their 'particularist' rejection of assimilationist universalism. Using the prevalent slogan '*Je Suis Charlie, Policier, Juif*' to examine the hierarchies of inclusion on which official anti-racism is constructed, Lentin argues that it is not enough to observe that Islamophobia plays the same role that antisemitism fulfilled in an earlier period of modernist nation-building. Their significance is also relational; state philosemitism, which positions the Shoah as the over-determining instance of modern racism, functions, to quote Bouteldja, to ultimately demonstrate that "'Jews' as a category are still not a fully legitimate part of the nation and its identity" (p. 272).

Aurélien Mondon and Aaron Winter also argue for attention to the relationality of racisms, as the key to understanding the force of the current formation is to recognise its polyvocality – or, put another way, to grapple with how anti-Muslim racism is produced through the synthesis of a plurality of tendencies: from the appropriation of *laïcité* as an essentially French characteristic and bulwark against 'Islamism' and Islam by the Front National, to the reactionary nationalist political space created by Nicolas Sarkozy, to the permeation of a transnational discourse of anti-Muslim animus circulated during the 'war on terror' era, to the coloniality immanent in Republicanism. The force of Islamophobia in France, they argue, emerges from the potency of the interplay of 'liberal' and 'illiberal' forms, and not – as is often argued in a context where the far right has added concern for the civilisational qualities of sexual freedom, gender equality and liberal freedoms to its repertoire of racialisation – because the latter has appropriated and thus warped the former.

Their approach has a wider heuristic value, for while this 'Islamophobic spiral' (Wolfreys 2015) is built in part on a narrative of exceptionalism, it is far from exceptional. It is not just that anti-Muslim racism has become normalised, if not yet normal, across those states that self-define as 'the West', but that the combination of securitarian prerogative and culturalist assimilationism discussed by Khiabany has become pronounced far beyond its particular French articulation. The demand, reflected on in many chapters here, that 'you must integrate yourself' captures the dual drive of this relation. To 'integrate' is to take responsibility for yourself, to produce yourself as a flexible individual in a context of prolonged neoliberal retrenchment of the welfare state. Yet it is also to prove yourself capable and worthy of integration, as this diminished social contract intensifies the compensatory and cohering dynamics of culturalist politics, as Khiabany's chapter explores. But as Lentin's argument makes clear, the legitimacy of these racialising arrangements is based in part on their status as 'not-racism': that is, when compared with the exterminationist and pseudo-scientific 'frozen racism' that provides official state anti-racisms with their safely repudiated past.

The readings

The aftermath of the attacks witnessed a semiotic blizzard, an intensive spectacle of identification and dis-identification mediated by the shifting invitation to identify proffered by #JeSuisCharlie, and driven by the reverential sharing of cover images and cartoons from the newspaper in a dispersed ritual of Google-enabled mourning and tribute. This combination, inevitably, generated a proliferation of political assessments of the publication itself – who is the Charlie to be identified with? For some, the speed of this second-order response was a problem *in and of itself*; the cartoonist Tom Spurgeon summarised this position in tweeting to "please reconsider riffing on the ideas, concepts, signifiers, comparisons of people being murdered until the bodies are cold". For others, imposing solemnity on a political actor, even in death, is no less disrespectful, for, as Javier Arbona argued, it means "ventriloquizing with their corpses ... they are actually being used as blunt tools against dissenting thought and radical ideas" (2015).

Yet, 'Charlie Hebdo' took shape because forms of ventriloquism and projection were inevitable in a context where a tiny proportion of participants in the communicative event had any relationship with *Charlie Hebdo* as an actual publication. *Berliner Zeitung*'s mistaken inclusion, in an 8 January front-page montage of front covers, of an antisemitic parody version, *Charlo Hebdo*, provided an egregious if hardly isolated example of what happens when intense symbolic energy rushes into a practically empty space. Consequently, a weird and intensive spectacle of interpretation took shape around establishing the correct meaning of *Charlie Hebdo*'s most notorious covers and cartoons. Weird, because despite its transnational unfolding, its dominant hermeneutic tendencies were deeply parochial. Intensive, because what was at stake was not solely textual disagreement, but a political question as reductive as the interpretative terms on which it was mainly conducted. Were *Charlie Hebdo*'s caricatures of the Prophet Muhammed, and assorted adventures in racialised imagery – and, by extension, the newspaper itself – to be considered *racist or anti-racist*?

The prolonged intensity of this focus is reflected in the decision, in April 2015, of a stellar cast of writers – including Junot Díaz, Teju Cole and Michael Ondaatje – to object to the award by PEN of its Freedom of Expression Courage Award to *Charlie Hebdo*, arguing that "there is a critical difference between staunchly supporting expression that violates the acceptable, and enthusiastically rewarding such expression"

(Yuhas 2015). Deborah Eisenberg, in her open letter to PEN America, took issue with precisely this folding of support into valorisation; why not give, she argued, "the award retroactively to Julius Streicher's *Der Stürmer* and its satirical anti-Semitic cartoons" if there is no difference in these positions? Eisenberg's general argument is a useful one, for this distinction is continuously elided in the repetitive, set-piece rituals that constitute the periodic outbreak of 'freedom of speech wars' (see Grantham and Miller's chapter for an untangling of these positions). Yet, while not drawing an exact parallel, Eisenberg's trans-historical trump card of a Nazi parallel also evades the careful work of opening out how, precisely, *Charlie Hebdo*'s images express the "anti-Islamic and nationalistic sentiments already widely shared in the Western world". A better question embraces the kind of contradiction posed by Jason Farago when he asked: "[H]ow did anti-racist, anti-military, anti-church artists end up, in the late 2000s and early 2010s, producing images that antagonized some of France's most vulnerable citizens?" (2015).

If far too much Anglophone criticism was content to cast *Charlie Hebdo* as some form of openly racist agitator, its defenders were equally liable to evade the implications of Farago's question, content to cast it as an anti-racist champion, fully and sorely misunderstood in the hour of its tragedy. In this argument, France is conjured up as a hermeneutically organic community, unified by a shared reverence for satirical codes so peculiarly French that informed reading is simply not possible beyond the Hexagon. The crowd-sourced site 'Understanding Charlie Hebdo', for example, which took shape in the weeks after the attack, offered detailed information on contextual references and step-by-step guides to unlocking the 'codes' of particularly notorious images.[2] Describing the publication's humour as a form of absurdism 'somewhat unique to French people', the 'understanding' on offer is doctrinal. It disciplines not only Anglophone misreading, but also membership of the imagined community, eliding the alternative readings of the not-quite-French who refuse to accept the idea that blithely contributing to the relentless focus on 'problem populations' can simply be declared 'anti-racist' because of an insistence on satirical intentionality, or on an idealist distinction between religion in the public sphere and racialised identities in national publics.

It is certainly the case that images, in a digital media environment characterised by mobility and bricolage, will travel and make meaning beyond the original *lieu d'énonciation*. Context collapse is a condition and result of networked and interactive media. But it is also the case that the travels of orientalist caricatures, colonial tropes and dehumanising, simianised imagery began long before their digital circulation, taking shape in and through the colonial networks that traverse the 'interpretative community' of France. This repertoire cannot be simply brushed down and deployed in the services of 'anti-racist' satire, at least without some open reckoning with its historical weight, and recognition of the opposition to its use by people indexed to the human hierarchies these images enunciate. Ultimately, however, the contributors to this book have elected not to spend much time unpicking these controversies in order to take positions, preferring to approach them as symptomatic of the wider struggles concerning Republicanism and (post-racial) racism at the heart of the book.

The same holds for the mesh of investments mediated by the proliferation of #JeSuisCharlie in the hours, days and months after the attacks. Used on average 6,500 times a minute during the afternoon of 7 January, to date this is one of Twitter's most intensively used and globally dispersed hashtags. A 'Je suis Charlie' app was made available on Apple's App Store within an hour of CEO Tim Cook being personally requested to approve it. A hashtag does more than organise data; it seeks to organise, however momentarily, a transnational public. Hashtags are also memetic, they invite meta-commentary, adaptation, parody. "We live," as Limor Shifman argues, "in an era driven by a hypermemetic logic in which every major public event sprouts a string of memes" (2014). As hashtag publics shift in composition, so too does the accentuality of the hashtag. This hashtag initially proposed an ephemeral form of human identification, an affective reaction to violent death. But it soon became freighted with value-driven identifications, with the contest over who Charlie was and what it stood for. As a social media, hashtags also invite endless self-differentiation: *I am Charlie but I am also this, I am not Charlie because I am actually that.*

The formulation #JeSuisCharlie rapidly produced *extensive forms* – I am also Ahmed Merabet – and *antagonistic forms* – I am not Charlie, I am *other* – providing what Romain Badouard described as a vector of identity construction that was inescapably both individual and collective (2016). It is the shifting constitution and dynamics of the 'ad hoc publics' formed around the viral hashtags #JeSuisCharlie and #JeNeSuisPasCharlie that forms the basis for Simon Dawes' exploration of public debate after the attacks. Despite the apparent polarity suggested by these formulations – and assumed, as Dawes shows, by a mainstream French press that ignored this 'polyphony' for days, only to then position any dissent or difference as a deviation from 'national unity' – the hashtag facilitated the "formation of different issue publics", characterised not so much by criticism of the newspaper but of the dominant media framing of the debate, in particular the hypocrisy inherent in the state and political class claim to cherish freedom of speech as a defining value (see also De Genova's chapter for key instances of this).

This pronounced dis-identification with the insistent themes of 'Charlie' rather than *Charlie* is also discussed in Des Freedman's chapter, where he examines how the intensive international media focus on the January attacks was taken up, in wider networked communicative space, as a real-time barometer of hierarchies of newsworthy and grievable life (a memetic reflex which became far more pronounced after the November attacks, and Facebook's provision of a tricolour filter for profile pictures to its users to display solidarity). By focusing on press and broadcast media coverage, Freedman's analysis, following Dawes', emphasises that the apparently encompassing 'freedom of speech debate' that rapidly took shape in the aftermath is better approached as a lattice of intersecting discussions and conflicts, shifting between recursive invocations of the abstract principle and positional negotiations of what is concretely at stake.

As Freedman argues, understanding an attack on media workers as an attack on freedom of speech makes sense, and could have been productively linked to the increased political targeting of journalists in conflict zones and unstable political contexts (according to Reporters without Borders, 101 journalists were killed in 2015, with much of the violence against journalists constituting deliberate, silencing attacks on journalism). However, the adoption of the civilisational discourse preferred by French political figures was of particular sectional value to media players happy to position themselves as 'fearless defenders' of liberty, and at a moment – particularly in Britain – when public levels of trust in the mainstream media are in flux.

A claim not just to defend freedom of speech, but, in some shape or form, to embody it, informed countless attempts to generate political capital from the attacks. Among the most blatant was the far-right attempt to extend the event chain by staging public acts of apparent solidarity with the magazine, including transnationally memetic attempts to stage 'draw the Prophet' competitions. That several of these events were arranged quickly and independently of each other in the aftermath of the attacks is probably because this tactic first emerged after the 2005–2006 *Jyllands-Posten* cartoon conflict (see Carolina Sanchez Boe's chapter for a detailed account of *Charlie Hebdo*'s history with the *Jyllands-Posten* cartoons, and wider press debates in Denmark and France about the ethics of publishing the cartoons in solidarity). There was also a broadly mediated attempt to establish an 'Everybody Draw Mohammed Day' in 2010 after online threats were made to the creators of the cartoon *South Park*.

One of the first to attempt to organise a 'Mohammed cartoon competition' was the youth party of the *Perussuomalaiset* (True Finns), which had announced a competition and subsequent exhibition online on 14 February because the attacks "once again show us the true nature of Islam" and "the defence of freedom of speech concerns us all". The competition was abruptly cancelled on 22 February without comment. In April 2015, the small extreme-right Pro-NRW party in Nordrhein-Westfalen successfully organised a competition entitled 'Freedom instead of Islam', with the winning entries posted on the 'free speech website' *Politically Incorrect*, a hugely successful 'counter-jihad' blog that was established in response to the *Jyllands-Posten* cartoon controversy, and thus one of an important network of sites that have shaped a space for overt anti-Muslim racism by framing its 'honesty' as a refusal to surrender any more territory on freedom of speech.

By far the most significant attempt to further the event chain through imitation garnered global headlines when two people were shot dead at a 'Muhammad Art Exhibit and Cartoon Contest' hosted at the Curtis Culwell Center in Garland, Texas in May 2015. The event was sponsored by Robert Spencer's website *Jihad Watch* and organised by the front group American Freedom Defense Initiative, established by Spencer and Pamela Geller and previously best known for a series of anti-Muslim subway ads in US cities which were designed to trigger legal challenges and thus First Amendment defences. After the attack in Texas, other smaller tribute events were staged in Arizona, but this particular event also had transnational responses. Sharia Watch UK, fronted by the former UKIP candidate Anne Marie Waters, attempted to host a UK 'Draw Mohammed Competition and Exhibition' in August 2015. The event was to be co-hosted with *Vive Charlie*, an 'online satirical magazine' established in April 2015 to 'exercise our rights to freedom of expression and freedom of speech', and which in practice acts as an online clearing house for material from the wider network of the 'counter-jihad' and anti-Islam blogosphere. The event was cancelled in August 2015, citing security concerns, although it is likely that this provided some compensatory publicity for the fact that the exhibition did not appear to be coming together.

A more successful event adaptation was staged by Geert Wilders and his Party for Freedom (PVV) in the Netherlands. Wilders has been a speaker at the event in Texas a day before the attack on the exhibition centre, and used this connection to demand of the Board of the Dutch Parliament that the winning cartoons from the Texas exhibition be displayed in the parliament. This request was refused,[3] but Wilders used the broadcast time allocated to the PVV by the Dutch Public Service Broadcaster to exhibit the winning cartoons on live television, on 24 June 2015, with the message: "I do not broadcast the cartoons to provoke; I do it because we have to show that we stand for freedom of speech and that we will never surrender to violence. Freedom is our birth right. Freedom of speech must always prevail over terror and violence."

Far-right attempts to weaponise liberal values are, of course, of limited credibility. However, whatever purchase they have stems less from the successful appropriation of a discordant vocabulary than an opportunistic intensification of a racio-civilisational identity politics that has been welded into shape from a much broader spectrum of political positions. As Ghassan Hage pointedly argues in his contribution:

> 'democracy', 'tolerance' and 'freedom of speech' all can become – and are increasingly becoming in the Western world – *fin d'empire* colonial, racialised strategies of phallic distinction. They are what Westerners 'flash' to the racialised Muslims to say: "Look what we have and you haven't got. At best, yours is very small compared to ours." And this is at the very same time as Western societies are becoming less democratic, tolerant, and committed to freedom of speech. (p. 260)

This book's engagements with the question of freedom of speech are not driven by the desire to refashion a normative theory for our times. Instead, they underline the importance of reclaiming free speech, as a radical political freedom, from the spectacles of 'phallic distinction' that have become routinised in Western public cultures.

Notes

1 The archive website is http://cahl.io/.

2 See www.understandingcharlieheb
do.com/. After an initial burst of energy
and publicity, the website does not
appear to be well maintained or regularly
updated at the time of writing.

3 Wilders, of course, is attempting
to replicate the successful strategy of
his 2008 film *Fitna*, a short, YouTube
response-style video that expressly
positioned itself in an event chain
narrative, as its opening shots
reference Theo van Gogh and Ayaan
Hirsi Ali's 2004 film *Submission*, and
the 'turban-shaped bomb' cartoon by
Kurt Westergaard that was included in
the *Jyllands-Posten* culture supplement
cover from 2005. No Dutch broadcaster
would accept *Fitna*, and it was
broadcast online from April 2008, and
subsequently became the subject of
a freedom of speech roadshow, with
Wilders, for example, being refused
entry to the UK for a screening of his
film in the House of Lords in February
2009.

References

Arbona, J. (2015) '#JeSuisCharlieHebdo?' https://aljavieera.wordpress.com/?s=hebdo.

Badouard, R. (2016) '"Je ne suis pas Charlie". Pluralité des prises de parole sur le web et les réseaux sociaux' in P. Lefébure and C. Sécail (eds) *Le Défi Charlie. Les medias à l'épreuve des attentats*. Paris: Lemieux.

Bowen, J. R. (2008) *Why the French don't like Headscarves: Islam, the State and Public Space*. Princeton NJ: Princeton University Press.

Challand, B. (2015) 'When the Far Enemy Becomes Near: Reflections on the Charlie Hebdo Killings', *Public Seminar*, 10 January, www.publicseminar.org/2015/01/when-the-far-enemy-becomes-near.

Chamayou, G. (2015) *Drone Theory*. London: Penguin.

Eyerman, R (2008) *The Assassination of Theo Van Gogh: From Social Drama to Cultural Trauma*. Durham NC: Duke University Press.

Farago, J. (2015) 'Image Conscious', *Art Forum*, 17 January. www.artforum.com/slant/id=49810.

Fassin, D. (2015) 'In the Name of the Republic: Untimely Meditations on the Aftermath of the *Charlie Hebdo* Attacks', *Anthropology Today* 31 (2): 3–7.

Faucher, F. and L. Boussaguet (2017) 'The Politics of Symbols: Reflections on the French Government's Framing of the 2015 Terrorist Attacks', *Parliamentary Affairs*, 22 June.

Fernando, M. (2015) 'France after Charlie Hebdo', *Boston Review*, 24 February.

FIDH (2016) *Quand l'exception devient la règle: Mesures antiterroristes contraires aux droits humains*. www.fidh.org/IMG/pdf/rapportfrance-hd1_def.pdf.

Gifford, P. (2016) 'The Charlie Hebdo Affair in Senegal', *Canadian Journal of African Studies/Revue canadienne des etudes africaines*, 21 January, pp. 479–92 [online].

Goldberg, D. T. (2009) *The Threat of Race: Reflections on Racial Neoliberalism*. Malden MA: Wiley-Blackwell.

Graham, D. A. (2015) 'What is France Doing in Syria?', *The Atlantic*, 15 November. www.theatlantic.com/international/archive/2015/11/france-syria-iraq-isis/416013.

Graham, S. (2011) *Cities Under Siege: The New Military Urbanism*. London: Verso Books.

Hollande, F (2015) 'Attack against Charlie Hebdo Statement by Mr François Hollande President of the Republic January 7th 2015'. *France Diplomatie.* www.diplomatie.gouv.fr/en/the-ministry-and-its-network/events/article/attack-against-charlie-hebdo.

Kassem, R. (2016) 'France's Real State of Emergency', *The New York Times*, 4 August.

Klug, B. (2016) 'In the Heat of the Moment: Bringing "Je Suis Charlie" into Focus', *French Cultural Studies* 27 (3): 223–32.

Lentin, A. and G. Titley (2011) *The Crises of Multiculturalism: Racism in a Neoliberal Age.* London: Zed Books.

Pitcher, B. (2009) The Politics of Multiculturalism. Basingstoke: Palgrave Macmillan.

Plenel, E. (2016) *For the Muslims: Islamophobia in France.* London: Verso.

Riemer, N. (2015) 'France and its War on Terror and Intellectuals', *New Matilda*, 2 December. https://newmatilda.com/2015/12/02/france-and-its-war-on-terror-and-intellectuals.

Saeed, S. (2015) 'The Charlie Hebdo Affair and the Spectre of Majoritarianism', *Economic and Political Weekly* 23: 37–41.

Shatz, A. (2015) 'Moral Clarity', *LRB Blog*, 9 January. www.lrb.co.uk/blog/2015/01/09/adam-shatz/moral-clarity.

Shifman, L. (2014) *Memes in Digital Culture.* Cambridge MA: MIT Press.

Toor, A. (2015) 'France's Sweeping Surveillance Law Goes into Effect', *The Verge*, 24 July. www.theverge.com/2015/7/24/9030851/france-surveillance-law-charlie-hebdo-constitutional-court.

Volkmer, I. (2014) *The Global Public Sphere: Public Communication in the Age of Reflective Interdependence.* Cambridge: Polity.

Wolfreys, J. (2015) 'After the Paris Attacks: An Islamophobic Spiral', *International Socialism: A Quarterly Review of Socialist Theory*, 11 April. http://isj.org.uk/after-the-paris-attacks.

Yuhas, A. (2015) 'Two Dozen Writers Join Charlie Hebdo Award Protest', *Guardian*, 29 April.

PART I

THE CONTESTED REPUBLIC

1 | *CHARLIE HEBDO*, REPUBLICAN SECULARISM AND ISLAMOPHOBIA

Aurélien Mondon and Aaron Winter

The attack against *Charlie Hebdo* in Paris on 7 January 2015 took place in a context in which Islamophobia had become increasingly mainstream in France.[1] The widespread albeit uneven use of the slogan 'Je Suis Charlie' across France and the Western world represented for many an assertion of solidarity, and more specifically identification, with *Charlie Hebdo* and its championing of liberal Enlightenment and Republican values of freedom of speech. This reaction, we were told, was in response to the threat posed by Muslim extremists and terrorists. However, the boundaries between a critique of extremism and terrorism and that of Islamophobia (and anti-Muslim hate), as well as that between the defence of liberal values, Islamophobia and securitisation, have become increasingly blurry. The string of deadly attacks by those identified or self-identifying as 'Islamist' and linked to IS (however tenuous that link may be) which have taken place since in Paris, Nice and Saint-Etienne-du-Rouvray have rendered them ever fuzzier. It is for this reason, and the mapping of these discourses and practices as they relate or are deployed in relation to Islam and Muslims, however loosely defined, that we employ our concepts of illiberal and liberal Islamophobia (Mondon and Winter 2017).

The illiberal articulation of Islamophobia, or 'anti-Muslim' hate, is closest to traditional racism based around exclusivist notions and concepts of race, ethnicity, gender, sexuality and religion, as well as identity itself, and is commonly associated with the extreme right and authoritarian treatment of minority groups and rights. Liberal Islamophobia, on the other hand, apparently rejects but in fact displaces and conceals traditional racism and overt prejudice by constructing a pseudo-progressive binary and narrative. It constructs a stereotypical notion and image of Muslim or Islamic belief and culture inherently opposed to some of the core values espoused in a mythical and essentialised culturally homogeneous, superior and enlightened West, or specific Western nation. In this fantasised picture, the West is argued to embody progress, such as democracy, human rights, free speech, and gender and sexual equality, and, ironically, particularly in terms of the way in which Muslims were and are targeted, tolerance. Although liberal Islamophobia claims to target religion and belief (Islam) on behalf of liberalism as opposed to people (Muslims) to claim its liberal credential and non-racist defence, it does retain the same target – Muslims – as its illiberal counterpart, often under the auspices of 'culture', and is part of a long legacy of anti-Muslim hate in France and wider Europe, dating to colonialism. It can also be used to justify illiberal practices, such as the racialisation, profiling and securitisation of Muslims and Muslim communities, as the boundaries between the two are at times functional and thus blurry. Even before the attack, *Charlie Hebdo* used its satirical cartoons of the Prophet Mohammed to prove the point about a fantasised version of Islam and Muslims' 'backwardness' (recalling, in a French context, not just liberal Enlightenment Republican ideals, but racist colonial and neo-racist particularist 'cultural' discourses), in an expression of free speech.

In the aftermath of the attack, *Charlie Hebdo* appeared as a flagbearer for such a civilisational project: 'Je Suis Charlie' was the assertion that the West and France in particular identified with the magazine as its symbol or proxy for freedom of speech, and stood together in solidarity with the West and France for freedom of speech and the attack on it/them/us. However, this was accompanied by developments that would seem contradictory to the liberal values of freedom that *Charlie Hebdo* allegedly championed and to which Islamists posed a threat: securitisation, states of emergency in which civil liberties would be suspended, a crackdown on so-called 'extreme' speech and a boost for the extremists on the right. In this context, the extreme right Front National (FN), long the standard-bearer of racist hate and right-wing authoritarianism, was able to normalise itself further. By strategically embracing a liberal form of Islamophobia in defence of the Republic, the FN has now placed itself in perfect alignment with the mainstream.

This chapter will examine these developments, focusing on the rise of the FN and the mainstreaming of Islamophobia and anti-Muslim hate in France under the banner of liberalism. It will argue that, while Islamophobia has often taken an illiberal shape, a more mainstream, acceptable and accepted form within a liberal framework has become commonplace within the mainstream political discourse of twenty-first century France, particularly in relation to discourses about Republicanism. It will examine such developments in light of tensions in the Republican tradition between liberalism and reactionary politics that go back to the founding of the Republic and throughout French history. These are revealed and articulated in responses to social and political crises: for example, the transformation and mainstreaming of Islamophobia in the context of and response to the *Charlie Hebdo* attack, and the debate surrounding freedom of speech, which should be seen in the context of a wider crisis of faith in democracy that lends itself to hate and scapegoating, as well as extreme-right opportunism. Finally, it will examine the development and changes to this discourse in response to attacks that followed the one on *Charlie Hebdo*.

The Republic has fallen, long live the reactionary Republic!

To understand the current situation and the normalisation, if not normalcy, of Islamophobic discourses, both liberal and illiberal, in mainstream political debates, it is essential to place the return of reactionary politics in France in a broader historical context. Since the late nineteenth century, France's history has been marred by the struggle between the Republic and its own contradictions, and reactionary ideologies and movements, such as those based on various iterations of racism. From the Dreyfus Affair and the role played by Charles Maurras' Action Française and colonialism, to the interwar fascist leagues and the failed coup of February 1934; from the Vichy Regime to the post-war nostalgic and anti-decolonisation movements, the French extreme right's virulent opposition has played a key part in defining the Republic as the progressive alternative, despite its own shortcomings and responsibility with regard to systemic racism (see Selim Nadi's chapter in this book). In this context and with more radical alternatives in disarray, the Republic was constructed as the ultimate symbol of progress in mainstream discourse, but also as the strongest barrier against the extreme right: where the Republic prevailed, it was argued, the forces of reaction would be defeated. This led, in the second half of the twentieth century, to the creation of a Republican Front against parties of the extreme right, which took its real meaning in the 1980s and 1990s as the FN began to gather momentum. The idea of a Republican Front was particularly prominent when Jean-Marie Le Pen, the leader of the extreme right FN, reached the second round of the 2002 presidential elections. Interestingly, despite media hype

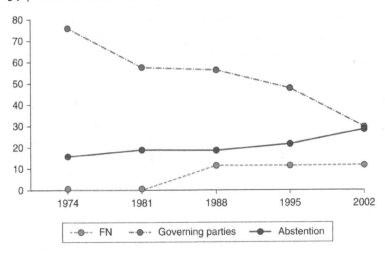

Figure 1.1 Presidential election results per registered voters

Note: Governing parties include the centre left and centre right parties.

around the rise of the FN, the novelty was not so much Le Pen's results (similar to 1988 and 1995), but the fall of the traditional governing parties and the rise of abstention (see Figure 1.1). In 2002, almost as many people turned to abstention as those who trusted the three traditional governing party families.

In an era of post-democracy (Crouch 2004), this concerning trend was for the most part ignored and solace was found in the phantasmatic fight staged by almost all parties between good and evil, between the Republic and the fascist menace.[2] In the second round, *la 'bête immonde'* was defeated and Jacques Chirac, at the time involved in various corruption scandals, was re-elected with 82.21 per cent of the vote. Here again, French commentators praised Republican unity in the face of what was advertised as the irresistible rise of the FN, once more ignoring Le Pen's party's failure to appeal to more than 17.79 per cent of voters (or 13.4 per cent of registered voters) when faced with a less than popular candidate. Left-wing newspaper *Libération*'s front pages were symptomatic of the amalgamation of extremely diverse ideologies within the Republic, stressing the vital necessity to vote for right-wing Chirac "For the Republic's sake". At the same time, popular magazine *Paris Match*'s front pages praised the 'hope' triggered by 'Republican enthusiasm' "to say no to Le Pen": 'the wounded Republic' was ultimately victorious.[3] Apocalyptic language abounded, with words such as 'shock', 'bomb', 'catastrophe', 'nightmare' across front pages and throughout the news. *L'Express* (25 April 2002) summarised the union of the press against the FN, calling for a vote for Chirac "for France, for the Republic, for Democracy". *Le Monde* (2 May 2002) concluded that it was not so much Chirac, but 'the Republic being re-elected'. That abstention now equalled the same number of votes as the main governing parties in post-war France was ignored in the mainstream debate. The threat to the Republic and French democracy was thus not to be sought within the failure of mainstream parties, but rather in the exaggeration of the 'success' of the FN, and in turn in the legitimisation of its discourse as a prominent political alternative.

As it seemed to triumph over fascism in 2002, the Republican Front and the legitimation of the FN as the alternative to 'politics as usual' made Nicolas Sarkozy an appealing candidate on the right. Sarkozy's aims were clear: no more compromises with the old order; he would instead choose to bring FN voters back to his party even if it meant he had to go and get them 'one by one' (Sarkozy 2006). By positioning himself in opposition to the establishment, despite being very much part of it, Sarkozy successfully appealed to many of those who had chosen the FN as a protest vote, and in doing so dealt a lethal blow to the Republican Front. His insistence on breaking taboos freed much of the neo-racist discourse central to the FN's strategy, particularly with regard to Islam. The presence of the Republican Front had not negated racism in its many guises, but prior to the arrival of Sarkozy, such utterances had remained marginal and overwhelmingly condemned in the mainstream political discourse, albeit useful to appeal to parts of the electorate (Mondon 2013: 7–8).

The creation of what Thomas Deltombe termed 'Imaginary Islam' can be traced back to the 1970s (Deltombe 2005; see also Hajjat and Mohammed 2013); however, its positioning as the natural enemy of the secular Republic in the mainstream discourse fully took hold in the 2000s. Following the polemics around the same issue in 1989 and 1994, the 2004 law on 'conspicuous' religious symbols in schools was not so much about secularism as it was about an essentialised view of Islam: Muslim communities were assumed to be worthy of suspicion and those most affected were not given the space to express concerns or agency (Tévanian et al. 2008). As highlighted by Pierre Tévanian amongst others, this was very much a non-issue at the time, since "the number of headscarf-related disputes, according to the French Ministry of Education, fell from 300 in 1994 to 150 in 2003 [with] 146 of these incidents quickly resolved through compromise" (Tévanian 2005). Nevertheless, the Republic and secularism increasingly became repressive tools used to entrench discrimination, in opposition to more emancipatory meanings (Mondon 2015). Mention of *laïcité* and the law of 1905 on the separation of church and state no longer referred to the text itself and its focus on the protection of individual rights. Both were used to pursue some identitarian project based on an imagined clash of civilisations. Such debates were reminiscent of the *mission civilisatrice* central to the French colonial project and processes and to the Third Republic's self-righteous outlook on the world and its duties to civilise all, even against their will. It is telling that when the 2010 law against the burka was passed in France, the office of Éric Besson, then Minister of Immigration and National Identity, commented that this law was necessary for "life in society and civilisation to be explained" to those guilty of wearing the attire (Leprince 2010). Nuance was nowhere to be seen; Republican emancipation was to be imposed and agency limited to those like 'us'.

In a global context where Islam was constructed as the global threat, Sarkozy's campaigns and presidency normalised this neo-racist perspective in much of the political discourse in France. He brought with his leadership of the centre-right UMP two elements central to this mainstreaming. On the one hand, contrary to his predecessors and mainstream opponents, his use of such tropes was unrepentant and his stance based on the constant struggle against so-called 'political correctness' and taboos imposed by a self-righteous elite. On the other hand, while much of his discourse on immigration and Islam was borrowed from the FN's repertoire, his position as leader of a mainstream party and his subsequent presidency added legitimacy to such themes and gave them an aura of authority and acceptability, if not normalcy. For Sarkozy, the Republic was no longer the rampart against the extreme right, but a nationalist project based on an emotional attachment to *la patrie*: "to become French is to subscribe to a form of civilisation, values and mores" (Sarkozy 2009).

Sarkozy's discursive strategy based on nationalism and the stigmatisation of Islam proved successful in 2007,[4] but played a part in his demise in 2012 as he was ultimately unable to satisfy the deeply divided parts of his electorate. By the end of his presidency, Sarkozy had shifted the line between what was acceptable and what was not, what could be discussed and envisaged by the President, what was taboo and what was the new normal. In his attempt to outbid the FN in promising that no debate would be out of bounds for his government, Sarkozy allowed for extreme right discourse to both gain an increased amount of coverage and, more importantly, to become part of the Republican and democratic sphere from which it had been excluded since the Second World War. In 2012, Sarkozy could break the ultimate Republican taboo, saying what no other mainstream party's leader had dared and what the media in unison had revolted against in 2002: that the FN was part of the 'Republic'; it was a 'democratic' party (Mondon 2013).

As the Republican Front weakened, the FN evolved. In the twenty-first century, and even more so under the new leadership of Marine Le Pen, the party has continued to redefine its discourse, if not its ideology, in its ongoing attempt to reclaim key concepts of the French national psyche (Crépon et al. 2015). This change required a refining of the old narratives that had been core to Jean-Marie Le Pen's politics, placing him throughout his political life as the 'outsider'. The rise of Islamophobia within the mainstream allowed the FN to join the Republican camp and to reshape key concepts such as *laïcité* in its own image. Marine Le Pen has thus positioned herself as champion of the hegemonic values seemingly abandoned by mainstream parties, forcing them in turn to toe the line. This shift has seen a further escalation in the 'vocabulary war' the party launched in the late 1980s, under the influence of *Nouvelle droite* think tanks and their right-wing appropriation and use of Antonio Gramsci's theories. In her counter-hegemonic struggle, Marine Le Pen has made the themes of the Republic and secularism central to her discourse: the Republic is now understood as the nation in the traditional extreme right manner, and secularism as the weapon against the divisions caused by the nation's new primary enemy: Islam.

The rise of the secularist crusaders: Islam versus freedom of speech

The growing acceptance of liberal Islamophobia in France and the West in general was greatly aided by the rise of media-savvy commentators whose broad access to a mainstream media hungry for cheap polemics has allowed them to publicise their message. Somewhat ironically, self-appointed rebels and taboo-breakers such as Éric

Zemmour have benefited from the support of most mainstream TV channels, magazines, radios, newspapers and publishing companies to convince their audience that it was censorship which had prevented their argument from being discussed, rather than because it was simply wrong and retrograde. As a result of this disproportionate coverage, an array of reactionary ideas have made their way back from the margins, and have targeted groups whose demands for equal treatment were turned into attacks against 'our' values and civilisation. Through a recasting of 'our' history, the West is no longer described as the cradle of equal rights, but as the greatest civilisation put in jeopardy by so-called minorities, and aided by a self-righteous and self-loathing intelligentsia. If 'our' great achievements are to be saved from destruction, then those trying to divide us must no longer be allowed to demand emancipation. In this apocalyptic argument, Muslims, loosely defined, have come to play the part of the invader, whose culture and laws are to replace ours. When pushed to its extreme, women and homosexuals are equally characterised as enemies from the inside, whose demands for equality have led to a feminisation of society, which has in turn facilitated the invasion of virile barbarians (Zemmour 2006). While the most extreme forms of such illiberal Islamophobia, sexism and homophobia remain theoretically anchored in the extreme right, and are as such denounced by much of the media, the spectral presence of an imagined homogeneous and politically unified Muslim community has become a mainstream concern in France and Europe.

This was made clear in 2005 when the editors of Danish conservative newspaper *Jyllands-Posten* asked cartoonists to submit a picture of the Prophet Mohammed, something which is discussed at length in Carolina Sanchez Boe's chapter. This was rationalised with claims that a Danish author had been unable to find someone to illustrate his children's book as potential artists feared reprisals. Despite having contacted forty-two cartoonists, only twelve drawings were submitted, some of which criticised the newspaper's stance (Klausen 2009). Yet what was supposed to be 'a summer-time prank' soon created a media storm. Fleming Rose, the editor of the newspaper, claimed that the aim of the cartoons' publication was to test "the boundaries of censorship in a time of war" (Battaglia 2006: 29). For Rose, freedom of expression was under threat, and the war analogy resonated within part of the French elite who had just passed and supported the banning of the hijab in schools. For Ferruh Yilmaz, *Jyllands-Posten* was extremely successful in (a) creating an intense debate that can easily be described as a 'moral panic' about Islam's compatibility with 'Western' values, (b) making freedom of speech the central question in the debate, and (c) mobilising sides on the basis of Muslim and Western 'identities,' regardless of what their own identifications and arguments are otherwise. (Yilmaz 2011: 11)

In France, the battle against perceived religious censorship helped rekindle the idea of a glorious past when a fantasised version of the nation was the vanguard of universal (secular) emancipation. The fact that secular France is no longer threatened by an all-powerful Catholic church has been lost on the new soldiers of the secularist crusade. Their enemy instead is a minority, and one that is constantly and systematically discriminated against. This is particularly striking with regard to the very argument about freedom of speech which excludes opponents of the caricatures, whatever their rationale, as "it becomes clear that, dissenters, or the 'censors', are posited as illegitimate in their claim to legal recourse, immoral in their attack on the public good, and undemocratic in their politics" (Battaglia 2006: 29).

The cartoons affair therefore allowed right-wing voices to rework their neo-racist argument into part of the fuzzy Enlightenment project: the new crusades would be between innately reactionary Muslims and indiscriminately progressive Western societies. This line of argument was extremely successful, creating deep divisions within and throughout the left as intellectuals and activists wrongly felt forced to choose between secularism and racism: in order to defend universalism and secularism, the essentialisation and exclusion of part of the population were deemed necessary. The choice was a false flag, as pointedly argued by Christine Delphy with regard to sexism and racism (Delphy 2006). It was in this context that *Charlie Hebdo*, a niche left-wing libertarian weekly magazine whose financial situation at the time was dire, decided to republish the cartoons in support of freedom of speech (Miera and Sala Pala 2009). The solidarity expressed by a French left-wing magazine with a right-wing newspaper in Denmark demonstrated that the fight against Islam trumped any other political consideration.

Large parts of the left and their uncritical support of secularism and the Enlightenment were therefore caught on the wrong side of a debate led by the right and based on the neo-racist essentialisation of the Muslim community. As highlighted by Adria Battaglia in the case of the United States, "the narrative becomes a hegemonic device, or a way of controlling how [we] view the debate: this is an issue of protecting our freedoms, not recognizing that our freedoms are not equally shared amongst all people" (Battaglia 2006). This was equally applicable to the situation in France, where complaints about the cartoons were ignored or denounced without any consideration of their relevance with regard to the legal system. For Pascal Mbongo (2007: 147), the filing of a complaint against *Charlie Hebdo*'s publication of the cartoons should not have been problematic since it was received by the tribunal as valid, even though the magazine was later found not guilty. Therefore, while various Muslim and anti-racist associations placed the fight against intolerance and racism within the Republican jurisdiction, they were nonetheless considered as the enemies of a mythological vision of *laïcité*. Furthermore, as they virulently denounced the associations for what they argued was a religious trial, the so-called defenders of freedom of speech failed to acknowledge that *Charlie Hebdo* was sued for only three of the cartoons, which they did not attack as blasphemous, but rather as incitement to racial hatred (Miera and Sala Pala 2009: 398).

The debate about freedom of speech was no longer about whether it is even possible in a deeply unequal society where public discourse is within the reach of very few. Instead, the discussion centred on the necessity to uphold absolute freedom of speech against one particular threat. The racist rationale behind the publication of the cartoons, and more importantly behind the support *Charlie Hebdo* received – from the left in particular – was clear. The publication of the cartoons and their defence had little to do with freedom of speech; it was yet another attack on Islam and anyone even remotely associated with the religion. As Roy et al. argued:

> No major newspaper would publish cartoons mocking blind people, dwarfs, homosexuals or Roma people, more because they fear bad taste than because of potential legal pursuits. But bad taste does not seem to be an issue with Islam because public opinion is more permeable to Islamophobia (which often hides behind a rejection of immigration). One can make jokes about Muslims we would not make about others. What shocks Muslim people is not the way the Prophet is portrayed but rather that there are double standards. (Roy et al. 2006: 323)

Charlie Hebdo's supporters claimed that the magazine was an equal opportunity offender, but failed to acknowledge the relative power (or powerlessness) of targets, and the potential impact on Muslims and Muslim communities came at a time of growing Islamophobia and anti-Muslim hate throughout politics, media and civil society, often cloaked in such liberalism. It is this context that lent itself to the power and popularity of the images and provided a ready-made framing and response for the 'Islam versus Western liberal values/freedom of speech' discourse.

Islamophobia in mainstream French politics: the *Charlie Hebdo* attacks and their aftermath

While the liberal form of Islamophobia, pitting a progressive West against a reactionary Islam, has become increasingly prevalent in France, the series of attacks that have taken place since January 2015 have made the distinction between liberal and illiberal forms in the mainstream increasingly blurry. After the November 2015 attacks in which 130 were killed, most politicians reiterated that France was 'at war', something highlighted by former Prime Minister Dominique de Villepin (Huet 2015). The then Prime Minister Manuel Valls (*L'Obs* 2012) went as far as discussing the 'enemy within' – a phrase with clear connotations with the Second World War. Still reminiscent of France's darkest hours, prominent politicians on the right called for any suspect to be imprisoned without trial in 'interment camps' (Clavel 2015). By responding in such a violent manner, French politicians have played right into the hands of terrorists (Benzine 2016). They have provided Islamic State with the opportunity to stand falsely righteous when the inevitable civilian casualties will be found under the rubble left by French bombs. Strengthening further the state of suspicion towards Muslim communities, the attacks on the Bataclan and wider sites of Parisian nightlife were taken by some to represent an attack by Muslims on the liberal culture and lifestyle of the young in France (Saadia 2015). However, while this liberal version of Islamophobia prevailed after the *Charlie Hebdo* attacks, the element of repetition and the apparent failure of the government to protect its citizens have rendered illiberal discourses and measures increasingly prevalent.

It was thus not surprising that terrorism, retaliation and securitisation were central to the reaction to the 14 July attack in Nice. The defence of so-called liberal values was no longer the focus of political discourses, and the false unity which had brought most politicians together after the *Charlie Hebdo* attacks was replaced by a race to the bottom in relation to both Muslims and liberty. Despite a clear lack of evidence during the early stages of the investigation, the government and opposition denounced a terrorist attack and demanded ever more stringent measures to be implemented. Positioning himself for the 2017 presidential election as the alternative to the Front National, Nicolas Sarkozy demanded that all suspects of terrorism be given an electronic bracelet (Laurent 2016). While this measure was already considered ineffective at the time and thus sheer demagoguery, it was further discredited on 26 July as the bearer of such a device murdered a priest and gravely injured another parishioner.

However, far from discouraging an ever more brutal discussion of the situation in France, the opposition continued to push for more securitisation. Sarkozy soon declared that this latest attack "show[ed] the extent to which we must change the scale of our retaliation to Islamist terrorism" (Bordenave et al. 2016). This may mean extraordinary measures, be they against the constitution: "our system must protect potential victims rather than probable perpetrators of a future terrorist attack". In this demagogic and increasingly authoritarian climate, the government's call for unity and use of '*our* democracy as shield' failed to convince (Bekmezian 2016). Hollande declared that "restraining our liberties and infringing upon our constitution would not be efficient in the struggle against terrorism and would weaken the all so precious cohesion of our nation. Our country must avoid indulging in one-upmanship, polemics, amalgams, suspicions' (ibid.). This shift in discourse demonstrated the tensions between the illiberal and liberal strategies the government had been trying to balance. As the President demanded calm, unity and respect of *our* rights and freedoms and Prime Minister Valls denounced the 'Trumpisation of minds', the government extended the state of emergency until January 2017 and implemented further anti-terrorist legislation despite their clear inefficacy and their discriminatory nature, at the expense of more long-term policies tackling the socio-economic roots of the problem (Bredoux 2016). Illiberalism, previously the extreme right form of anti-Muslim hate, but replaced by the increasingly mainstream liberal Islamophobia targeting the so-called illiberalism of Islam and Muslims, was now the state's response to terror in defence of liberal values.

And it has been as ineffective as it is contradictory. In February 2016, Amnesty International (2016) highlighted that only one person had been arrested on terrorism charges, out of 3,210 often violent interventions. Again, the government's reaction played right into the hands of so-called Islamic State as such policies and the associated rhetoric were likely to feed into their propaganda machine, as they will no doubt highlight the unfair treatment Muslims are subjected to in France. In a long opinion piece in the *Journal du Dimanche*, five days after the Saint-Etienne-du-Rouvray attack, Valls (2016) pushed the contradictions in the government's discourse further, calling for a rebuilding of the Islam of France, praising the second religion in France for having "found its place in the Republic" and telling Muslims indiscriminately that they "have an immense responsibility to uphold".

Conclusion

Islamophobia and racism more generally have been part of the Republican narrative for a long time in France. However, with the sanitisation of the Front National and the mainstreaming of many of its ideas by politicians, the media and pundits, seeing Islam and Muslims, however loosely defined, as suspicious has become commonplace in elite discourse. In the wake of the *Charlie Hebdo* attacks in January 2015, France appeared falsely unified in its defence of freedom of speech and other liberties seen as central to the French Republican culture, identity and democracy, despite early moves from the state to increase security measures and curtail basic rights. The subsequent attacks in Paris in November 2015 and in Nice and Normandy in July 2016 shifted the balance in the struggle between Republican liberalism and its associated form of Islamophobia and reactionary forces (acknowledging as we have that the two were always intertwined), as, at the same time, securitisation, a state of war and emergency, the introduction of a National Guard, and hardened positions became central to much of the public discourse.

What also cannot be ignored in these responses is that France was preparing for the 2017 presidential elections, and that three of the main candidates – Hollande, Sarkozy and Le Pen – were playing each other off and appealing to their constituencies as well as trying to capture more of the vote. Perhaps most striking in this context has been Marine Le Pen's behaviour in the aftermath of the attacks. As mainstream politicians attempted to outbid each other in a race towards securitisation and suspicion, at the expense of civil liberties and fostering further discrimination against Muslim communities, Le Pen has steered away from polemical grounds and simply claimed that mainstream politicians have failed in their duty to protect their citizens. Having poorly navigated the aftermath of the *Charlie Hebdo* attack, setting herself and her party apart from the unified movement, she became much more cautious in her approach. After the Saint-Etienne-du-Rouvray attack, Le Pen appeared even more moderate than the *Républicain* opposition, declaring that the rule of law should be respected.

Despite this, it is clear that these attacks have shifted the political debate further to the right. It seems that the pre-campaign has been increasingly fought on the right's territory: the Socialist party appears to have given up on inclusive politics and forfeited its alternative position to the Front National, and much of what has been discussed and proposed on both sides of the mainstream political spectrum since the attacks could just as well be borrowed from their programme.

Notes

1 While the attack also included targets such as a Jewish grocer in Paris, this chapter focuses on the role of the attack on *Charlie Hebdo* and discourses surrounding freedom of speech and 'Je Suis Charlie'.

2 Only Arlette Laguiller from the Trotskyite *Lutte Ouvrière* refused to give her support to Jacques Chirac in the second round.

3 *Paris Match*, 2, 9 and 16 May 2002.

4 Surveys suggested that between 21 and 38 per cent of Le Pen's 2002 electorate voted for Sarkozy in the first round of the 2007 elections (Evans and Ivaldi 2007). In the second round, two-thirds of Le Pen's voters transferred to the UMP candidate (Shields 2010).

References

Amnesty International (2016) *France: l'impact de l'état d'urgence*. Paris: Amnesty International.

Battaglia, A. (2006) 'A Fighting Creed: The Free Speech Narrative in the Danish Cartoon Controversy', *Free Speech Yearbook* 43 (1): 20–34.

Bekmezian, H. (2016) 'L'opposition veut durcir les lois contre le terrorisme', *Le Monde*, 27 July.

Benzine, R. (2016) 'Les déchirements français font partie du plan de Daech', *Le Monde*, 25 July.

Bordenave, Y., N. Chapuis and M. Goar (2016) 'Saint-Etienne-du-Rouvray, Nice: Nicolas Sarkozy demande la "vérité" au gouvernement', *Le Monde*, 27 July.

Bredoux, L. (2016) 'Après Nice, des polémiques parfois indignes face à un pouvoir faible', *Médiapart*, 26 July.

Clavel, G. (2015) 'Attentats de Paris: Laurent Wauquiez veut ouvrir des "centres d'internement" et c'est illégal', *Le Huffington Post*, 14 November.

Crépon, S., A. Dézé and N. Mayer (eds) (2015) *Les faux-semblants du Front National: Sociologie d'un parti politique*. Paris: Sciences Po Les Presses.

Crouch, C. (2004) *Post-Democracy*. Cambridge: Polity Press.

Delphy, C. (2006) 'Antisexisme ou antiracisme? Un faux dilemme', *Nouvelles Questions Féministes*, 26 (1): 59–83.

Deltombe, T. (2005) *L'islam imaginaire: la construction mediatique de l'islamophobie en France, 1975–2005*. Paris: La Découverte.

Evans, J. and G. Ivaldi (2007) 'L'extrême droite à la dérive: recomposition à droite', *Revue Politique et Parlementaire* 109 (1044): 113–22.

Hajjat, A. and M. Mohammed (2013) *Islamophobie. Comment les élites françaises construisent le 'problème musulman'*. Paris: La Découverte.

Huet, S. (2015) 'Villepin: "Le piège, c'est l'idée que nous sommes en guerre"', *Le Figaro*, 15 November.

Klausen, J. (2009) *The Cartoons that Shook the World*. New Haven, CT, and London: Yale University Press.

L'Obs (2012) 'Terrorisme: Valls met en garde contre "l'ennemi intérieur"', *L'Obs*, 12 October.

Laurent, S. (2016) 'Après Nice, Nicolas Sarkozy entre intox et postures martiales', *Le Monde*, 18 July.

Leprince, C. (2010) 'Burqa: la France invente la loi "pédagogique"', *Rue89*, 16 September.

Mbongo, P. (2007) 'Les caricatures de Mahomet et la liberté d'expression', *Esprit* 5: 145–9.

Miera, F. and V. Sala Pala (2009) 'The Construction of Islam as a Public Issue in Western European Countries through the Prism of the Muhammad Cartoons Controversy', *Ethnicities* 9 (3): 383–408.

Mondon, A. (2013) 'Nicolas Sarkozy's Legitimisation of the Front National: Background and Perspectives', *Patterns of Prejudice* 47 (1): 22–40.

Mondon, A. (2015) 'The French Secular Hypocrisy: The Extreme Right, the Republic and the Battle for Hegemony', *Patterns of Prejudice* 49 (4): 1–22.

Mondon, A. and A. Winter (2017) 'Articulations of Islamophobia: From the Extreme to the Mainstream?', *Ethnic and Racial Studies*, 40 (13).

Roy, O., A. Bidar and O. Mongin (2006) 'Les caricatures de Mahomet', *Esprit* 3: 323–35.

Saadia, M. (2016) 'The Paris Attackers Hit the City's Young, Progressive Core', *Fusion*.

Sarkozy, N. (2006) 'Nicolas Sarkozy répond aux lecteurs du Parisien, Entretien de Nicolas Sarkozy', *Le Parisien/Aujourd'hui en France*, 28 March.

Sarkozy, N. (2009) 'Discours à La-Chapelle-en-Vercors'. UMP, Speech at La-Chapelle-en-Vercors, 6 November.

Shields, J. (2010) 'Support for Le Pen in France: Two Elections in Trompe L'Oeil', *Politics* 30 (1): 61–9.

Tévanian, P. (2005) *Le voile médiatique. Un faux débat: 'l'affaire du foulard islamique'*. Paris: Éditions Raisons d'Agir.

Tévanian, P., I. Chouder and M. Latrèche (2008) *Les filles voilées parlent*. Paris: La Fabrique Édition.

Valls, M. (2016) 'Reconstruire l'islam de France', *Journal du Dimanche*, 31 July.

Yilmaz, F. (2011) 'The Politics of the Danish Cartoon Affair: Hegemonic Intervention by the Extreme Right', *Communication Studies* 62 (1): 5–22.

Zemmour, E. (2006) *Le Premier Sexe*. Paris: J'ai lu.

2 | THE MEANING OF 'CHARLIE': THE DEBATE ON THE TROUBLED FRENCH IDENTITY

Philippe Marlière

In the aftermath of the killings in Paris in January 2015, the French media, the government and most politicians delivered an emphatic verdict on those barbaric assassinations: what was at stake, they concurred, was the issue of freedom of speech. In other words, through their actions, the murderers had attempted to silence free speech, a cardinal value in French society.

From the outset, it was clear that the deeply unpopular socialist executive was trying to rally public opinion under the 'Je Suis Charlie" banner. To some extent, President François Hollande and Prime Minister Manuel Valls managed to achieve this objective. The 'Charlie Effect' – as it was called in the French media – did not last long though. The grand march in Paris on 11 January brought together large segments of the nation: up to 1.6 million people from various social, religious and ethnic backgrounds took peacefully to the streets of Paris (and up to 3.7 million in various cities across France) (*Libération* 2015).

But what was the meaning of those peaceful demonstrations? Was it really in defence of freedom of expression and the 'right' to ridicule believers and their beliefs, as it was argued by the French media and most politicians? Did the public demonstrate with a view to supporting the 'right' to blasphemy? It would be hard to answer those complex issues unequivocally; however, one can certainly challenge some of the official assumptions of the nebulous 'Nous Sommes Charlie' movement. In short, one can attempt to contextualise and objectify the government narrative on the matter.

The aim of this chapter is to reflect upon and look beyond the 11 January march. This piece discusses and assesses the controversial debate about the 'Je Suis Charlie' movement. Why did this march fail to heal the entire nation? In its aftermath, it sparked instead a heated discussion which involved frontline politicians, the media and high-profile intellectuals. In short, what was the actual meaning of the 'Charlie' debate?

The Hollande–Valls narrative

The only way not to concede victory to terrorists is to remain calm (Laborde 2015). This is not what George W. Bush did after 9/11, and this is not what the French government did either. The point here is not to draw a parallel between the two situations which were, in many respects, dissimilar. But what was striking in the hours following the Paris attacks – and this was somehow reminiscent of the American reaction – was the public outpouring of emotion, and the active role played by the media and the government in conveying this sentiment. The fact that the attack was perpetrated by French jihadists against a left-libertarian publication certainly struck a chord with large sections of the public. Although *Charlie Hebdo*'s 'anti-Islamic' stance was increasingly seen as divisive and politically ambiguous by some on the left (Cyran 2013), the cartoonists who were killed – notably the elder ones such as Cabu and Georges Wolinski – were held in high esteem by the public.

There were unusual reactions in France the days following the attacks: in the 'unity marches', people were seen flying the tricolour flag (for most French people, to do any such thing seems to represent rather cheap nationalism); they sang *La Marseillaise* (a song normally associated nowadays with the right or the extreme right, despite recent attempts on some parts of the left to somehow 'reclaim' it). More extraordinary still, citizens on the streets cheered and praised the police, a public institution which is traditionally fairly distrusted by the population. Marching with other heads of state – some of them open enemies of free speech at home – François Hollande declared on 9 January that: "Paris is today the capital of the world."

Manuel Valls, with similar self-restraint, affirmed: "France carries free speech everywhere." This was, in a way, the expected Gallic response to those tragic events: a brand of patriotism, which mixes abstract statements about the 'Country of the Rights of Man and the Citizen' and references to the so-called 'universal values' of the French 'Republican model'. This imperial rhetoric is reminiscent of that used by the US establishment when describing the United States as the 'Land of the Free' or as the self-appointed 'leader of the Free World'.

Once a guerrillero in the Bolivian forest alongside Ernesto 'Che' Guevara, now a conformist writer, Régis Debray summed up the national mood in his trademark grandiloquent manner:

> There were 4 million good citizens marching in the streets of France [on 11 January]; rightly proud to be there; unbelievers [in God]. This is admirable, but let's think that there are one billion believers in the world; people who do not think like us. We cannot ignore this reality. (Debray 2015)

Régis Debray's interpretation of the historic show of unity was as follows: the crowd marching through the streets of Paris was celebrating 'French exceptionalism' – that is, the *Voltairian* spirit of the French Revolution and its associated values: reason and free thinking (which for some in France are synonymous with anticlericalism if not anti-religious sentiments).

However, in line with the movement of '*déclinologues*' (politicians, journalists and intellectuals who lament France's economic and geopolitical decline or loss of influence over the past decades), the writer acknowledged that outside France, few people in the world understood, let alone embraced, the values of *laïcité à la française*: that is, French-style secularism. Since the law of 1905, *laïcité* constitutionally separates the state and the church and mandates strict neutrality from the state in regard to religions.

Re-establishing 'Republican values'

The defence of *laïcité* against what Manuel Valls has labelled 'Islamofascism' (Riché 2015) was, for some, a key component of the mass support after the Paris attacks. A few days after the Paris killings, Jean-Luc Mélenchon, the 2012 presidential candidate for the Left Front (a radical left coalition of parties) gave a public conference (Mélenchon 2015).

At that public event, Mélenchon argued that the attacks had aimed to undermine *laïcité*. According to this line of reasoning, the attacks had allegedly taken place because some could not tolerate the idea that religions – in this instance, Islam – should be made the butt of mockeries or blasphemous cartoons. Blasphemy – as it was argued almost unanimously in France at the time – constitutes a fundamental right as *laïcité* allegedly protects all kinds of beliefs including the right not to believe and to deride religions.

The day after the shooting, the French Ministry of Education decided that a minute of silence would be observed in all secondary schools across France to honour the victims. Teachers were invited to talk about the values of the Republic – notably *laïcité* – that had allegedly been threatened by the killings. In the days that followed the massacres, a twelve-year-old girl was temporarily excluded from school for saying in the playground that "all Muslims are friends with jihadists".

An eight-year-old was interrogated for two hours at a police station for allegedly refusing to respect the mandatory minute's silence and to join a 'chain of solidarity' on the playground in support of *Charlie Hebdo*. He also allegedly declared that he was "on the side of the terrorists" (those claims were strongly denied by the child's parents and lawyer). About 200 incidents of that nature were reported to the Education Ministry. When no incidents took place, Najat Vallaud-Belkacem, the Education Minister, still lamented that "too much questioning came from pupils", hinting that it was suspicious on the part of youngsters to discuss critically what had taken place in Paris or not to express full solidarity with *Charlie Hebdo*.

On 22 January, Vallaud-Belkacem presented a series of measures which were to constitute a "great mobilisation for schools around the values of the Republic". Several of those measures focused on *laïcité*. It was decided that a day of *laïcité* would be celebrated every 9 December to mark the passing of the law separating the church and the state on 9 December 1905.

Other measures included explaining *La Marseillaise*, the French national anthem, or the flag in order "to re-establish teachers' authority and Republican rites" in the classroom. Teachers were on the whole not impressed. Some regretted that those measures were ill-conceived and ineffectual as it was like imposing "something from the outside to kids who don't understand it". Some even challenged the reference to *laïcité* seen as a tool "that could be perceived as Islamophobic" by some pupils (Costa-Kostritsky 2015).

Sociological studies have shown that Islam has given some youngsters from the *banlieues* a chance to socialise at the mosque; it has helped them to steer out of delinquency and focus on their studies. In short, Islam has provided them with a way to find some dignity (Truong 2013). The importance that Islam today holds in the suburbs is the consequence of failed promises and policies from the 1980s onwards.

In 1983, a march for equality was organised: people walked from Marseilles to Paris. This was the first time that second-generation immigrants – mostly from Maghreb and former French colonies – publicly spoke up in favour of a multicultural and more inclusive France. After being initially courted by the socialist government, they were rapidly ignored. This generation was failed and was never represented by the political system as a whole.

When Manuel Valls described France as experiencing a "territorial, social and ethnic apartheid" on 20 January 2015 (*Le Monde* 2015), most politicians were outraged: how could the Prime Minister compare the country of the Rights of Man with the institutionally racist South African regime? Valls, however, did not intend to suggest that France has failed to integrate the population of foreign descent.

It is true that he unwittingly admitted that, in France, there is indeed 'race politics': contrary to the elites' Republican discourse, successive French governments from the left and from the right have implemented policies that have stigmatised and discriminated against those populations.

For example, while serving as Interior Minister in March 2013, Manuel Valls crudely stated that the Roma population (hardly 2,000 people in France) could not integrate because its culture was 'incompatible' with 'French values' and 'lifestyle'. This commentary was perceived as blatantly discriminatory and also arguably racist by anti-racist associations (*Le Monde* 2013). Yet the reaction of mainstream media and of political parties was tame if not inexistent.

The sanctification of *laïcité*

Given the size of the Muslim population, the French authorities cannot be as dismissive as they are with the Roma people. In France, one does not refer to 'Blacks' or 'Arabs', but to 'people from immigration'; one talks about universal values, and, although one alludes to Islam, one mentions *laïcité* instead. In other words, race politics in French politics is heavily understated and codified (Fassin 2015).

What had Valls intended, then, with his unsubtle comment about apartheid in France? After recognising that France was an 'ethnic apartheid', did the Prime Minister plead guilty for France's social failures, and for treating sections of its population as second-class citizens? He did not in the least do that. Rather than saying that the French government had imposed 'apartheid policies' on some individuals, the Prime Minister argued that some (notably Muslim) 'communities' had imposed apartheid on the rest of society. In short, the population 'of migration background' allegedly creates isolated 'ethnic areas'.

The French call it *communautarisme* (communitarianism – not to be confused with the word as it is used in English), a notion that refers to communities (racial or sexual, for instance). It has a very negative connotation in French public life as it entails that individuals allegedly separate themselves from the rest of society instead of mingling with it. This self-imposed segregation is a cardinal sin, as the French Republic is arguably 'indivisible'. Therefore, it cannot accept segregated populations because they represent a 'threat' to the unity of the nation. What this discourse fails to acknowledge, of course, is that those 'segregated' populations do not choose to live in poor suburban areas - successive governments put them there in the first place (Hussey 2014).

Banished from the physical as well as political and economic centres of French society, many 'French Muslims' have sought acknowledgement of their culture. The promotion of a 'Muslim identity' has been for some a strategy to receive attention and some form of recognition. The political reaction to these new demands has been to radically redefine French secularism in terms of a normative set of rules and boundaries (Bowen 2015).

Throughout the whole process of demonisation and segregation of individuals of Muslim faith, French 'Republicans' of late emphatically – some would say obsessively – refer to the notion of *laïcité*. The great universalist values of *laïcité* – freedom of conscience for all, common rules for everyone and equality between men and women – have become the instrument used to distinguish between 'us' (the 'good' French citizens who abide by French law and customs) and 'them' (those who do not) (Rancière 2015).

This is not what *laïcité* and the law of 1905 was intended to achieve (Marlière 2013). In the nineteenth century, *laïcité* was a political concept that allowed Republicans to free schools from the grip exerted by the Catholic Church. From the 1980s, it has become a kind of universal – and, in a sense, religious – principle: a rule that every individual has to obey (Baubérot 2006). It is up to the immigrants (first and second generations) and to the Muslims to conform to a kind of 'Frenchness', a set of unwritten rules of conduct and lifestyles which are compatible with 'being French' or simply with living in France.

In this respect, Catholicism is largely integrated in this new *laïque* space; Judaism and Protestantism are tolerated, but Islam is seen and portrayed as an alien and incompatible body within the French nation. Worse, Islam is described as a 'threat'. For women, to wear a hijab is a threat to *laïcité* because the majority of the population disapproves of the norms and values they ascribe to the garment. No pluralistic accommodation of those minority practices may possibly be found. In this situation, the role of the state is to intervene to 'liberate' and 'emancipate' women; to challenge decisions that most have made freely.

The state interference into people's privacy goes as far as controlling women's dress code and physical appearance. This explains why, since the late 1980s, the wearing of the hijab (first in school but now in the public sphere at large) and, more recently, the controversy about the burkini (a beach costume for women) (Marlière 2016) have become a thorny issue for the tenants of this holistic interpretation of *laïcité* (Fouteau 2015a). Such a take on *laïcité* relies on a false universalism while proposing in fact a 'majority *communautarisme*' (Marlière 2004), meaning a set of Franco-centred values and norms that are compatible with the views and culture of a majority of French citizens. After the ban on the hijab in state schools in 2004 (Bowen 2007) came the ban on the face veil in the street (in 2010). More recently, girls in secondary education who were not wearing a hijab were expelled from schools on the grounds that the 'long dark dress' which they were wearing constituted a "conspicuous religious [Islamic] sign" (Marlière 2015a).

The public narrative on 'Islam' and 'the Muslims' (as opposed to 'the Arabs', the more widely used term until the 1990s) by French politicians, the media and intellectuals/writers has shaped very negative representations of Islam in general. It can be argued that there has been an attempt – deliberate or not – to vilify and ostracise people who are Muslims (Fredette 2014).

'Freedom of expression'

Obviously, everyone was horrified by the Paris attacks and everyone agreed to condemn them. But this is not to say that everyone agreed with *Charlie Hebdo*'s cartoons, nor that the great marches across France were determined by their support for 'freedom of expression'.

Free speech is obviously an essential component of liberal societies. It follows that the state cannot prevent dissenting views being expressed unless they break the law. The 'Charlie Hebdo effect' and the show of national unity were short-lived exactly because French citizens did not take to the streets in support of an unqualified conception of free speech. People know that some ideas and viewpoints are suppressed. For instance, France has the most draconian laws in Europe to fight anti-Semitism. So everyone understands that one can defend free speech in theory, but without having to publish, let alone embrace, offensive ideas.

This is the main reason why the whole nation could not possibly come out in support of the *Charlie Hebdo* cartoons, which were seen by many as crude and offensive. On the left, there was unease with the emphasis on anti-Islamic criticism, as Muslims have virtually no representation and no political clout in society. Simply put, people took to the street to express their disgust at the cold-blooded killings. They sent a simple message: it is not right to shoot someone because you do not like what they have to say.

This underlying principle of tolerance sets the terms of how individuals can live together and learn to respect each other. The French authorities, however, chose instead to polarise the debate in terms of freedom of expression with, on the one hand, partisans of the Republic, *laïcité* and free speech (the 'good' citizens), and, on the other, the first- and second-generation immigrants (the 'bad' citizens), who are 'communitarian', culturally backward, sexist and Islamist.

Reducing the Charlie Hebdo attacks to a question of freedom of speech allows the government to ignore the disastrous socio-economic context in which some young French people become murderers. In truth, the obsessive reference to Islam in French society can be seen as a proxy for class and race. Muslims are discriminated against owing to their religion, but also because they belong to the lowest socio-economic segments in French society: they live in deprived areas where school and public service provisions are poor, and where there are few job opportunities. They are stigmatised due to the colour of their skin. In those hostile circumstances, Muslims in France were urged by the government and the media to pledge their allegiance to the Republic by publicly stating 'Nous Sommes Charlie'.

In a pluralist society, *laïcité* should not involve banning religions from the public sphere, but should enforce equality of all – believers or not – before the law. Under those circumstances, minority religions should only be limited when they break the law or when they do not respect the principles of liberty and equality for all. Religions should not be banned on the grounds that they do not please, or even offend, the majority of the population (Laborde 2009). The ban on 'conspicuous' religious signs in schools (the hijab notably with the 2004 law) and in the street (the 2010 law) is not 'Republican' as it goes against the underlying Republicans values of liberty (to decide how to appear in public) and equality (the 2004 and 2010 laws primarily discriminate against Islam). For some, a new Republicanism – pluralistic and strongly egalitarian – should be founded (Laborde 2010).

Since the January 2015 killings, France has not become more tolerant and more united; if anything, the opposite has happened, and this can be traced back to the initial state responses, from the condemnation of those – at school and elsewhere – who would not join the 'Je Suis Charlie' movement to the silencing of those who dissented from the claim that the public was mobilising in favour of free speech. Of more serious and lasting consequence, however, was the development of new legislation restricting freedom of expression and dissent as well as drastic internet surveillance in the name of the 'fight against terrorism' (Fouteau 2015b).

Since January 2015, the French government has robustly reigned in vocal support for terrorism: up to 100 people have been under investigation for "making or posting comments that support or try to support terrorism". The Valls government prepared its own Patriot Act 'to fight terrorism', a move described by critics from all political persuasions as the 'single most important attack' on French civil liberties since the end of the Second World War (Plenel 2015).

Those were the 'official' reactions in the political and media fields in the aftermath of the attacks. But the first major citizen contribution to the 'meaning of Charlie' came from Emmanuel Todd, a high-profile left-wing intellectual. Todd, a demographer and a historian, and also a staunch 'French Republican', published a vitriolic essay on the 'Je Suis Charlie' march four months after the event. The book took the media, political and intellectual worlds by storm (Todd 2015a).

Emmanuel Todd and the great Charlie Hebdo 'sham'

Todd was the first prominent intellectual figure to come out against this intolerant and illiberal drift, calling the march of 11 January an 'imposture': "This neo-Republic is a weird socio-political object which keeps shaking the grand rattles of liberty, equality and fraternity which have made France famous all over the world, whereas, in fact, our country has become unequal, ultra-conservative and closed" (Todd 2015a: 251). In the aftermath of the Paris killings, it is not free speech that is dominant, but a brand of French Republican McCarthyism.

Emmanuel Todd's main thesis is, indeed, quite provocative, as it blows to smithereens the French government's doxa of national unity. In a nutshell, Todd's central argument is that the January demonstrations across France were not, as the world was led to believe, a display of national unity and solidarity after the crimes committed by the Kouachi brothers and Amedy Coulibaly. They were, conversely, a 'sham' (Lancelin 2015), an act of 'collective hysteria', and a 'Europeanist happening' mainly enacted by white middle-class citizens. In a heated debate with 'pro-Charlie' proponent and *Libération* director Laurent Joffrin, Todd affirmed that the days following the killings were like a 'totalitarian flash'. For the first time in his life, he felt that free speech had deserted France, and he conceded that he "was afraid of expressing his views publicly" (Biseau and Daumas 2015).

Todd contends that the demonstrators were not upholding the values of the 1789 Revolution – liberty, equality, fraternity – but represented the counter-Revolution of 1815; they embodied the traditionalist Catholic France. To say that Emmanuel Todd's thesis is 'counterintuitive' is a major understatement. The first chapters of *Qui Est Charlie?* (2015a) provide an in-depth analysis of the 11 January marches. In order to engage with Todd's take on the January demonstrations, one must not be put off by some of his abrasive comments, which are often self-defeating, as they tend to undermine his own credibility as a 'serious' researcher. Todd has acknowledged in various media interviews that the "tone of the book was not academic". But it is one thing to denounce the 'implicit Islamophobia' of the crowds (an allegation that he substantiates throughout the book) and another to label the marchers 'Vichyssois', with reference to the French collaborationist regime during the Second World War. If one sets aside the more vitriolic and hyperbolic remarks, his analysis is interesting.

Todd points out that working-class people and members of ethnic minorities (who are often the same) were overwhelmingly underrepresented in the massive crowds that took to the streets on 11 January 2015. This is a contentious point, as several commentators were prompt to remark that no tangible data are available to substantiate this claim with certainty. Todd – who did not participate in the demonstrations – relies on 'intuition' and people's empirical observations. Critics may argue that the social or ethnic background of demonstrators is not essential to grasp the meaning and intentions of a march. What characterises a demonstration is what it stands for, supports, or opposes (Johsua 2015). In May 1968, students showed solidarity with blue-collar workers although most of them were petit bourgeois. The youngsters supported the cause of working-class emancipation all the same.

'Zombie Catholics'

Emmanuel Todd's book compares various maps to account for the intensity and nature of the demonstrations across France. This offers a 'geography of marches', a 'landscape of demonstrations', with quite strong variations in terms of popular mobilisation from one city to another. Thus, Todd observes that more people demonstrated in Paris, Grenoble, Lyon, Brest and Cherbourg than in Marseille, Lille, Béziers and Saint-Nazaire. Todd is certainly right in stressing that demonstrators were largely 'white, middle-class people', a socially, economically and politically hegemonic population in France that he refers to as MAZ ("*classes Moyennes, personnes Âgées, catholiques Zombies*", or "middle classes, elderly people, zombie Catholics"). He is less convincing, though, when he emphatically concludes that, overall, those marches were the expression of an "old French brand of Catholicism" embodied by "selfish and repressive" middle-class people. In other words, these demonstrators were not the egalitarian children of 1789 but 'zombie Catholics', a recurring expression throughout the book that Todd uses to refer to marchers from "de-Christianized regions of France". He argues that, in those areas, Christian roots are traditionally more resistant to the Republican values of tolerance, solidarity and secularism (*laïcité*).

The differences in the sizes of the marching crowds – the more egalitarian cities were less supportive of the movement than the inegalitarian ones – were allegedly evidence that those demonstrations were driven by selfish, individualistic and Islamophobic sentiments. Todd remarks that the greatest attendance records were achieved in cities that supported the European constitutional treaty that was rejected by 55 per cent of French voters in 2005. The opponents of the treaty argued at the time that it would set in stone 'neoliberal' policies and principles at the heart of European integration. Although Todd was criticised for making rather loose and unscientific use of his maps, cartographic experts, despite pointing to some factual errors, agreed that the correlation established between the number of marchers and the sociology of the populations studied was basically correct (Joliveau 2015; Cassely 2015).

By comparing several maps of France, Todd is able to draw on an overall picture of the demonstrations to point to the hotbeds of 'pro-Charlism', which run from Normandy (north-west) down through Brittany to the Pyrenees, then up to the Alps region and to Alsace (north-east). According to Todd, these are the bastions of zombie Catholics, the staunchest battalions of the 'Je Suis Charlie' movement. Although in these areas Catholicism has dramatically declined since 1960 – notably its social influence – it nonetheless still continues to structure the political and social life of citizens, even those who are not believers or worshipers. This is the meaning of the provocative label 'zombie Catholics' – undead creatures, typically depicted as mindless, reanimated corpses.

Militant *laïcisme* and inegalitarian views

With the exception of Paris – historically, ground zero for all upheavals and therefore an egalitarian city – the other cities with a high turnout have historically been seen as 'conservative' and deeply attached to the Catholic Church. Zombie Catholics may not be churchgoers or even believers, but they are fundamentally under the influence of the inegalitarian views of the church. What is more, Todd lambasts the middle-class 'militant *laïcisme*' directed against the poor, uneducated immigrants of Muslim faith. He regards the increasingly anticlerical, antireligious and Islamophobic stand of the *laïcistes* as deeply disturbing.

It is for him one of the perverse effects of de-Christianisation and of the rise of socio-economic inequalities in France. He points to the negative role of the Parti Socialiste (PS), which has given up on constructing a society in which wealth is fairly distributed and in which those in need can be supported by the state. After sabotaging the very idea of socialism in France, Todd argues that the PS is now on course to "destroy the Republic" and its egalitarian ideals (Todd 2015b). For Todd, 'genuine' Republicanism belongs to all: it means universal suffrage and pursuit of equality and solidarity through the 'Social Republic'. What he calls 'neo-republicanism', conversely, turns its back on this demanding type of universalism and has been 'confiscated' by the privileged few in French society.

Since the Revolution, the left has had to fight the power and hegemony of the Catholic Church in French society. Until the 1960s, the church was deeply hostile to the Republican regime and to the 1905 law separating the state and religions in France (*laïcité*). According to Todd, the new religion of the MAZ is a virulent *Voltairianism*, a militant atheism that looks down upon working-class Muslims. The demographer here 'essentialises' groups of people and argues that regional cultures impact in a quasi-deterministic manner on people whatever their personal background. These cities and regions, Todd argues, thrive on growing economic inequalities and the widening gaps between people in terms of wealth and career opportunities. Furthermore, the 'Je Suis Charlie' movement comes across as "intolerant and largely Islamophobic". The zombie Catholics have become key supporters of the governing PS, a party that Todd describes as uninterested in addressing rampant inequalities in France as well as racism and anti-Semitism.

Emmanuel Todd's central thesis is that those at the 'Je Suis Charlie' gatherings are 'neo-republicans' who support a 'neo-Republic'. However, this neo-republicanism has nothing to do with the ideals of the 'true' Republic because it has marginalised the poor and immigrants. Todd finds it repulsive that, on 11 January, the so-called zombie Catholics demonstrated in order to affirm the "absolute right to mock, caricature, and to blaspheme" a minority religion, one practised by some of the most vulnerable members in French society. Todd seems to have a point here: 'the right to blasphemy' in the context of the *Charlie Hebdo* killings seems to boil down to the right of the majority to ridicule people from a poor background. Todd notes that such ridicule is cowardly, as Muslims comprise only about 5.6 per cent of the entire population (El Karoui 2016) and have been strongly discriminated against in France for the past three decades.

Todd's analysis has been the subject of significant criticism. The geographer Jacques Lévy argues that, on a theoretical level, Emmanuel Todd is a 'culturalist' in that he tends to dismiss far too easily the influence of historical processes on individuals' actions (Lévy 2015). In Todd's analysis, human behaviours tend to be 'essentialised', explained through deeply engrained cultural patterns – types of 'habitus', as Pierre Bourdieu would have put it. There is little room for 'historicity' – for making history, conflicts, or class struggles. Todd neither belongs to the Anglo-American liberal left nor does he think as a European Marxist: he is above all a French Republican. The

French Republican tradition – in its revolutionary left and reformist conceptions – has always been ideologically 'Jacobin'. Mainstream Jacobins hold a strong belief in representative democracy as opposed to popular democracy; in a 'unitary' and 'indivisible' nation; in centralised institutions and a top-down approach to power and politics (Marlière 2015b). John Stuart Mill, who did not think much of this 'abstract Republican mind', described it as proceeding "from an infirmity of the French mind, which has been one main cause of the miscarriages of the French nation in its pursuit of liberty and progress; that of being led away by phrases, and treating abstractions as if they were realities which have a will and exert active power" (Mill 2013 [1910]: 347).

More recently, a robust rebuttal of Todd's analysis came from Mayer and Tiberj (2016). According to their study, 'Charlie' in the streets was over-represented among young, urban, educated, left-wing and tolerant citizens: i.e., they had the usual profile of demonstrators mobilised on post-materialist issues. They had no hostility to Muslims or minorities: on the contrary, the most inclined to join the rallies were those with the lowest scores on the scales of Islamophobia and xenophobia. As for religion, once controlled by all the other individual characteristics (age, gender, residence, party proximity, attitudes), being a Catholic, whatever the level of practice, showed no statistically significant effect on the actual participation in the rallies. The authors also note that this tolerant mood, after the bloody attacks against *Charlie Hebdo* and the Hyper Cacher, was not only a characteristic of those who took part in the rallies, it was shared by French society at large.

Conclusion

Thus, what was the meaning of 'Charlie'? Following the Paris attacks of January 2015, it started off as a mass movement of citizens aggrieved and shocked by the atrocious killings. It rapidly descended into a political football: the weak and unpopular socialist executive tried to regain the political initiative by promoting a kind of official and mandatory 'Je Suis Charlie' line. It quickly became obvious to some that the 'Charlie' narrative meant much more than a robust defence of free speech and the 'right to blasphemy'.

Underneath the surface of a tribute to the dead, there was an authoritarian streak that ethnicised and stigmatised the Muslim population. The whole chain of events reinforced Islamophobic stereotypes.

Muslims were regarded with even more suspicion in different constituencies of the media and politics.

In this chain of subsequent events, this chapter considers Emmanuel Todd's vitriolic attack on the whole 'Je Suis Charlie' movement, for while Mayer and Tiberj's study has largely undermined Todd's main assertions, Todd's contribution framed a number of key issues in relation to French identity. Indeed, Todd's book unveiled a number of disturbing truths as to France's increasingly intolerant and narrow-minded reaction to cultural pluralism and religious freedom. This critique helped underline the failure of the Republican polity to integrate and treat all citizens as equal and autonomous individuals.

References

Baubérot, J. (2006) *L'Intégrisme Républicain Contre la Laïcité*. La Tour d'Aigues: Éditions de l'Aube.

Biseau, G. and C. Daumas (2015) 'Emmanuel Todd: "Le 11 janvier est un tour de passe-passe"', *Libération*, 3 May. www.liberation.fr/politiques/2015/05/03/le-11-janvier-est-un-tour-de-passe-passe_1287114 (last accessed on 22 September 2016).

Bowen, J. (2007) *Why the French Don't Like Headscarves. Islam, the State, and Public Space*. Princeton NJ: Princeton University Press.

Bowen, J. (2015) 'France's Own Political Traditions Can Accommodate Visible Islam and Heal Social Divisions', *Boston Review*, 3 March. http://bostonreview.net/forum/john-bowen-france-after-charlie-hebdo (last accessed on 17 September 2016).

Cassely, J.-L. (2015) 'Manifestations du 11 janvier: Qui était vraiment Charlie?', *Slate*, 6 May. www.slate.fr/story/101221/11-janvier-qui-etait-vraiment-charlie (last accessed on 22 September 2016).

Costa-Kostritsky, V. (2015) 'Forced to be "Charlie"', *Precarious Europe*, 17 February. www.precariouseurope.com/lives/forced-to-be-charlie (last accessed on 17 September 2016).

Cyran, O. (2013) 'Charlie Hebdo pas raciste? Si vous le dites …', *Article 11*, 5 December. www.article11.info/?Charlie-Hebdo-pas-raciste-Si-vous (last accessed on 17 September 2016).

Debray, R. (2015) 'Après Charlie, le risque d'un McCarthysme démocratique', *Mediapart*, 20 April. www.mediapart.fr/journal/france/200415/apres-charlie-le-risque-d-un-maccarthysme-democratique (last consulted on 17 September 2016).

El Karoui, H. (2016) 'Un Islam français est possible', Fondation Montaigne, September. www.institutmontaigne.org/fr/publications/un-islam-francais-est-possible (last accessed on 22 September 2016).

Fassin, É. (2015) 'Apartheid: aveu ou dénégation?', *Libération*, 1 February. www.liberation.fr/politiques/2015/02/01/apartheid-aveu-ou-denegation_1193483 (last accessed on 17 September 2016).

Fouteau, C. (2015a) 'Des crèches aux universités, Vingt-cinq ans de fixation contre le voile', *Mediapart*, 22 March. www.mediapart.fr/journal/france/220315/des-creches-aux-universites-vingt-cinq-ans-de-fixation-contre-le-voile (last accessed on 17 September 2016).

Fouteau, C. (2015b) 'Valls touche à la liberté d'expression pour lutter contre le racisme et l'antisémitisme', *Mediapart*, 17 April. www.mediapart. fr/journal/france/170415/valls-touche-la-liberte-d-expression-pour-lutter-contre-le-racisme-et-l-antisemitisme (last accessed on 17 September 2016).

Fredette, J. (2014) *Constructing Muslims in France. Discourse, Public Identity, and the Politics of Citizenship.* Philadelphia PA: Temple University Press.

Hussey, A. (2014) *The French Intifada. The Long War Between France and its Arabs*, London: Granta.

Johsua, S. (2015) 'Todd, impair et passe', *Mediapart*, 6 May. https://blogs. mediapart.fr/samy-johsua/ blog/060515/todd-impair-et-passe (last accessed on 22 September 2016).

Joliveau, T. (2015) 'Où était Charlie? Ce que montrent réellement les cartes d'Emmanuel Todd', *Slate*, 22 May. www.slate.fr/story/101827/ou-est-charlie-cartes-emmanuel-todd (last accessed on 22 September 2016).

Laborde, C. (2009) 'Républicanisme critique vs. républicanisme conservateur: repenser les "accommodements raisonnables"', *Critique Internationale* 3 (44): 19–33.

Laborde, C. (2010) *Français, Encore un Effort pour Être Républicains!* Paris: Éditions du Seuil.

Laborde, C. (2015) 'Don't Let the Paris Murderers Win', European Institute, UCL, 25 February. www.ucl.ac.uk/ european-institute/analysis/2014-15/ paris-murderers (last accessed on 17 September 2016).

Lancelin, A. (2015) 'Emmanuel Todd: "Le 11 janvier a été une imposture"', *L'Obs*, 29 April. http://bibliobs.nouvelobs. com/actualites/20150428.OBS8114/ emmanuel-todd-le-11-janvier-a-ete-une-imposture.html (last accessed on 22 September 2016).

Le Monde (2013) 'Le MRAP porte plainte contre Manuel Valls pour ses propos contre les Roms', *Le Monde*, 12 November. http://abonnes.lemonde. fr/politique/article/2013/11/12/le-mrap-porte-plainte-contre-manuel-valls-pour-ses-propos-sur-les-roms_ 3512261_823448.html (last accessed on 17 September 2016).

Le Monde (2015) 'Manuel Valls évoque un "apartheid territorial, social, ethnique" en France', *Le Monde*, 20 January. http://abonnes.lemonde. fr/politique/article/2015/01/20/pour-manuel-valls-il-existe-un-apartheid-territorial-social-ethnique-en-france_ 4559714_823448.html (last accessed on 19 September 2016).

Lévy, J. (2015) 'Un Todd stimulant, mais brouillé avec la réalité', *Libération*, 3 May. www.liberation. fr/politiques/2015/05/03/un-todd-stimulant-mais-brouille-avec-la-realite_1287119 (last accessed on 20 September 2016).

Libération (2015) 'Marche républicaine à Paris: une marche sans précédent', *Libération*, 11 January. www.liberation. fr/societe/2015/01/11/en-direct-la-place-de-la-republique-noire-de-monde_1178277 (last accessed on 17 September 2016).

Marlière, P. (2004) 'La laïcité en France, un communautarisme majoritaire', *Politique, Revue de Débats* 33 (February). www.revuepolitique. be/france-un-communautarisme-majoritaire/ (last accessed on 17 September 2016).

Marlière, P. (2013) 'La *Laïcité*, un principe de non-domination', *Mediapart*, 30 October. http://blogs.mediapart. fr/blog/philippe-marliere/301013/ la-laicite-un-principe-de-non-domination (last accessed on 17 September 2016).

Marliere, P. (2015a) 'Charlie Hebdo and the dawn of French McCarthyism', *openDemocracy*, 17 August. https://www.opendemocracy. net/can-europe-make-it/philippe- marli%C3%A8re/charlie-hebdo-and- dawn-of-french-mccarthyism (last accessed on 24 August 2017).

Marlière, P. (2015b) 'The Paris Commune: Globalisation before Globalisation', *London Review of Books* 37 (13): 21–2.

Marlière, P. (2016) 'L'hystérie anti-burkini, symptôme d'un mal profond', *L'Obs*, 31 August. http://leplus.nouvelobs. com/contribution/1555055-l-hysterie- anti-burkini-symptome-d-un-mal- profond-non-a-un-republicanisme- autoritaire.html (last accessed on 20 September 2016).

Mayer, N. and V. Tiberj (2016) 'Who Were the "Charlie" in the Streets? A Socio- political Approach of the January 11 Rallies', *International Review of Social Psychology* 29 (1): 59–68. www.rips- irsp.com/articles/10.5334/irsp.63/ (last accessed on 22 September 2016).

Mélenchon, J.-L. (2015) 'Conférence *laïcité* et paix civile', *Le Blog de Jean-Luc Mélenchon*, 12 January. www.jean-luc- melenchon.fr/2015/01/12/conference- laicite-et-paix-civile/ (last accessed on 17 September 2016).

Mill, J. S. (2013 [1910]) *The Letters of John Stuart Mill*. Vol. 2. London: Forgotten Books.

Plenel, E. (2015) 'Contre la surveillance, la question démocratique', *Mediapart*, 29 April. www.mediapart. fr/journal/france/290415/contre- la-surveillance-la-question- democratique (last accessed on 17 September 2016).

Rancière, J. (2015) 'The Front National's Useful Idiots', VersoBooks.com, 13 April. www.versobooks.com/ blogs/1936-jacques-ranciere-the- front-national-s-useful-idiots (last accessed on 17 September 2016).

Riché, P. (2015) 'Le clin d'oeil néo- conservateur de Manuel Valls', *L'Obs*, 16 February. http://tempsreel. nouvelobs.com/edito/20150216. OBS2604/islamo-fascisme-le-clin-d- oeil-neo-conservateur-de-manuel- valls.html (last accessed on 17 September 2016).

Todd, E. (2015a) *Qui Est Charlie ? Sociologie d'une Crise Religieuse*. Paris: Éditions du Seuil.

Todd, E. (2015b) 'Ce livre, c'est aussi la révélation du rôle du PS dans la destruction de la République', *Atlantico*, 17 May. www.atlantico.fr/decryptage/e- todd-livre-est-aussi-revelation-role-ps- dans-destruction-republique-qui-est- charlie-2146250.html (last accessed on 22 September 2016).

Truong, F. (2013) *Des Capuches et des Hommes*. Essais et Documents. Paris: Buchet-Chastel.

3 | AFTER THE DRAMA: THE INSTITUTIONALISATION OF GOSSIPING ABOUT MUSLIMS

Valérie Amiraux and Arber Fetiu

Introduction

In January 2015, political violence broke out in the heart of Paris. The massacre at *Charlie Hebdo*, the assassination of police officers and a hostage-taking in a kosher supermarket were perpetrated by three Frenchmen in the name of Al Qaeda and Daesh. Two years later, it is still difficult to grasp the entire scale of the political consequences of these events.[1] The subsequent attacks in Paris (November 2015) and Nice (July 2016), as well as other heinous incidents – murders of religious figures and police officers committed in the name of similar causes – further complicate the task of understanding the overall situation. Yet, an impression of strange familiarity emerged from the ways in which public discussions were set in motion, particularly in political arenas and in the media, while trying to make sense of these events. In the aftermath of the collective shock came a call to share the effects in the form of what politicians later referred to as 'national unity'. This call was initiated from a desire to create an emergency response that matched the seriousness of these events. Drawing on the 'social sharing of emotions' – reciprocal affection, perpetuating bonds of attachment and the guarantee of social integration for everyone (Rimé 2010) – we will examine the public conversation that emerged immediately after the incidents via a corpus of works published in France 'as a reaction' to the events that took place at the *Charlie Hebdo* editorial office.

This chapter argues that, notwithstanding the violence and the emotional impact of the Paris attacks against *Charlie Hebdo*, nothing truly original has emerged in the way in which public narratives on the 'Muslim problem' have been displayed in France since January 2015. The terms of the public discussion sparked by these events have merely updated the various strata on which the 'Muslim problem' has gradually been constructed in France since the late 1980s and early 1990s (Amiraux 2004; Hajjat and Mohammed 2013). In fact, these publications have merely fed into previous public discussions on Islam and Muslims which have been ongoing in France since the late 1980s. These violent events have legitimised the intensification of securitarian discourse and paved the way for political decisions to implement new policies in so-called 'priority sectors' such as urban policy and education. These intensifications are best understood in contrast to the pattern of public conversation that has been occurring in France for nearly fifteen years. These are the same discussions that laid the foundation for the way in which French citizens talk about Islam and their Muslim co-citizens.

To elaborate on this idea of a continuity, we decided to look empirically at the material that has emerged since January 2015 under the form of a series of new books (both fiction and non-fiction). This heterogeneous corpus has been published in the aftermath of the attacks, taking the 'Charlie events' as their main justification. In this chapter, we will begin by presenting the contents descriptively, and then will map the main topics that emerge, before examining how this publishing logorrhoea contributes to the consolidation of a gossip pattern that has become the dominant form of public conversation about Muslims and Islam in France. Here, gossip is used to refer to an informal form of personal communication built around those who are absent, or, more tellingly, are simply treated as such.

The corpus: responses to the event

Eighty-three books were published in France between the immediate aftermath of the attacks of January 2015 and July 2016: that is, an average of 4.6 books were published on Charlie Hebdo every month during this period. Some also refer to the Paris attack of November 2015. We have identified this database through various channels, for example by tracking them through the book sections of newspapers and magazines such as *Le Monde*, *Libération* and *Nouvel Obs*.[2]

We read each book, paying attention to the data used, the genre and the main narrative lines. From a discourse analysis perspective, our corpus is composed of diverse literary genres including fiction and non-fiction, from which we get a sense of the enormous diversity of narrative models employed to respond to the attacks: comic books, philosophical and political essays, novels, edited books containing letters or comments written by diverse authors, professional and personal journals, collected drawings, fieldwork essays, collected chronicles, books by witnesses present at the attack scenes, survivor testimonials, posthumous essays by victims, close friends and family memory books, biographies, volumes by sociologists and political scientists, and even poetry dedicated to events or, more precisely, to *Charlie Hebdo*.[3]

The gender ratio of the publications is clearly dominated by male authors, who produced fifty-one of the publications compared with just fifteen by female authors. Five publications were co-authored by male and female authors, nine were co-authored by male authors and three were collective volumes. Some of these authors are frequently published writers, including philosophers such as Onfray (2016), Badiou (2016) and Viveret (2015); journalists such as Ginori (2016), Birnbaum (2016) and Mas-Pionnier (2016); and public figures and polemicists such as Fourest (2015), Joffrin (2015), Montbrial (2015) and Polony (2015) cohabitating with relatively unknown authors and newcomers such as Bathily (2016). Bathily, one of the protagonists of the Hyper Cacher attack who helped save the hostages, wrote his book to describe his life before, during and after the incident at Hyper Cacher. The ethnic diversity of authors is another significant feature of the corpus, as self-declared Muslim authors are but a tiny minority (among these few are al Malik 2015; Bathily 2016; Baouz 2016). Similar comments could also be made about the generational variation.

From this initial corpus of books, we specifically focused on the forty publications listed at the end of the chapter. Some of the initial publications were excluded as we thought their content, or the nature of the work, did not precisely correspond to the objectives of this research – for instance, we decided not to work on books published by academics since our research is not interested in the discourse that emerges from experts (especially in the fields of anti-terrorism, sociology of violence, Islamic studies, education, etc.).[4] We also put aside books that were collections of chronicles published before Charlie Hebdo and re-edited to fit the after-events (Schneidermann 2015; Pelloux 2015). A few books were unavailable (Vaquette 2015) or hard to find (Etchian 2016). The unity of our corpus is mostly based on the founding aspect of the Charlie attacks, even though some authors folded in the November attacks to expand their comments.

From the selected publications, there are: twenty-six essays, five edited volumes (Attali 2015; Duhamel 2015; Mas-Pionnier 2016; Maxence 2015; Collectif 2015), one comic book (Luz 2015), two novels (Berton 2015; Ginori 2016), and six testimonials/autobiographies (Baouz 2016; Bathily 2016; Bouazar 2015; Ibn Ziaten and Jouve 2016; Lamoureux 2015; Wolinski 2016). Some of the selected publications have proven to be quite popular. Only one month after its publication, Michel Onfray's *Penser l'Islam* sold 28,000 copies. Luz's 'Catharsis' (2015) published 90,000 copies, holding the number one comic book position on the 'Top fifteen comics' for quite some time.[5]

Genericity: main topics identified in the corpus

In this section we address this literary production in relation to the notion of 'genericity' (Adam 2011). Genericity encompasses the idea of common characteristics shared with other volumes in the same category and highlights connections between the books, but also emphasises the possibility of their expressing a singular voice. In the two years following the attacks, 'Charlie' has certainly acquired the status of a signifying category. It condenses an extensive body of information, and conveys images and visual memories of scenes that have been circulating through the media since day one. It concentrates a complex set of heterogeneous representations. 'Charlie', as a discursive category, has turned into a trigger for a memory of the event with its associated horror, factual basis and political outcomes.

The corpus revolves around three topical axes. The first looks at the traumatic events (*Charlie Hebdo* attacks, 7–9 January) as a *theatre of facts*. Authors relate to this factuality but deliver rather surgically detailed descriptions of scene(s). The general impression after the reading of these books oscillates between having watched a suspenseful thriller or being a detective working on a high-profile murder case. They, in a way, translate or transpose the continuous flow of images that invaded private homes from 7–9 January into writing. While some authors are direct protagonists, others engage in the description of scenes and events in absentia through fiction and non-fiction, grounding their narratives in the media by delving into institutional narratives and facts or by providing a fictional reconstruction of the events from a distance. Some writers, such as Bathily (2016), were direct protagonists of the events. Their story is told in the first person. So is the semi-fiction by Anaïs Ginori (2016). She tells of Patrick, the newspaper seller located on Boulevard Saint-Germain who, on the morning of 7 January, sold Cabus and Wolinski their daily newspapers, as usual. The real story is striking: Patrick met the Kouachi brothers a couple of hours later, after they massacred the people at *Charlie*. They stole his car trying to escape the police.

Federbusch (2015), on the other hand, partially reconstructs the events at *Charlie Hebdo* and the Hyper Cacher from a distance. In another register, Berton's (2015) novel offers a fictional description of the events through the voice of a hypothetical survivor named Charif Kouachi. Bruno Dive (2016) digs into the channels of French institutions to reconstruct the events of *Charlie Hebdo* and Hyper Cacher, through interviews and investigations with figures such as François Hollande and Manuel Valls. Mas-Pionnier co-authored an ambitious fact-checked inquiry inspired by Lapierre and Collins' book *Paris brûle-t-il?* (1960), which later inspired the French-American movie by René Clément in 1966,[6] based on a script by Francis Ford Coppola and others. Duhamel (2015) collected quotes that popped up in the public sphere after the massacre, expressing the wish to place the reader in touch with the spirit of citizens displayed a few hours after the events.[7] Attali (2015) offers a collection of comments from 'the day after', provided by members of the Livre de Poche (a French publishing house) expressing their feelings about the event and including paragraphs from several authors. Many of the authors cited here are connected through diverse temporal and spatial proximity with the events (Bathily 2016; Ginori 2016; Luz 2015).

The second axis approaches the events as an occasion to raise certain issues and speak out about them. Here, we found a range of topics and themes being tackled in multiple ways, sometimes antagonistically. The first theme of this axis deals with religion and Islam. While Federbusch (2015) talks about the failures of the police force to protect *Charlie Hebdo* as a critique of the institutions and the party in power, Birnbaum (2016) and Onfray (2016) are more interested in debating the compatibility of Islam in a Republican context. The question of Islam and violence is significant in Joffrin (2015) as well as in Baouz (2016), Bouazar (2015), Abd al Malik (2015), Bathily (2016) and Ibn Ziaten and Jouve (2016). These texts embody the more traditional dichotomy of public conversation regarding Islam in France. On the one hand, an argument is made that 'Islam is the religion of peace' and that those who commit acts in its name are an unrepresentative, and even a condemnable, minority inside a largely peaceful and convivial majority. They argue that the attacks are a deformation of Islam by those who have hijacked it, or that they are simply a derailment of the religion.

On the other hand, other authors also claim that there is an intrinsic connection of Islam with violence, thus raising the issue of the legitimacy of Islam's presence in the French Republic and therefore of Muslims as co-citizens in connection with the events in Paris. Onfray for instance, reflects upon the tie that intrinsically binds religion and violence in the founding texts of Islam. His genealogical approach, based on his reading of Islamic traditional texts – referring to the Qur'an as the main source for understanding the contemporary behaviour of terrorists and radical figures – is a direct critique of those who tend to dismiss religion as an independent variable.

A second thematic section focuses on what the authors identify as a crisis of French identity. Polony (2015) emphasises the multiple breaches and fault lines that affect the French identity. Her book focuses exclusively on identity being defined as a 'mode of being', an inherited content of norms and values to which citizens pay tribute and demonstrate their attachment. The idea of an identity based on a community of practice, or to *do* rather than to *be*, is absent in her proposal. Morin and Singaïny (2015), Ory (2016) and Viveret (2015) consider that this crisis encompasses society as a whole, while Baouz (2016) limits the notion of the identity crisis to specific urban locations (the suburbs), and Storti (2016) warns against the risks of using 'identity' as a political category. Polony (2015) shares similar concerns: who is the *we* in the 'We are France' slogan that was espoused as the national motto after Charlie? Identity, she says, has turned into a dirty word and to some extent has become a taboo. France needs a new narrative to be shared by everyone.

In a few cases, authors expressed their anxieties through a belligerent analogy with war, an approach that corresponds with statements made by the Prime Minister immediately after the events. Emphasising geopolitical connections, 'France is waging a foreign war', according to Onfray (2016) and Joffrin (2015). Yet this fight also resembles a civil war according to Boucheron and Ribolet (2015) and Morin and Singaïny (2015). Public debate, moreover, also appears to be a war zone, with different intellectual projects and agencies held to account. Pierrat (2015) and Colosimo (2016), along with Val (2015), Birnbaum

(2016) and Federbusch (2015), for instance, take the opportunity to criticise sociological approaches that, in their opinion, make it hard and confusing for us to look at and analyse the events and their consequences appropriately. Others, such as Storti (2016), Joffrin (2015), Viveret (2015) and Ory (2016), critique those they term 'reactionaries' – Zemmour, Onfray, Camus and Finkielkraut in particular – who replicate the obsession of the far right with 'immigrants', 'Muslims', the 'violent suburbs' and 'communitarianism', as the basis for rather pessimistic and dystopian views (such as Renaud Camus' theory of 'grand replacement') about the future of French society.

Several publications, such as those by Birnbaum (2016), Colosimo (2016), Federbusch (2015), Val (2015, 2016), Pierrat (2015), Guirous (2016) and Onfray (2016), unleash a critique of what they see as the incapacity of the left to consider religion as an 'independent agent'. Others have more specific targets, including Storti (2016), who criticises feminism and postcolonial studies, while Lamoureux (2015) and Guirous (2016) tackle multiple problems they identify as the fault of the educational system. Federbusch (2015) evokes the failure of the police force to protect *Charlie Hebdo* and critiques the institutions and the party in power. Ginori (2016) connects her sensational story based on the real facts with larger comments on the state of the press and the particular conditions that affect journalists.

Philippe Val (2015, 2016) prefers to stick to his intimate knowledge of *Charlie Hebdo*. In both books, he narrates the ups and downs of the magazine, the multiple challenges faced by the members of the team, along with an autobiography that distils the need to safeguard the spirit of the Republic as incarnated by himself, the journal and its free spirit. Colosimo (2016) and Pierrat (2015) also take the approach that freedom of expression was the main victim of the terrorist attack against *Charlie Hebdo*. These works focus on blasphemy and the legal cases of freedom of expression. Val (2015, 2016), Ory (2016), Guirous (2016), Fourest (2015) and Federbusch (2015) also touch upon this approach in a more general manner.

On a more optimistic note, few books are presented to the reader as calls for a better future. Bidar (2015) begins with the idea that Islam is experiencing a crisis while putting an emphasis on the question of freedom of expression, and urges the reader to develop a more universal and pragmatic '*fraternité*'. Ibn Ziaten (Ibn Ziaten and Jouve 2016) also takes freedom of expression as a central point of her plea for a tolerant society. In doing so, she also emphasises the necessity of developing tolerance as an ethic of respect. Viveret (2015) also closely follows Bidar in emphasising '*fraternité*', and Abd al Malik (2015), in his letter addressed to his co-citizens with an emphasis on the Muslim community, calls for a better future based on proactive and committed communities. Hansen-Löve and Tomei (2015) also take a similar line, while putting the emphasis on the generational gap that may bridge a common path to a better future. While these books present a plea for an improved future, they recognise the reality of the challenges and problems in French society and underline that it would be vain to consider statements about the importance of identity as sufficient to engage younger citizens.

The third topical axis includes recurring themes that frame public discussion about Muslims and Islam in France. The most commonly discussed issues are predictable: the status of *laïcité*, the danger of communitarianism, the fragility of Republicanism, and the larger topic of integration as related to immigration, security threats and radicalisation (Guirous 2016; Lamoureux 2015; Ory 2016; Colosimo 2016). The Charlie-related books do not really offer anything properly new or specific here, as these questions are the usual suspects that have framed public discussion about 'Muslim others' since the end of the 1970s. Charlie is the excuse to rephrase a series of narratives that sound very familiar to a French audience. Some authors have, in fact, made a career of these discourses, including Onfray, a regular author of bestsellers on the topic. *Laïcité*, however, now takes on a new shape as a sanctified item, one that carries the burden of being a renewed solution to all the problems associated with the trajectories of the French terrorists and their attacks on the symbols of 'French culture' (Guirous 2016; Ory 2016; Federbasch 2015; Fourest 2015).

As against this, several authors deplore the impulse towards the *intégrisme laïque* (secular fundamentalism) as manifested in the discourse of groups such as *Riposte laïque* in the French debates around Muslims, who use *laïcité* as a blunt instrument against Muslims. These authors insist on more openness and flexibility regarding *laïcité* (Storti 2016; Joffrin 2015; Viveret 2015). Discussion of 'Islamophobia' is found in several of these publications. Some deny its existence or consider it as a silencing instrument against a criticism of Islam (Guirous 2016; Ory 2016; Federbusch 2015; Val 2015, 2016; Fourest 2015) while others, although they recognise potential misuses of it, affirm the existence of the phenomena (Joffrin 2015; Storti 2016; Morin and Singaïny 2015; al Malik 2015). There is also a third wave that remains deeply sceptical about it, considering it conceptually wrong or inoperative (Colosimo 2016; Glucksmann 2016).

Muslim communities – and the young male segment of them in particular – are identified as being *failed citizens*. They are the ones who show explicit disrespect for French society, its culture and Republican values at school. They are also accused of not paying enough respect to the memory of the victims, of not expressing clear contrition and not engaging properly with the national rites, post-Charlie. Their refusal to participate in the minute of silence organised in French public institutions, mostly in schools and universities, is discussed by Polony (2015) as the tip of the iceberg, representing a broader breakdown of the relationship between individuals and institutions. Colosimo (2016) and Guirous (2016) lament the putative lack of presence of Muslims in the public demonstrations in January, after they decided that they were not present, or were insufficiently visible.[8] Ironically, the Janus face of this argument was blatant. While Muslims were asked to make their 'Muslimness' invisible while engaging the public, they were also blamed for not taking part in the public space as 'Muslims' (Colosimo 2016; Guirous 2016). The media broadly speculated on the 'missing Muslims', absent from the scene in the post-attack protests.

This push-and-pull dynamic pressures Muslim citizens, who, on the one hand, are asked not to intervene as Muslims in public – as this is perceived as a sign of communitarianism or identity politics – while also blaming them for not demonstrating as 'Muslims' in the commemorative events of January 2015. The Muslim community, therefore, is continually reproduced in accordance with the paradoxical imaginations of these interventions, treated as a homogeneous body, and thus ironically 'communitarised' through these speech acts. Since January, there has been heated discussion regarding who should be invited to comment on events alongside experts and politicians on televised platforms. Who should speak on behalf of French Muslims when community leaders are non-existent? Should it be imams, representatives from the French Council for the Muslim Faith, academics, intellectuals, artists or sports personalities? This politics of representation extends beyond media inclusion; what type of leadership will the French authorities include in the implementation of collaborative measures to effectively counter radicalisation and jihadism as advocated by the Minister for the Interior since January 2015,[9] and especially given that, in a liberal democracy, visibility is directly associated with citizen participation and recognition? This makes way for the possibility of providing access, a voice and visibility within public and political spheres while also allowing for evaluation by others – in other words, recognition. In our corpus, there was a clearly disproportionate absence of the population that is most directly affected by the issues being debated, those who were spoken about *as if they were absent*, as the subjects of gossip.

Writing after Charlie: gossiping as the French art of (public) conversation

The arguments we identified in the corpus coalesce into a unifying defence of secularism and a preservation of national values. It is useful to think of these multiple voices as constituting a gossip circuit. Gossip is an informal form of personal communication built around those who are absent or are simply treated as such (Bok 1982). Legitimate and illegitimate forms of knowledge intersect in these gossip circuits. The legitimacy of voice is related to their position vis-à-vis Charlie (were they protagonists, friends, family, survivors?) but also regarding their position, and therefore visibility, in the media (are they regular columnists?). Gossip usually takes the form of conversations between people who know and trust one another (Spacks 1985; Ayim 1994). Indeed, gossip circuits function by maintaining an elevated level of alert and reinforcing the discretionary authority of some social actors over others. It consolidates the subjects as authorities over 'objects'. Gossip ultimately creates a kind of authority, regardless of its initial source. "As the rumour process moves toward forming agendas for actions intended to protect culture against a potential threat, it contributes to political decisions that, for better or worse, can lead to long-lasting social consequences" (Fine and Ellis 2010: 204–5). Our corpus produced a slew of authoritative declarations triggered by Charlie that are reminiscent of the social function of gossip.

Gossip produces several effects that find their way into the debate at hand. Above all, it makes us feel familiar with a subject removed from ourselves (Spacks 1985). The first axis of the corpus, sticking to a surgical storytelling of the events, contributed to this familiarity. It allows us to establish connections, to link events and locations regardless of their temporal, emotional or geographical distance. Ultimately, it helps circulate assertions that, as they move away from the source and time of issue, begin to function as ways to validate and objectify authority. Gossip facilitates the soft imposition of dominant ideas that subsequently become almost impossible to contest (Birchall 2006; Miller and McHoul 1998) and are quasi-hegemonic. It is essential here to highlight that all levels of knowledge, expertise and status engage in gossip circuits and that they are likely reinforced by the fact that the most recent books of our corpus include comments on previously published ones. In a way, our corpus constitutes a conversation, a battlefield of gossip in which some of the protagonists are more powerful than others because of status, visibility and rhetorical skills. Gossip circuits ultimately emphasise the authority of face-to-face discussions taking place behind the backs of absent people whose character and behaviour are being singled out for characterisation and criticism.

Being a Muslim in France means having to cope with regularly being the object of public debate and being discussed as a sensitive topic by non-Muslim co-citizens. This was the case before Charlie and it still is the case two years later. To put it bluntly, the governance of Islam and Muslims is implemented either as a security issue or as a matter of conflicting cultural, political and social values. The corpus of books studied here clearly confirms this. The public gaze constantly directed towards Muslims in France is multidimensional. This public eye on Islam and Muslims brings to the fore the idea that the public sphere is where controversies, polemic discussion and collective debate unfold and where public problems are often embodied. From this proceeds the idea of a 'public problem' that did not exist before the 'disturbances' and concerns under discussion, although Islam is not a public problem in and of itself. The media, politicians, civic associations, lawyers, public intellectuals, philosophers, judges and citizens as a whole take part in this processes of public problematisation.

The term *public* makes the experiences of individual citizens secondary in importance by creating paths that lead directly to legal, political and civil contexts that act as a network of constraints and courses of action. It tends to favour a set of disagreements, experiences and conflicts that Islam and Muslims are held to practically incarnate as a public problem to be defined and resolved. In the liberal idea of the public, *publicness* is exercised in a political space that is a sphere for opinion formation, an arena where rational debates, disputes and controversies between citizens are broached to reach an agreement.

However, if religious beliefs "are relevant in the public sphere, they must however be kept far from the space occupied by the State" (Portier 2013: 42). Free and equal citizens deliberate, oppose each other and argue over subjects that affect them either directly or indirectly. The timespan for this conversation is one that will engage everyone, every day, forever, as it is a condition of 'living together'.

The public space of liberal secularism is based on the exercise of 'freedom of conscience' – everyone can believe or disbelieve as they like in private without being exposed to public consequences. Religious organisations, however, are asked to abstain from political ambition and not act as facilitators for parties in the public sphere and to respect the law. Contact between religious institutions, Islam, other faiths and political instances take differing paths for the mutual rejection of radicalisation and reciprocal instrumentalisation. The religious lives of individuals, separate from these institutions, tend to be modest and discrete. The public sphere is therefore perceived as being a product of cultural consensus that upholds the primacy of individual freedoms and reduces religious practice to personal preference and choice. In this sense, it becomes a space for the projection of citizenship and the political community through the lens of visibility – a good citizen has nothing to hide. However, what becomes of this public space in the context of religious pluralisation, the violent expression of political convictions and the unveiling of power relationships that affect social relationships as in the wake of January 2015?

Acknowledgements

This work has been made possible thanks to the financial support of PLURADICAL and the Canada Research Chair for the Study of Religious Pluralism (SSHRC).

Notes

1 References in this text to 'Charlie' include the attacks on journalists at the *Charlie Hebdo* offices as well as on the police officers and on the customers of a kosher supermarket that took place in Paris and its surroundings, between 7 and 9 January 2015.

2 We also visited bookshop websites online (amazon.fr, fnac.fr), online book vendors (such as www.chapitre.com and www.lalibrairie.com) as well as web searches (Google Books). Our search used specific keywords: i.e. 'Charlie Hebdo + livre + attentats'; 'Paris + terrorisme + livre'; 'France + attaques + terroristes + publication'; 'Livres + terrorisme + France'; 'JesuisCharlie + livres + publications'; 'jihad + livre + France +

attentats'; 'laicite + France + terrorisme + publication'; 'attentats terroristes + France + ouvrages'; and other analogous keywords. The variety of website types also proved to be very helpful in discovering a few publications by unknown publishers that would otherwise have remained invisible.

3 These publications are drawn from works produced by some of the most prominent French publishers: Grasset, Flammarion, Le Seuil, Stock, l'Harmattan, Plon, Gallimard, Hachette, Fayard and Albin Michel, to mention but a few. Other publishing houses with more than one book in the identified corpus are Éditions de l'Atelier, Édilivre, Éditions de l'Aube, Les Échappées, Ovadia and PUF.

4 This selection was not based on the publishing house but rather on the academic profile of the authors. We chose therefore not to include Kepel (2015), Durpaire and Mabilon-Bonfils (2016) or Todd (2015), even though their books addressed issues directly related to *Charlie Hebdo*. For instance, we had doubts about including Durpaire and Mabilon-Bonfils (2016) and Todd (2015) in our corpus; in both books, *Charlie* works as a trigger event to extend an academic analysis on exclusion and racism at school as well as the #JesuisCharlie protests and national unity march of 11 January 2015. On 8 January 2015, a solemn national minute of silence was organised to pay a tribute to the memory of the victims, in which 60,000 schools and educational institutions were involved. The refusal to perform this minute of silence (which happened in roughly seventy schools) rapidly became both a sign of a resistance to the injunction #JesuisCharlie, and a demonstration of the deep fault line separating the 'unified nation'. The topic was intensely discussed on TV and radio shows and on blogs by teachers and parents. Durpaire and Mabilon-Bonfils (2016), both in the field of education

studies, took these incidents as a motive for presenting their work on systemic racism and discrimination of students in French public schools. We excluded the book from the sample for two main reasons: the authors are academics who are experts on the topic discussed in the book (as mentioned earlier) and the sources they use were prior to the Charlie events.

5 Taubira's *Murmures à la jeunesse* published in early 2016 was left out of the corpus as the book was published after her resignation from the government, and due to it being a rather brief appeal to French youth to keep trusting the Republican institutions. She was a political protagonist of both the Charlie and the November 2015 attacks, although Charlie does not appear to be the main motive for her writing the book. The argument goes beyond this occurrence, and therefore we felt it did not respond to our central selection criteria.

6 The film is a three-hour meticulous historical epic focusing on the anti-Nazi resistance and its role in the liberation of Paris.

7 This approach resembles the 'Charlie archive' constructed at Harvard University (see http://cahl.io/).

8 This absence has been the matter of very heated discussion following publication of Todd's opus on the 11 January demonstration. Todd's controversial book pointed to the confiscation of #JesuisCharlie by a part of the French population (middle-class, mostly white, older) that is deeply attached to 'freedom' but less committed to 'equality'. Yet, there is certainly a lot of fluidity in this discussion regarding the absence of 'Muslims', as it is built on speculation, it disregards proportionality (since this is difficult if not impossible to measure) and it presupposes a somewhat larger burden on certain citizens to manifest themselves and who

are isolated from the rest of the society by their distinctiveness. Why would one problematise the (non-)participation of Muslims compared with all others and not the participation of Buddhists or the

LGBT community, for example, if not because of certain expectations that presuppose a necessity for some to show off?

9 See www.stop-djihadisme.gouv.fr.

References

Adam, J.-M. (2011) *Genres de récits. Narrativité et généricité des textes.* Louvain-la- Neuve: Academia.

al Malik, A. (2015) *Place de la République: pour une spiritualité laïque.* Paris: Indigène.

Amiraux, V. (2004) 'Expertises, savoir et politique. La constitution de l'islam comme problème public en France et en Allemagne' in B. Zimmermann (ed.) *Les sciences sociales à l'épreuve de l'action.* Paris: EHESS, pp. 209–45.

Attali, J. (2015) *Nous sommes Charlie.* Paris: Librairie Générale Française.

Ayim, M. (1994) 'Knowledge Through the Grapevine: Gossip as Enquiry' in R. F. Goodman and A. Ben – Ze'ev (eds) *Good Gossip.* Lawrence KS: University of Kansas Press.

Badiou, A. (2016) *Notre mal vient de plus loin penser les tueries du 13 novembre.* Paris: Fayard.

Balongana-Louzolo, R. (2015) *Les fleurs poétiques à 'Charlie hebdo'.* Saint-Denis: Édilivre.

Baouz, K. (2016) *Plongée au coeur de la fabrique jihadiste.* Paris: Éditions First.

Bathily, L. (2016) *Je ne suis pas un héros.* Paris: Flammarion.

Berton, B. (2015) *J'étais la terreur.* Paris: Christophe Lucquin Éditeur.

Bertrand, G. (2015) *Terrorisme, émotions et relations internationales: essai d'actualité.* Bordeaux: Myriapode.

Bidar, A. (2015) *Plaidoyer pour la fraternité.* Paris: Albin Michel.

Birchall, C. (2006) *Knowledge Goes Pop: From Conspiracy Theory to Gossip.* Oxford: Berg.

Birnbaum, J. (2016) *Un silence religieux: La gauche face au djihadisme.* Paris: Seuil.

Bok, S. (1982) *Secrets: On the Ethics of Concealment and Revelation.* Oxford: Oxford University Press.

Boniface, P. (2015) *Les pompiers pyromanes: ces experts qui alimentent l'antisémitisme et l'islamophobie.* Paris: Max Milo.

Bonnet, D. (2016) *Je suis Charlie Chaplin.* Lyon: Jacques André Éditeur.

Boucheron, P. and M. Riboulet (2015) *Prendre dates: Paris, 6 janvier–14 janvier 2015.* Lagrasse: Verdier.

Bouquillon, G. (2015) *Toulouse est Charlie.* Photographs by Gilles Bouquillon, Thierry Bordas, Frédéric Charmeux, Xavier de Fenoyl et al.; text by Pierre Escudé, Magyd Cherfi, Jean-Pierre Denis et al. Portet-sur-Garonne: Empreinte Éditions.

Bouterfa, S. (2016) *Droit de réponse, nous sommes Charlie ou le triomphe de l'imaginaire nationaliste.* Paris: Édilivre.

Bouzar, D. (2015) *La vie après Daesh.* Ivry-sur-Seine: Les Éditions de l'Atelier.

Buffier, D. and P. Galinier (2015) *Qui est vraiment Charlie?: ces 21 jours qui ébranlèrent les lecteurs du Monde.* Paris: Éditions François Bourin and Le Monde.

Cardon, D. and M. Bouvet (2015) *1000 crayons pour la liberté d'expression.* Marseille: Bec en l'air.

Cayat, E. (2015) *Noël, ça fait vraiment chier! Sur le divan de Charlie Hebdo.* Paris: Les Échappés.

Charbonnier, S. (Charb) (2015) *Open Letter on Blasphemy, Islamophobia, and the True Enemies of Free Expression.* Paris: Hachette.

Cohen, C. (2015) *Charlie For Ever*. Nice: Les Éditions Ovadia.

Collectif (2015) *Je suis Charlie: Ainsi suit-il ...* Paris: Éditions l'Harmattan.

Collectif (2016) *Pour saluer Bernard Maris*. Paris: Flammarion.

Colosimo, A. (2016) *Les bûchers de la liberté*. Paris: Stock.

Crouzet, D. and J.-M. Le Gall (2015) *Au péril des guerres de religion: réflexions de deux historiens sur notre temps*. Paris: PUF.

Cyrulnik, B. (2016) *Je dessine: la jeunesse dessine pour Charlie Hebdo après le 7 janvier*. Paris: Les Échappés.

Dive, B. (2016) *Au coeur du pouvoir: l'exécutif face aux attentats de janvier 2015*. Paris: Plon.

Dorai, Y. and M. Taubmann (2016) *Hyper caché: quatre heures dans la tête d'un otage, ses révélations sidérantes avec Michel Taubmann*. Paris: Éditions du Moment.

Droumaguet, Y. (2015) *L'humain et le barbare*. Rennes: Éditions Apogée.

Duhamel, J. (2015) *Je suis Charlie liberté, j'écris tes mots*. Paris: Éditions First.

Durpaire, F. and B. Mabilon-Bonfils (2016) *Fatima moins bien notée que Marianne ... L'islam et l'école de la République*. La Tour d'Aigues: Éditions de l'Aube.

Etchian, A. (2016) *Charlie Hebdo 7 janvier 2015 et si les caricatures du Prophète Mohammed n'étaient pas le vrai mobile?* Paris: Éditions l'Harmattan.

Federbusch, S. (2015) *La marche des lemmings ou la deuxième mort de Charlie*. Brussels: Ixelles Publishing Editions.

Fine, G. A. and B. Ellis (2010) *The Global Grapevine: Why Rumors of Terrorism, Immigration, and Trade Matter*. Oxford: Oxford University Press.

Foulot, M. (2015) *Le complot Charlie plongée dans l'imaginaire conspirationniste*. Neuilly: Atlande.

Fourest, C. (2015) *Éloge du blaspheme*. Paris: Grasset.

Fourquet, J. (2015) *Janvier 2015: le catalyseur*. Paris: Fondation Jean Jaurès.

Garnot, B. (2015) *Voltaire et Charlie*. Dijon: Éditions universitaires de Dijon.

Ghannūshī, R. and O. Ravanello (2015) *Au sujet de l'islam*. Paris: Plon.

Ginori, A. (2016) *Le Kiosquier de Charlie*. Paris: Éditions des Équateurs.

Glucksmann, R. (2016) *Génération gueule de bois. Manuel de lutte contre les réacs*. Paris: Allary Éditions.

Guirous, L. (2016) *#Je suis Marianne*. Paris: Grasset.

Hajjat, A. and M. Mohammed (2013) *Islamophobie. Comment les élites françaises construisent le 'problème musulman'*. Paris: La Découverte.

Hansen-Löve, L. and C. Tomei (2015) *Charlie, l'onde de choc: une citoyenneté bousculée, un avenir à réinventer*. Nice: Éditions Ovadia.

Ibn Ziaten, L. and A. Jouve (2016) *Dis-nous, Latifa, c'est quoi la tolérance?* Ivry Sur Seine: Éditions de l'Atelier.

Jean-Louis, B., L. Bouzar and S. Grzybowski (2015) *L'après-Charlie: 20 questions pour en débattre sans tabou*. Paris: Éditions de l'Atelier.

Joffrin, L. (2015) *Le réveil français: pour en finir avec les défaitistes, les déclinistes et autres prophètes de la décadence*. Paris: Stock.

Kepel, G. (2015) *Terreur dans l'Hexagone: genèse du djihad français*. Paris: Gallimard.

Lamoureux, M. S. (2015) *Je ne capitule pas – Après les attentats de Charlie Hebdo: à quoi ça sert un prof?* Paris: Éditions Quichotte.

Lefébure, P. and. C. Sécail (2016) *Le défi Charlie: les médias à l'épreuve des attentats*. Paris: Lemieux Éditeur.

Lehman, S. (2016) *L'Esprit du 11 janvier. Une enquête mythologique*. Paris: Guy Delcourt Productions.

Luz (2015) *Catharsis*. Paris: Futuropolis.

Manent, P. (2015) *Situation de la France*. Paris: Desclée de Brouwer.

Maris, B. (2016) *Et si on aimait la France*. Paris: Pluriel.

Marsel, C. (2015) *Psychologie de l'inconscient et hypermodernité essai d'interprétation du paradigme 'Je suis Charlie'*. Paris: L'Harmattan.

Mas-Pionnier, M.-L. (2016) *Et soudain ils ne raient plus les trois jours où tout a basculé*. Paris: Les Arènes.

Maxence, P. (2015) *Face à la fièvre Charlie: des catholiques répondent*. Paris: Éditions de l'Homme Nouveau.

Mercier, D. (2016) *Vive Charlie!* Saint-Denis: Société des Écrivains.

Miller, T. and A. McHoul (1998) *Popular Culture and Everyday Life*. London, Thousand Oaks CA and New Delhi: Sage.

Montbrial, T. D. (2015) *Le sursaut ou le chaos*. Paris: Plon.

Morin, E. and P. Singaïny (2015) *Avant, pendant, après le 11 janvier: pour une nouvelle écriture collective de notre roman national*. La Tour d'Aigues: Éditions de L'Aube.

Onfray, M. (2016) *Penser l'Islam*. Paris: Grasset.

Ory, P. (2016) *Ce que dit Charlie. Treize leçons d'histoire*. Paris: Gallimard.

Pelloux, P. and Charb (2015) *Toujours là, toujours prêt préface de Gérard Mordillat dessins de Charb*. Paris: le Cherche-Midi.

Pierrat, E. (2015) *La liberté sans expression?: jusqu'où peut-on écrire, tout dire, écrire, dessiner*. Paris: Flammarion.

Pol, P. (2015) *Jésus est Charlie et Muhammad n'est pas Mohammed: les substitutions d'Othman*. Saint-Denis: Édilivre.

Polony, N. (2015) *Nous sommes la France*. Paris: Plon.

Portier, P. (2013) 'Démocratie et religion. La contribution de Jürgen Habermas', *Revue d'Éthique et de Théologie Morale* 4 (277): 25–47.

Rimé, B. (2010) 'Les émotions, conséquences cognitives et sociales' in S. Masmoudi and A. Naceur (eds) *Du percept à la décision. Intégration de la cognition, l'émotion et la motivation*. Brussels: De Boeck, pp. 179–95.

Riss (2015) *Charlie Hebdo: tout est pardonné*. Paris: Les Échappés.

Robert, D. (2015) *Mohicans*. Paris: Julliard.

Schneidermann, D. (2015) *On n'a pas fini de rire. Quelques mots à ma nouvelle famille*. Paris: Le Publieur.

Spacks, P. M. (1985) *Gossip*. New York: Alfred A. Knopf.

Stora, B. (2015) *Que sont mes amis devenus … Les Juifs, Charlie, puis tous les nôtres*. Lormont: Le Bord de l'Eau Éditions.

Storti, M. (2016) *Sortir du manichéisme. Des roses et du chocolat*. Paris: Michel de Maule.

Taubira, C. (2016) *Murmures à la jeunesse*. Paris: Philippe Rey.

Ténor, A. (2016) *Je suis charliberté ! toute vérité est bonne à dire!* Paris: Scrineo.

Todd, E. (2015) *Qui est Charlie?: sociologie d'une crise religieuse*. Paris: Éditions du Seuil.

Truc, G. (2016) *Sidérations. Une sociologie des attentats*. Paris: PUF.

Truong, N. and J. Julliard (2015) *Penser le 11 janvier*. La Tour d'Aigue: Éditions de l'Aube and Le Monde.

Val, P. (2015) *Malaise dans l'inculture*. Paris: Grasset.

Val, P. (2016) *C'était Charlie*. Paris: Grasset.

Vaquette, T. E. (2015) *Je ne suis pas Charlie, je suis Vaquette*. Huriel: Poignon.

Viveret, P. (2015) *Fraternité, j'écris ton nom*. Paris: Éditions Les Liens qui Libèrent.

Weston Vauclair, J. and D. Vauclair (2016) *De Charlie Hebdo à #Charlie: enjeux, histoire, perspectives*. Paris: Eyrolles.

Wolinski, M. (2016) *Chérie, je vais à Charlie*. Paris: Éditions du Seuil.

4 | A DOUBLE-BIND SITUATION? THE DEPOLITICISATION OF VIOLENCE AND THE POLITICS OF COMPENSATION

Abdellali Hajjat

There are processes where the experience of an imminent danger is so overwhelmingly strong that relative detachment and the control of fear become, for most people, unattainable, even though the process itself, as they might see if they could collect themselves and reflect with a measure of detachment, still offers them chances of control and thus remaining whole. There are, however, also critical processes which have gone so far that, for those involved in them, no chance remains of keeping their physical and mental integrity intact or even of securing their survival. Great as may be their detachment, their capacity for realistic reflection, for them the process has reached the point of no return. They cannot save themselves, whatever they might think or do. (Elias 2007: 110–11)

French society is facing an unprecedented double-bind situation similar to that theorised by Norbert Elias. The French government and takfiri groups, such as Al Qaeda and ISIS, are tied in a violent relationship where mass murder attacks on French soil 'respond' to massive airstrikes in the Middle East and Africa, and vice versa. Caught in the middle of that escalation of violence, civil casualties are the "collateral damages" of a war that was not explicitly desired by French, Syrian, Iraqi or Libyan citizens, among others. In France, few people support the government's foreign policy and no Muslim organisation supports ISIS terror attacks. The idea of a gap between politicians and citizens has been epitomised with the slogan '*Leurs guerres, nos morts*' ('Their wars, our dead'), which became prominent in social media after the January and November 2015 attacks.

As Elias noted, some double-bind situations have gone so far that the possibility of detachment and rational reflection becomes extremely difficult, until the point of no return is reached. This tipping point is getting closer in France: on the one hand, French people are murdered by takfiri fighters because they are supposedly complicit with the government's foreign policy, and, on the other hand, Islamophobic acts have dramatically increased since the January 2015 attacks and French Muslims are overtly targeted by law enforcement, mainstream politicians and far-right groups as the disloyal 'fifth column' of the Republic. Unfortunately, the mediocrity of most French politicians has impeded a true process of detachment and reflection on the real causes of political violence. After the national trauma following the attacks, no public debate has been possible about foreign policy and the army's involvement in the wars of Afghanistan, Syria, Libya, etc. Nor was there a discussion about the many failures of the French intelligence agencies and their inability to prevent such mass attacks.

Instead of dealing with the social and political roots of violence at home and abroad, most politicians consider, as former Prime Minister Manuel Valls put it, that "to explain is to excuse" (*"expliquer, c'est excuser"*). Thus, social scientists, especially those who analyse Muslim communities, Islamic organisations and Islamophobia, have been criticised as 'naive' or 'incapable' of 'preventing' such violence, and even complicit with takfiri groups since they share their denunciation of Islamophobia. In other words, the 'gatekeepers' of rationality, detachment and reflection, which social scientists are meant to represent, have been overtly blamed, allowing political elites to turn to politics of emotion, fear and order, which have depoliticised the political violence and led to what I call the *politics of compensation*: while failing to address the real issues, the government must *seem* to address the problem of violence and find quick and visible solutions and compensate its political weakness by an increased focused on law and order. Thus, the politics of compensation is based on political communication rather than on policy informed by social science.

Using collected material from print and television media, observations and statistics, this chapter aims to show that the double-bind relationship between the takfiri political violence and the French government has led to an escalation in the level of violence towards the point of no return: indiscriminate mass physical violence and persecutions against Muslims. I would like to show how this vicious double-bind has provoked a complete depoliticisation of political violence and the politics of compensation, which converts a political problem – state violence in the Middle East and discrimination against Muslims – into a racial/religious problem: is Islam compatible with French society?

The depoliticisation of political violence is the Trojan horse of the racialisation of Muslims, which might be identified in various phenomena: the idea of Muslims' 'hidden solidarity' with the killers, the lack of recognition of Muslim organisations' statements against the attacks, the invisibility of Muslim heroes and victims, the kinds of 'collective punishment' implemented against Muslims, and the *néo-laïc* (secularist) framework that impedes any effort at a clear analysis of takfiri political violence.

The discourse of *hidden solidarity*

In 1903, W. E. B. Dubois wrote: "How does it feel to be a problem?" That is the nagging question that so-called 'Muslims', both French citizens and foreigners living in France, have asked themselves for the past three decades. Recent attacks have served as morbid realisations of prophecies for both literary (Michel Houellebecq) and journalistic (Eric Zemmour, Alain Finkielkraut) Islamophobes who conceive of the 'Muslim community' as 'a people within a people', and whose problematic presence can only be remedied by what Renaud Camus calls 'remigration', a euphemism for deportation. Many other intellectuals, who may not link Islam to terrorism, have argued nonetheless for a 'reformation of Islam' that ought to be initiated by theologians and Muslim leaders. This solution is proposed by intellectuals such as Abdennour Bidar, Laurent Bouvet and Gilles Kepel, according to whom the 'disease of Islam' can explain political violence.

Both of these approaches fail to take into account the most basic sociological evidence: the 'Muslim community' does not exist. Muslim organisations do not represent so-called Muslims. So-called Muslims constitute a diverse population in terms of social class, nationality, and political and ideological leanings, all of which are erased entirely by the call for *désolidarisation*. This neologism assumes that there already exists solidarity between the killers and all other supposed Muslims. In other words, so-called Muslims are presumed guilty by their simple association with Islam, and being Muslims automatically makes them part of the problem.

This guilt by association prevails despite all Muslim organisations, including the Salafi ones, univocally condemning the attacks. After the ISIS-related assassination of two police officers in 2016 in Magnanville by Larossi Aballa, a demonstration against takfiri political violence was organised by local Muslim leaders, gathering thousands of people in

Mantes-la-Jolie, in front of the town's police headquarters. Considering that many politicians have accused Muslims of not being vocal enough against the attacks, one could have expected full media coverage. However, only one journalist covered the event (Aubenas 2016) and revealed that the organisers had not been invited to come into the police office, as if public statements against takfiri violence were not sincere enough and were in fact an instance of duplicity (ibid.). The idea of hidden solidarity remains unquestioned even when Muslims are in the line of fire as victims or heroes – such as Ahmed Merabet, a police officer killed in cold blood in front of the *Charlie Hebdo* office, and Lassana Bathily, a former illegal immigrant who saved several lives in the hostage situation in the kosher supermarket in 2015. In the Nice attack in 2016, more than a third of the eighty-four people killed were Muslims (Mediapart 2016).

The idea of hidden solidarity and the types of discourse associated with it – Islam as a threat or as 'diseased' – draw their power from updated racialised relationships: the immigrants of yesterday have become the so-called Muslims of today (Hajjat and Mohammed 2016). After the 'problem of immigrant integration', French elites have moved on to the 'Muslim problem', although both of these 'problems' share the same stakes: do they (the so-called Muslims) have the right to live in France? While deporting unemployed French citizens would never be considered the solution to the 'unemployment problem', deportation becomes somehow a viable option when applied to the 'Muslim problem'. Reducing the identity of so-called Muslims to their association with Islam conceals a shameful truth: they remain '*Français de papiers*' (French citizens on paper only) and thus morally liable for deportation.

Let us now turn to the reasons behind the general blindness that followed the attacks. The emotional response on both the national and international levels incited by the killings tends to discredit social science researchers and journalists whose job it is to deconstruct the mechanisms behind this violence. They are discredited for being 'excessively idealistic' or 'politically correct' or because of their perceived 'inability to see what is directly in front of them'. The historical context is similar to that of post-9/11, when pundits gave geography lessons to political scientists, sociologists and journalists who had for years conducted research on violent groups. For instance, the former director of *Charlie Hebdo*, Philippe Val, published an essay after the January 2015 attacks to denounce what he calls 'sociologism', since it is supposed to "make individuals [such as takfiri fighters] totally irresponsible [for their acts]" (Val 2015: 83; see also de Montlibert 2015). Social scientists are accused of legitimating the violence and attenuating takfiri fighters' responsibility since they try to find the social causes of the violence. What is at stake here is the possibility of producing a rational discourse based on empirical research, at the very moment when Islamophobes are taking advantage of a window of opportunity to proclaim the return of the concept of 'the clash of civilisations'.

With the blame solidly placed on so-called Muslims, journalists and commentators criticising the editorial choices of *Charlie Hebdo* were generally scorned. For example, the journalist Caroline Fourest (2015) and the politician Jeanette Bougrab called out associations such as *Les Indivisibles*, founded by Rokhaya Diallo, for having armed the killers with ideology: "by saying that Charlie Hebdo is Islamophobe, [Les Indivisibles] are of course guilty".[1] According to them, anti-Islamophobia activists might even be 'responsible' for the killings and ought to explain themselves, as if their articles and speeches against racism had somehow inspired the killers. This accusation attributes to these activists a media influence that they do not actually have, since reaching a larger public is in fact much more difficult than that. Furthermore, to make such an accusation is to misunderstand the real ideological influences of the killers, which are rooted in the writings of sheiks and the nebula that is Al Qaeda and ISIS. With emotion prevailing over reason, there is a risk of censoring all types of university, journalistic and protest speech denouncing the very real social phenomenon that is Islamophobia. The risk is that collective responsibility becomes collective punishment, which takes three forms: Islamophobic hate speeches and crimes; the biased implementation of the law against the 'apology of terrorism'; and the way in which government policy under the state of emergency targeted the so-called Muslim community.

Collective punishment

The proliferation of anti-Semitic acts committed during periods of violence in Palestine clearly shows that so-called Jews are punished collectively and held responsible for Israeli war crimes (Sieffert 2004). Similarly, as well as the extremely problematic perceived 'defence of terrorism' already discussed, so-called Muslims have been subjected to a form of collective punishment, which has manifested itself in an increase in Islamophobia. Data from the Ministry of the Interior show that almost as many Islamophobic acts were committed in January 2015 (128) as in the entirety of the year 2014 (133). Police sources recorded thirty-three acts committed against mosques and ninety-five threats, some of these acts involving grenades or firearms (CNCDH 2016). This racist violence was nourished by the 'fascist sphere' within social media that relayed calls to murder (Chapelle 2015). However, considering the extreme tension that blanketed the country, one cannot help being struck by the difference between Islamophobic and anti-Semitic acts. Although anti-Semitic acts have become less frequent over the last decade, they are more violent, and have often involved murder (the Toulouse killings by Mohamed Merah in 2012, for instance).

Conversely, Islamophobic acts occur much more frequently, and while they can be very violent (the Ajaccio mosque was burnt in November 2015), only rarely do they lead to homicides. The only case recorded after the Charlie Hebdo events is that of Mohamed El Makouli, a forty-seven-year-old Moroccan killed at his home in Le Beaucet (Vaucluse) on 14 January 2015 by his neighbour, who stabbed him seventeen times while screaming, "I am your god, I am your Islam" (the offender was not prosecuted since he was considered 'irresponsible' because of mental illness) (Ferhallad 2016). Islamophobia-related physical attacks are thus more common, relatively less violent, more anonymous, and generally directed at women wearing a hijab (CNCDH 2016). This is where the point of no return becomes clear: by exacerbating existing social tensions, ISIS aims to provoke far-right appeals to murder. As the director of the French home intelligence service, Patrice Calvar, told the National Assembly in July 2016:

> We will have, at one time or another, to provide resources to deal with other extremist groups because the confrontation is inevitable. This confrontation, I think will take place. Even one or two attacks and it will happen. It therefore behoves us to anticipate and block all those groups who would, at one time or another, trigger communal clashes. (Albertini 2016)

This discrepancy between anti-Semitic and Islamophobic violence is reinforced by the differing levels of legitimacy assigned to different types of racist speech: whereas anti-Semitic speech is largely denounced by the entire French elite, as the 2015 dismissal of Jean-Marie Le Pen from the Front National demonstrated, Islamophobic speech appears to be much more acceptable. Indeed, certain public figures, such as the philosopher Elisabeth Badinter, do not hesitate to label themselves as Islamophobic, arguing that "we mustn't be afraid to be labelled as Islamophobes" (Hausalter 2016). Nevertheless, while the link between the level of physical and symbolic violence is not easy to determine, the mainstream media's reluctance to court it could be witnessed in the aftermath of the *Charlie Hebdo* attack and may have prevented even more physical violence.

For example, the commercial radio station RTL broadcast on 7 January 2015 a daily show hosted by Marc-Olivier Fogiel (Graulle 2015) in which the extreme right-wing *Le Figaro* editorialist Yvan Rioufol called upon the so-called Muslim journalist Rokhaya Diallo to "*désolidariser*" herself from the killers. Diallo began to weep and was comforted by the other participants, including Fogiel and Laurence Parisot, the former head of the French employers union MEDEF. This kind of situation, which we find elsewhere in the media sphere, can bring about a call to stop symbolic Islamophobic violence for fear of provoking a civil war. It was as if the link made between terrorism and Islam, which is usually the bread and butter of the mainstream print and television media, had been suspended for the short time around the killings in order to avoid sinking further into an ever widening hole of violence.

The second form of collective punishment relates to the law against the apology for terrorism and its increasingly tough implementation. Until the anti-terrorism law of 14 November 2014, this offence fell within the guidelines of the 1881 law concerning the freedom of the press: proceedings were usually very long and handled by a special judicial committee, because freedom of expression could be limited only in very special cases. This offence is now included in the penal code (Article 421-2-5), can be invoked by any judge in a criminal court, and can compel an immediate court appearance. The violent reaction in response to the attacks in January and November 2015 led the Syndicat de la Magistrature (2015) – a national association of judges – Amnesty International, and prominent attorneys such as Maître Eolas to sound the alarm and denounce the 'swift justice' being enacted in contradiction to the original goal of the law.

What little information is available is enough to show that the implementation of the anti-terrorism apology law after the January

2015 killings has mostly affected those who had nothing to do with violence relating to Islam. Out of a total of forty-six cases reported by the press – there are actually about 117 (Soullier 2015) – only the three following cases related to people who subscribed directly to the ideology of the Islamic State. On 13 January in Elbeuf, Franz Petermann, a temp worker and Muslim convert, told police officers during an altercation: "I'm not gonna move, asshole … it's not enough for you that we killed three cops? There are a lot of us and we have AK-47s." Petermann was placed under arrest for "criminal association with intent to commit acts of terrorism" in Syria. Although the charge of 'defence of terrorism' was dropped, he received a three-month suspended prison sentence and five years' probation for insulting an officer and for issuing a death threat.

On 19 January in Lille, a fifty-eight-year-old bookseller allegedly sold Islamic State flags and then declared at the police station: "I am not Charlie, I am Coulibaly, I am a terrorist." He was given a suspended prison sentence of one year for 'apology for terrorism'. On 22 January in Valence, a divorced forty-five-year-old man allegedly forced his children to look at 'extremely violent' images that 'defended terrorism', with the supposed goal of indoctrinating them (unknown verdict). It should be noted that these sentences are lenient for a crime that can lead to up to five years in prison and a €75,000 fine or, in the case of defence of terrorism online, up to seven years in prison and a fine of €100,000. The real targets of the law were, in the end, given suspended sentences.

On the other hand, severity is the norm for all other cases. For example, an eighteen-year-old man who made an 'offensive gesture' towards a police station and screamed "100 per cent Kouachi!" several times in Nice on 9 January was sentenced to a one-month mandatory prison sentence. In Valenciennes on 10 January, a thirty-four-year-old man was charged with driving under the influence of alcohol, refusing multiple times to take a breathalyser test, involuntary assault, and defending terrorist acts by screaming: "There should be more Kouachis. I hope you will be next … You are holy bread for terrorists." He received a four-year mandatory prison sentence, his driver's licence was taken away for two years, and he was stripped of his civil and family rights for three years. Between these two extremes, most of those convicted were given a prison sentence – rarely suspended – of a few months.

Victims of this disproportionate reaction were numerous: an eight-year-old third-grader named Ahmed was referred to the police by his school in Nice for having allegedly declared: "I am with the terrorists" (*La Dépêche* 2015); another student, nine years old, was referred to the police after another student's ill-intentioned tattling, and accused of breaking the minute of silence in Villers-Cotterêts (*Le Parisien* 2015); a left-wing activist and high-school philosophy teacher in Poitiers, Jean-François Chazerans, was accused by students' parents of defending the attacks, and was suspended from teaching for several months and finally moved to another high school (Lejay 2016); a metal worker represented by the SUD union was fired for having allegedly made some 'shocking' remarks defending the attacks while working at the Bombardier factory in Crespin (*La Voix du Nord* 2015).

In the first case, the child did not even know what the word 'terrorism' meant, but nevertheless suffered stigmatisation at the hands of faculty, which, if those remarks really had been genuine, should have turned the situation into a 'teachable' moment. The second and the third are the victims of what amounts to gossiping by a student and by the parents of a student respectively. The fourth is the result of union pressure within the context of a serious conflict with management. The accusation of defence of terrorism has become an easy weapon to wield when one wishes to spread rumours about an enemy, whether on the playground, in the political sphere, or in the workplace. Similar accusations were made by waiters at an Angoulême restaurant against four men later released by a judge, then jailed for two months after the prosecutor contradicted the first judge's decision. Accused of 'celebrating 7 January in a bar', they were, in fact, celebrating a successful bet at a horse race (*Rue89* 2015).

The gap between the spirit of the law and its application in reality is even more surprising when we take into account the conditions which led these people to 'defend terrorism'. At least twenty cases were related to a direct challenge to police authority (BAC, CRS, police, gendarmerie) or to public transport controllers. In other words, the new crime of 'defence of terrorism' is used as a crime of contempt and rebellion, which is a classic judicial tool used by police to maintain social order. The only difference is the use of words such as 'AK-47' or 'Allahu Akbar' (God is great) – as if 'Allahu Akbar' were synonymous with the defence of terrorism – and the explicit reference to the Kouachi brothers or to Coulibaly. Far from being ideologues of ISIS, these individuals made crude and intemperate but hardly ideologically motivated reference to the killings in order to taunt, insult, and provoke those who represent the authorities of social control.

The height of absurdity was reached when judges dealt extremely severe sentences to seven people under the influence of alcohol. One intoxicated thirty-one-year-old man got a ten-month mandatory prison term for saying, while in a police station on 11 January, "Dirty Africans, Allah Akbar, fuck France, the Arabs are here" and "That's not good, AK-47 better, I'll smoke you with an AK-47." The lawyers tried to argue that the state of drunkenness was responsible for these stupid comments, but the judges were unmoved. They were unmoved as well in the case of two people with serious mental health issues. One of them, a thirty-eight-year-old Moroccan man from Paris, who insulted police officers on 15 January, was given a three-month mandatory prison sentence despite psychiatric evidence proving his mental health condition. In the end, the law of 14 November 2014, as it has been applied after the January 2015 killings, has been used to compensate for the inability of the government to deal with the problem of takfiri political violence. Government authorities have convicted around fifty people, most of Maghrebi origin or of Muslim faith. Those cases that have been made public, especially the case of young Ahmed, show that so-called 'Muslim' men and women are rendered as suspects from an early age.

The third form of collective punishment deals with the state of emergency. The politics of compensation is at the core of the state of emergency as it has been implemented since 13 November 2015. As was the case in January, the condemnation of the November killings was massive, the desire to show solidarity with the victims was unanimous. But, in the so-called Muslim community, these feelings were mitigated with the fear of retaliation from far-right groups and of the brutal government response during the state of emergency. According to the Ministry of Interior (Halissat 2016), 3,021 administrative searches (*perquisitions*) and 318 home arrests were conducted between 15 November 2015 and 7 January 2016. While 464 offences were discovered (from illegal weapon carrying to drug dealing), only twenty-five were terrorism-related. Ultimately, the anti-terrorism prosecutor initiated only four proceedings. Again, aberrations have dominated the news: a Muslim humanitarian organisation (Baraka City), a practising Catholic, environmental activists, protesters against the state of emergency and others were arrested or put under house arrest despite them having no links with any armed group.

Néo-laïc framework

We cannot understand the logic of collective punishment and the politics of compensation in France without what I call 'the *néo-laïc* framework'. *Laïcité* as defined by the 1905 law corresponds more or less to the separation of church and state and the guarantee of the freedom of religion and worship, even in public spaces. *Néo-laïcité* distinguishes itself by expanding the realm governed by *laïcité*, which now includes the use of public services (no longer only public service workers) and religious practice not only in public areas, but also in private companies. The defining characteristic of *néo-laïcité* is that since 1989 it has strived to eliminate Islam from public view, framing the persistent belief in and practice of Islam by the children of postcolonial immigrants as a perceived threat to 'national identity'. From an assimilationist point of view, which is precisely the type of perspective that has inspired *néo-laïcité*, this persistence is considered an anomaly within the 'Republican model' and constitutes the source of the 'Muslim problem'. It is therefore not an accident that the first institution summoned to 'respond' to the killings was the national school system and that the first tenet called upon was that of *laïcité*.

From that point of view, the solution to the problem of political violence might lie in teaching about *laïcité* in public schools: hence the extensive teacher training programme, the institution of 9 December as 'National *Laïcité* Day' and the 'counter-radicalisation' policy in public schools. Moreover, other parts of the public sector, from the 'left hand' of the state, have been involved in the 'counter-radicalisation' policy. For instance, the Ministry of Interior, the 'right hand' of the state, asked the Juvenile Protection Administration (Chassat-Philippe 2015), which is supposed to help youngsters with family difficulties to integrate in society, to prevent any "new Kouachi brothers" and detect any "radicalisation indicators" such as wearing a beard, starting to pray, etc., invented by the so-called Islam expert Dounia Bouzar (Delaporte 2014). Some municipalities and *Caisses d'allocations familiales* even closed community centres, where many social activities are organised for working-class families and young people, because of a suspicion that some rooms may be used as a prayer space.[2] The *néo-*

laïc framework acts as the Trojan horse of the racialisation of Muslims in the public sector.

This *néo-laïc* framework has also appeared in the legislative branch of the government. On 18 February 2015, the UMP National Assembly representative Eric Ciotti proposed a bill seeking to extend the principle of *laïcité* to include public institutions of higher education. On 2 March, Pascale Boistard, Secretary for Women's Rights, went further, declaring that the veil might not belong in a university setting. On 12 March, a bill adopted by the Senate in January 2012 in response to the 'Baby Loup' affair,[3] and subsequently relegated discretely to the fringes of the legislative agenda, resurfaced and was again submitted for adoption by the National Assembly in May 2015. The bill sought to ban the wearing of religious symbols in private day-care facilities that receive any government funding – which is to say the vast majority of centres in France. It is thus apparent that representatives on both the right and the left have conflated the killers with women who wear the hijab in universities and nurseries; this conflation holds those women responsible for acts that they did not commit but are suspected of secretly supporting. Thus, one of the likely effects of the killings has been a process of entrenched legal discrimination that aims to construct a special legal statute that subverts the right to education and the right to work.

Towards an substantive analysis of political violence related to Islam

In order to avoid the unfortunate blindness brought about by the *néo-laïc* framework, we must return to the facts themselves and adopt a substantive analysis of political violence. Those responsible for the attacks are not the only ones who make use of violence: other groups do it in the name of other ideologies and in response to other conflicts. In order to fully understand the basic mechanisms behind the violence related to Islam and – for lawmakers – to prevent this sort of violence from happening, we must consider this violence from a range of perspectives. Clear questions must be asked: How does one embark on the career of a combatant? Under what conditions is political violence likely to occur?

The personal histories of the members of the terrorist groups give us a few clues. Their struggle originated in the political quagmires provoked by Western military intervention before and after 9/11 (Syria,

Yemen, Iraq, etc.). After being supported by the United States against the Soviet Union, the 'freedom fighters' who consisted of Taliban and future Al Qaeda leaders took aim at their former American allies after the fall of the Wall. In Afghanistan they imposed their own politico-religious order with the help of foreign powers, and created a haven for every fighter in the world who shared their ideology and wished to easily learn techniques for death and destruction. This political violence is the offspring of Western intervention, nursed by the power struggles in Algeria, Chechnya, Bosnia and elsewhere. It struck at the heart of Western political powers in 1995 in Paris, 2001 in New York, 2004 in Madrid, and 2005 in London.

After the accumulation of military capital since the 1970s, a significant wave of violence has washed over these Western powers, perpetrated by these seasoned combatants. Whereas these violent groups were initially confined to a few countries, the 'war on terror' in fact led them to expand into countries that had previously been spared or at least hardly affected by their presence: Iraq, Syria, Libya, Yemen, Mali, Pakistan. A new generation, embodied by the leaders of the organisation dubbed 'Islamic State', radicalised by what they have seen in the prisons at Abu Ghraib and Guantanamo, has undertaken military training for combat against Western occupation and now moves freely within a truly transnational network that extends from Africa to Asia. In other words, the primary source of political violence relating to Islam lies in the state-sponsored violence in the Middle East and the disastrous consequences of wars waged precisely in the name of the 'fight against terrorism'.

The second source of violence is linked to the social anomie that is worsening in working-class neighbourhoods in France. Contrary to the implication of the Islamophobic demand for '*désolidarisation*', the three perpetrators of the *Charlie Hebdo* attacks were 'free electrons' attached to no one and nothing in particular; they were the products of traumatising life events, social marginalisation and systemic inequality, all of which led them towards lives of delinquency and membership of violent groups. These 'free electrons' '*désolidarized*' themselves from their own peers, especially from their extended families and fellow worshippers at the local mosque; they were never given a second chance in school and were drawn in by preachers convinced of the imminence of the 'clash of civilisations', who acted as objective allies to their neoconservative counterparts. These children of working-class families internalised a high level of violence that turned them into tortured souls who no longer found existential meaning within traditional structures, but found it in a nihilistic and murderous ideology that promised them power and recognition. This type of ideology was, and still remains, popular only among a tiny minority in working-class neighbourhoods.

We can distinguish between multiple trends within the Islamic landscape in France: non-affiliated mosques, large organisations that maintain close ties with their country of origin (Maghreb and Turkey), fellowship societies such as the Muslim Brotherhood, the Tablighi Jamaat, the 'Salafi' of both the purist and the apolitical type, the Sufis, etc., and finally the violent sub-groups labelled 'takfiri'. Every day, residents, activists and local politicians struggle almost unnoticed against the influences of these violent sub-groups without ever making front-page news. For example, the members of the Buttes de Chaumont Network, to which the Kouachi brothers belonged, were banned from pro-Palestine protests by immigration and antifascist activists in the early 2000s.[4]

The grand irony of the story is that the very people who used to fight on the ground against violent sub-groups are the same people who are now held responsible or complicit when they denounce Islamophobia. The existence and the resilience of these violent sub-groups are thus directly linked to power struggles within working-class communities. They gain influence when other political forces, specifically those led by the heirs of the marches for equality and against racism, have now begun to lose momentum and have left behind a relative political void from which terrifying alternatives are emerging. This phenomenon is also supported by the disconcerting ease with which weapons from the former USSR can be bought and the constant mobilisation by takfiri networks to recruit via social networking sites, transmitting ideology and military know-how beyond geopolitical borders (Bonelli 2015).

The conditions of possibility for the political violence of 2015 are many. Analyses by sociologists deserve to receive more attention from lawmakers, and yet it is the experts in 'Islam and terrorism' who have had the ever indulgent ear of the President, his advisers, and the media. The failure of the intelligence services, which had detected and interrogated the killers, seems to be hidden behind their aura of 'neutralisation'. The initial political reactions appear to be heading towards the worst outcome: the adoption of a French 'Patriot Act' to add to already stringent terrorism laws; the return of the debate about the death penalty and *ius soli*; the targeting of the 'enemy within' – that is, Muslims who resist assimilation; and the politics of segregation against Muslims in public spaces such as the beach and the streets. In brief, the lessons of post-9/11 policies do not appear to have been learned: political violence continues to feed on state-sponsored violence and social violence.

Notes

1 BFM TV, 8 January 2015. See Les Indivisibles, 'Non-coupables', 1 February 2015. www.lesindivisibles. fr/non-coupables.

2 Interview with a CAF director, 20 July 2016.

3 Baby Loup was a private day-care facility in which a female employee was fired in 2008 for wearing veil to work.

4 Interview with Mohamed, activist in Paris, January 2015.

References

Albertini, D. (2016) 'Terrorisme: la crainte d'une réplique de l'ultradroite', *Libération*, 13 July.

Aubenas, F. (2016) 'Magnanville: les fractures françaises au grand jour', *Le Monde*, 20 June.

Bonelli, L. (2015) 'Les chemins de la radicalisation', *Le Monde diplomatique*, February.

Chapelle, S. (2015) 'Incitations à la haine, racisme, intox: des élus et cadres du FN se lâchent', *Bastamag*, 23 January.

Chassat-Philippe, S. (2015) 'Les missions locales et la PJJ mobilisées pour la prévention de la radicalisation', Directions.fr, 19 May.

CNCDH (Commission nationale consultative des droits de l'homme) (2016) *La lutte contre le racisme, l'antisémitisme et la xénophobie. Année 2015*. Paris: La Documentation française.

de Montlibert, C. (2015) 'Philippe Val et la haine de la sociologie', *Le Monde*, 21 April.

Delaporte, L. (2014) 'Radicalisation religieuse: l'Education nationale dérape', *Mediapart*, 21 November.

Elias, N. (2007) *Involvement and Detachment*. Dublin: University College Dublin Press.

Ferhallad, M. (2016) 'Meurtre de M. El Makouli: l'irresponsabilité pénale requise', *La Provence*, 16 June.

Fouest, C. (2015) *Éloge du blasphème*. Paris: Grasset.

Graulle, P. (2015) 'Attentat: Rioufol ouvre le bal des "dérapages"', *Politis*, 8 January.

Hajjat, A. and M. Mohammed (2016) *Islamophobie. Comment les élites françaises fabriquent le 'problème musulman'*. Paris: La Découverte.

Halissat, I. (2016) 'Etat d'urgence: les perquisitions en chute libre', *Le Monde*, 14 January.

Hausalter, L. (2016) 'Elisabeth Badinter: "Il ne faut pas avoir peur de se faire traiter d'islamophobe"', *Marianne*, 6 January.

La Dépêche (2015) 'Nice: le petit garçon, entendu par la police pour apologie du terrorisme, témoigne', *La Dépêche*, 5 February.

La Voix du Nord (2015) 'Bombardier Crespin: menacé de licenciement parce qu'il n'est pas "Charlie"?', *La Voix du Nord*, 29 January.

Le Parisien (2015) 'Un enfant de 9 ans entendu pour "apologie de terrorisme", son père porte plainte', *Le Parisien*, 30 January.

Lejay, L. (2016) 'Dans le tourbillon médiatique', *La Nouvelle République*, 3 January.

Mediapart (2016) 'A Nice, plus d'un tiers des victimes de confession musulmane', *Mediapart*, 19 July.

Rue89 (2015) 'Deux mois de prison ferme pour apologie d'acte terroriste', *Rue89 Bordeaux*, 16 December.

Sieffert, D. (2004) *Israël-Palestine, une passion française. La France dans le miroir du conflit israélo-palestinien.* Paris: La Découverte.

Soullier, L. (2015) 'Apologie du terrorisme: la justice face à l'urgence', *Le Monde*, 22 January.

Syndicat de la Magistrature (2015) 'Apologie du terrorisme: Résister à l'injonction de la répression immédiate!', *Syndicat de la Magistrature*, 20 January. www.syndicat-magistrature.org/Apologie-du-terrorisme-Resister-a.html.

Val, P. (2015) *Malaise dans l'inculture*. Paris: Grasset.

PART II

THE LONG 'WAR ON TERROR'

5 | THE WHITENESS OF INNOCENCE: *CHARLIE HEBDO* AND THE METAPHYSICS OF ANTI-TERRORISM IN EUROPE

Nicholas De Genova

Here shines still the whiteness of innocence. (Drinnon 1997 [1980]: viii)

A boy named Charlie Brown

In *A Boy Named Charlie Brown* (1969), the first feature film based on the 'Peanuts' comic strip and television specials, Charlie Brown is deeply troubled about being a loser, wracked with self-doubt and an inferiority complex. Eventually, he discovers the one thing that he's good at – spelling – and then does so well in the school spelling bee that he's sent to a national competition in New York City, which will be televised. In the end, he loses and has to return home in disgrace. In an attempt to console him, Charlie Brown's friend Linus tells him, "But did you notice something, Charlie Brown? The world didn't come to an end." When Charlie Brown goes outside, he sees life going on as normal. Then, when he sees Lucy playing with a football, he sneaks up behind her to kick it, but as she always does, Lucy snatches it away at the last second and he falls flat. The film ends with Charlie Brown lying on the ground, humiliated, as Lucy leans over and says, "Welcome home, Charlie Brown."

This vignette seems to supply a fitting analogy for the European experience of decolonisation – and for present purposes, the French experience in particular. The crucial difference, of course, is that France has generally suffered from the opposite malady. It has been vexed by a superiority complex. France congratulates itself with the notion that many of the essential categories of what is taken to be our global political 'modernity' – concepts of citizenship, individualism, the idea of the subject, the rule of law, equality before the law, justice, liberty, human rights, democracy, popular sovereignty, the distinction between the state and civil society, public and private, secularism, scientific rationality, humanism, Enlightenment – all can somehow be credited as having their origins, to some significant degree, in France. In the colonial context, this heritage purportedly bequeathed to humanity by Europe, and by France in particular, was called 'civilisation' (Chakrabarty 2000: 7). Therefore, upon returning from its colonialist adventure in the great big world in the aftermath of decolonisation, humiliated and disgraced, France desperately needed to resuscitate its narcissistic delusions of grandeur.

Now, however, in a classic act of postcolonial historical amnesia, France's universalist ambitions would have to be nurtured with the revised sort of self-aggrandisement that could be derived strictly from 'national' insularity. As Achille Mbembe argues, in the wake of its postcolonial demise, France withdrew into the narrow epistemic confines of its presumptive 'national' borders, "which became its filter for narrating itself and the world" (2011: 90). As for all the other European colonial powers, France would have to grapple with the fact that, with the loss of its global power and prestige, 'the world didn't come to an end'. Furthermore, as with Lucy's surprise humiliation of tricking Charlie Brown with the football, reconfirming that he is really a loser after all, France's desire to retreat into a sanitised narrative of national greatness, miraculously cleansed of the filth of its colonial legacy, has been met with the postcolonial boomerang effect that presents itself in the form of mass migration, above all from the countries formerly subjugated by France. "Welcome home, Charlie Brown."

A boy named Charlie Hebdo

On 7 January 2015, the evening of the shootings that left twelve people dead at the offices of the magazine *Charlie Hebdo* as well as five more dead at a Jewish grocery, approximately 35,000 people gathered in Paris holding 'Je Suis Charlie' signs. In addition, smaller but significant gatherings were reported in Bordeaux, Grenoble, Lyon, Marseille, Nantes, Nice, Rennes, and Toulouse. In total, more than 100,000 people gathered across France to take part in these virtually instantaneous rallies on the evening of the events. Similar demonstrations and candlelight vigils also spread to cities outside France, including Amsterdam, Barcelona, Berlin, Brussels, Copenhagen, Ljubljana, London and Washington DC.[1] The next day, the headline of the national daily newspaper *Le Monde* proclaimed the events to be "The French 9/11" (Fassin 2015: 3). Indeed, in a manner reminiscent of the headline in *Le Monde* the day after the events of 11 September 2001 in New York City, proclaiming to its French readership, "We are all Americans. We are all New Yorkers,"[2] the 'Je Suis Charlie' affirmation went viral and became the obligatory international expression of identification and sympathy. In this context, President François Hollande proclaimed Paris to be the "capital of the world" (Fassin 2015: 3). Hollande described the shooting as a "terrorist attack of the most extreme barbarity", called the slain cartoonists and journalists "heroes", and declared a day of national mourning on 8 January.[3]

With widespread endorsement of the call for demonstrations of 'national unity' from across the political spectrum, there emerged the official slogan: "Against barbarity, let us defend the values of the Republic!" (Fassin 2015: 3). On Sunday 11 January, approximately 2 million people (demonstrably led by more than forty heads of state) rallied for national unity in Paris, and over the weekend of the 10th and 11th, an estimated total of 3.7 million people joined demonstrations across France. These 'Republican marches', as they quickly came to be known, were the biggest in French history, and, notably, also the largest public rallies in France since 1944, when Paris was liberated from Nazi occupation. Following the National Unity rally, the front page of the national centre-left daily newspaper *Libération* was dominated by an image of thousands of people gathered under a banner that declared 'Je Suis Charlie'. The newspaper announced: "We are one people" (Fassin 2015: 3). Indeed, the nation appeared to now have only one name – Charlie.

Although the sheer scale of violent calamity was in no sense comparable to the events of 11 September 2001 in the United States, which had served so efficiently to usher in the bombastic proclamation of the Global War on Terror, this so-called French '9/11' – much like the Australian and Canadian ones that had transpired just a short while earlier, as well as the Danish one that would soon follow – served to institute a traumatic rupture in time that severed the events from any prior history and ensnared the nation as unwitting witnesses in a spectacular present (cf. De Genova 2013). Moreover, the French spectacle of the attacks, the manhunt and the final showdown enshrouded the very invocation of *Charlie Hebdo* in a halo of sanctity. Exactly like the quasi-hieroglyphic ideogram '9/11'(Heller 2005: 3; cf. Simpson 2006), the name '*Charlie Hebdo*' now crystallised and encapsulated a whole ideological script, such that the mere mention of the name became virtually self-evident and sufficient to signal the new hegemonic consensus.[4]

Following this massive spectacle of French nationalist exuberance and international solidarity, Prime Minister Manuel Valls solemnly asserted that France is indeed "at war with terrorism" (Fassin 2015: 3). Predictably, during the week after the shootings, fifty-four anti-Muslim incidents were reported in France. These included twenty-one reports of shootings or grenade throwing at mosques and other Islamic centres, and thirty-three cases of threats of violence or verbal abuse.[5] Furthermore, in the town of Beaucet, near Avignon, Mohammed El Makouli, a Moroccan, was murdered after being stabbed seventeen times by a neighbour who invaded his home, shouting anti-Muslim slogans. (His wife was also slashed with the assailant's knife before fleeing the scene with their young child.) In addition, despite the celebration of *Charlie Hebdo*'s notorious racist/anti-Muslim cartoons (see Cyran 2013) as an icon of the freedom of expression, a reanimated political climate commanding conformity with the sacralisation of the *Charlie Hebdo* victims and the sanctity of the official values of the Republic culminated in the widespread suppression of free speech and reprisals against those who were perceived to show disaffection for the new consensus. Some lost their jobs and others were reported to the police for refusing to honour the official moment of silence promulgated to commemorate the victims.

Because of at least 200 reported incidents of defiance or irreverence with regard to the moment of silence by schoolchildren, mainly from 'immigrant' (non-white) communities, the government announced new plans to invest €71 million to more assiduously propagate and reinforce secularist values in classrooms, including the singing of the national anthem. Notably, the Minister of Education, Moroccan-born Najat Vallaud-Belkacem, suggested that measures must also be taken to enforce respect for the authority of teachers (de la Baume 2015). As many as 100 people, including controversial comedian Dieudonné M'bala M'bala, came under police investigation for making or posting comments online that purportedly justified or glorified terrorism, and several were quickly convicted and sentenced to prison terms of as long as four years.[6] When police in Nice subjected an eight-year-old boy to questioning concerning allegations of 'justifying terrorism', it seemed indisputable that the official intolerance towards any disaffection for the fetishisation of *Charlie Hebdo* as an icon of Republican virtue had reached the point of hysteria (de la Baume and Bilefski 2015).

Houria Bouteldja and Malik Tahar Chaouch of the Parti des Indigènes de la République (PIR) have astutely depicted this as "a political climate of institutional violence" and repression intended to subordinate "the people on the receiving end of structural racism" in France to the mandates of a "national unity" that "serves to exclude them and to demand their submission" and thereby reinforces the very same "social order that engendered the spiral of violence".[7] Thus, they argue incisively, "'freedom of expression' becomes a pretext for silencing those who have the least access to it ... and is being used instead to impose a reign of intimidation and fear", while "national unity serves ... above all to consolidate the white consensus" (Bouteldja and Chaouch 2015; see also PIR 2015). Directly indicting the pretence that *Charlie Hebdo*'s anti-Muslim cartoons could somehow be upheld as a pure manifestation of the freedom of speech or subversive anti-clerical satire, Bouteldja (2015) has called this into question: "I blame them for having stripped satire of its meaning, for directing it against the oppressed (which is a form of sadism) instead of against power and the powerful (which is a form of resistance)." Meanwhile, Jeannette Bougrab – daughter of a Berber Muslim Algerian 'Harki' (a loyalist volunteer soldier who served as an auxiliary in the French colonial army fighting to defeat Algeria's national liberation struggle), attorney and law professor, right-wing (UMP) politician, former junior minister under President Nicolas Sarkozy, and also the self-proclaimed romantic companion and virtual widow of *Charlie Hebdo* editor-in-chief Stéphane ('Charb') Charbonnier, but publicly repudiated by his family – went on the attack against the anti-racist left, particularly the PIR, as 'guilty' and 'responsible' for the shootings by having previously accused *Charlie Hebdo* of Islamophobia.[8] She declared: "those who denounce Islamophobia have armed the assassins".[9]

Notably, that same week, the new far-right anti-Muslim movement in Germany, Pegida (Patriotic Europeans against the Islamisation of the West), dedicated its weekly Monday evening march in Dresden to the commemoration of the *Charlie Hebdo* victims, and rallied a record-high turnout of 25,000 supporters for its cause on 12 January. Alongside such lurid crypto-fascist millenarian nationalist mantras as "Germany is awakening. For our fatherland, for Germany, it is our country, the country of our ancestors, descendants and children!",[10] however, Pegida's explicit assertion of what we may instructively call 'patriotic Europeanism' – in this instance, in solidarity with French 'national unity', against the putative menace of 'Islamisation' – authorised themselves not only as the authentic and organic expression of 'the German nation' but also as the voice of 'the people' of Europe. Notably, the rise of Pegida in Germany was in fact assisted by the German branch of a far-right anti-immigrant, anti-Muslim movement that actually began in France, the Bloc Identitaire, and its youth wing Génération Identitaire, which, like Pegida, is committed to an explicitly and emphatically Europeanist project (De Genova 2015; cf. De Genova 2016).

The general political climate in France leading to the events of 7 January 2015 was already one of escalating postcolonial racial tension. In October 2014, the AGRIF (General Alliance against Racism and for the Respect of French and Christian Identity), a far-right group, brought a legal complaint against leftist sociologist Saïd Bouamama and rapper Saïd Zouggagh, aka Saïdou, of the hip-hop group Z.E.P. (Zone d'expression populaire), for their anti-racist and anti-colonialist song 'Nique la France' ('Fuck France') and their eponymous book-length manifesto, both published in 2010, celebrating the "duty of insolence" and unreservedly denouncing French nationalism and its equation with white racial identity.[11] The complaint was lodged in the wake of the public debate initiated by prominent right-wing (UMP) politician Jean-François Copé's book *Manifeste pour une droite décomplexée* ('Manifesto for a right-wing without inhibitions', 2012), popularising the contention of 'anti-white racism', a notion that had previously been explicit only within the far right. Indeed, in September 2012, when Copé began to 'break taboos' by making his case against 'anti-white racism'[12] as a presidential candidate aspiring to become the successor to Nicolas Sarkozy, National Front leader Marine Le Pen accused him and his party of invading the ideological territory of the National Front in a cynical tactical manoeuvre to capitalise on their unprecedented electoral success during the spring of that year, when they garnered more than 6.5 million votes. (In May of that same year, the National Front had already called for a law to explicitly prohibit 'anti-white' prejudice.) These moves by Copé notably followed Sarkozy's declarations, during the desperate electoral campaign of 2012, that there were "too many foreigners" on French territory, and that "all civilisations are not equal in worth", as well as his Interior and Immigration Minister Claude Guéant's pronouncement that it is natural for the French to "want France to remain France" (Mondon 2012a). Notably, Copé – publicist of the insidious notion of 'anti-white racism' – is himself the son of a father of Romanian Jewish origin and a mother of Algerian Jewish origin.

Thus, over the period of several months before and after the *Charlie Hebdo* attacks, the far-right campaign to legally punish the anti-racist, anti-colonial audacity of Saïd Bouamama and Saïdou, for their song and manifesto 'Fuck France' ('*Nique la France*') marked an important tactical improvisation within the wider field of French racial/cultural politics. Here is a sample from the text of the book:

> We encounter massive racial discrimination – systemic, structural, institutional – that touches every sphere of life (school, vocational training, employment, housing, relationships with the police, etc.). It turns us into a stigmatised social group, deprived of rights and assigned to the most precarious, most degraded and most unequal positions in French society.
>
> We are the target of regular ideological campaigns branding us as 'barbarian', 'homophobic', 'anti-Semitic', 'intolerant of secularism', 'terrorist' and so on. Islamophobia is steadily gaining ground, making us 'the enemy within' to be monitored, hunted, punished ...
>
> This systematic humiliation of a whole social group is ongoing and getting worse. The organisation of the French social structure confines us within frontiers [borders] that are no less real for being invisible ...
>
> From the counter of the immigration and nationalisation office to the police identity check, from educational selection to employment discrimination, our everyday life is a constant reminder of these frontiers [borders]. We are constantly required to show our allegiance, our submission, our deservingness, our politeness, our worthiness, our unobtrusiveness, our invisibility. And this when our human dignity can be safeguarded only by rebellion, by struggle, by visibility, by impoliteness, by irreverence, by insubordination, by egalitarian impatience. We are called on to love the system that oppresses us. We are accused of 'communitarianism' when we seek to organise autonomously. In the context of our oppression, however, this demonised 'communitarianism' is a defence against depersonalisation, decomposition, self-hatred.
>
> Why the hell should we be ashamed to be Arab, Black, Muslim ...? To be non-White? We are accused of 'victimology' when we do no more than denounce the massive racial discrimination we suffer and

insist on being treated as equals. We are, objectively, the victims of a racist system that finds expression in massive, systemic discrimination.

Who is this 'We', then? This we is both the legacy of colonisation and the ongoing product of today's French social system ... This we is made up of the Blacks, Arabs and Muslims of France, whatever their status, whatever their nationality ... To abandon all illusions in the face of the false promises, the sympathy and the good intentions, and the myths of the Republic – equal opportunity, fraternity, Enlightenment and all – that are recited to us to make us go to sleep ...

Given [debates on the burqa and on national identity, with the expulsion of undocumented immigrants amid general indifference, with the multiplication of racist crimes, with discrimination as a system, all evidence of the failure of the quest for inclusion], there is only one conclusion to be drawn: the need to break radically and unambiguously with all the mystifying discourses produced and circulated in order to legitimate and to maintain the inequalities and injustices of this society, of this France never decolonised ...

That is why we say, calmly, imperturbably: Fuck France! [*Nique la France!*] Fuck colonial, racist, unequal France! If the phrase emerged spontaneously on the lips of the young people of the *quartiers populaires*, and then appeared in the titles and lyrics of songs, it was not because of a taste for vulgarity ... For a long time now, the phrase has simply meant a refusal to tolerate the intolerable, to stay where you're told, to be the object of speech rather than a speaking subject. All the laws and sanctions of the world can do nothing against this refusal of the life of a slave, of a [colonised] native ...

'Fuck France' doesn't say 'I am X or Y' but rather 'I refuse to be X!', 'I will not be Y!', 'I refuse the place I have been allotted in life!'

'Fuck France' is the refusal to be invisible, to be discreet; it is the assertion of our right to be who we are, and not to have to hide it.

'Fuck France' is the refusal to defer and to be polite in the face of a social system that oppresses us, exploits us, stigmatises us, and marginalises us.

'Fuck France' is the assertion that we alone are responsible for our own emancipation, rejecting the 'integration', the 'assimilation', the 'civilisation' that others have defined for us as if we were mere modelling clay, to be shaped at will.

'Fuck France' will be with us as long as there is inequality. It will not disappear, so long as there is oppression and discrimination. It is continuously produced by our conditions of existence, by the physical, social and symbolic violence that characterises them ...

We no longer want to be on the defensive, we no longer want
to justify ourselves, for these attitudes spring from internalised
oppression. We will not complain, or negotiate, but simply insist on
equality now.[13]

Bouamama and Zouggagh, aka Saïdou, were indicted in Lille on 20
January 2015 for 'public insult' and 'incitement to discrimination, hate,
or violence'. (They were finally judged to be not guilty of the spurious
charges on 19 March 2015.) Concurrently, just three weeks before the
Charlie Hebdo shootings, prominent right-wing television and radio
commentator and columnist Éric Zemmour, son of Algerian Jewish
parents who migrated to France in the 1950s and author of the anti-
immigration bestsellers *Mélancolie française* (*French Melancholy*, 2010)
and *Le Suicide Français* (*The French Suicide*, 2014), had to be fired by the
twenty-four-hour news channel i-Télé after a scandal over revelations of
an interview, published in Italy, in which he endorsed the idea that all
Muslims, including second- and third-generation French citizens, should
be deported from France in the interests of avoiding 'chaos and civil
war'.[14] In this regard, refusing to acknowledge the French nationality
of the country's 'Muslim' (non-white) citizens, Zemmour was merely
recapitulating the folksy racist common sense of National Front founder
Jean-Marie Le Pen, who has never tired of insisting that 'a goat born in
a stable is not a horse', and thus 'immigrants' (particularly Muslims)
are often "of a race, religion, and mores very different from that of true
French [*Français de souche*]" (Mondon 2012b). Earlier in 2014, Zemmour
had remarked that the barbarian pillage of Europe after the fall of Rome
was being re-enacted by "thieving violent gangs of Chechens, Romas,
Kosovars, North Africans, and Africans" (Lichfield 2014). Hence, the
discourse broadly affiliating Muslims – and migrants, more generally –
with 'barbarity', so pronounced in the wake of the shootings, has been part
of an extended controversy over the qualifications of France's migrant
(non-white) 'minorities', especially Muslims, for proper inclusion within
French 'civilisation'.

It is important here to note nonetheless that, contrary to the
widespread notion that what we are witnessing is the re-entrenchment
of a 'clash of civilisations' thesis as the dominant ideological grammar of
an era of intensified and aggravated 'Islamophobia', what is really
operative fairly consistently is the mobilisation of diverse manifestations
of anti-Muslim racism that serve to coercively sort and rank Muslims as

'good' ones (those who are docile, obedient, assimilationist) versus 'bad' ones whose 'barbaric' proclivities disqualify them from 'Civilisation' altogether. This latter outlook corresponds in fact to the thesis, associated with Francis Fukuyama, of 'the End of History', for which there is finally one and only one possible pathway of Civilisation and 'progress'. The difference is a significant one. The 'clash of civilisations' argument posits a plurality of essentially incompatible and fundamentally inimical 'cultures' or 'civilisations' in a conflict for planetary dominance, embroiled inextricably in a constitutive antagonism that, by implication, is inherently a struggle to the death. Roughly speaking, the perspective of someone like Zemmour does indeed articulate this view, whereby Muslims in Europe are universally and automatically presumed to be the foot soldiers of an enemy camp, and mass expulsion is the only plausible solution to an intractable and irreconcilable conflict. However, the dominant theme is actually a mandate for (secular, Republican) 'assimilation'. Rather than positing a pluralist scenario of rival 'cultures' or 'civilisations', it understands there to be only one Civilisation, and commands (and expects) the subordination and submission of all cultural or religious differences within a hegemonic framework of secularist and multiculturalist 'integration'.

This perspective actually compels the repeated performative collusion of Muslims who aspire to verify their deservingness, credibility and civility through obligatory pronouncements of disapproval and disavowal of 'terrorism' and all manner of 'fundamentalist' excesses. It also helps to explain the high visibility and strategic importance of so many persons of proverbial 'immigrant background' who have been prominent and vociferous defenders of the imperatives of the French political establishment. Indeed, every iteration of the 'clash of civilisations' argument in this manner invites its own repudiation, summoning 'good' Muslims to refute the bald allegations against 'Islam' in general and thereby uphold the multiculturalist dogma whereby Muslims can also be loyal and dutiful liberal subjects of the secular Republic. The alleged tendency among Muslims toward 'communitarianism' may be persistently held as worthy of suspicion and constantly subjected to vigilance, but this kind of superintendence is precisely *disciplinary*: it is dedicated to training those whose 'civility' is deemed to be incomplete or defective for fuller 'integration'; it is, in short, a 'civilising mission'. This is why, for example, a violation of France's 2010 ban on wearing the burqa or niqab in public is penalised not only with a fine but also the mandate to attend citizenship classes. It is also why the then presiding Interior Minister Guéant instructed police that women arrested for wearing full facial coverings should be tactfully informed of the law's motivations in a spirit of education.[15] Of course, these gestures of police 'sensitivity' were frequently accompanied by vilification, abuse, and sporadic violence on the part of anti-Muslim racists who were re-energised in their self-righteous confidence to perpetrate attacks against veiled Muslim women following the enactment of the ban.

The proliferation of diverse manifestations of anti-Muslim derision and discrimination in France is plainly a systemic postcolonial racism that seeks to subjugate Muslim/migrant/non-white 'difference' within a racial socio-political order of white supremacy and nationalist prerogative, but its dominant logic is one of (hierarchical) assimilation and domestication. Rather than a pluralist metaphysics of absolute incompatibility and incommensurability, with its segregationist logic, as would be implied by the 'clash of civilisations' thesis, this anti-Muslim racism ought instead to be understood to epitomise a dynamic of subordinate inclusion, or what I have elsewhere depicted as "inclusion through exclusion" (De Genova 2010b). Thus, it is ultimately only the incorrigible remainder of Muslims, the truly 'radical(ised)' fringe, who get castigated as atavistic and irredeemably 'barbaric'. For these, who are effectively disqualified from any possible inclusion within the one and only (global, neoliberal) Civilisation, there remains no other recourse than expulsion, or, indeed, extermination. (For a fuller discussion, see De Genova 2010a; cf. De Genova 2010b.)

Here we recognise the metaphysics of anti-terrorism, famously promulgated by George W. Bush in his ultimatum to the Taliban government in Afghanistan in 2001, which was simultaneously an ultimatum to the whole world: "You are with us, or you are with the terrorists." (For a fuller discussion, see De Genova 2007, 2011, 2013.) It is within this emphatically and explicitly globalist metaphysics of Civilisation, in its millenarian showdown with barbarism, that forthright critiques of *Charlie Hebdo*'s grotesque and extravagant hostility to Muslims or refusals to embrace the 'Je Suis Charlie' mantra become tantamount to complicity with, justification of, or apology for the abominable 'terrorist' enemy.

It is crucial, here, to distinguish between the more psychologistic notion of Islamophobia and what is truly an anti-Muslim racism. The productivity of racism in this instance derives precisely from its capacity to racialise a category that ostensibly refers to religious difference or 'culture'. In other words, anti-Muslim racism is a premier example of the kind of culturalist, differentialist racism (Balibar 1991a) that overtly dissimulates race and appears to be about something else (e.g. religion). It becomes clear that this is not strictly or primarily about Islam (as a religion) so much as it is about Muslims as a group, as a racialised category, who may be conveniently associated with some of the more visible and identifiable accoutrements or paraphernalia of Islamic practices, but need not be committed in any substantive doctrinal or practical sense to Islam as such. Notably, this was always true of the category 'Muslim' in the French colonial context:

> the designation as Muslim did not strictly correspond to a religious affiliation. Even the few thousand of those who converted to Catholicism remained 'Muslims' under the French law, since according to a 1903 decision of the Court of Appeal of Algiers, the term 'does not have a purely denominational meaning, but designates all individuals of Muslim origin, without necessity to distinguish whether they belong to the Islamic religion'. (Fassin 2015: 6)

Thus, historically and still today, the category "'Muslim' has long been the generic term to name the colonial subjects of North Africa" (Fassin 2015: 6). Hence, Houria Bouteldja, spokesperson for the PIR, has unpacked the contemporary Muslim question in ways that fundamentally exceed and destabilise any narrow fetishisation of religious difference as such. She explains:

> I would even say that 'Muslim' also denotes 'resident of a poor neighborhood.' It is sometimes a euphemism for '*banlieue.*' Its meaning is pejorative … In France, Islam is above all a religion of the poor and of immigrants and therefore of a part of the population that has no political, economic or media power … The white European identity that dominated the world for 500 years is in decline.
> The voices – often hysterical – raised in the media against Islam fundamentally express a fear of this decline … Whites are losing their historical centrality … and they see all these non-whites, wrongly identified with Islam, as a threat to their identity. (Bouteldja 2012)

In short, 'Muslim' operates as a category that condenses both racial and class derision, encompassing non-white 'foreigners' who are not necessarily foreign-born or migrants, and may not even be Muslims. The Muslim question in France (and much of the rest of Europe) today is therefore not reducible to Islamophobia or even to any specific antagonism directed exclusively toward Muslims as such. Rather, the Muslim question is merely a refraction of what may be best apprehended, in fact, to be a question about 'Europe' and 'European'-ness as a racial problem of postcolonial whiteness: what I call the 'European' question (De Genova 2016).

In extravagant juxtaposition with France, 'Europe' or 'the West' – rather than Christianity, for example – this aversion to Muslims and this heightening intolerance towards Islam can only really be apprehensible as a matter of religion to the extent that nationalism itself may be understood to be a religion, the veritable theology of the (nation-)state. There is, after all, considerable basis for theorising nationalism as a kind of religion. Notably, in his classic study of nationalism, Benedict Anderson astutely notes the national project's cult of death and nationalism's need to reanimate itself by means of sacralised corpses, such as the victims of the *Charlie Hebdo* attack. Anderson suggests, furthermore, that nationalist concerns with death and immortality are indicative of "a strong affinity with religious imaginings" (1991: 10), which transform "fatality into continuity" (ibid.: 11). Anderson elaborates:

> The century of Enlightenment, of rationalist secularism, brought
> with it its own modern darkness. With the ebbing of religious belief,
> the suffering which belief in part composed did not disappear.
> Disintegration of paradise: nothing makes fatality more arbitrary.
> Absurdity of salvation: nothing makes another style of continuity more
> necessary. What then was required was a secular transformation of
> fatality into continuity, contingency into meaning. As we shall see,
> few things were (are) better suited to this end than an idea of nation.
> If nation-states are widely conceded to be 'new' and 'historical,' the
> nations to which they give political expression always loom out of
> an immemorial past, and still more important, glide into a limitless
> future. It is the magic of nationalism to turn chance into destiny.
> (ibid.: 11–12)

Similarly, Hannah Arendt refers specifically to the 'sentimental' role of nationalism in symbolising the 'essential community' of citizens otherwise atomised by the ascendancy of bourgeois individualism and the cleavages of class conflict, encompassing state sovereignty with the "pseudomystical aura ... [of] a 'national soul'" (1968 [1951]: 230–1). Nationalism thereby became, in Arendt's account, "the precious cement for binding together a centralized state and an atomized society" and substantiated a precisely "pseudomystical" (quasi-religious) but vital connection between individuals in and through the state, which would now be taken to embody the putative will of 'the nation' (ibid.: 231). In this manner, nationalism aspires to verify the elusive promise of what Anderson memorably depicts as a "deep horizontal comradeship" (1991: 7), or, in other words, what Étienne Balibar discerns to be a circumscribed egalitarianism that is "first and foremost, an equality in respect of nationality" (1991b: 50). In spite of the fact that "the members of even the smallest nation will never know most of their fellow-members, meet them, or even hear of them", Anderson contends, "in the minds of each lives the image of their communion" (1991: 6) – the "community in anonymity which is the hallmark of modern nations" (ibid.: 36).

Here, it is useful to note the resonance of these features of modern nationalism with Émile Durkheim's classic discussion of religion in the example of totemism among so-called 'primitive' Australian aboriginal peoples organised on a clan basis:

> It even seems as though the clan could not exist, in the form it has taken in a great number of Australian societies, without the totem. For the members of a single clan are not united to each other by a common habitat or by common blood, as they are not necessarily consanguineous and are frequently scattered over different parts of the tribal territory. Their unity comes solely from their having the same name and the same emblem, their believing that they have the same relations with the same categories of things, their practicing the same rites, or, in a word, from their participating in the same totemic cult. (Durkheim 1965 [1912/1915]: 194)

The example of "a plurality of individual consciousnesses [that] enter into a communion and are fused into a common consciousness" verifies the non-utilitarian and 'sentimental' (non-rational) form of association that Durkheim deems to be the essence of religion (quoted in Alexander 1982: 242). For our purposes, therefore, the beleaguered project of postcolonial French nationhood today may be seen to have been newly rejuvenated through the totemic cult of *Charlie Hebdo*. The events of 7 January have bestowed a sentimental communion upon a (white) 'nation', emphatically disarticulated from the phantasmatic figure of 'Muslim' 'terrorism', by endowing the whole atomised aggregate of alienated ('modern', 'secular') individuals with the same name and the same emblem: *Je suis Charlie.*

"Welcome home, Charlie Brown."

Notes

1 http://en.wikipedia.org/wiki/Charlie_Hebdo_shooting#cite_ref-Pech_84-0.

2 The headline is attributed to Jean-Marie Colombani, editor-in-chief of *Le Monde*. The headline was published on 12 September 2001, but its official dateline was 13 September 2001.

3 http://en.wikipedia.org/wiki/Charlie_Hebdo_shooting#cite_ref-Pech_84-0.

4 The intensity of this new consensus is evidenced in the subsequent meltdown within the National Front, where the movement's founder Jean-Marie Le Pen's knee-jerk anti-Semitism and belittling of the Holocaust have been deemed utterly anathema to the political necessity to be aligned with the victims of the attacks, including, of course, those targeted at the Jewish supermarket. "Jean-Marie Le Pen seems to have descended into a strategy somewhere between scorched earth and political suicide," said his daughter and current National Front leader, Marine Le Pen. "His status as honorary president [of the party] does not give him the right to hijack the National Front with vulgar provocations" (Daley 2015).

5 http://en.wikipedia.org/wiki/Charlie_Hebdo_shooting#cite_ref-Pech_84-0.

6 The new anti-terrorism law was passed on 4 November 2014, and includes provisions for fast-track convictions.

7 For a more general account of racist policing disproportionately directed at 'minorities' in France, see Human Rights Watch (2012).

8 www.lepoint.fr/societe/charlie-hebdo-le-temoignage-de-jeannette-bougrab-compagne-de-charb-08-01-2015-1895054_23.php.

9 http://oumma.com/219542/jeannette-bougrab-sujet-de-charlie-hebdo-indigenes-de.

10 Spiegel Online International, 4 November 2014.

11 http://mrzine.monthlyreview.org/2015/zep130115.html.

12 www.lefigaro.fr/politique/2012/09/26/01002-20120926ARTFIG00428-cope-denonce-l-existence-d-un-racisme-anti-blanc.php.

13 http://en.wikipedia.org/wiki/Racism_in_France#Racism_against_white_French.

14 www.english.rfi.fr/france/20120927-right-wing-leader-claims-anti-white-racism-growing-france.

15 http://en.wikipedia.org/wiki/French_ban_on_face_covering.

References

Alexander, J. C. (1982) *Theoretical Logic in Sociology. Volume Two: The Antinomies of Classical Thought: Marx and Durkheim*. Berkeley CA: University of California Press.

Anderson, B. (1991) *Imagined Communities: Reflections on the Origins and Spread of Nationalism*. Revised edition. New York: Verso.

Arendt, H. (1968 [1951]) *The Origins of Totalitarianism*. New York: Harvest/Harcourt.

Balibar, É. (1991a) 'Is There a "Neo-Racism"?' in É. Balibar and I. Wallerstein (eds) *Race, Nation, Class: Ambiguous Identities*. New York: Verso, pp. 17–28.

Balibar, É. (1991b) 'Racism and Nationalism' in É. Balibar and I. Wallerstein (eds) *Race, Nation, Class: Ambiguous Identities*. New York: Verso, pp. 36–67.

Bouteldja, H. (2012) 'Islamophobia: When the Whites Lose Their Triple A Rating', Decolonial Translation Group, 26 November. Available in English translation at: www.decolonialtranslation.com/english/islamophobia-when-the-whites-lose-their-triple-a-rating.html.

Bouteldja, H. (2015) 'Charlie Hebdo: The Sacred of the "Wretched of the Earth" and its Desecration', Decolonial Translation Group, 26 January. www.decolonialtranslation.com/english/harlie-hebdo-the-sacred-of-the-wretched-of-the-earth-and%20oits-desecration.html.

Bouteldja, H. and M. T. Chaouch (2015) 'The Unity Trap', *Jacobin Magazine*, 4 February. www.jacobinmag.com/2015/02/charlie-hebdo-racism-movement; http://indigenes-republique.fr/the-unity-trap.

Chakrabarty, D. (2000) *Provincializing Europe: Postcolonial Thought and Historical Difference*. Princeton NJ: Princeton University Press.

Copé, J.-F. (2012) *Manifeste pour une droite décomplexée*. Paris: Fayard.

Cyran, O. (2013) '"Charlie Hebdo", Not Racist? If You Say So ...' Translated by Daphne Lawless. Originally published in *Article 11*, 5 December. http://posthypnotic.randomstatic.net/charliehebdo/Charlie_Hebdo_article%2011.htm; www.leninology.

co.uk/2015/01/charlie-hebdo-not-racist-if-you-say-so.html.

Daley, S. (2015) 'Marine Le Pen, Leader of France's National Front Party, Splits With Her Father, Its Founder', *New York Times*, 8 April. www.nytimes.com/2015/04/09/world/europe/marine-le-pen-leader-of-frances-national-front-party-splits-with-her-father-its-founder.html?emc=edit_th_20150409&nl=todaysheadlines&nlid=44765954.

De Genova, N. (2007) 'The Production of Culprits: From Deportability to Detainability in the Aftermath of "Homeland Security"', *Citizenship Studies* 11 (5): 421–48.

De Genova, N. (2010a) 'Antiterrorism, Race, and the New Frontier: American Exceptionalism, Imperial Multiculturalism, and the Global Security State', *Identities* 17 (6): 613–40.

De Genova, N. (2010b) 'Migration and Race in Europe: The Trans-Atlantic Metastases of a Post-Colonial Cancer', *European Journal of Social Theory* 13 (3): 405–19.

De Genova, N. (2011) 'Spectacle of Security, Spectacle of Terror' in S. Feldman, C. Geisler and G. Menon (eds) *Accumulating Insecurity: Violence and Dispossession in the Making of Everyday Life*. Athens GA: University of Georgia Press, pp. 141–65.

De Genova, N. (2013) 'The Securitarian Society of the Spectacle' in Z. Gambetti and M. Godoy-Anativia (eds) *Rhetorics of Insecurity: Belonging and Violence in the Neoliberal Era*. New York: New York University Press, pp. 213–42.

De Genova, N. (2015) 'In the Land of the Setting Sun: Reflections on "Islamization" and "Patriotic Europeanism"', *Movements: Journal für kritische Migrations- und*

Grenzregimeforschung (Journal for Critical Migration and Border Regime Research) 1 (2). http://movements-journal.org/issues/02.kaempfe/15. de-genova--pegida-islamization-patriotic-europeanism.html.

De Genova, N. (2016) 'The European Question: Migration, Race, and Postcoloniality in Europe', *Social Text* 34 (3) [Issue #128]: 75–102.

de la Baume, M. (2015) 'Paris Announces Plan to Promote Secular Values', *New York Times*, 22 January. www.nytimes.com/2015/01/23/world/europe/charlie-hebdo-attack-leads-to-changes-in-french-schools.html.

de la Baume, M. and D. Bilefsky (2015) 'French Police Question Boy, 8, After Remarks on Paris Attacks', *New York Times*, 29 January. www.nytimes.com/2015/01/30/world/europe/french-police-questions-schoolboy-said-to-defend-charlie-hebdo-attack.html?_r=0.

Drinnon, R. (1997 [1980]) *Facing West: The Metaphysics of Indian-hating and Empire-building.* Norman, OK: University of Oklahoma Press.

Durkheim, É. (1965 [1912/1915]) *The Elementary Forms of the Religious Life.* Translated by Joseph Ward Swain. New York: The Free Press/Macmillan.

Fassin, D. (2015) 'In the Name of the Republic: Untimely Meditations on the Aftermath of the *Charlie Hebdo* Attack', *Anthropology Today* 31 (2): 3–7.

Heller, D. (2005) 'Introduction: Consuming 9/11' in D. Heller (ed.) *The Selling of 9/11: How a National Tragedy Became a Commodity.* New York: Palgrave Macmillan, pp. 1–26.

Human Rights Watch (2012) *The Root of Humiliation: Abusive Identity Checks in France.* Human Rights Watch, 26 January. www.hrw.org/reports/2012/01/26/root-humiliation.

Lichfield, J. (2014) 'Sacking of Islamophobic Television Presenter Provokes Free-speech Row in France', *Independent*, 21 December. www.independent.co.uk/news/world/europe/sacking-of-islamophobic-television-presenter-provokes-freespeech-row-in-france-9939085.html.

Mbembe, A. (2011) 'Provincializing France?', *Public Culture* 23 (1): 85–119.

Mondon, A. (2012a) 'France 2012: Sarkozy's Ugly Campaign', *The Conversation*, 20 April. https://theconversation.com/france-2012-sarkozys-ugly-campaign-6465.

Mondon, A. (2012b) 'Le Pen's Attacks on Islam Are No Longer Veiled', *Independent*, 27 September. www.independent.co.uk/voices/comment/le-pens-attacks-on-islam-are-no-longer-veiled-8181891.html.

PIR (Parti des Indigènes de la République) (2015) 'No to the "national union" backing imperialists! Yes to an anti-racist and anti-imperialist "political union"!', PIR, 10 January. http://indigenes-republique.fr/no-to-the-national-union-backing-imperialists-yes-to-an-anti-racist-and-anti-imperialist-political-union.

Simpson, D. (2006) *9/11: The Culture of Commemoration.* Chicago, IL: University of Chicago Press.

6 | THE VISIBLE HAND OF THE STATE

Gholam Khiabany

I

The dominant narrative for understanding the murderous attack on *Charlie Hebdo*'s office in January 2015 has insisted that this is a war – a war between two rival civilisations. On the one side stands a free, tolerant, secular, progressive and advanced civilisation that is increasingly under siege by another, a violent, backward, bigoted and inferior civilisation. In a statement released immediately after the murder of *Charlie Hebdo*'s staff, François Hollande declared that the attack on Charlie Hebdo was an attack against the Republic as a whole:

> The Republic equals freedom of expression; the Republic equals culture, creation, it equals pluralism and democracy. That is what the assassins were targeting. It equals the ideal of justice and peace that France promotes everywhere on the international stage, and the message of peace and tolerance that we defend – as do our soldiers – in the fight against terrorism and fundamentalism. (Hollande 2015)

Comparing the struggle to protect the Republic's value with what 'our soldiers' do in the fight against terrorism and fundamentalism reanimated the narrative of war. The language of war became more explicit after a second terrorist attack in Paris in November 2015. The French President immediately declared a state of emergency and promised to wage a 'merciless' war. But against who and which enemy state, and who will suffer from this 'pitiless war'?

The model that emerged to explain and motivate the response to the catastrophe of 11 September has become the universal model to explain all atrocities that have taken place on European shores since 2001. All acts of terror are now domestic 9/11s. The US government misleadingly compared the violence that was unleashed on 11 September to the bombing of Pearl Harbor. If that attack in December 1941 precipitated the United States' entry into the Second World

War, the declaration of a 'war on terror' after 11 September paved the way for the disastrous invasion of Afghanistan and Iraq. The promise of simple repetition in this historical analogy ignores some important and uncomfortable details, not least that the attack in 2001, unlike the bombing of Pearl Harbor, could not be identified with a single recognised state.

The 'war on terror' has taken many forms, gone through many phases, unleashed many forces, and turned many countries into battlefields with enormous human costs. If wars are not simply rhetoric, and the 'war on terror' has been deadly, then the declaration of war is about allocating resources and mobilisation to defeat the enemy. France's declaration of war is no exception. Immediately after the *Charlie Hebdo* tragedy, the French Prime Minister Manuel Valls announced that more than €700 million ($990 million) would be spent over the next three years on 'the fight against terrorism', and 2,600 more jobs would be created to monitor and prosecute 3,000 people who, according to the French Prime Minister Manuel Valls, had ties with jihadis (Lichfield 2015). Valls also indicated the direction of his government by declaring that his goal was to fight 'Islamofascism', a term which has been used by neo-cons and the far right. Real wars, no matter how horrific, have a beginning and an end. The 'war on terror', however, has no end, no clearly identified enemy and, very much like terrorism itself, is not bound by any international law or national border. Targeting a loosely defined enemy scattered over loosely defined territories has allowed the declaration of war to be used as a mandate for the expansion of a form of state power that is increasingly defined in terms of its security function. The security state can do what it wants, attack who it wants, and accepts no limits on its power.

If the attack on *Charlie Hebdo* was an attack on the Republic as a whole, then the state of emergency and the constant state of the war is dismantling the very values that Hollande claims the Republic stands for. The call and march for 'unity' in the aftermath of the attack against *Charlie Hebdo* echoes the rhetoric of Bush and Blair but such calls paradoxically also mimic the terrorist language of 'profane' versus 'holy' while charging those who call for reflection with 'treason'. Is this merely a coincidence or are we seeing two fundamentalisms, the imperial and the religious, converging and colliding? But there is more. The biggest paradox is the transformation of the word 'terrorism' itself. As Badiou has pointed out, "it is remarkable that the word 'terrorism', which clearly qualified a particular figure of exercise of the state power, has succeeded, little by little, in coming to signify exactly the contrary" (2006: 18).

It is the state, the ultimate body with monopoly over the legitimate use of force, that is designating violent acts as terrorism precisely because they are committed by non-state adversaries/actors. The term 'Islamic fascism', as Katha Pollitt (2006) has pointed out, has also received a linguistic makeover. The term was used for the first time by Malise Ruthven in 1990 to describe the authoritarian states in the Middle East. A decade later and after 9/11, the term was employed to cover a diversity of political practices by a broad swathe of Muslims. Yet this is not a mere linguistic makeover. 'Culture' has always, and even more so now, been used to legitimise power, oppression and domination while veiling that very function, and in particular the violence and coercion of the state.

There are other ways of putting this. The 'Republic' is staring at itself in the mirror of terror. If 'Islamofascism', as Valls puts it, is the enemy, then mobilising for war is a mobilisation against those who 'essentially' carry that 'identity'. If Islam is the 'identity' of those who carried out the hideous and calculated acts of terror on French soil in January and November 2015 as well as in July 2016, the responses by the state in France (and elsewhere in Europe) leave no doubt that anti-Muslim identity has become one of the core values of the Republic. It is precisely in such a climate that anti-Muslim racism and campaigns against immigrants have made the battle for protecting 'real' European and citizens a key battle between the far right and mainstream political parties in France and elsewhere. Some examples of the violence against Muslims in France are discussed in the first section of this book. Such acts of violence, of course, are not considered as terror. Neither is the imperialist aggression that François Hollande, without a hint of irony, labels as "the ideal of justice and peace that France promotes everywhere on the international stage".

It is precisely this transformation in the use of the word that has made it possible to designate that only one horrific act of violence committed on 11 September is considered as terrorism, given that the CIA planned and sponsored a coup against the democratically elected government of President Salvador Allende on 11 September 1973. It was also on 11 September that Anwar Sadat surrendered to the United States and Israel in 1977 by accepting the Camp David Accords (Wright

2014). A year later Anwar Sadat and Menachem Begin received the shared Nobel Peace Prize while Palestinians, who had no voice or representation in the negotiations, remained – and continue to remain – at the mercy of Israel. It was also on 11 September that George Bush Sr made his 'New World Order' speech to a joint session of Congress and announced the war against Iraq in 1990. This history of this date alone requires us to ask if it is only jihadis who target 'democracies' and make no distinction between civilians and non-civilians in their violence.

II

Asserting the anti-Muslim identity of the Republic is extending and expanding anti-Muslim racism across Europe. Situating and justifying racism in relation to cultural difference is nothing new, and neither is the statement that 'they are not like us'! But today this coincides with a wholesale attack on multiculturalism and a drive towards assimilation. Since 11 September, all European countries have realigned their 'race' policies towards an assimilationist, monocultural approach to integration. In the drive towards 'assimilation', racism is justified in terms of cultural 'values', and this in turn justifies an increasingly violent and authoritarian state. As the regressive attacks on public spending and the increasing gap between rich and poor eat away at the existing legitimacy of the state, the image of a 'great nation under threat' has been nurtured in the media and in the world of politics in order to attach the public to a new authoritarian state by providing an anti-Islamic 'common purpose'. Throughout history, various communities have served this purpose; Muslims are simply the latest of such 'suspect' communities.

There is an undeniable link between the domestic and foreign interests of imperial states. Indeed, it is worth remembering that when Huntington pointed at Muslims and Islam as the principal threat to what he calls 'Western Civilisation', he was in fact concerned not only with Muslims and Islam in the Middle East and North Africa but also large Muslim communities (of all nationalities and ethnicities) who were living in the West. That his next major project, *Who Are We?* (2004), turned to immigrants in the United States, and specifically to members of its Hispanic communities, should thus be no surprise. And one of his admirers, Francis Fukuyama, was similarly disturbed by demographic changes within North America and Europe. Indeed, even when he began to distance himself belatedly from the disastrous invasion of Iraq, he argued: "Meeting the jihadist challenge needs not a military campaign but a political contest for the hearts and minds of ordinary Muslims around the world. As recent events in France and Denmark suggest, Europe will be a central battleground" (Fukuyama 2006). The clash of civilisations was no longer going to take place 'out there' but at home!

In evoking the essence of the Republic as one uninterrupted history, Hollande and others not only skate over the reality that cultures and identities are less than stable or fixed, but more crucially that the so-called clash of cultures is deeply rooted in a material history. 'National characters' are constantly constituted and reconstituted by selective readings of 'tradition' and images of social memory. Nations and states have historically been each other's projects, and this most recent attempt at regulating 'cultural diversity' demonstrates the contradictions in the attempts of neoliberal states to impose a monopoly over the legitimate use of violence (symbolic or otherwise). How nations and cultures (as ideologies) are produced and reinforced, who are identified as enemies, and what classed, racialised and gendered groups are visible in or absent from this new attempt at managing 'difference' and drive for social legitimacy are significant issues.

Today, neoliberal states in Europe are pushing for even more deregulation of corporations and are attacking welfare systems and public services under the banner of 'downsizing the state' whilst at the same time invoking the idea of a great nation with a glorious past. Under neoliberalism, many of the state's responsibilities have been removed and privatised. Indeed, as Wendy Brown (2005) has argued, in contrast to classic market liberalism, neoliberalism starts from the state itself. But, in the process, the state "rather than being provider and guarantor of public welfare, becomes 'a parasite' on the population, concerned only for its own survival, demanding more and more and giving less and less in exchange" (Bauman and Bordoni 2014: 17–18). It is important to remember that the period between the end of the Second World War and the ascendancy of neoliberal states was marked by two significant factors: a period of economic growth and prosperity that enabled and maintained welfare systems, and also a period in which the world witnessed the rise of anti-colonial, anti-imperialist struggle and liberation movements across the world. Internationally, many of the movements for liberation and independence either became co-opted into the structures of capital and/or were defeated.

By the 1980s, a shift to the right in European and North American politics deepened the attacks on the welfare aspects of the state. How do states deal ideologically with their attempts to eradicate those social institutions upon which they have based their legitimacy? David Harvey argues that in such climates neoliberal states face a major dilemma. They must simultaneously take a back seat and "simply set the stage for market functions" and they must also act as a collective corporation in order to promote their competitive edge. For Harvey, "nationalism is an obvious answer" to the problem of ensuring citizen loyalty (2005: 79). Similarly, Liz Fekete suggests that "neoliberalism and the promise of abundant riches and freedom no longer provide a plausible script ... Hence the comfort of the sticking-plaster of nationalism and the narrative of anti-multiculturalism and anti-immigration" (2017: 5). Paradoxically, and perhaps not surprisingly, the perceived threat of immigration is used, on the one hand, to introduce measures and policies (structural adjustments) that have until now been imposed predominantly on developing countries (Swenson 2015), and, on the other, to impose colonial-style emergency laws (Fekete 2017).

In a country such as France in which minority ethnic communities have never been treated as equal citizens, the history of colonialism still weighs like a nightmare. Was it a mere coincidence that one of the attackers of *Charlie Hebdo* was a French Algerian? The current crisis is not just an economic crisis in exactly the same way that neoliberalism is not just an economic project. This crisis is also a crisis of the state and nationalism. Far from challenging neoliberalism, it is a path through which the final transformation of a 'social state' to a fully fledged neoliberal market state is taking place. Nationalism, "far from representing a break with neo-liberalism, provides the climate that allows for its break from democracy" (Fekete 2017: 18).

One significant outcome of this transformation has not only been a form of statism without the state, at least in terms of welfare, but also an increased emphasis on the main historical function of the state: that is, disciplining its subjects. The incorporation of social democracy into a neoliberal project has paved the way for a more authoritarian rule. Such a shift, as Jessop has argued, "could be explained in terms of the logic of capital (requiring more state intervention) and/or the logic of class struggle (requiring more state repression and legitimation measures)" (2007: 238). More repressive measures are needed in order for the state to maintain and control an impoverished and weak citizenship. It is exactly this reconfiguration of state power that should be the focus of attention, including the basis on which these newly reconfigured states claim legitimacy.

III

The unity of the state under a nationalist or nativist flag will not be complete without 'national unity'. Indeed, the survival of the state depends on homogeneity from within. We know that nations are imagined communities (Anderson 2006) and yet historically the state has been crucial in offering ways of imagining nations. Communities, imagined or otherwise, are necessarily bound up with borders and states, and, despite a significant discursive erasure of place in much of the literature on globalisation (Dirlik 2001), borders are proliferating and there are more demands for sovereignty and recognition. Equally problematic is the thesis which claims that the power of the state has declined with the formation of 'Empire'. Hardt and Negri's prophecy that capital, in its latest incarnation, has neither a centre nor a periphery, neither home nor an abroad exist (2001: 239), merely echoes a variant on the theory of globalisation.

There have been changes in the priority of the state, including surrendering some of its economic functions to the private sector (such as making its central banks 'independent'), restricting the role of the parliament and representative institutions, and the undeniable growth of state authoritarianism. However, rather than representing the decline of state power, this reflects a shift in the balance of power and the fact that states are declaring war against their own citizens and democracy. This expansion of the repressive dimension of the state has happened in tandem with an amputation of its welfare functions.

The rapid expansion of the repressive apparatus, and the upgrading of colonial measures and policies with digital and biometric technology, are justified by the imperatives of the fight against terrorism. The various pieces of anti-terrorism legislation and 'Patriot Acts' implemented in the name of providing 'security' for domestic society (Khiabany and Williamson 2012), pigeonholing citizens into the binary of patriots and terrorist sympathisers, the limitation on civil and democratic rights, and the subordination of everything and everyone to the perceived ideals of the 'free world', 'the Republic' or 'Western civilisation' are all part of a process which Frances Webber (2016) has aptly called 'the inversion of accountability'. The state has not only imposed monitoring obligations on education, welfare and health professionals, but has also promoted the act of citizens spying and informing on each other as the very definition of good citizenship and patriotism. Having designated a number of regimes (including many in the Middle East) as 'rogue states' which threaten the very fabric of the progressive, tolerant and free world, imperial states themselves have 'gone rogue' and actively become failed states in relation to the welfare of their own population.

The formation of nations is a colonial process; those that do not fit in the 'imagination' and those that are not part of a defined homogeneous population are marginalised, suppressed and excluded. All states are keen to determine ways – perhaps a singular way – of imagining a community. The name of the nation is also the name of the state, and questions of who belongs, who is excluded, what are the boundaries and what are accepted cultures, customs and languages are all determined by the state. This does not mean that a nation cannot exist without a state as such. That the Kurds, Basques and Palestinians, for example, can mount such a struggle to be recognised and to have their own state is clear evidence of the significance of the state. However, only a narrow nationalist concept can imagine the imagined community as an abstract entity that is beyond and above the state.

> If the nation is the name, the state is the body that bears it; if the nation is the end, the state is the means of achieving it. A nation without a state would appear to be a name without a bearer, without anyone worthy of bearing it with the requisite glory and splendour, and so it remains a damaged name, which may well dissipate, becomes assimilated among the languages or scattered among the peoples of the world. (Ophir 2010: 90)

The state not only actively reconstructs the past but also imagines the present and attempts to set the scene for the future. Jessop insists that nation and state are distinct concepts and that conflation of the two in the ambiguous concept of the nation-state is confusing. As far as the question of nationhood is concerned, it is important to remember that national imaginaries have always involved "more than the question of nationality" and that they are shaped by other types of ideal and material interests, including class, gender and race (Jessop 2016: 156). For Bourdieu (1999), the state is a concentration of different forms of capital, including physical force as well as economic, informational and symbolic capital. The concentration of a symbolic capital of recognition, or legitimacy, goes hand in hand with the concentration of armed forces and financial resources. He suggests that, parallel with a unified army and unified taxation, there has to be a unified 'culture'.

It is in this process of promoting a 'particular' culture and language to the status of 'universal' that all others fall into particularity. As such, any serious discussion of 'national' culture needs to avoid ahistorical analyses of certain 'characters' and realise the importance of the state in constructing that sense of a 'national character'. It is usually the case that when the advocates of 'authentic culture' refer to the notion of collective identity, they fail to address exactly whose identity is being defined and by whom. It is precisely this imposing of 'norm' (the so called 'universal') on a whole population that "enables the state to separate certain groups from collectivity" (Badiou 2012: 92). According to Badiou, those who do not resemble the fictive identitarian object can range from Muslim to Islamist, immigrant to Roma, or simply youths from the *banlieues* – 'identity politics' par excellence!

IV

The state has been central to paving the way for the emergence and articulation of racism. The history of racism is also the history of state policy on race relations (Sivanandan 2008; Kundnani, this volume). Lentin and Lentin also argue that racism and state are interdependent and that racism in its historical formation and in the present "is inextricably linked both to the policy instituted by states and to the political climate engendered by governmental leaders playing the proverbial 'race card'" (2006: 2). For them, racism, rather than being a pathological problem or an aberration of the politics of democracies, is in fact inseparable from the modern project. The reified notion of national cultures is the product of modernity, which, from the beginning, has produced and sustained, under the banner of 'universalism', different variations and forms of parochialism.

Indeed, modernity has always been described using the language of progress, creativity, freedom and emancipation. Hollande and others, in the aftermath of the attacks, merely fell back on this myth. Such formulations always ignore what Walter Mignolo has described as "the darker side of Western modernity" (2011), which has been and continues to be responsible for the historical devastation wrought by exploitation, insecurity, intolerance and genocide. When examining racism, an historical approach to modernity is crucial for interrogating not only the hegemonic assumptions of Euromodernity but also new forms of cultural reification and competing nativisms.

Racism (of various kinds) is not just a product of economic crisis nor does it arise simply as a response to immigration, although these are used to justify it. Rather, it is linked to the very core of European modernity and the colonial project. In fact, the very 'modernity' that is constantly lined up against the 'uncivilised' was also about contempt towards the 'Other'. This 'Other', of course, was not always racialised as understood in the contemporary sense, and neither did contempt against the 'Other' begin with colonisation. Indeed, as Balibar has suggested, the contempt and discrimination against 'labouring classes' was (and is) similar with those of categories of blacks. He demonstrates this by showing that the white/native working class can also be victims of racism – *class racism*. It was much later that the "notion of race was 'ethicized', so that it could be integrated into the nationalist complex, the jumping off point for its successive subsequent metamorphoses. Thus it is clear that, from the vey outset, racist representations of history stand in relation to the class struggle" (Balibar 1991: 207–8).

Balibar is right to insist that the narrative of the modem nation-state and modernity cannot be separated from capitalism and the organisation of labour. Anna Curcio similarly argues that, under capitalism, racism and class domination have always been intertwined: "to talk distinctly about race means both calling up a whole system of historically constructed inequalities and highlighting the *material* and *structural* nature of racism – that is to say, its strong connection to the relations of production and their transformation" (Curcio 2014). In her examination of state formation in Italy, she shows that Italian racism (and indeed European racism) was developed along two paths.

On the one hand, within Europe, Italy, Spain, Greece and Portugal, for example, were racialised; considered as primitive and explained in precisely those terms of exoticness and backwardness that were later used to describe the colonies. The recent coverage of economic crisis in Spain, Portugal and in particular Greece leaves no doubt that southern Europe has remained the 'Other' within Europe (Bickes et al. 2014). In portraying Greeks in particular as lazy, corrupt and incapable of governing themselves, the political and media elites pushed the debate away from structural concerns towards a 'culturalisation' of crisis that generated hostile and racist sentiments against the Greek population. What this crisis shows again is that the so-called Western civilisation and culture is itself torn between the hollow universalism and the narrow particularism of the 'culture' of capital. The 'unity' of the West crumbles under the disastrous weight of 'market competition'.

If southern Europe was the racialised 'Other', southern Italians became the racialised, inferior and 'negroid' to the 'Aryan and Caucasian' in the north. From the outset, the modern nation-state in Italy was founded on the idea of 'Two Italies'. Curcio argues:

> As a result, the existence of 'Two Italies,' each one inhabited by a different racial group, signified the existence of two different moral and socio-political inclinations, where the 'Negroid' ancestry of southern Italians becomes the evidence of their inferiority and criminal behaviour, as well as the justification for brutal repression of social uprisings in the South. (Curcio 2014)

The particular case of France gives us more insight. The very idea of modernity is explicitly linked with the 'bourgeois revolutions' in general and the French Revolution in particular. The French Revolution, by highlighting the issue of political rights for the masses, generated a significant problem for the idea of 'natural' differences between individuals. Yet the equality of birth was and is contradicted by the structural inequality that has continued to naturalise social divisions and antagonism in capitalist modernity. There are two important issues that are worth highlighting. First, the much celebrated 1789 Declaration of the Rights of Man and of the Citizen, a foundational Enlightenment document, did indeed define the individual and collective rights of all the estates of the realm as universal. These 'rights' were qualified as 'natural, unalienable and sacred', and the first article proudly announced that "Men are born and remain free and equal in rights. Social distinctions may be founded only upon the general good." Yet the declaration neither revoked slavery nor recognised the equal rights of women. Why were the calls and petitions for recognising equal rights not applied to all people? Was this a simple accident or an omission? How compatible is the universalism of liberal ideology with the system of hierarchies that is preserved and maintained in contemporary capitalist societies? How do we understand these significant exclusive clauses in such a highly regarded and era-defining historical document?

Another significant exclusive clause can be seen in article 11 of the same document: "The free communication of thoughts and of opinions is one of the most precious rights of man: any citizen thus may speak, write, print freely, *except* to respond to the abuse of this liberty, in the cases determined by the law." That *except* has proved a major problem, for, throughout this document, the right appears as a bundle. This bundle and its 'universal' gloss have historically been used to camouflage the particularism of liberal ideology and to take away the very political liberty against the state. The law and the very definition of that little 'except' are determined not in a vacuum but by the state. Witness the French government clampdown on the internet in the aftermath of *Charlie Hebdo*'s tragedy.

Such exclusive clauses in the 'universal' rights of man were also hideously and brutally applied and safeguarded inside and outside France (and other imperial powers). The abstractions of individuals and nations have been the key to a distinctly French concept of universalism. The unified totality of the nation is, of course, fictitious, and it is precisely this fictitious entity that has been regarded as the defining feature of French universalism. To be admitted to this universal entity, various groups had to relinquish their own individual and collective identity for the abstract common goal of the Republic (Scott 2004: 35).

The state refusal to expand the constituencies and scope of democratic rights is a well-known fact. Indeed, the assumption of the 'equality of men' as a central tenet of the French Revolution has coexisted with structural inequality and the brutal exclusion of significantly large sections of the population (the working class and women in particular), as well as with slavery and colonialism, and thus represents the basic contradiction of capitalist modernity. The 'ideal of justice and peace' that Hollande claims France has promoted on the international stage is airbrushed of such colonial atrocities as those in Indochina (1930–33), the massacre in Madagascar (1947–48), and the brutal suppression of the Algerian struggle for liberation:

> Estimates of those the French killed include a million Vietnamese and a million Algerians. As for Madagascar, estimates have it that upwards of 100,000 people were killed by the French. These are just a few examples of French colonial barbarities in some colonies and not an exhaustive list by any means. French colonialism, under the grandiose heading of a *mission civilisatrice*, has clearly failed to civilize, most of all, the French themselves. The *mission*, it would seem, remains unaccomplished! (Massad 2015)

The ravages of colonialism did, of course, rebound within European borders – the celebration of Western economic, cultural and moral superiority simply cannot acknowledge that Nazi Germany represents an essential part of the 'West'. "Genocide is the absolute integration," remarked Adorno. For him, in some ways Auschwitz was the outcome of an 'identitarian' logic that violently supresses the non-identical: "It is on its way wherever men are levelled off – 'polished off,' as the German military called it – until one exterminates them literally, as deviations from the concept of their total nullity. Auschwitz confirmed the philosopheme of pure identity as death" (Adorno 1973: 362). In connecting the colonial dots of Western civilisation, Domenico Losurdo (2015: 242) rightly suggests that Hitler's attempt to enslave the Slav and to exterminate Jews should be seen as part of a cycle of Western colonialism that began with the genocide of Native Americans and continued with the horror of slavery. Racism is not modernity's 'Other', or external to it.

V

In thinking about history at this time, it is impossible not to recall Walter Benjamin's assertion that "there is no document of civilisation which is not at the same time a document of barbarism". If state racism is a product of modernity, then there can be no innocent invoking of an imagined past and an imagined 'culture' that does not serve to feed reactionary nostalgia and hatred.

The "Cross faced down the Crescent, the West had come to the Orient never to leave", Said wrote in *Orientalism* (1994: 91). The European states in general and France in particular are now busy trying to face down a very small slice of the Crescent that took on the invitation to come and rebuild the Cross. At the time in which the sovereignty and the borders of many countries in the Middle East and North Africa are being questioned and undermined in the name of the 'war on terror', the issue of assimilation and integration, as Lentin and Titley argue, has become "a border practice beyond and inside the territorial border" (2011: 204). It is precisely this obsession with 'integrating' European Muslims into 'national culture' and 'our way of life' which is used simultaneously to combat multiculturalism and demand and secure loyalty from the wider population.

Ironically, this move to make citizens into grateful dependants of the security state happens at a time in which citizens are also chided moralistically for being too dependent on the state for jobs, housing, health and education. It is within this context that, by focusing on 'culture', the alien is transformed into an enemy. It is for that reason that Balibar suggests that the "reduction of the figure of the stranger to that of the enemy is perhaps one of the clearest signs of the crisis of the nation-state" (2010). Yet the concerted attack on civil liberties and measures introduced by European security states has effectively meant that states have begun to suspend democracy with the excuse of saving it. The focus on 'culture' and the attempts by some European states to resolve 'the Muslim question' has been part of an effort to justify an increasingly authoritarian state by substituting cultural difference for the class divisions and antagonisms that underlie the current crisis.

References

Adorno, T. (1973) *Negative Dialectics*. Translated by E. B. Ashton. New York: Continuum.

Anderson, B. (2006) *Imagined Communities: Reflections on the Origin and Spread of Nationalism*. London: Verso.

Badiou, A. (2006) *Polemics*. London: Verso.

Badiou, A. (2012) *The Rebirth of History: Times of Riots and Uprising*. London: Verso.

Balibar, E. (1991) 'Class Racism' in E. Balibar and I. Wallerstein, *Race, Nation, Class: Ambigous Identities*. London: Verso.

Balibar, E. (2010) 'At the Borders of Citizenship: A Democracy in Translation?', *European Journal of Social Theory* 13 (3): 315–22.

Bauman, Z. and C. Bordoni (2014) *State of Crisis*. Cambridge: Polity.

Bickes, H., T. Otten and L. C. Weymann (2014) 'The Financial Crisis in the German and English Press: Metaphorical Structures in the Media Coverage on Greece, Spain and Italy', *Discourse & Society* 25 (4): 424–45.

Bourdieu, P. (1999) 'Rethinking the State: Genesis and Structure of the Bureaucratic Field' in G. Steinmetz (ed.) *State/Culture: State-formation after the Cultural Turn*. Ithaca NY and London: Cornell University Press.

Brown, W. (2005) *Edgework: Critical Essays on Knowledge and Power*. Princeton NJ: Princeton University Press.

Curcio, A. (2014) 'Paths of Racism, Flows of Labor: Nation-state Formation, Capitalism and the Metamorphosis of Racism in Italy', *Viewpoint Magazine* 4. https://viewpointmag. com/2014/10/12/paths-of-racism-flows-of-labor-nation-state-formation-capitalism-and-the-metamorphosis-of-racism-in-italy.

Dirlik, A. (2001) 'Place-based Imagination: Globalism and the Politics of Place' in R. Prazniak and A. Dirlik (eds) *Places and Politics in the Age of Globalization*. New York: Rowman and Littlefield.

Fekete, L. (2017) 'Flying the Flag for Neoliberalism', *Race & Class* 58 (3): 3–22.

Fukuyama, F. (2006) 'Neoconservatism Has Evolved into Something I Can No Longer Support'. www. informationclearinghouse.info/article12024.htm.

Hardt, M. and A. Negri (2001) 'Adventures of the Multitude: Response of the Authors', *Rethinking Marxism* 13 (3–4): 236–43.

Harvey, D. (2005) *A Brief History of Neoliberalism*. Oxford: Oxford University Press.

Hollande, F. (2015) 'Attack against Charlie Hebdo Statement by Mr. François Hollande, President of the Republic', 7 January. www.diplomatie.gouv. fr/en/the-ministry-of-foreign-affairs/ events/article/attack-against-charlie-hebdo.

Huntington, S. (2004) *Who Are We?: The Challenges to America's National Identity*. New York: Simon & Schuster.

Jessop, B. (2007) 'Statism', *Historical Materialism* 15 (2): 233–42.

Jessop, B. (2016) *The State: Past, Present, Future*. Cambridge: Polity.

Khiabany, G. and M. Williamson (2012) 'Terror, Culture and Anti-Muslim Racism' in D. Freedman and D. Thussu (eds) *Media and Terrorism: Global Perspectives*. London: Sage.

Lentin, A. and R. Lentin (2006) *Race and State*. Newcastle: Cambridge Scholars Press.

Lentin, A. and G. Titley (2011) *The Crises of Multiculturalism: Racism in a Neoliberal Age*. London: Zed Books.

Lichfield, J. (2015) 'French Prime Minister Announces 736m Euros to Combat Terrorism in Wake of Charlie Hebdo Attacks', *Independent*, 21 January. www.independent.co.uk/news/ world/europe/french-prime-minister-announces-736m-euros-to-combat-terrorism-in-wake-of-charlie-hebdo-attacks-9992520.html.

Losurdo, D. (2015) *War and Revolution: Rethinking the Twentieth Century*. London: Verso.

Massad, J. (2015) 'Assimilating French Muslims', *Electronic Intifada*, 22 January. https://electronicintifada. net/content/assimilating-french-muslims/14205.

Mignolo, W. (2011) *The Darker Side of Western Modernity: Global Futures, Decolonial Options (Latin America Otherwise)*. Durham NC: Duke University Press.

Ophir, A. (2010) 'State', *Mafte'akh* 1: 67–96.

Pollitt, K. (2006) 'The Trouble with Bush's "Islamofascism"', *Alternet*, 25 August. www.alternet.org/story/40850/the_ trouble_with_bush's_'islamofascism'.

Said, E. (1994) *Orientalism*. New York: Vintage Books.

Scott, J. W. (2004) 'French Universalism in the Nineties', *differences: A Journal of Feminist Cultural Studies* 15 (2): 32–53.

Sivanandan, A. (2008) *Catching History on the Wing: Race, Culture and Globalisation*. London: Pluto.

Swenson, H. (2015) 'Anti-Immigration as Austerity Policy: The Rejection of Maternalist Governance in Arizona's SB 1070 Immigration Law', *Feminist Formation* 27 (2): 98–120.

Webber, F. (2016) 'The Inversion of Accountability', *Race & Class* 58 (2): 55–63.

Wright, L. (2014) *Thirteen Days in September: Carter, Begin, and Sadat at Camp David*. New York: Alfred A. Knopf.

7 | SYMBOLIC POLITICS WITH BRUTALLY REAL EFFECTS: WHEN 'NOBODIES' MAKE HISTORY

Markha Valenta

It took an attack of terrifying determination, the brutal death of twenty people, to understand the materiality and political dimension of the defiled sacred. Not the sacred of the dominant – the flag, the national anthem (highly protected and only subject to one-way criticism within particular power relations) – but the sacred of the 'wretched of the earth' ... When, first, we are killed socially ('you're the scum who deserve the power hose'), and then we are finished symbolically (e.g., the caricatures of the Prophet), believe me, you have to fear the worst. Yes, I was scared. (Bouteldja 2015)

When I was conducting workshops at a high school in a city in northern France, the teachers asked me to avoid too delicate themes: the notion of the future for example. 'Here,' they said, 'we are trying to manage the present. The future is anxiety for these young people.' (Marc Cheb Sun)[1]

The vast rush of emotion and meaning-making in response to the attacks on *Charlie Hebdo* even now constitute a dense, enveloping field when writing about it. Wave upon wave of charged affect. Some vast, tsunami-like, cresting master-narrative of dramatic assertions, fears, and fury: that this entailed an attack on Our Free Speech, on Our Democracy, on Our Freedom, on Our Way of Life. The widespread conviction that not only fury and disgust with the attackers but also, flowing from this, identification with the victims, with 'Charlie', could be the only natural, moral, decent response. All this left precious little room for the smaller seething waves: those who disagreed publicly, did not performatively identify, did not feel endangered. As if to disagree, to not identify, was to desecrate the dead. And to desecrate the living who perceived the precarity of their lives, their country and civilisation played out in the violent execution of *Charlie Hebdo*'s journalists.

And yet a minority did disagree, vociferously. Unleashing a fierce debate on whether or not, on how and how not, *Charlie Hebdo* is racist, Islamophobic, Orientalist, sexist, or simply the dated, puerile, atrophying product of a gaggle of (mostly) white men who in the 1960s may once have been creative in challenging much that was taboo but today have become irrelevant predictable bores, or worse – deluded hypocrites who mistakenly imagine it takes courage to attack the sacred of the 'wretched of the earth'.

For the French state, as for all our states and political representatives in the West, there were no such questions, no such debates in the days and weeks after the attack. The political estate identified itself and 'us' with those killed, in a fashion at once fervent, simplistic and blind to its own role. And translated this identification into action equally fervent, simplistic and blind. Prime Minister Valls declared war 'against Jihadism, against radical Islam' (Bilefsky and De La Baume 2015). President Hollande gave body to the claim by mobilising 10,000 troops to patrol the streets, and another 5,000 police to patrol Jewish communities and synagogues (Silva 2015), as well as some mosques, with the Defence Minister noting that "this is the first time that our troops have been mobilized to such an extent on our own soil" (Marsden 2015). The police were given further powers to carry out searches and place citizens under house arrest; electronic surveillance was expanded; as were anti-terror operations in schools. Plans to curb the defence budget were reversed and instead it was increased by nearly €4 billion. Seeing the executions at *Charlie* literally as a reflection of comprehensive mortal danger facing it as a whole, French society was militarised at the cost of billions of euros. This is a crucial dimension of '*Charlie Hebdo*' as event: the chain of violence, of action and reaction in which that day's violence is embedded as one link among many (see Sreberny, this volume).

Some months later, emergency armed street patrols were made permanent. A new bill was approved by a parliamentary vote of 438 to 86 allowing intelligence agencies to tap phones and emails without seeking permission from a judge, to place cameras in homes, install keylogger devices on computers and vacuum up metadata, even as €425 million was earmarked to recruit thousands of extra police, spies and investigators (Chrisafis 2015). In effect legalising what French spies already were doing illegally, the new digital mass surveillance produces more data than French security organs and their staff – operating at one-hundredth the budget of the US intelligence community, whose approach they are reproducing – can process (Groll 2015). In effect, the expansion entails a shift from targeted to mass surveillance; from comprehensive oversight of the domestic security apparatus to drastic deregulation, limited attention to human rights and decreased transparency; and from rationalised security targets to mapping and tracking a much more fluid, undefined field of activities that might potentially threaten 'public order' and French 'Republican institutions' in political, economic, scientific and foreign policy domains (ibid.).

The drastic expansion of the security state, however, failed to prevent a further, much more deadly attack by a French-Belgian-Moroccan network of Syria fighters in November 2015 at the Bataclan theatre and the Stade de France, killing 130. Hollande then declared a state of emergency, banned public demonstrations, announced that France will "lead a war which will be pitiless" (Doherty 2015), and dropped some twenty bombs on Daesh in Raqqa, Syria (Walt 2015; Doherty 2015). This intensified repression fared little better, and there was a further attack in Nice in July 2016, killing eighty-four. Carried out by a divorced, abusive Tunisian living in France, with a history of drugs and mental instability, the response to this attack by Hollande was more of the same, extending the state of emergency and intensifying bombing in Iraq and Syria.

This is the longest state of emergency France has experienced since the Algerian war. By August 2016, nearly 3,600 raids and 400 house arrests, all without warrants, had taken place. Pre-trial detention for the most serious (suspected) offences was extended from two to three years, including for minors older than fifteen years. The impact of the raids, often carried out in a ruthless fashion in the middle of the night, also on families with small children, and of warrantless house arrests extending at times to a year, has been highly disproportional. Overwhelmingly targeting Muslims and those of North African descent, they leave in their wake a string of lives disrupted through lost jobs, bodies randomly battered by unrestrained police, traumatised children, businesses and homes brutally entered and damaged, humiliating public body searches and an intensified blanket of discrimination. A raft of human rights violations have been documented by Human Rights Watch, Amnesty International and Défenseur des Droits, creating and expanding a deep distrust of the French state and police.

The net result of all this denigrating, multi-million-euro force unleashed on France's (Muslim/North African) minorities by August

2016 was a mere *six* terrorism-related criminal investigations, only *one* of which had led to prosecution, and negligible improvements in national security. Most home raids have been unrelated to terrorism and instead are being carried out by narcotics units. It is unclear if the house arrests are any more closely related to anti-terrorism actions: in the days leading up to the Paris Climate Conference, for example, the new measures were instead used to detain twenty-four environmental activists (Kassem 2016; Fédération internationale des ligues des droits de l'Homme 2016). While massive and egregiously expensive, the state of emergency's pre-eminent motive appears to be to performatively visualise the state acting as if it is securing the nation. Prime Minister Manuel Valls rather deceptively has asserted that "every day intelligence services, police, foil attacks, dismantle networks" (BBC 2016).

The lived effects of these actions are the psychic, social, economic and physical brutalisation of more vulnerable citizens in the interests of legitimising politicians in the eyes of those citizens who 'count', while expanding the state's powers to police at will. Even as 'security' is used to legitimate such state violence and invasion (recalling here that the bill expanding the state's surveillance apparatus was set in motion more than a year *before Charlie Hebdo* and then was fast-tracked), its net effect is to perform the state's dominance over minorities in conjunction with a hyped international war on Daesh.

In other words, the French state's security operations – in combining vast reach, devaluation and 'lawless' invasion of minority lives, and few comprehensive security results – entail a symbolic politics with brutally real effects. This is a logic complementary to the one that drove the Bush administration's invasion of Iraq, alongside its criminalisation and invasive surveillance of US domestic Muslim populations. It is the state's dance of (in)security, in which minorities are roughly criminalised and structurally alienated, even as society at large is kept in a sensitive, reactive state of fear and crisis, in a fashion that both narrows and shores up the state's mandate to control and tightly bind the social collective to itself in an age of otherwise dispersive, mobile, multitudinous globalism.

Ostensibly, the state is here carrying out its classic function of securing the lives of its citizens from internal threats and external enemies. Yet the external enemy is not a (neighbouring) state, but an emergent, multinational 'caliphate' (Daesh) and a multi-sited global jihadist franchise (Al Qaeda) – hybrid, innovative formations at the intersection of politics, corporate marketing, multinationalism, social media, petrodollars, and religion – engaged in an international war for power primarily, but not exclusively, in the Middle East. Likewise, the domestic threat is neither a classic social movement, a political party, an organisation, a particular ethnic group, a network or even a religion, but instead unevenly dispersed little pockets of self-activated, entrepreneurial cells and individuals, some with experience in Syria or elsewhere in the Middle East, but others very local small-time criminals, playboys, dealers and part-time workers. Most have extremely limited knowledge of Islam as a religion, tradition, jurisprudence and form of sociability and declare an allegiance to one of Daesh's or Al Qaeda's international branches only a mere few weeks, days or hours before committing violence in their name. That is to say, if we take the French state to be performing a largely symbolic politics of security with real repressive effects, many of those entering the public domain as terrorists are similarly performing a largely symbolic politics of 'Islamic' identity with real violent effects.

While the French state targets especially those of Muslim descent, conviction or affiliation, it has no effective means of measuring the content, extent or lack of religiosity among those it targets. Those targeted by the state, then, range from atheist to reformist to conservative to separatist to violent and it is, in effect, the state's brutalisation, invasion and humiliation of them which make them 'Muslim'. To be interpellated by the state as 'Muslim' makes one subject to the treatment meted out to 'Muslims', locking into place these citizens' public-political subjectivity regardless of the subject's own identification. The fact that the majority of those who have committed jihadist violence were born and raised in the West, including converts, constitutes a polymorphous muddle of postcolonial reality the state neither can accept nor engage.

In particular, there is intense resistance to the fact that these are 'French' and 'Western' men and women enacting violent attacks. This is perhaps the ultimate brutality, in the context of modern democracy whose foundation is the state's obligation to 'represent' the citizen and be answerable to that citizen. Here, instead, the state apparatus makes a symbolic, political 'representation of' the citizen as 'Muslim' that minoritizes him, negates his Western culture, identity and citizenship, and effectively deprives him of his public and political subjectivity as a full French citizen – all in the interests of shoring up the subjectivity of the state as the guarantor of security. Those designated 'Muslim' are in effect sacrificed to the imperative pressing down on the state to be seen to be 'doing something'. On all this, however, the world has been largely silent. In stark contrast to the sea of debates on the identity politics of *Charlie Hebdo* and on the meaning and significance of the extremist Islamist attack carried out against its journalists – as this drew in masses of commentators from across the world – there has been little visible, heated international debate on the dramatic militarisation, securitisation and repressive response of the French state.

This is particularly striking in two regards. Firstly, there is the fact that the structural violation of civil rights, liberties and national fraternity which the expansion and militarisation of the French state entails goes much farther and deeper than did the extremist Islamist attacks to which they are said to respond. And secondly, there is the fact that the disruptions of French Muslims' and minorities' lived daily lives are much more brutal, destructive and comprehensive than the impact of anything anti-Islamic that *Charlie Hebdo* itself published. In other words, the French state is institutionalising the violation of French democratic freedoms, civil rights and the rule of law in a consistent, intensified fashion, whereas the attacks of the Kouachi brothers only did so in a highly episodic, momentary fashion; even as this institutionalised securitisation by the French state is much more grossly detrimental to Muslim lives, having the full power of the state behind it, than *Charlie Hebdo* ever managed to achieve.

This means that the foremost danger to citizen liberties, rights and ways of life, on the one hand, and to Muslim minorities, on the other, resides in one and the same entity: the (securitising) state. Indeed, what we are seeing is the assertion of crude state power at the expense of that democratic rule of law which is regularly presented as constituting the core of Western culture, values and identity; *and* at the expense of the Muslim minorities said to pose the most significant threat to this Western culture, values and identity. In other words: the better to fight what is presented as the violent Islamist threat to national culture and values, the state sacrifices precisely that culture and values. At that moment, the state reveals that it represents not the people, not Western values, not a culture of Republican *laïcité*, freedom and democracy but, first and foremost, itself. And one other thing: Western hegemony over the (former) colonial. In this regard, developments in France parallel those throughout the West.

To put this in another way: given the choice between preserving Republican democracy, pluralism and the rule of law *or* reinforcing control of and dominance over the postcolonial minority, citizens of democracies are increasingly tempted by the latter – our surging anti-Islam populist movements are successfully instigating a growing, though not yet consolidated, preference for cultural-economic hegemony over an (im)migrant underclass rather than democratic, constitutional equality.

Racism and xenophobia, as such, continue to be embedded in the deepest bowels of the nation-state, persisting in primordial, biological, racialised understandings of the 'nation' that are both profound and subtle, repressed and aggressive. This inclination towards preserving racialised (cultural-economic) hegemony at the expense of (constitutional) democracy is, however, neither inevitable nor particularly 'natural'. It takes tremendous labour, the investment of funds, affect and organisation to persist, also in the face of significant multicultural, anti-racist, pluralist activism since the 1960s. The return of an influentially vicious, denigrating nationalism in the West's public domain today attests to the persistence of race and biological politics as a politics of social Darwinism. Correspondingly, that return is produced by politicians, pundits and intellectuals who effectively are framing the choice facing our nation-states as one of existential survival.

And, indeed, they are right in terms of the existential challenge: what is at stake is the continued persistence (or, alternatively, the dismantling and reconfiguration) of the fundamentally inegalitarian, undemocratic framework for ordering the world's relations of peoples that has undergirded our societies for the past 150 years. Migration of the world's peoples to the West since the 1960s has meant that those inegalitarian, undemocratic dynamics of global relations are becoming a crucial element of our *domestic* social and political relations. In the process, precisely that which was once a solid, steady line on the ground or on our maps – both national borders and the West–East divide – becomes mobile, moving down into the nooks and crannies of our cities and out into the world. Rather than clear borders between national spaces, our countries now are tapestries of overlapping borderlands, with the borders themselves hop-skipping this way and that, following shifts in migrant streams, border checks, political controversies and financial crises (Balibar 1998; Balibar 2009; van Houtum and van Naerssen 2002).

And it is this that is *Charlie Hebdo*: an eruption of the wounded borderland in the offices of an old (white) Europe indifferent to the violence it does. "The ... border," writes Gloria Anzaldúa, "*es una herida abierta* where the Third World grates against the first and bleeds. And before a scab forms it hemorrhages again, the lifeblood of two worlds merging to form a third" (Anzaldúa 2007: 25). The significance of *Charlie Hebdo* as event – and this includes the attacks by Frenchmen of Algerian descent affiliating themselves with Al Qaeda in Yemen; the highly mediatised debates about the attacks' meaning and significance; the French state's response; and international mobilisations for and against *Charlie Hebdo* (in Niger, Pakistan and Mali) – lies in the way it enacts and channels this fundamental question: what is to be our future? This is, of course, always-already the question of modernity. So, the argument developing below is that what is new here, what is remarkable here, is the way in which socio-cultural, economic 'nobodies' from Western Europe's margins – margins that are at one and the same moment domestic *and* global – in claiming the right to 'avenge the Prophet' and exact judgement and justice in Europe's very heartland, are making history. It is the moment, if you will, of colonialism's inversion ... as ugly, inhumane and brutal in that brief moment as colonialism itself was for centuries on end.

Under colonial modernity, as we have inherited its logic in the system of global relations that give shape to our world today, it has been the West's privilege to draw, redraw and remake the world, to asymmetrically penetrate the other at will, without being penetrated in turn. This logic, deeply embedded in global structures and Western identities, narratives and fantasies, is now under pressure *within the West* from new migration streams and new global, mediatised identities. It is this which is distinctive of the contemporary moment relative to earlier anti-colonial moments of the 1960s and 1970s: that within the West, postcolonial/post-migration generations have come of age that are now fully *of the West* by birth, even as this beautiful mongrel *métissage* leaves them open to mix and match their favoured lines of filiation as these run deep into Europe's soil *and* stretch across the world.

The rise of populist, xenophobic, nationalist movements throughout the West are documents to significant resistance to such developments. Their fears are not imaginary but very real. Current events are blowing holes, puncturing, rupturing and redrawing the lineaments holding in place the global geopolitical system that took shape when the West went 'out' into the world, but the world did not come 'in' to the West. Crucially, this is to offer a framework for analysing *Charlie Hebdo* that is incommensurable with one that takes as its central starting point the 'Islamic' identity and argument of the attackers. This aspect, which has been taken as defining and central by many, is incidental rather than fundamental. To make this point fully would take another chapter. So instead I will here merely note the fact that the practice of exacting justice and sacrificing one's life in the name of a higher political ideal, whether patriotic or anarchist or anti-colonial – or, alternatively, to sow terror – is one of the most modern of inventions: the latter, political terror, an invention of the French Revolution. The fact that the executioners of *Charlie Hebdo* variously name their ideal 'the Prophet' or 'Allah' rather than 'France' or 'Freedom' or 'Democracy' is insignificant relative to the deeply modern political practice in which they are engaged in which the material, social and ideological aspects of political conflict are continually translated through each other.

This argument builds on the comprehensive set of arguments developed by William T. Cavanaugh in *The Myth of Religious Violence* (2009) that there is no essential or fundamental difference between religious and secular violence under modernity, and on that of Talal Asad in *Genealogies of Religion* (1993) and *Formations of the Secular* (2003) that the constitution of the category of 'religion' in distinction to that of 'the secular' has a modern history, political context and effect that are, among other things, both constituted through and constituting to colonialism. Under high modernity – post-1850, say – absolutist creedal political standpoints are not so much the mark of the religious, but of intensely politicised, polarised conflicts in which different sides are mobilised via arguments that their ways of life and existential futures are endangered (Whitman 2014). While the language of such mobilisation may be religious, it may also be secular. This fluidity and interchangeability emphasises that what is crucial is the existential aspect of political mobilisation, rather than the religious. It is modernity's tendency to turn politics into a matter of conflicting ideologies and ways of life – its ideational and existential inclinations – that makes religion so useful, rather than the other way around. *Charlie Hebdo* is one further, contemporary, globalised, postcolonial, Islamic example of this, but nothing more, as far as religion and politics are concerned. (See Olivier Roy's *Jihad and Death* (2017) for the complementary argument that jihadism entails not so much the radicalisation of Islam but the Islamisation of radicalism.)

Which is not to say that it is irrelevant that those who killed at *Charlie Hebdo* did so in the name of Islam. Of course, this matters. But not because of what it can tell us about 'religion' or 'religion and violence' or 'Islam and political violence' (Cavanaugh 2009). Instead, it matters because 'Islam' has become a name, a sign, a gesture through which to rally, to act, to make history (Asad 1993). The story of how and why this has happened just now, at this moment, in this place and in this way is overdetermined and too complicated to tell here. Understanding 'Islam' as a name and as a discourse, however, allows us to approach the term as a conceptual and political tool, as it were, a tool that allows those who take hold of it to act in ways that will insert them into the contemporary political and media field in certain predictable ways.

The core argument of this chapter, then, is that '*Charlie Hebdo*' as event shows what happens when the global system has been enfolded within our nation-states. These have – in a completely unplanned and by many undesired fashion – in point of fact become multi-national states. Yet the overwhelmingly dominant conceit of the moment is that they might return to the condition of bounded nation-states. This structural contradiction means that Western societies are now faced with the existential choice of whether to abandon defining elements of their (globalised) democracies – notably equality and inclusive diversity – or, alternatively, to give up their fantasies of purist (national) unity.

This may sound rather overblown, so let me step back to explain more carefully what I mean: how it is that the attacks on *Charlie Hebdo* make history. In order to do this, I want to draw on three ideas. The first of these is that the structure of global relations which we have inherited from colonial modernity is one that combines five key features: 1) ever tightening relations of global interconnection and interdependence; 2) profound inequality in power, welfare and status among global societies, constituted over the course of high imperialism and continuing to fundamentally structure contemporary global relations; 3) the structural tension this produces in the West between ideals of constitutional democracy, pluralism and equality 'at home' and realpolitik power politics 'in the world', at the expense of the labour, lives and bodies of the world's poor, vulnerable, and unlucky; 4) such that the West structurally violates its core ideals and values when going to work in the world, even as it seeks to prevent the majority of the world's peoples living under conditions of exploitation, precarity and repression from coming to the West to escape such conditions; while 5) the tensions this produces for the West are contained through narratives, frameworks and sensibilities that obscure the extent and nature of global interdependence, naturalise global inequality, and regularly blame the world's poor for their poverty, wars and bad luck through culturalist explanations. (While this is a distillation of what is now a vast and dynamic body of scholarship on globalisation under modernity, see Buzan and Lawson's *The Global Transformation* (2015) for one of the most comprehensive and detailed arguments in alignment with the one made here.)

Correspondingly, the situation in which we find ourselves now, in which populations of 'the rest' are being unevenly incorporated into Western Europe, feels to many, under such conditions, unnatural, confronting, disruptive and dangerous. Most disruptive of all is the growing extent to which the domestic/nationalised/incorporated 'rest' are simultaneously constituting a racialised, segregated urban underclass *and* gaining access to the centres of political, cultural and symbolic power: the highest levels of government; the welfare and subsidy coffers of the state; the mechanisms of democracy; the education, jobs, institutions and lifestyles of the middle class and high elite. Correspondingly, the increasing pluralisation of the West, its increasing organisational multiculturalism, multiracialism and multinationalism, proceeds in lockstep with a simultaneously increasing xenophobic, racist, reactionary nationalism. Achille Mbembe (2009), for example, offers an evocative account of the ways in which the urban uprisings in the suburbs of Paris of October–November 2005 confronted France with the beast of race as an inheritance of colonialism's violence and the 'plurality of memory' it generated.

The second idea is that the complex of global relations might be called the world's 'geo-body'. The Thai historian Thongchai Winichakul (1994) coined this term originally to name the way in which a sense of nationhood is constituted through practices of modern mapping that visually delineate the body of the nation, clearly demarcated from other bodies/other nations by borderlines. In circumscribing the territory of the nation, borderlines visualise and mark its domain, its beginning and end as a body in space, differentiating what it is from what it is not (the other side of the border and all that contains). Even as the nation *pace* Anderson is imagined and narrated, that imagination is undergirded by both the materiality and geopolitics of bounded territory. It is this material boundedness – in conjunction with particular military organisation, (re)productions of knowledge, mapping operations, regimes of control and administrative integration – that concretely enables notions of national 'sovereignty' and 'independence', along with practices of loyalty, attachment, sacrifice and history-making, to take material shape.

While Winichakul uses the term 'geo-body' to refer to the body of the nation-state, I shift scales upward and use it to refer to our global geopolitical body as a whole: the world's geo-body as this is constituted by territorialised states arranged in space relative to each other across the globe. Not only are not all the globe's states equal, as we know all too well, but that inequality in turn means that some states have had much more say than others in giving shape to the delineation of the geo-body both as a whole and in terms of the constitution, delineation and relation of its parts (the ostensibly sovereign states constituting it). One of the sites at which this is most visible and obvious is the Middle East.

Here, the West – in its British and French guise – colluded to carve out states as it saw fit from the crumbling Ottoman empire in a fashion rife with arrogant caprice. Of course, all nation-states are the offspring of artifice, of circumstance and luck. The difference in the Middle East is that the states created in this fashion – crafted by external, colonial powers for their own benefit in a region lacking any tradition of territorially bounded nation-states – correspondingly lacked the most vital and essential ingredient of all: popular consent (Kelidar 1993). The states' spanking new borders – newly drawn lineaments in the colonial geo-body – amputated a host of communities, tribes, allegiances, memories and histories while ruthlessly thrusting together other unrelated and antagonistic ones. Lacking popular consent, however, its governments lacked legitimacy.

Woven through and across the new tapestry of Middle Eastern countries surrounding Israel was the persistence of a Muslim political ethos that was both indigenous and deeply rooted. Here, sovereignty comes not from the people (however Islamic they may be) and is not territorially delimited, but is divine and extends across the Ummah, the realm of Muslims. This older notion of political community was forced to 'cohabit', as it were – in the words of Elie Kedourie – with the new state structures that the colonial powers superimposed (Kedourie 1987 cited by Kelidar 1993). These colonial structures failed, however, to create institutional frameworks for peacefully resolving – rather than autocratically containing and manipulating – political and social conflict. "It is not surprising," remarks Abbas Kelidar,

> that the arrangement was so vehemently rejected by rulers and ruled alike ... The states of Iraq, Syria, Lebanon and Jordan had no wish to be what they have become ... Each and every communal unit of the mosaic felt alienated, as they did not want the state imposed on them in the form in which it was created ... As such, the nation-state has sown the seeds of a challenge to, rather than acceptance of, its authority. (Kelidar 1993: 319, 321, 322–3)

It is to this condition that Daesh's grandly mediatised gesture of literally cutting through the Sykes-Picot borderline owes its potency, as it cuts through history and disempowerment, turns shame to agency, displaces fracture with the aspiration to unification, replaces artificial, insufficient, incomplete sovereignty with the political ethos and community of the Ummah. Hyping its performance far and wide, Daesh reclaimed for itself not just the territory beneath its feet, but the authority and power to insert itself forcefully into a geo-body it redraws in the process.

Crucially, the attack on *Charlie Hebdo* extended this 'gesture' to the heart of Europe. A fundamental element of the (post)colonial geo-body has been that the violence of the colonial encounter and of the (post)colonial extractive global economy has been reserved, as it were, for 'there'. While 'here' has been the domain of an increasingly pluralist democracy undergirded by the welfare state, 'there' has remained – as far as the West was concerned – the domain of realpolitik, ruthless extraction, covert and overt intervention, a site at which to go to work through militarised, deadly and quite illegal 'shock and awe' as opposed to the rule of law. It was this logic that undergirded the Bush doctrine of pre-emptive intervention against *emerging* and potential threats anywhere in the world. That is to say, the Bush doctrine claimed global sovereignty to enact violence in its own interests.

Now Al Qaeda and Daesh claim this same sovereignty over the world's geo-body: the authority to judge, to sentence, to intervene and to commit violence anywhere in the world where Muslim interests (as constituted by Al Qaeda and Daesh, respectively) are actually or potentially threatened, *as this includes Europe and the US*. Herein lies the symbolic potency and political threat of 'Charlie Hebdo'. Not in an attack on an abstract 'freedom of speech' that in fact continues overwhelmingly unmolested; and not in an attack on 'democracy' and 'our way of life', as the rule of law, political organisation and secular consumer culture in the West are anything but fundamentally disrupted (excepting by the security state itself). What has been disrupted instead has been the fundamental conceit that it is the West's right and might to make history; to write the geo-body; to judge the world's people and find them lacking; to go 'there' while restricting their right to come 'here'; to be wealthy and secure while they are doomed to poverty and precarity; to make use of the world – its resources, its labour, its hearts and minds – for our own ends but not to have them make use of us. All this the universalist claims of Daesh and Al Qaeda invert, even as 'Charlie Hebdo' brings home, literally and figuratively, the fact that this is no mere fantasy but very possibly an ineradicable, real element of our present and future. (For the related argument that the object of Al Qaeda's militancy is global humanity as such, much like that of humanitarianism and contemporary politics more generally, see Faisal Devji's *The Terrorist in Search of Humanity* (2009).)

And this brings me to the third and final core aspect of making sense of Charlie Hebdo. Begoña Aretxaga, a feminist anthropologist of violence and former Basque activist, argues that we should take seriously what she calls the existential quality entailed in making history. "To miss [this], both as event and narrative, is to disown history of agency and leave the creative force of human emotion unaccounted for or reduced to structural determinism." The existential is a "predicament that gives meaning to people's lives, legitimizing their politics and charging their actions with emotional power." Within such a framework, history, then, IS "a continuous attempt to resolve existential paradoxes" (Aretxaga 1997: 36). The key aspect here is the way in which Aretxaga's argument delicately negotiates the tension between structure and agency, where violence is a central element of both.

All too often, analyses of violent jihadist actions, when they do not trace the source of such violence back to Islam, alternatively argue that the violence emerges as a response to structural conditions of poverty, exclusion and denigration and/or as a response to highly particular, individual psychological pain, trauma or imbalances. While useful and to some extent persuasive, these approaches, much like those that see violence as the expression of (totalitarian-like) religion, are very limited in their ability to conceive and engage the agency of the perpetrators. Either it is an undirected irruption of psychological instability or it is the rational – yet structurally produced – response to structural discrimination. While the first is too individual to tell us more that could be of general use, the latter is too structurally determined to tell us more about the ways in which, as individuals, we engage injustice and violence, yearning for community, and fantasies of redemption and coherence.

Yet these elements, too, are central and vital if we are to understand the deep power of a grotesquely violent jihadism 'far away' to speak to some of us 'here' by opening the door to a future we thought closed, impossible, beyond reach. Putting the future in our hands as something that is ours to make is a profoundly powerful gesture. The fact that the West would deprive its internal and external 'rest' of that is not only violently unjust in its own right but existentially untenable. 'Charlie Hebdo' – as symbolic politics with brutal effects on real lives – was one possible response. The securitised racism of the 'old' nation-states is another possibility. Neither will give us the world we want, however. So that now it is up to us: to create another possible response, equally as redemptive, as capable of engaging our world's existential violence, not through further violence but through that radicalism that "make[s] hope possible, rather than despair convincing" (Williams et al. 1988: 118).

Note

1 Personal communication, 12 December 2016. Translation from the French by author.

References

Anzaldúa, G. (2007) *Borderlands: The New Mestiza = La Frontera*. 3rd edition. San Francisco, CA: Aunt Lute Books.

Aretxaga, B. (1997) *Shattering Silence: Women, Nationalism, and Political Subjectivity in Northern Ireland*. Princeton, NJ: Princeton University Press.

Asad, T. (1993) *Genealogies of Religion: Discipline and Reasons of Power in Christianity and Islam*. 2nd edition. Baltimore, MD: Johns Hopkins University Press.

Asad, T. (2003) *Formations of the Secular: Christianity, Islam, Modernity*. Stanford, CA: Stanford University Press.

Balibar E. (1998) 'The Borders of Europe' in P. Cheah and B. Robbins (eds) *Cosmopolitics: Thinking and Feeling Beyond the Nation*. Minneapolis, MN, and London: University of Minnesota Press, pp. 216–29.

Balibar, E. (2009) 'Europe as Borderland', *Environment and Planning D: Society and Space* 27 (2): 190–215.

BBC (2016) 'France Foiling Terror Plots "Daily" – Prime Minister Manuel Valls', BBC News, 11 September. www.bbc.com/news/world-europe-37334836 (accessed 15 December 2016).

Bilefsky, D. and M. De La Baume (2015) 'French Premier Declares "War" on Radical Islam as Paris Girds for Rally,' *New York Times*, 10 January. www.nytimes.com/2015/01/11/world/europe/paris-terrorist-attacks.html (accessed 14 December 2016).

Bouteldja, H. (2015) 'Charlie Hebdo: The Sacred of the 'Wretched of the Earth' and its Desecration', Mondoweiss, 30 January. http://mondoweiss.net/2015/01/charlie-wretched-desecration/ (accessed 15 December 2016).

Buzan, B. and G. Lawson (2015) *The Global Transformation: History, Modernity and the Making of International Relations*. New York: Cambridge University Press.

Cavanaugh, W. T. (2009) *The Myth of Religious Violence: Secular Ideology and the Roots of Modern Conflict*. New York: Oxford University Press.

Chrisafis, A. (2015) 'France Passes New Surveillance Law in Wake of Charlie Hebdo Attack', *The Guardian*, 5 May. www.theguardian.com/world/2015/may/05/france-passes-new-surveillance-law-in-wake-of-charlie-hebdo-attack (accessed 14 December 2016).

Devji, F. (2009) *The Terrorist in Search of Humanity*. London: Hurst.

Doherty, B. (2015) 'France Launches "Massive" Airstrike on Isis Stronghold of Raqqa', *The Guardian*, 16 November. www.theguardian.com/world/2015/nov/16/france-launches-massive-airstrike-on-isis-stronghold-in-syria-after-paris-attack (accessed 14 December 2016).

Fédération internationale des ligues des droits de l'Homme (2016) *Quand l'exception devient la règle: mesures antiterroristes contraires aux droits humains*. Paris: FIDH. www.fidh.org/IMG/pdf/rapportfrance-hd1_def.pdf (accessed 14 December 2016).

Groll, E. (2015) 'Le Petit Problème with France's new big brother', *Foreign Policy*, 5 May. http://foreignpolicy.com/2015/05/05/le-petit-probleme-with-frances-new-big-brother/ (accessed 15 December 2016).

Kassem, R. (2016) 'France's Real State of Emergency', *New York Times*, 4 August. www.nytimes.com/2016/08/05/opinion/frances-real-state-of-emergency.html?_r=0 (accessed 14 December 2016).

Kedourie, E. (1987) 'The Nation-State in the Middle East', *Jerusalem Journal of International Relations* 9 (3): 1–9.

Kelidar, A. (1993) 'States without Foundations: The Political Evolution of State and Society in the Arab East', *Journal of Contemporary History* 28 (2): 315–39.

Marsden, C. (2015) 'France Deploys 10,000 Troops in Wake of Charlie Hebdo Attack', World Socialist Web Site, 13 January. www.wsws.org/en/articles/2015/01/13/fran-j13.html (accessed 14 December 2016).

Mbembe, A. (2009) 'The Republic and its Beast: On the Riots in the French *Banlieus*'. Translated by J. M. Todd. In C. Tshimanga, D. Gondola and P. Bloom (eds) *Frenchness and the African Diaspora: Identity and Uprising in Contemporary France*. Bloomington, IN: Indiana University Press, pp. 47–54.

Roy, O. (2017) *Jihad and Death: The Global Appeal of Islamic State*. London: Hurst.

Silva, C. (2015) 'French Soldiers Flood Streets of Paris after Charlie Hebdo Attack, Jewish Community on Alert', *International Business Times*, 1 December. www.ibtimes.com/french-soldiers-flood-streets-paris-after-charlie-hebdo-attack-jewish-community-alert-1781058 (accessed 14 December 2016).

van Houtum, H. and T. van Naerssen (2002) 'Bordering, Ordering and Othering', *Tijdschrift voor Economische en Sociale Geografie* 93 (2): 125–36.

Walt, V. (2015) 'France Strikes ISIS Targets in Syria as Manhunt Underway',

Time, 15 November. http://time.com/4113706/paris-terror-syria-bombings/ (accessed 14 December 2016).

Whitman, J. Q. (2014) *The Verdict of Battle: The Law of Victory and the Making of Modern War*. Cambridge, MA: Harvard University Press.

Williams, R. and R. Gable, with an introduction by R. Blackburn (1988) *Resources of Hope: Culture, Democracy, Socialism*. New York: Verso.

Winichakul, T. (1994) *Siam Mapped: A History of the Geo-body of a Nation*. Honolulu, HI: University of Hawai'i Press.

8 | EXTREMISM, THEIRS AND OURS: BRITAIN'S 'GENERATIONAL STRUGGLE'

Arun Kundnani

In Eqbal Ahmad's 1998 lecture 'Terrorism, theirs and ours', the legendary Pakistani scholar and activist demonstrated that, in official US literature on terrorism, definitions of the term are necessarily vague, the word's use is selective and inconsistent, terrorism's causes are left mysterious, and yet terrorists can be named with complete certainty. The word is bent out of shape for a purpose: in order that 'their' (Muslim) terrorism be highly visible, the subject of moral outrage, a threat to civilisation itself, while 'our' terrorism, the terrorism of the Ku Klux Klan, of the Contras, along with the state terrorism of the US and its allied governments, is hidden (Ahmad 2006). Ahmad died in the year after he presented his analysis; he did not witness in 2001 the emergence of the so-called Global War on Terror and its subsequent expanding vocabulary of terms such as 'extremism' and 'radicalisation', both sharing with 'terrorism' the same selective application. Even more so than 'terrorism', 'extremism' and 'radicalisation' are nebulous words that give "an appearance of solidity to pure wind" – as George Orwell noted of political language designed to deceive (Orwell 1957b: 157). This appearance of solidity is essential if the words are to be deployed in law-making and institutional practice. But, as with 'terrorism', when closely examined, the terminology of 'extremism' and 'radicalisation' reveals itself to be a 'mobile army of metaphors' that is "rhetorically intensified, metamorphosed, adorned, and after long usage seems to a nation fixed, canonic, and binding" (Nietzsche 1954: 46–7).

By the time thousands marched through Paris to declare 'Je Suis Charlie' and defend freedom of expression on 11 January 2015, more than a decade of fixing meanings through rhetoric and adornment had already produced a Gramscian 'common sense' meaning to the word 'extremism': a set of images, stories and assumptions lodged in popular consciousness (Gramsci 2000). This common sense provided the dominant framing for the killing of *Charlie Hebdo*'s journalists, which was aligned immediately and seemingly spontaneously with the pre-existing binary grid of extremism versus freedom of speech, their fanaticism versus our liberalism. So powerful were the images, stories and assumptions giving meaning to the term 'extremism' that the word could paint a veneer of dignity over the open hypocrisy that followed, as pro-Palestinian demonstrations in France were banned, a permanent state of emergency declared, and the resulting powers used "to barge into places without warrants where French Muslims gather, shut mosques and coffee shops, detain people with no charges, and otherwise abolish basic liberties" (Greenwald 2016).

Meanwhile in Britain, six months after then Prime Minister David Cameron attended the Paris march for freedom of speech, his government's fast-tracked Counter-Terrorism and Security Act 2015 came into effect. It placed an obligation on public bodies – from universities and hospitals to nursery schools and optometrists – to surveil, identify and report to the authorities persons expressing 'un-British' cultural values. The word 'extremist' did the work of partially concealing the stark contradiction between holding freedom of speech to be an absolute value and, in the name of that very freedom, restricting what opinions can be expressed. Thus did those most vociferously defending freedom of speech in the aftermath of the attacks become enthusiastic censors. In what follows, the process by which the current usage of 'extremism' emerged in Britain is traced, and its practical implications explored.

Extremism redefined

Since at least the French Revolution, politicians have made accusations of extremism to denounce enemies on their flanks and present themselves as occupying a moderate centre. Used in this way, the concept is, of course, somewhat arbitrary: yesterday's extreme is today's centre and vice versa. In British political discourse, the term 'extremism' was first used at the beginning of the twentieth century. Police reports produced by the colonial administration in India categorised anti-colonial militants who favoured full independence as 'extremists', while those, such as the Indian National Congress, whose demands then were limited to administrative reform, were dubbed 'moderates'. English-language newspapers in India used the terminology before it spread to the British press (Backes 2010: 97–8). With the Cold War, the formula of the moderate centre was recontinued. Historian

Arthur M. Schlesinger Jr wrote in his 1949 book *The Vital Center* that American liberalism stood for a down-to-earth process of gradual reform, which was endangered by communist extremists on the left and anti-democratic extremists on the right – both ideologies captured men's minds by exploiting the "darker passions" (Schlesinger 1962: 40).

From the end of the Cold War to the 7/7 bombings of the London transport system in 2005, the term 'extremism' was generally used in UK government literature to refer to a range of extra-parliamentary political groups and movements: animal rights activism, radical environmentalism, anarchism, anti-fascism, communism, Trotskyism, Black nationalism, the peace movement, neo-Nazism, Islamic political movements, and Irish nationalism. The response of the state to these groups within the British mainland was to carry out surveillance, infiltration and criminalisation – tasks assigned to police special branches and the domestic intelligence agency MI5. As late as 2004, Islamic extremism in Britain was conceived in official literature as a matter of *membership organisations* that sought to *recruit* Muslims to participate in street-based activism. Their success in doing so was taken to be a function of social disaffection and alienation among young Muslims. Extremist groups themselves may not have carried out or advocated violence but they "provide an environment for some to gravitate to violence" (Home Office 2004: 2). The implicit opposite of extremism was a sense of national loyalty and a commitment to government institutions. It remained obscure how extremism was related to terrorism but there was at least an acknowledgement that the government's understanding of these matters was limited (ibid.: 1).

The concept of 'extremism' underwent a transformation following 7/7. It detached itself from references to formal groups and movements. It now emphasised attitudes, mindsets and dispositions. Above all, it referred to a free-floating ideology that did not work through recruitment but through radicalisation. 'Radicalisation' referred to the process by which extremist ideology captured the minds of the young and made them into potential terrorists. Extremism was pictured as a virus, flowing from radicaliser to radicalised, infecting, spreading, infiltrating (Bettison 2009: 130–1). Naively allowing Muslims too much separation and autonomy, in the name of multicultural tolerance, had encouraged the spread of the virus. The search for other social explanations for extremism was abandoned; the aim instead was to stem the flow of dangerous ideas. An extremist was now someone who held a particular kind of ideology, even if he was not involved in any group or movement, and that ideology was taken to be the underlying cause of terrorism. The content of extremist ideology was rarely spelled out except negatively as the rejection of British liberal values, even as members of the public – Muslims in particular – were called upon to block its spread by identifying and challenging it. This use of 'extremism' proliferated through the circuits of policymaking, journalism and popular culture, everywhere accompanied by the assumption that there was no explanation for terrorism beyond the rather mysterious extremist ideological messages that underpinned it.

The transformation and proliferation of the meaning of 'extremism' was not a simple and transparent reaction to the crisis event of 7/7. Rather, a series of agencies – government departments, police forces, intelligence agencies, think tanks and news organisations – used 7/7 to redefine the meaning of the term and expand its use. Stuart Hall and the co-authors of *Policing the Crisis* argued in their classic study of race and mediated crime panics that crisis events never appear in a 'pure' form to the public but are made sense of through vocabularies determined by whoever has the power to offer the primary definition of the event. In their analysis, these primary definers set

> the limit for all subsequent discussion by framing what the problem is. This initial framework then provides the criteria by which all subsequent contributions are labelled as 'relevant' to the debate or 'irrelevant' – beside the point. Contributions which stray from this framework are exposed to the charge that they are 'not addressing the problem.' (Hall et al. 1978: 59)

The ideological process of defining and explaining crises is about giving meaning to disturbing and troubling events and restoring a sense of control over the world. The 'lay' explanations that are given are not logical or coherent but are a way of giving meaning to shocking and apparently random events, to draw them into the framework of the rational order of things that can be worked on, addressed, handled, managed (Hall et al. 1978: 166).

Policing the Crisis has been criticised for neglecting internal divisions among the state institutions that act as primary definers and for downplaying the extent to which opposition can influence what definitions emerge (Miller 1993). In the process by which meanings were attached to 7/7, there were indeed tensions and divergences between conservative and liberal state factions, between central and local government, and between the security arm of the state and other branches of government. There was also prominent opposition to policies introduced in the aftermath of 7/7. The anti-war movement had demonstrated its strength in 2003 before that year's war on Iraq, enabling a counter-definition linking 7/7 to UK foreign policy rather than to religious fanaticism. This counter-definition had a certain presence but it nevertheless faltered over time in the face of the state's better organised capacity to assert a different narrative. Thus, a public consensus emerged across the state and mainstream media that read 7/7 as, above all, a matter of religious radicalisation enabled by a failure of British identity. This consensus remained solidly in place even as the counter-extremism policies that rested on it were routinely criticised. *Policing the Crisis* remains useful as a way to understand this consensus and the central role of the state in organising, if not unilaterally defining, the social process by which national security crises are made sense of.

This was achieved in part through newspaper columnists. A flurry of commentary on the 7/7 attacks established a relatively consistent framework, linking political violence to cultural values, separatism, and a failing multiculturalism. Alice Miles at *The Times* called for the government to "tear into those Muslim ghettos" (Miles 2005) and Anthony Browne in the same newspaper argued that multicultural tolerance of 'Muslim ghettos' needed to be abandoned so that arranged marriages, headscarves in schools and imams who supported the Muslim Brotherhood could be banned (Browne 2005). Boris Johnson – the current Foreign Secretary, then working as a columnist at the *Daily Telegraph* – demanded Muslims be made to 'acculturate' to 'our way of life' and more firmly embrace Britishness, as the best way to prevent future terrorist attacks (Johnson 2005). Melanie Phillips in the *Daily Mail* blamed 7/7 on a 'lethally divisive' multiculturalism (Phillips 2005).

Think-tank reports were also significant in establishing a fixed explanatory framework. Such reports are able to claim the validity of objective and substantial research while also connecting with policymaking and public debate in a way that makes them newsworthy. In the two years after 7/7, the think tank Policy Exchange published three reports arguing in various ways that multicultural tolerance had enabled the spread of extremist ideology, which in turn led to the risk of terrorism (Kundnani 2008). In 2007, a new 'counter-extremism' think tank, the Quilliam Foundation, was founded, which became a major source of ideological support for this new narrative of extremism. It argued forcefully that extremism was a 'conveyor belt' to terrorism and that Islamic political movements were inherently violent even when they appeared to take non-violent forms. The Foundation launched an extensive programme of 'radicalisation awareness' training sessions for thousands of police officers and officials working in local authorities around England and Wales, promoting this argument. With backing from government ministers, it also advised schools on the behaviours that could indicate a young person was being radicalised (Kundnani 2014: 173–4). In 2008, the leading military think tank, the Royal United Services Institute, released a report by a group of British former generals, senior diplomats and intelligence services officers bemoaning Britain's "fragmenting, post-Christian society, increasingly divided about interpretations of its history, about its national aims, its values and in its political identity ... misplaced deference to 'multiculturalism' [which] failed to lay down the line to immigrant communities", thus undercutting the fight against extremism and terrorism (Prins and Salusbury 2008: 23).

In the case of events involving political violence, the national security arm of the state has a particular authority to define those events because of its presumed role as defender of society from unknown threats and its claim to hold classified information unavailable to others. In Britain, the national security arm of the state is both centralised and able to influence all other spheres of government. It has used its power to help circulate its narrative of extremism, through ministerial speeches, statements and reports, and through its briefings to journalists. Since 2006, government ministers have repeatedly delivered what is essentially the same underlying narrative. Ruth Kelly (2006), Hazel Blears (2009), David Cameron (2011), Theresa May (2015) and David Cameron (Prime Minister's Office 2015b) have each conveyed the same basic message: that Britain is in crisis because a section of the Muslim population has cut itself off from the rest of society, advocated a distinct, extremist value system, and thereby created the conditions for terrorist violence. A series of links is thus produced from separatism and extremism to terrorism.

In this way, the new crisis of 7/7 – the first time that British Muslims carried out acts of terrorism within the UK – was attached to a pre-existing discourse of integration that had taken shape in the aftermath of the urban rebellions by Muslim youth in Oldham, Burnley and Bradford in the summer of 2001. That earlier moment of crisis, before 9/11, had been officially interpreted as a problem of Muslim separatism and excessive cultural differences that now needed hard-headed reining in through less multicultural tolerance and a tougher allegiance to British national identity (Kundnani 2007). As this story attained the ideological power of 'common sense', claims that other factors might be a part of the explanations for the summer 2001 rebellions (institutional racism) or the 7/7 attacks (the Iraq war) were dismissed as lacking in seriousness. When made by Muslims, such claims were themselves taken to be signs of an extremist mindset, rather than valid contributions to the public sphere.

Moreover, this account of extremism was not easily dislodged by factual contradiction. Close attention to the lives of Muslims (let alone others) involved in terrorist violence in Europe showed that they rarely matched the official narrative of religious radicalisation. Take, for example, Mohamed Lahouaiej-Bouhlel, the perpetrator of the Bastille Day attack in Nice in July 2016, in which eighty four people were killed. Prosecutors searched in vain for evidence of a process of radicalisation that involved his becoming more religiously extreme. What they found instead was someone with a range of mental health problems and no interest in religious ideology, radical or otherwise (Nossiter et al. 2016). Confronted with so many cases such as this, scholars who had developed religious radicalisation models after 9/11 revised their analyses a decade later. Marc Sageman, the leading academic supporter in the mid-2000s of a religious radicalisation model, moved away from his earlier emphasis on religious ideology as a significant factor in causing terrorism. In 2013, he suggested that governments should "stop being brainwashed by this notion of 'radicalisation.' There is no such thing. Some people when they're young acquire extreme views; many of them just grow out of them. Do not overreact – you'll just create worse problems" (Hasan 2013). Similarly John Horgan, director of the International Center for the Study of Terrorism at Pennsylvania State University, said that: "The idea that radicalization causes terrorism is perhaps the greatest myth alive today in terrorism research ... [First], the overwhelming majority of people who hold radical beliefs do not engage in violence. And second, there is increasing evidence that people who engage in terrorism don't necessarily hold radical beliefs" (Knefel 2013). But because the power of the official narrative of extremism had not rested on the authority of scholarship, so developments in scholarship made little difference to the narrative's prominence.

Neither did changes of government. In their essentials, there were more continuities than differences between New Labour's Ruth Kelly speaking on extremism in 2006 and the Conservative Party's David Cameron speaking on extremism in 2015 (Prime Minister's Office 2015b). The power of the discourse on extremism rests, in part, on this consistency of ministerial statements from 2006 to the present day. While this discourse has been adopted by Conservative ministers since 2010, its origins lie in the Labour Party leadership's ideological transformation in the 1990s. Tony Blair's embrace of neoliberalism differed from Thatcher's in his belief that the government had an active role to play in reshaping society in line with market values. This meant producing the kinds of cultural values and identities that would, it was hoped, sustain a neoliberal political economy. Where once Labour Party leaders had claimed to represent the working class, now they sought to transform its cultural life. The old images of unchanging Englishness that Blair's Conservative predecessor as Prime Minister, John Major, had invoked, quoting Orwell's "old maids biking to Holy Communion through the mists of the autumn mornings", were set aside (Orwell 1957a: 64). Instead, New Labour politicians advocated a 'third way' national identity based on liberal individualism. Britishness, they said, meant individual freedom and equality of opportunity. When David Cameron claimed in 2015 that what defines Britishness is "freedom of speech, freedom of the press, freedom of worship, equal rights regardless of race, sex, sexuality or faith", he was following Tony Blair's script (Prime Minister's Office 2015a). Since 2006, government ministers have repeatedly argued that multicultural tolerance has somehow prevented people from advocating for these liberal values in a sufficiently assertive way and that doing so is now essential to prevent extremism. In this discourse, Muslims were the Other to a new cultural nationalism, the screen upon which a refiguring of national identity could be projected, and the object of a surveillance gaze that aimed to regulate identity.

Condensing an image

With the Preventing Violent Extremism (PVE) policy introduced by Tony Blair's government in 2006, this concept of extremism was institutionalised in policy for the first time. A burden was placed upon Muslims and public service workers to identify those who seemed to support extremist ideology. Muslims were called upon to publicly denounce extremism; indeed, their community organisations received government money to do so (DCLG 2007). Alongside the investigations carried out domestically by police forces and MI5, which were focused on intercepting those whose activities were criminalised under the UK's wide-ranging anti-terrorist legislation, PVE policy aimed at addressing a wider population whose values and beliefs were not leading to criminal activity but, according to government officials, were indicative of extremism. Within a few years, thousands of local government and public service workers had received training that inculcated this account of extremism and embedded its assumptions in their working practices.

Muslims, who had been given the task of eradicating extremism within their families and communities, made the obvious point that, without a clear definition, they were unlikely to succeed. A 2009 speech by government minister Hazel Blears offered a first attempt to clarify the definition of extremist ideology: it is, she said, "belief in the supremacy of the Muslim people, in a divine duty to bring the world under the control of hegemonic Islam, in the establishment of a theocratic Caliphate, and in the undemocratic imposition of theocratic law on whole societies". This 'ideology', she said, is rooted "in a twisted reading of Islam" and is the underlying cause of terrorism (Blears 2009). In the same year, the government official in charge of PVE policy at the Home Office gave another definition. Extremism, he said, is "views in some quarters here that Western culture is evil and that Muslims living in this country should not engage with Western cultural organisations, for want of a better term, with Western culture itself" (Home Affairs Committee 2009: Ev 26). By now, millions of pounds of public money were being spent each year on various PVE initiatives. These were presented as efforts at identifying Muslims who held these views and beliefs, dissuading them from believing such things or expressing them in public, and countering those beliefs when they were expressed.

Two years later, another definition was produced by the government. Extremism was:

> vocal or active opposition to fundamental British values, including democracy, the rule of law, individual liberty and mutual respect

and tolerance of different faiths and beliefs. We also include in our definition of extremism calls for the death of members of our armed forces, whether in this country or overseas. (HM Government 2011: 107)

The same government document also defined extremism as believing that "the West is perpetually at war with Islam; there can be no legitimate interaction between Muslims and non-Muslims in this country or elsewhere; and that Muslims living here cannot legitimately and or effectively participate in our democratic society" (HM Government 2011: 20). Two years later, a government task force on extremism and radicalisation gave yet another definition of extremism:

It is an ideology which is based on a distorted interpretation of Islam, which betrays Islam's peaceful principles, and draws on the teachings of the likes of Sayyid Qutb. Islamist extremists deem Western intervention in Muslim-majority countries as a 'war on Islam', creating a narrative of 'them' and 'us'. They seek to impose a global Islamic state governed by their interpretation of Shari'ah as state law, rejecting liberal values such as democracy, the rule of law and equality. (HM Government 2013: 1–2)

These various descriptions were all consistent with the broader set of images, assumptions and narratives that had given shape to the concept of extremism since 2006. But, as objective definitions, they pointed in multiple, inconsistent directions. Is 'extremism' a belief in Islamic supremacy, in theocracy, the rejection of Western culture, rejection of liberal values, or Islamic resistance to Western wars? The word was being asked to do too much and forced into strange contortions as a result. If extremism were defined as rejection of liberal values, then its application would be so wide as to include vast swathes of the British population – from Home Counties conservatives and the Christian Right's opposition to LGBT rights, to the Hindutva movement in Britain, with its backing of the far-right Narendra Modi government in India, and the Zionist movement, with its fundraising and support for the war crimes of the Israel Defense Forces. Applying the term 'extremism' so widely, especially to non-Muslims, would, however, make it hard for it also to seem to refer to a step towards terrorism. For the term to have its political effects, it had to condense a mixture of concepts – separatism, illiberalism, theocracy, violence – into a single image of the dangerous Muslim. It had to be an image tied to acts of terrorism carried out by small numbers of people but also one diffuse enough to warrant alarm, mass surveillance and policy mobilisation across so many spheres – what Cameron called a "generational struggle" (Cameron 2014). The more precisely 'extremism' was defined, the harder it was for the word to carry off this double role. Thus the incoherence of the definitions was not a barrier to the term's proliferation in policymaking and public discussion but necessary for it. The consistency needed was not in the word's definition but in its political effects. And the consistency of those effects was secured by the consistency of those with the power to shape the word's meanings.

A new speech regime

The PVE programme – known as 'Prevent' for short – was not introduced through legislation but through the initiative of Tony Blair's office, from where it was passed through the various ministries of central government. The local authorities, schools, police forces, prisons, probation services, National Health Service trusts, colleges and universities in England and Wales, which were gradually drawn into participating in Prevent from 2006 onwards, and received central government funding to do so, were technically acting on a voluntary basis. As opposition mounted to Prevent, many of these agencies began to question their involvement. The government's response was to pass the Counter-Terrorism and Security Act 2015, which for the first time made participation in Prevent a statutory obligation on public bodies. Under the Act, schools, universities and health service providers could no longer opt out of monitoring students and patients for supposed radicalised behaviour.

The censorious trends already visible in the functioning of Prevent before the Act now intensified. Every teacher, lecturer, doctor and public service worker was expected to surveil Muslim populations for signs of the rejection of British values. Norms of confidentiality and trust between professionals and their students or patients were undermined, anti-Muslim suspicion and prejudice were institutionalised, and the space for free expression of political and religious ideas was narrowed. Never in peacetime Britain had national security surveillance of religious and political identity been so deeply embedded in the normal functioning of public life.

By 2015, almost 4,000 people a year were being reported as potential extremists under the Prevent programme (Halliday 2016). Three-eighths of the cases involved children under eighteen years old, an indication of the extent to which schools had been drawn into Prevent surveillance (Tran 2015). A sense of the behaviours taken to be suspicious can be gleaned from a sample of publicly reported cases of recent referrals to Prevent. In one school, a ten-year-old child was referred to Prevent for requesting a prayer room (*Telegraph* 2015). At a nursery school in Luton, a four-year-old boy faced referral after he drew a picture of his father cutting a cucumber with a knife, which staff misheard described by the child as a 'cooker bomb' (Quinn 2016). At a school in London, a teenager was referred after mentioning the word 'eco-terrorist' in a class discussion about environmental activism (Dodd 2015). There have been multiple reports of students being referred for wearing 'Free Palestine' badges (Broomfield 2016) or advocating in schools for the campaign to Boycott, Divest and Sanction Israel (Hooper 2015).

The overwhelming majority of referrals involve Muslim students, but the same procedures introduced through Prevent are also occasionally used in response to left-wing activism. A teenage student at a school in north London was reported as a suspected 'anarchist' on the grounds that he had criticised the running of the school on his personal blog. The headteacher who reported him said: "In the last year he has become more and more enchanted by anti-establishment ways of thinking and has even said that there is an inherent risk that every government is corrupt" (Amara 2013). In Manchester, a seventeen-year-old student active in Trotskyist political groups was referred for 'left-wing extremism' (Kundnani 2014: 153–6). At one primary school in east London, children as young as nine were asked to fill out a survey designed to identify signs of extremism. The data was collected as part of the Prevent programme and the results were therefore available to the police without the knowledge of parents (Taylor 2015a). Suspicion does not only fall on Muslim students but also on teaching staff. Around a hundred Muslim teachers and teaching assistants were investigated by the National College for Teaching and Leadership (NCTL) as potential extremists in 2015 and could be prevented from working in schools for life (Kerbaj 2015). Significantly, the National Union of Teachers passed a motion condemning Prevent policy at its 2016 conference.

Muslim children are also a target in France. Special measures introduced after the *Charlie Hebdo* attack require schools to report pupils for comments that are said to constitute an 'apology' for terrorism. Hundreds of such incidents were passed to the police in January 2015. France's Education Minister, Najat Vallaud-Belkacem, told the National Assembly: "Even in schools where no incidents took place, too much questioning came from pupils," labelling as suspicious even the act of discussion. Over a hundred were charged with expressing opinions considered too accepting of terrorism (Costa-Kostritsky 2015). In Nice, an eight-year-old Muslim boy was asked by his teacher to adopt the slogan 'Je Suis Charlie', to which he said he objected to the magazine's cartoons. He was summoned by the police and accused of condoning terrorism (Mouillard 2015).

In British universities and further education institutions, guidance issued in 2015 clarifies that there is now a legal duty that would-be speakers be vetted for extremism (HM Government 2015: 4). In order to meet this requirement, universities will likely outsource decision-making to the police, via a police-employed Prevent officer stationed on campuses, giving the police effective censorship powers in further and higher education. Opposition from universities (*Independent* 2015) and the National Union of Students has been strong (Wintour 2015).

So, too, do Muslim organisations continue to oppose and, in some cases, refuse to participate in the Prevent programme. The Waltham Forest Council of Mosques has described Prevent as "an ill-conceived and flawed policy" used to "spy and denigrate the Muslim community and cause mistrust" (Taylor 2015b). The chair of Birmingham Central Mosque has called for a boycott of Prevent after claiming it "unfairly targets Muslims and school children" (Finnigan 2016).

But the government ploughs ahead. At the time of writing, it is drawing up new legislation – the Counter-Extremism and Safeguarding Bill – to further embed the concept of 'extremism' in law, a process first begun with the 2015 Act. The new Bill will include 'civil orders' to restrict extremist activity – for example, by preventing extremists from posting material online or working with children – and new powers for the broadcasting regulator Ofcom to pre-emptively block broadcasts of interviews with extremists. As Home Secretary, Theresa May criticised the BBC's decision to screen an interview with radical activist Anjem Choudary on its *Newsnight* programme in 2013. The new Ofcom power is understood to be intended to prevent such interviews as well as to make it easier to shut down minor satellite channels accused of broadcasting extremist content (Dawson and Godec 2016).

Together with the 2015 Act, the Bill represents a significant shift in strategy from legislating against terrorism to what the government calls 'non-violent extremism', a term as clumsy as it is deceptive. As Theresa May stated in her 2014 Conservative Party conference speech, the government is proposing "a new counter-extremism strategy that goes beyond terrorism" (May 2014). What is being introduced is the selective criminalisation of a broad category of ideological speech – an entirely different legislative project from the existing laws on incitement of violence and glorification of terrorism (under the 2006 Terrorism Act). In effect, the new legislation will, for the first time, make it a crime to publicly express opposition to British values – especially for Muslims. Under this new speech regime, Muslim expression of radical views – such as support for the Palestinian cause – will not be treated as an act of dissent by fellow citizens but an indicator of terrorist potential, and criminalised as such. As with the term 'terrorism', what 'extremism' exactly is will remain necessarily vague, its causes unexplored, and the term selectively applied. Yet thousands of extremists will be confidently identified every year through an elaborate system of surveillance across public life. In essence, this will be no more than government censorship of political opinions it finds unacceptable. And, ironically, this will be done in the name of defending 'British' values of individual freedom.

References

Ahmad, E. (2006) 'Terrorism: Theirs and Ours' in C. Bengelsdoorf, M. Cerullo and Y. Chandrani (eds) *The Selected Writings of Eqbal Ahmad*. New York: Columbia University Press.

Amara, P. (2013) 'Headteacher Reports Teen Blogger Who Criticised School to Police', *Camden New Journal*, 5 September.

Backes, U. (2010) *Political Extremes: A Conceptual History from Antiquity to the Present*. Abingdon: Routledge.

Bettison, N. (2009) 'Preventing Violent Extremism: A Police Response', *Policing* 3 (2): 129–38.

Blears, H. (2009) 'Many Voices: Understanding the Debate about Preventing Violent Extremism'. www.lse.ac.uk/website-archive/publicEvents/pdf/20090225_HazelBlears.pdf.

Broomfield, M. (2016) 'Anti-terror Police Question Schoolboy for Wearing pro-Palestine Badge', *Independent*, 14 February. www.independent.co.uk/news/uk/anti-terror-police-question-schoolboy-for-wearing-pro-palestine-badge-a6873656.html.

Browne, A. (2005) 'Fundamentally, We're Useful Idiots', *The Times*, 1 August.

Cameron, D. (2011) 'PM's Speech at Munich Security Conference', 5 February. www.gov.uk/government/

speeches/pms-speech-at-munich-security-conference.

Cameron, D. (2014) 'This Poisonous Extremism Is a Direct Threat to Britain', *Sunday Telegraph*, 17 August.

Costa-Kostritsky, V. (2015) 'Forced to be "Charlie"', *Precarious Europe*, 17 February. www.precariouseurope. com/lives/forced-to-be-charlie.

Dawson, J. and S. Godec (2016) 'Counter-extremism Policy: An Overview'. Briefing Paper 7238. London: House of Commons Library.

DCLG (2007) *Preventing Violent Extremism – Winning Hearts and Minds*. London: Department for Communities and Local Government (DCLG).

Dodd, V. (2015) 'School Questioned Muslim Pupil about Isis after Discussion on Eco-activism', *Guardian*, 22 September.

Finnigan, L. (2016) 'Birmingham Central Mosque Chairman Calls for Boycott of "Racist" Prevent Programme', *Telegraph*, 23 January.

Gramsci, A. (2000) *The Gramsci Reader: Selected Writings 1916–1935*. Edited by D. Forgacs. New York: New York University Press.

Greenwald, G. (2016) 'Where Were the Post-Hebdo Free Speech Crusaders as France Spent the Last Year Crushing Free Speech?', *The Intercept*, 8 January.

Hall, S., C. Critcher, T. Jefferson, J. Clarke and B. Roberts (1978) *Policing the Crisis: Mugging, the State, and Law and Order*. London: Macmillan.

Halliday, J. (2016) 'Almost 4,000 People Referred to UK Deradicalisation Scheme Last Year', *Guardian*, 20 March.

Hasan, M. (2013) 'Woolwich Attack: Overreacting to Extremism "Could Bring Back Al Qaeda" Ex-CIA Officer Warns', *Huffington Post*, 28 May. www.huffingtonpost.

co.uk/2013/05/27/sageman-interview_n_3342206.html.

HM Government (2011) *Prevent Strategy*. Cm 8092. London: HM Government.

HM Government (2013) *Tackling Extremism in the UK*. London: HM Government.

HM Government (2015) *Prevent Duty Guidance for Further Education Institutions in England and Wales*. London: HM Government.

Home Affairs Committee (2009) *Project Contest: The Government's Counter-terrorism Strategy: Ninth Report of Session 2008–09*. London: Home Affairs Committee.

Home Office (2004) *Young Muslims and Extremism*. London: Home Office.

Hooper, S. (2015) 'Stifling Freedom of Expression in UK Schools', *Al Jazeera*, 23 July. www.aljazeera.com/ indepth/features/2015/07/stifling-freedom-expression-uk-schools-150721080612049.html.

Independent (2015) 'PREVENT Will Have a Chilling Effect on Open Debate, Free Speech and Political Dissent', *Independent*, 10 July. www. independent.co.uk/voices/letters/ prevent-will-have-a-chilling-effect-on-open-debate-free-speech-and-political-dissent-10381491.html.

Johnson, B. (2005) 'This Is a Turning Point: We Have to Fly the Flag for Britishness Again', *Daily Telegraph*, 14 July.

Kelly, R. (2006) 'Speech on Integration and Cohesion', *Guardian*, 24 August. www.theguardian.com/ politics/2006/aug/24/uksecurity. terrorism.

Kerbaj, R. (2015) '100 Islamist Teachers Face Ban', *Sunday Times*, 5 April.

Knefel, J. (2013) 'Everything You've Been Told about Radicalization Is Wrong', *Rolling Stone*, 6 May.

Kundnani, A. (2007) *The End of Tolerance: Racism in 21st Century Britain*. London and Ann Arbor, MI: Pluto Press.

Kundnani, A. (2008) 'How Are Thinktanks Shaping the Political Agenda On Muslims in Britain?', Institute of Race Relations, 2 September. www.irr.org.uk/news/how-are-thinktanks-shaping-the-political-agenda-on-muslims-in-britain.

Kundnani, A. (2014) *The Muslims are Coming!: Islamophobia, Extremism, and the Domestic War on Terror.* London and New York: Verso.

May, T. (2014) 'Speech to Conservative Party Conference 2014'. http://press.conservatives.com/post/98799073410/theresa-may-speech-to-conservative-party.

May, T. (2015) 'A Stronger Britain, Built on Our Values'. Speech to the Royal Institution of Chartered Surveyors, London, 23 March. www.gov.uk/government/speeches/a-stronger-britain-built-on-our-values.

Miles, A. (2005) 'Four Pathetic Young Bombers', *The Times*, 13 July.

Miller, D. (1993) 'Official Sources and "Primary Definition": The Case of Northern Ireland', *Media, Culture and Society* 15: 385–406.

Mouillard, S. (2015) 'L'enfant de 8 ans au commissariat pour "apologie du terrorisme"', *Liberation*, 28 January.

Nietzsche, F. W. (1954) 'On Truth and Lie in an Extra-moral Sense'. Translated by W. Kaufmann. In W. Kaufmann (ed.) *The Portable Nietzsche*. New York: Viking Press.

Nossiter, A., A. J. Rubin and L. Blaise (2016) 'Killer in Nice Long Drawn to Violence', *New York Times*, 25 July.

Orwell, G. (1957a) 'England Your England' in *Inside the Whale and Other Essays*. Harmondsworth, Middlesex: Penguin.

Orwell, G. (1957b) 'Politics and the English Language' in *Inside the Whale and Other Essays*. Harmondsworth, Middlesex: Penguin.

Phillips, M. (2005) 'This Lethal Moral Madness', *Daily Mail*, 14 July.

Prime Minister's Office (2015a) 'At Ninestiles School in Birmingham, Prime Minister David Cameron Set out his Plans to Address Extremism', 20 July. www.gov.uk/government/speeches/extremism-pm-speech.

Prime Minister's Office (2015b) 'Counter-extremism Bill – National Security Council Meeting', 13 May. www.gov.uk/government/news/counter-extremism-bill-national-security-council-meeting.

Prins, G. and R. Salusbury (2008) 'Risk, Threat, and Security: The Case of the United Kingdom', *RUSI Journal* 153 (1).

Quinn, B. (2016) 'Nursery "Raised Fears of Radicalisation over Boy's Cucumber Drawing"', *Guardian*, 11 March.

Schlesinger, A. M. (1962) *The Vital Center: The Politics of Freedom*. Boston MA: Houghton Mifflin Company.

Taylor, D. (2015a) 'Fury after Primary Pupils Are Asked to Complete Radicalisation-seeking Surveys', *Guardian*, 28 May.

Taylor, D. (2015b) 'Society of Mosques to Boycott "Racist" Anti-terror Prevent Programme', *Guardian*, 17 December.

Telegraph (2015) 'Teachers' Extremist Fears over Boy, 10, after He Complains about Lack of Prayer Room', *Telegraph*, 13 October.

Tran, M. (2015) 'Large Proportion of Those Referred to UK Deradicalisation Scheme Are under 18', *Guardian*, 7 October.

Wintour, P. (2015) 'Government Warns NUS to Stop Opposition to Prevent Strategy', *Guardian*, 16 September.

PART III

MEDIA EVENTS AND MEDIA DYNAMICS

9 | FROM *JYLLANDS-POSTEN* TO *CHARLIE HEBDO*: DOMESTICATING THE MOHAMMED CARTOONS

Carolina Sanchez Boe

On 30 September 2005, Danish newspaper *Morgenavisen Jyllands-Posten* published a set of political cartoons representing Prophet Mohammed. Over the next several months and years, the cartoons and stories about them circulated around the world, provoking pro- and anti-cartoon activities, more political cartoons, and reprints of some or all of the initial cartoons in various media throughout the world. In February 2006, when the cartoon controversy was 'brought home' to France with the publication of *Jyllands-Posten*'s cartoons by *France Soir*, the French media coverage was framed as a sudden outburst of disorder – "matter out of place" (Douglas 1966) – that was to be dealt with. French media producers, whether foreign correspondents, journalists or public intellectuals, offered a selective account of what had happened in Denmark, as the event was inserted into domestic debates that were already taking place in the French media well before the controversy. These narratives were appropriated by media producers and media consumers, who "recognize particular elements of texts as being shared by other texts they have seen and use this to construct particular 'readings' of these texts" (Peterson 2005: 134). As social anthropologist Mary Douglas puts it:

> In a chaos of shifting impressions, each of us constructs a stable world in which objects have recognizable shapes, are located in depth and have permanence. In perceiving we are building, taking some cues and rejecting others. The most acceptable cues are those which fit most easily into the pattern that is being built up. Ambiguous ones tend to be treated as if they harmonized with the rest of the pattern. Discordant ones tend to be rejected. *If they are accepted, the structure of assumptions has to be modified.* As learning proceeds objects are named. Their names then affect the way they are perceived next time: once labeled they are more speedily slotted into the pigeon-holes in future. (Douglas 1966: 37, emphasis added)

This chapter accounts for the ways in which media actors struggled over how to assign responsibility and over the appropriate responses that would restore order to what they had framed as a sudden, chaotic outburst of disorder. In the process, they defined the cartoon controversy by relating it to familiar patterns and common sets of assumptions, creating a simple narrative that could carry value judgements and references to other equally simple narratives, thus linking them to larger systems of meaning. It was a matter of only a week before the complexities of the original news stories about the cartoon controversy, as it had been reported by the centre-left *Le Monde* and left-wing *Libération*, were reduced to a simple narrative that accepted and even reinforced an *orthodox* discourse. This chapter analyses the competing *orthodox* and *heterodox* discourses (Bourdieu 1977) that underlay the debate on whether the cartoons should be – or should have been – published. Further, it attempts to identify the common sets of uncontested assumptions and frames of meaning behind the power struggles within the media and political fields in France which set the terms of debate and shape the ways in which media producers and consumers make sense of the world.

To publish or not to publish, the cartoons as foreign and domestic news – autumn 2005 to 8 February 2006

In autumn 2005, before the cartoons were first published in France, the French media treated the cartoon controversy as strictly international news, somewhat unrelated to domestic debates. These news articles show how foreign correspondents tend to draw on other journalists' work to contextualise and understand the news that they report. The foreign correspondents from two dailies, *Le Monde* and *Libération*, and one weekly, *L'Express*,[1] reported on the reasons why *Jyllands-Posten* had published the cartoons, and assigned responsibility for the consequences of the controversy in ways that reproduced the competing debates in Denmark over how to interpret the event (Hervik and Berg 2007; Hervik 2008). The correspondent of the centre-right *L'Express* reproduced *Jyllands-Posten*'s and the Danish Prime Minister's framing of the event as 'freedom of speech threatened by Islamists'. They assigned responsibility for the internationalisation of the crisis to eleven ambassadors to Denmark who had asked to meet with the Prime Minister of Denmark, Anders Fogh Rasmussen, and to a delegation of imams who had travelled from Denmark to the Middle

East with a portfolio containing the cartoons, arguing that they did not respect or did not understand fundamental democratic values. Both *Le Monde* and *Libération* clearly offered explanations and established responsibility in a similar fashion to the Danish daily *Politiken*: that is, by reproducing the stance of *Politiken* and notably of its editor-in-chief Tøger Seidenfaden, among others (Larsen and Seidenfaden 2006). They argued that the author Kåre Bluitgen, *Jyllands-Posten* and the Prime Minister and his spin doctors had successfully managed to stage the controversy as though it were a matter of freedom of speech when, in fact, the cartoon controversy was but one of many events where both *Jyllands-Posten* and politicians in power had acted in a deliberately provocative fashion towards the Muslim minority in Denmark. Media producers, after all, are also media consumers and tend to reproduce each other's interpretations of events, taking part in the 'circular circulation of information' observed by Bourdieu (1996: 22), and trusting the analysis offered by fellow journalists who work for newspapers that they identify as being at their end of the political spectrum.

This changed as the controversy was 'brought home' on 1 February 2006, when *France Soir*[2] republished all of *Jyllands-Posten*'s twelve cartoons, as well as a cartoon of its own making on its front page that showed Jehovah, Buddha, Mohammed and the Christian God, with the latter saying 'Don't moan Mohammed, we've all been caricatured.' As the cartoons suddenly became domestic news, journalists and editors from other French newspapers, public intellectuals and politicians as well as viewers, listeners and readers felt compelled to address their own position in favour of publishing the cartoons or not. Media producers published texts, articles, editorials and opinion pieces in which they engaged in self-referential analysis of an event that had become a story about the media, about journalists themselves (Hervik 2008; Peterson 2007: 253).

Within a few days, a field of opinions emerged that was soon to be dominated by a discourse that focused on *defending freedom of speech and protecting our civilisation*. Defenders of this orthodox discourse argued that freedom of speech is a value above all others, along with the notion of *laïcité*, or secularity, and that no special consideration should be shown towards religious minorities. An alternative, more marginal (or *heterodox*) counter-discourse argued that *freedom of speech comes with responsibilities* (Berthaut et al. 2007).[3]

Several media outlets were invested in the debate on whether it is permitted to draw the Prophet or not, according to the Qur'an (*Libération*, 5 January 2006; *Le Monde*, 30 January 2006; *Le Monde*, 2 February 2006). French journalists can rely on an already existing network of people who present themselves as being (or are believed to be) able to speak for or about France's Muslim minority. Whenever a journalist wishes to get an opinion on issues related to Islam, these actors are staged as representatives of Islam and are expected to express a 'Muslim' point of view on 'the veil', 'butchering sheep', 'forced marriage' and, in this case, 'drawing cartoons of the Prophet'. Journalists featured interviews with Muslim intellectuals and the usual experts on Islam, who gave examples of Persian miniatures of Prophet Mohammed, confirming that in 'real' – that is, intellectual – Islamic culture, there is no ban on pictures of the Prophet. These commentators distinguished between believers who do not know their own religion (simple minds who can be manipulated) and believers who do know that drawings *can* be made of the Prophet because they have a less emotional but more intellectual approach to Islam (Berthaut et al. 2007). This argument also reinforced the assumption that if Muslims were hurt by the cartoons, it was because they were angered by the ban on images of the Prophet Mohammed and not by the cartoons themselves or the context in which they had been published in Denmark or republished in France.

All papers inserted the cartoon controversy into a chronology of related events in order to legitimise or invalidate the choice of publishing the cartoons. Both opponents and proponents of publishing the cartoons engaged in "architextual practice" (Peterson 2005: 134–5), making indexical connections with other events and media texts from the past. In orthodox 'architextual practice', the cartoon controversy was staged under the headline 'Islam' and linked to a series of milestones in a 'chronology of violence', such as death threats and fatwas against cultural critique of Islam and of a certain representation of the position of women within the religion. For instance, *Libération* published an article that stated that "the Iranian fatwa against Salman Rushdie was on everybody's minds as well as the frequent tensions with religions other than Islam when the liberty to draw caricatures is at stake" (*Libération*, 4 February 2006). This allusion to recent actions by French Catholics to stop publications that they found insulting disappeared the following day when the event was contextualised with a list on 'Islam':

Islam. The Facts:

1988. A fatwa is launched by Imam Khomeini against Salman Rushdie, author of *The Satanic Verses*.

1993. A price is put on author Taslima Nasreen for her book *Shame*.

2004. Dutch filmmaker Theo van Gogh is assassinated by an Islamist after the release of his film *Submission* that denounced violence against women in the name of Islam.
(*Libération*, 4 February 2006)

Very few journalists challenged this dominant framework. Some did suggest heterodox or counter-discourses, arguing that freedom of speech and the law can conveniently be mobilised by debaters with a hidden agenda or that the press plays a part in playing groups of people against each other, whether deliberately or not. This stance was often expressed in some of the many letters to the editor published in February and March 2006 (except in *Le Figaro*) (Berthaut et al. 2007). Readers – who themselves become media producers when their letters are published – also engaged in architextual practice in order to mobilise proof of a general *Islamophobia* (Geisser 2003) in the French media. They argued that double standards apply in the media: that journalists are careful and considerate when they write about Catholics or Jews, whereas they regularly portray Muslims in France or abroad as fundamentalists and troublemakers. As a Catholic newspaper in a secular state, *La Croix*[4] tends to position itself as a defender of the cause of religious minorities generally. For instance, during the public debates that took place before the passing of the law on 'secularity and conspicuous religious symbols' in 2004, the paper defended a point of view close to that of various Muslim organisations concerning the wearing of the hijab in schools (Berthaut et al. 2007). During the cartoon controversy, the paper argued against publishing the cartoons and instead carried many contributions and letters to the editor that spoke in favour of tolerance towards religious minorities. Also, *La Croix* kept publishing all articles related to the cartoons – even after they had been published in France – in the 'International' section, as though the paper wouldn't acknowledge the event as domestic news (Berthaut et al. 2007).

Daily newspapers *Libération* and *Le Monde* chose to publish a selection of the cartoons, arguing that they wished to give their readers a chance to see what the controversy was about. Neither paper, however, decided to publish the cartoon of Mohammed wearing a bomb as a turban, taking the stance that 'with freedom of speech comes responsibilities'.

Charlie Hebdo's special issue: re-positionings in the media field – 8 February 2006

On 8 February, one week after *France Soir* initially published the cartoons, the left-wing anti-clerical satirical magazine *Charlie Hebdo* chose to publish them in a special issue, along with new cartoons and texts drawn or written by its usual contributors and editors. The front cover was a cartoon of the Prophet saying: "It's hard to be loved by fools." *Charlie Hebdo*'s editor Philippe Val stated that the paper had no choice but to publish the cartoons after the firing of *France Soir*'s editor: "The question is not whether these cartoons were good or not but whether we have the right to publish them."[5] *Charlie Hebdo* collaborator, journalist and academic Caroline Fourest established responsibility for the beginning of the cartoon controversy by reproducing *Jyllands-Posten*'s explanations, with articles such as 'Who Is after *Jyllands-Posten*?' In other words, in Fourest's framing, *Jyllands-Posten* was to be perceived as a *victim of* rather than *responsible for* the cartoon controversy.

To newspapers such as *Libération* and *Le Monde*, *France Soir* represents the sensational end of French journalism and ought not to be taken too seriously, whereas *Charlie Hebdo* is closer politically speaking to *Le Monde*'s and *Libération*'s readers. Even though both papers had initially pointed out that *France Soir* was facing major financial problems and that its choice to publish the cartoons might have been motivated by commercial reasons more than by a commitment to freedom of speech, they chose not to dwell on *Charlie Hebdo*'s possible commercial motives even though the special edition on the cartoon controversy quickly became its best-selling issue. While its normal print run was 140,000 copies, *Charlie Hebdo*, facing financial troubles, published 160,000 copies on 4 February and, when these quickly sold out, reprinted and sold an additional 400,000 copies.

Furthermore, newspapers that positioned themselves as critical of the government, such as *Libération* and *Le Monde*, were immediately faced with having to choose what stance to take in relation to the then President Jacques Chirac, who condemned the publication of the cartoons and called *Charlie Hebdo*'s special issue "a manifest provocation towards Muslims" (quoted in Berthaut et al. 2007). Chirac's stance explains why *Le Figaro*,[6] close to the government, chose not to publish the cartoons and never justified this choice with an official statement, neither in an editorial nor in an interview, even though the newspaper regularly publishes articles and letters to the editor that are both essentialising and very critical of Muslims and Islam. In what was most likely a deliberate strategy to distance their paper from the controversy, *Le Figaro*'s journalists never referred to the 'freedom of speech' frame. Like *La Croix*, *Le Figaro* chose to publish all articles related to the cartoon controversy in its international news section.

Charlie Hebdo's position in the media field and Chirac's stance pushed journalists from the left and centre-left press, notably *Le Monde* and *Libération*, largely to accept the terms of the debate set by the satirical paper and to support the republication of the cartoons. This happened only a week after both papers had explicitly distanced themselves from interpretations stressing the 'defence of freedom of expression' as the main motive behind publishing the cartoons. In the weeks that followed, however, the papers insisted on an alternative explanation to that of *Charlie Hebdo* in terms of what had really triggered the controversy in Denmark, with headlines such as 'There Is Something Racist in the State of Denmark' (*Libération*, 13 February 2006), or references to *Politiken*'s condemnation of *Jyllands-Posten*'s hypocritical attitude towards blasphemy given that the paper had previously refused to publish a cartoon of Jesus (*Le Monde*, 11 February 2006).

In the weeks and months that followed, *Charlie Hebdo* successfully staged the publication of the cartoons as a matter of defending free speech and protecting our 'civilisation'. It insisted that freedom of speech is a value, along with the notion of *laïcité*, above all others and that no special consideration should be shown towards religious minorities, thus reinforcing its previous stance during the debates on the law on secularity and conspicuous religious symbols. The paper covered the controversy as a choice between 'resistance' to self-censorship and the reintroduction of laws against blasphemy in a secular state. On 1 March 2006, *Charlie Hebdo* printed the manifesto 'Together Facing the New Totalitarianism', signed by 12 French and international public figures, among them the paper's editors, Philippe Val and Caroline Fourest, along with Ayaan Hirsi Ali, Bernard-Henri Lévy, Mehdi Mozzafari, Salman Rushdie and Taslima Nasreen. The manifesto defines Islamism as a form of totalitarianism that endangers democracy, comparing it to Fascism, Nazism and Stalinism.[7] The rhetoric of the manifesto and its association with figures such as Ali, Rushdie and Nasreen, identified as 'Muslim apostates' (Boe and Hervik 2008), made it even more difficult to argue against the republication of the cartoons.

After the cartoons controversy: an 'epidemic of self-censorship'? – post-March 2006

After the cartoon controversy had blown over in the French press, it reappeared in foreign news on Denmark or as news coverage relating to art and self-censorship. On 6 October 2006, *Le Monde* mentioned the cartoon controversy in an article arguing that 'an epidemic of self-censorship' was spreading. Between March and autumn 2006, journalists, public intellectuals and authors of letters to the editor had started referring to the cartoon controversy exclusively in terms of how Islamists were threatening freedom of speech. This de-contextualised story line (Hannerz 2004) was inserted in their architextual practice, in a chronology of allegedly similar events, mobilised as proof that cases of self-censorship were becoming more and more frequent in relation to Islam. *Jyllands-Posten*'s and the Danish Prime Minister's version of what had happened was inserted into a chronology, starting either with the Battle of Tours in 732 AD or with the fatwa against Salman Rushdie, and ending with what was presented as the latest case of self-censorship facing Islam. To quote just one of numerous examples, *Le Figaro* published an article about the cancellation of Mozart's opera *Idomeneo* in Berlin and wrote: "Since 2003, there has been the murder of Theo van Gogh, the Mohammed Cartoon Affair, and, very recently, the controversy following Pope Benedict XVI's declarations on Islam" (*Le Figaro*, 28 September 2006).

In 2006, two books and a documentary on the cartoon controversy attracted a huge amount of media attention. Both aimed to establish what had *really* happened in Denmark. French ethnographer Jeanne Favret-Saada's book (2007a) and her articles in the critical left-wing paper *Vacarme* (2006, 2007b) provided a thick contextualisation of the cartoon controversy, including an account of a hostile debate on minorities. Her situated interpretation of what had really happened originally in Denmark, however, is strikingly close to *Jyllands-Posten*'s, as suggested by the title of her book: 'How to Produce a World Crisis with Three Little Drawings'. Journalist Mohamed Sifaoui asks the same question as Fourest did in *Charlie Hebdo* – 'Who Is after Jyllands-Posten?' – in his book from 2006 and responds that Danish imams wished to create "a climate of hate against *Jyllands-Posten*" (Sifaoui 2006: 138).

A domestic affair: the court case against *Charlie Hebdo* – March 2007

Three organisations[8] had pressed charges against *Charlie Hebdo* for 'racist slurs', and during the court case in March 2007, the cartoon controversy became domestic news again. Once more, the paper's staff mobilised the explanation of what had *really* happened in Denmark as legitimisation for having chosen to publish the cartoons. *Jyllands-Posten*'s cultural editor, Flemming Rose, who had initially asked Danish cartoonists to draw cartoons of Prophet Mohammed, and journalist Mohamed Sifaoui testified in support of *Charlie Hebdo*. References to the hostile Danish debate against minorities disappeared and were replaced by a 'free speech' frame that argued that the initial publication had been justified as an act of resistance to self-censorship in the face of Islam. *Le Monde* supported *Charlie Hebdo* with headlines such as 'A Court Case from Another Age' and 'Respect of Beliefs or Manipulation by Islam?' (both 8 February 2007), while *Libération* published a special issue, 'Charlibération', in solidarity with the satirical newspaper. When *Charlie Hebdo*'s staff won the trial, editor Philippe Val called it a 'European victory', and 'revenge' for the murder of Theo van Gogh in the Netherlands, the cancellation of Mozart's *Idomeneo* by the Berlin Opera, and what he called 'a Munich attitude' (*Libération*, 23 March 2007), thus reproducing the rhetoric of an anti-totalitarian 'us' that resists 'them' – that is, '*Islamo-fascism*'.

Even though several titles had reported on some of the complexities of the Danish context in which the cartoons were originally published, they soon neglected to account for the intricacies of the original event, and the 'cartoon controversy' was elevated to a monolithic story in which details of the original event now mattered little. This de-contextualised story about the cartoons has now become the reference point for other stories, used by media producers in their architextual practice in order to express and resolve certain contradictions, whether they are about self-censorship, double standards or France's Muslim minorities. Indeed, another important change occurred between March 2006 and the court case against *Charlie Hebdo* in March 2007 in relation to media coverage of French Muslims who had criticised the publication of the cartoons.

Legitimate Muslim reactions?

In February 2006, when the cartoon controversy was 'brought home', French journalists and commentators had often emphasised that there were no violent reactions from French Muslims to the publication of the cartoons. The reactions of 'our' French Muslims – in letters to the editor, demonstrations, or the legal responses from Muslim representatives – were described as calm, moderate and democratic. The French press thus distinguished between 'bad' Muslims – backwards and irrational Muslims abroad who resort to violence when they protest – and 'good' Muslims, 'rational', modern Muslims in France, who have been educated in democracy and who accept the separation between public sphere and religion. The following editorial provides an example of this celebration of 'our' French Muslim minorities:

> It is, however, reassuring to see that the majority of Muslims in France stay calm in spite of being outraged or shocked. It is a sign of Reason gaining ground … This is *France Soir*'s battle. (Serge Faubert in *France Soir*, 4 February 2006)

This celebration of 'our' Muslim minorities against 'theirs' disappeared during the court case against *Charlie Hebdo* a year later, in March 2007. The cartoon controversy had now become a strictly domestic matter, and Muslims were distinguished as 'good' Muslims only if they actively supported *Charlie Hebdo* and free speech, whereas 'bad' Muslims were those who had pressed charges against *Charlie Hebdo* and who argued that freedom of speech is not absolute. The protesters who took *Charlie Hebdo* to court and used the legal system in order to express their discontent were accused of wishing to 'reinstate the law against blasphemy' and thus of undemocratic behaviour. This is a strong rhetorical weapon in France as it provides a reminder of undemocratic times before the French Revolution or of the culture that 'bad' Muslims have allegedly brought with them from the despotic, totalitarian regimes from which they have migrated. In this scenario, Muslims who celebrate their religion in the privacy of their homes without asking for any special treatment from the French press or French justice prove that they are integrated and, as such, that they are 'good' Muslims. In contrast, Muslims who criticised the publication of the cartoons or who supported the court case against *Charlie Hebdo* were depicted as though they did not understand the 'French tradition of satire'. In this discourse, humour and satire are linked to integration and to belonging, thus becoming essential markers of a new 'we', characterised by 'humour and democracy', in opposition to a 'them' characterised by 'dictatorship and violence', as Philippe Val argued in a debate that followed the documentary 'Why Democracy? Bloody Cartoons'[9] on the French/German TV channel Arte.[10]

Media professionals and public intellectuals who defended the publications thus successfully set their opponents in a rhetorical trap, as all resistance to, or criticism of, publication, even through democratic means such as participation in media debates or using the justice system, became proof of their lack of integration or allegiance to the French Republic – and even spread suspicion that they might support Islamic fundamentalism. This rhetorical trap has been reinforced during the past decade and continues to contribute to expose contradictions within the progressive left in France, which seems to have become only more divided on analyses of racism and Islamophobia.

Conclusion

When the debate on whether to republish the cartoons was at its height in the French press in February 2006, the French weekly magazine *L'Express* wrote that: "The bell tolls at the church of the global village. McLuhan's metaphor has become reality" (9 February 2006). To *L'Express*'s journalists, as to many other media professionals, political commentators and academics around the world, the 'cartoon crisis' was the perfect example of a global media event that, as Annabelle Sreberny discusses in her chapter, proved the existence of incommensurable cultural differences and a fundamental opposition between 'Western freedom of expression' and 'Islamic fundamentalism'. According to this reading, the 'crisis', or even the 'cartoon wars' (Howden et al. 2006; Puddington 2006), had been spurred by images and stories flowing across geographical and civilisational boundaries, unaltered, and with unexpected consequences. It could only be understood as the ultimate proof of a 'clash of civilisations' between 'the West' and 'Islam' (Peters 2007; Spencer 2007) and of the pernicious effects of Muslim immigration to Europe (Laqueur 2007).

An alternative analysis has emerged that has focused on the central role of media professionals and politicians in enhancing or even creating the 'Mohammed cartoon controversy' (Larsen and Seidenfaden 2006; Kunelius et al. 2007; Hervik 2008) and framing it as an 'imagined clash of civilisations' (Eide et al. 2008). This literature pays close attention to the ways in which images and stories get interpreted, appropriated and put to work within local contexts and is based on case studies of media coverage of the controversy in national print media in a large number of countries (Kunelius et al. 2007).

As more than a decade has passed since the initial media coverage of the cartoon controversy, this critical stance appears to have been increasingly difficult to defend in the face of a dominant reading of the controversy as symptomatic of an attack on Westerns notions of freedom of expression. For example, the Danish newspaper *Politiken*, which had been very critical of *Jyllands-Posten*'s initial publication of the cartoons (the paper's editor-in-chief had even published a book about it), chose to republish the cartoons in February 2008, some two years later.

This chapter has questioned the processes that can lead media professionals and academics to accept and even actively take part in promoting interpretations of news events that they had earlier contested, through an analysis of the domestication of the 'cartoon crisis' in the French media.[11] When foreign news coverage spoke of Denmark only, the cartoon controversy tended to be spoken of as a strictly Danish problem, somewhat unrelated to the French context, and no mention was made of the positions the French media had taken towards publishing or not. In a similar fashion, the foreign news coverage of the consequences of the cartoon controversy spoke of 'their' Muslims as violent and irrational and of 'our' Muslims as peaceful, democratic and rational – until the cartoon controversy became strictly domestic with the trial against *Charlie Hebdo*. However, when the context in which the cartoons were initially produced in Denmark and the ways in which they circulated became central as justifications in a debate for or against publishing, this had more to do with local interests and power struggles than with the events that originally triggered the cartoon controversy. Stories about how the Danish Prime Minister or *Jyllands-Posten* were defending freedom of speech were used as arguments to support a domestic orthodox discourse. It showed how the reactions to the cartoon controversy were as much an outcome of the journalists' and papers' situated positions, notably within the domestic media and political fields (Bourdieu 1996: 46–7), as they were an outcome of their individual positions in relation to the question of freedom of speech or press freedom.

When the cartoon controversy is inserted into a chronology of related events in order to legitimise or invalidate the choice of publishing the cartoons, journalists rarely select 'facts' in a vacuum, and as different actors engage in struggles to link one event to another, these contextualisations always carry value judgements. Whether the event was associated with the fatwa against Salman Rushdie or *Jyllands-Posten*'s stance in the debates on Muslim minorities in Denmark, these decisions are far from value neutral. The cartoon controversy was inserted into already existing local narratives related to issues such as the independence of the press, and to *laïcité*, religious minorities in general, and Islam in particular. They echoed and reinforced the debates on the wearing of hijabs in French state schools that had been present since the early 1980s and, most notably, the ones leading up to the passing of the law against conspicuous religious symbols in French state schools in 2004 (Berthaut et al. 2007). A decade later, in 2016, the cartoon controversy has now been inserted into new debates on the alleged irreconcilable cultural differences (Stolcke 1995) of a minority that, once again, is argued to threaten national unity.

It has become difficult, if not impossible, not to choose sides in the debates between an orthodox and a heterodox discourse. These stories about minorities that create disorder, that are "matter out of place" (Douglas 1966), are productive elements in the generation of the "fear of small numbers" (Appadurai 2006). Whether the stories point to one minority or another as problematic, and whether they adhere to the orthodox or the heterodox discourse, media producers and consumers seem time and again to tell stories about the irreconcilable cultural differences between majority and minority populations. As time passes, and mediated, de-contextualised stories such as that of the 'cartoon crisis' fade from memory, it becomes more and more difficult, although increasingly important, to question the fundamental terms of the debate.

Notes

1 *Le Monde* was founded in 1944. Politically, it is centre-left to centre-right, depending on the parties in power at the moment. *Libération* was founded in 1970, and is a left-wing newspaper. *Libération*'s opinion pages, *Rebonds*, however, publish views from very varied political standpoints. *L'Express* was founded in 1953, and is a centre-right weekly paper.

2 *France Soir* was founded in 1944, prospered during the 1950s and became the top-selling newspaper in France in 1961 with a peak circulation figure in excess of 1 million. Its last print edition was in 2011.

3 In the week following the publication of the cartoons by *France Soir*, weekly newspapers *L'Express*, *Le Nouvel Observateur* and *Courrier International* each published a selection of them, just as television stations TF1 and France 2 did.

4 *La Croix*, founded in 1880, is a Catholic newspaper.

5 Interviewed on Radio France Inter, 7 February 2006.

6 *Le Figaro* was founded in 1846 and is the oldest French newspaper published today.

7 For an analysis of the comparison between Islamism and totalitarianism, see Boe and Hervik (2008).

8 L'Union des organisations islamiques de France (Uoif), la Grande mosquée de Paris and the Muslim World League.

9 *Denmark 2007*, directed by Karsten Kjær.

10 Philippe Val, Arte, 16 October 2007.

11 This chapter draws on the analysis of published media text articles, op-eds and letters to the editor published by French print media on the cartoon controversy from September 2005 to autumn 2010. Due to limited space, I can refer only to the methodological accounts exposed in Berthaut et al. (2007) and Boe and Hervik (2008).

References

Appadurai, A. (2006) *Fear of Small Numbers. An Essay on the Geography of Anger*. Durham, NC: Duke University Press.

Berthaut, J., C. Boe, C. Hmed, S. Jouanneau and S. Laurens (2007) 'France: Should Voltaire be a Prophet in his Own Country?' in R. Kunelius, E. Eide, O. Hahn and R. Schroeder (eds) *Reading the Mohammed Cartoons Controversy: An International Analysis of Press Discourses on Free Speech and Political Spin*. Working Papers in International Journalism. Bochum/Freiberg: Projekt Verlag, pp. 53–63.

Boe, C. and P. Hervik (2008) 'Integration Through Insult?' in E. Eide, R. Kunelius and A. Phillips (eds) *Transnational Media Events: The Mohammed Cartoons and the Imagined Clash of Civilizations*. Gothenburg: Nordicom, University of Gothenburg.

Bourdieu, P. (1977) *Outline of a Theory of Practice*. Cambridge and New York: Cambridge University Press.

Bourdieu, P. (1996) *Sur la television*. Paris: Raisons d'Agir.

Douglas, M. (1996) *Purity and Danger. An Analysis of the Concepts of Pollution and Taboo*. London and New York: Routledge.

Favret-Saada, J. (2006) 'Le petit pays qui se croyait seul', *Vacarme* 36 (summer).

Favret-Saada, J. (2007a) *Comment produire une crise mondiale avec douze petits dessins*. Paris: Éditions Les prairies ordinaires.

Favret-Saada, J. (2007b) 'L'affaire des caricatures de Mahomet', *Vacarme* 38 (winter).

Geisser, V. (2003) *La nouvelle islamophobia*. Paris: Éditions la Découverte.

Hannerz, U. (2004) *Foreign News. Exploring the World of Foreign Correspondents*. Chicago, IL: University of Chicago Press.

Hervik, P. (2008) 'Original Spin and its Side Effects: Freedom of Speech as Danish New Management' in E. Eide, R. Kunelius and A. Phillips (eds) *Transnational Media Events: The Mohammed Cartoons and the*

Imagined Clash of Civilizations. Gothenburg: Nordicom, University of Gothenburg.

Hervik, P. and C. Berg (2007) 'Denmark: A Political Struggle in Danish Journalism' in R. Kunelius, E. Eide, O. Hahn and R. Schroeder (eds) *Reading the Mohammed Cartoons Controversy: An International Analysis of Press Discourses on Free Speech and Political Spin.* Working Papers in International Journalism. Bochum/Freiberg: Projekt Verlag, pp. 25–39.

Howden, D., D. Hardaker and S. Castle (2006) 'How a Meeting of Leaders in Mecca Set off the Cartoon Wars around the World', *Independent*, 10 February. www.independent.co.uk/news/world/middle-east/how-a-meeting-of-leaders-in-mecca-set-off-the-cartoon-wars-around-the-world-6109473.html (accessed 3 February 2011).

Kunelius, R., E. Eide, O. Hahn and R. Schroeder (eds) (2007) *Reading the Mohammed Cartoons Controversy: An International Analysis of Press Discourses on Free Speech and Political Spin.* Working Papers in International Journalism. Bochum/Freiberg: Projekt Verlag.

Laqueur, W. (2007) *The Last Days of Europe: Epitaph for an Old Continent.* New York: Thomas Dunne Books.

Larsen, E. R. and T. Seidenfaden (2006) *Karikatur Krisen. En undersøgelse af baggrund og ansvar.* Copenhagen: Gyldendal.

Peters, R. (2007) *Wars of Blood and Faith.* Mechanicsburg, PA: Stackpole Books.

Peterson, M. A. (2005) 'Performing Media' in E. W. Rothenbuhler and M. Coman (eds) *Media Anthropology.* Thousand Oaks, CA: Sage Publications.

Peterson, M. A. (2007) 'Making Global News: "Freedom of Speech" and "Muslim Rage"', *Contemporary Islam* 1: 247–64.

Puddington, A. (2006) 'Freedom of Expression after the "Cartoon Wars"', Freedom House. www.freedomhouse.org/template.cfm?page=131&year=2006&essay=24 (accessed 3 February 2011).

Sifaoui, M. (2006) *L'affaire des caricatures. Dessins et manipulations.* Paris: Éditions Privé.

Spencer, R. (2007) *Religion of Peace?: Why Christianity Is and Islam Isn't.* Washington, DC: Regnery Publishing.

Stolcke, V. (1995) 'Talking Culture: New Boundaries, New Rhetorics of Exclusion in Europe', *Anthropology* 36 (1): 1–24. Special Issue: 'Ethnographic Authority and Cultural Explanation'.

10 | #JESUISCHARLIE, #JENESUISPASCHARLIE AND AD HOC PUBLICS

Simon Dawes

Introduction

The attack at the offices of *Charlie Hebdo* on 7 January 2015 happened at about 11.30am local time. At 12.52pm, Joachim Roncin, a designer and journalist who lived in the neighbourhood, posted a tweet on his @joachimroncin Twitter profile featuring an image with the words 'JE SUIS CHARLIE' written in white and grey letters on a black background in a typography that called to mind that of the magazine's logo. By 22.50 his tweet had been favourited 500 times; by 8.33 the following morning, more than 1,000 times.

Meanwhile, from 12.59 onwards, just 7 minutes after Roncin's original tweet, the hashtag #JeSuisCharlie began to circulate – sometimes with, sometimes without the image. By 21.30, it was being tweeted 6,500 times a minute; in one day, the hashtag was used 3.4 million times; in less than a week it was used more than 5 million times. Both slogan and image were appropriated and transformed: 'JE SUIS – POLICIER, JUIF, MUSULMAN, CHRETIEN, ATHEE, FRANÇAIS, CITOYEN DU MONDE'. The morning after the attack, the front page of *Libération*, the French left-wing newspaper, declared simply 'NOUS SOMMES TOUS CHARLIE'. Roncin's image and adaptations of it were used as avatars on Facebook and Twitter, and, on the evening of the attack and during the Republican march the following weekend, variations were chanted and displayed on banners. The rapidity with which the 'JE SUIS CHARLIE' slogan flowed over from social media onto the streets and into the mainstream media framing of the event elevated the status of the slogan to that of the emotive symbol of national unity (Badouard 2016).

Beneath the façade of unanimous solidarity with Charlie, however, discordant voices sought to make themselves heard to say that, although they also condemned the attacks, they were not Charlie. It took several days for traditional French media to even acknowledge this polyphony and question the reasons for it. The opposite was the case online, however, as the #JeNeSuisPasCharlie hashtag (and equivalents), as well as Facebook groups and blogposts, were heard instantaneously (Badouard 2016). Although the popularity of the #JeNeSuisPasCharlie hashtag was nowhere near as great as #JeSuisCharlie – being tweeted 'only' 74,000 times in the days following the attacks (Giglietto and Lee 2015) – its virality nevertheless also constituted it as a trending topic. When the mainstream media did eventually pick up on the phenomenon, it was to denounce 'apologies for terrorism', making little attempt to distinguish between those condemning and those celebrating the attacks through their diversion from the dominant frame. And when effort was made to give voice to those who were clearly condemning the violence but nevertheless saying that they were not Charlie, it was to try to understand why so many (young) people did not 'share Republican values' or 'believe in free speech'.

The hostility towards (and perhaps genuine incomprehension of) alternative frames was echoed in elements of the French media's reactions to open letters from left-wing academics condemning the hypocrisy of the Republican march, and to the Anglo-Saxon media's internal debates on whether or not to reprint images from *Charlie Hebdo*. The political and journalistic focus, for perhaps understandable reasons, has been to insist on 'national unity' in the face of recurrent acts of mass violence. But as well as the obvious risks of such a strategy being used to suppress any criticism of the government or security forces, or of the open-ended state of emergency and proposed surveillance measures, the insistence on national unity has also diverted attention away from sociological inquiry into the backgrounds of the assailants and debates on social inequality in France. In Republican and laic France, generally, national unity is invoked by the mainstream media at the expense of recognising difference between ethnic communities within the French citizenry. In the particular case of the aftermath of the murder of the editors of *Charlie Hebdo*, the framing of national unity in terms of identification with a magazine that many people find offensive – and holding up the magazine as a symbol of free speech when many see it as synonymous with the stigmatisation of the Muslim community – ignores the feelings and opinions of a large minority of the population and promotes a highly selective interpretation of free speech.

While I have addressed elsewhere the differences between free speech and counter-speech, and between French- and English-language mainstream media framing of this event (Dawes 2015a, 2015b, 2015c), this chapter focuses on the viral and memetic spread of the #JeSuisCharlie and #JeNeSuisPasCharlie hashtags. Considering the extent to which use of the latter hashtag contributed to a subversion of the dominant media frame and an expression of the voice of a marginalised community, the chapter also discusses the extent to which these Twitter discussions can be considered in terms of the emotive and value-driven identity-building of 'hashtag communities', as well as their significance for public discourse and media participation. In the first part, I discuss the wider literature on the general emergence of such communities and the role of social media in their formation. In the second, I turn to recent analyses of the Twitter data that has been collated post-Charlie.

Hashtags, hashtag communities and ad hoc publics

In the days and weeks after the shootings at the offices of *Charlie Hebdo*, both #JeSuisCharlie and #JeNeSuisPasCharlie hashtags constituted trending topics, which is to say that they were discussions on Twitter that were simultaneously dense (lots of tweets) and viral (rapidly propagating) (Badouard 2016). As well as going viral, however, they were also memetic. Although internet virals and memes tended to be conflated in early social media research, a distinction has more recently been made between virals – which comprise a single cultural unit that propagates in many copies – and memes – which are better understood as collections of texts that function as part of remix and participatory culture (Shifman 2014). Although memes share common characteristics of content and form, they are circulated, imitated and/or transformed – sometimes parodied – via the internet by many users. Memes, and in this case the diverse variations on the model of the original #JeSuisCharlie hashtag and typography, may subvert dominant media messages or have implications for identity-building, public discourse and commentary in a participatory media environment (Huntington 2013). As such, it is important to analyse memes as socio-cultural practices of creation and sharing that are embedded within and beyond digital culture (Shifman 2014).

Social media offer opportunities to people, opinions and feelings that are otherwise hardly visible in the public sphere – for instance, even though Islam is a recurrent theme in French media, Muslim voices are largely absent from such debates (Badouard 2016). The differences between the mainstream media framing of post-Charlie France, on the one hand, and the discussions and debate that were taking place on social media, on the other, prompt us to consider how dominant media frames privilege and legitimise certain perspectives, and marginalise and delegitimise others. They also prompt us to analyse the forms of political participation that are unique to social media, wherein opinion flows and collective actions are often made through informal and everyday discussions on a relatively more horizontal plain (ibid.). The 'social' part of social media refers to its distinction from 'traditional' media (Murthy 2011, 2012), and its capacity to facilitate social interaction, collaboration and the sharing of digital media. Social *networks* provide one way of disseminating information through social *media*. Within social networks – that is, web services that enable users to maintain a "public or semi-public profile within a bounded system" and through which they can "articulate a list of other users with whom they share a connection" (boyd and Ellison 2007) – 'ordinary' people in ordinary social networks (as opposed to professional journalists, for example) can create user-generated 'news' (Murthy 2011, 2012) which they can share among their respective networks. One way of disseminating news through social media beyond one's own social networks is to use hashtags.

There is no limit or classification system for Twitter hashtags. Like many Twitter innovations, they are a user-led innovation, developing as ad hoc 'channels' out of user requests for 'groups' based on interests or relationships (Bruns and Burgess 2011). Because discussions on Twitter are speedy and unstructured, hashtags are necessary for organisational purposes (Giglietto and Lee 2015). They are commonly used to keep up with media events and spectacles (#royalwedding), for which original tweets are more likely, and crises and emergency events (#tsunami), for which retweets and the inclusion of URLs are more common (ibid.). They are also used for contributions to contemporary political developments (#Brexit) and for commentary on popular television programmes (#GameofThrones), to coordinate emergency relief (#SandyHelp) and even to form ad hoc issue publics (#imwithcorbyn) (Bruns and Burgess 2011).

Twitter hashtags enable the indexing and collation of disparate tweets under the same topic, thus structuring discussion between isolated users on a particular subject (Badouard 2016). Prefixing short keywords with the hash symbol '#' is a means of coordinating a distributed discussion between more or less large groups of users who are not connected through existing 'follower' networks. Specific hashtags are visible not only to the user's own followers, but also to anyone else following the hashtag conversation (Bruns and Burgess 2011), and retweets of material from the hashtag conversation, or the addition of the hashtag to other (re)tweets, are also visible to the conversation-follower network. As well as enabling diverse and subtle uses of information within a limited textual space (currently 140 characters per tweet), the hashtag thus constitutes the insertion of the text into a much greater *con*text (Merzeau 2015). To say #JeNeSuisPasCharlie, therefore, is not just to declare as such to your own networks, but to participate in a much larger conversation with others to which you are not otherwise connected.

As shared conversation markers, hashtags are useful and even essential for organising and participating in such discussions and as part of such networks (Bruns 2008). But hashtags can be much more than simply conversation markers; they can also perform as discursive devices, facilitating the construction of self- and collective identity. Those who use the hashtag become not just participants in the hashtag conversation but also temporary members of the 'hashtag community', with the potential to act as a bridge between this community and their own follower network (Bruns and Burgess 2011). By rendering such conversations searchable, hashtagging enables users to connect with an impermanent community by bonding around evolving topics of interest (Zappavigna 2011) and collectively producing shared values and understandings (Rieder 2012).

They can even be useful for structuring *connective*, if not *collective*, action (Bennett and Segerber 2012). The logic of connective action applies increasingly to life in late-/reflexive-/liquid-/post-modern socie-ties (Maffesoli 1996; Bauman 2000; Beck and Beck-Gernsheim 2002), in which formal organisations are losing their grip on individuals, and group ties are being replaced by large-scale, fluid social networks (Cas-tells 2000). These networks are particularly suited to the organisational processes of social media such as hashtag conversations, and their logic does not require strong organisational control or even the symbolic con-struction of a united 'we' (Bennett and Segerber 2012). While there is evidence of both homophily and polarisation in hashtag-based discus-sions (Giglietto and Lee 2015), a tendency has been noted for people to participate increasingly through large-scale personal expressions of identity, which can be accommodated on multiple layers within social media-based discussions (ibid.). The individual expressions of emotional response to the dominant and exclusionary frame of #JeSuisCharlie, for example, enabled the formation of a 'weak tie' network (Granovetter 1973) typical of individualised societies. Such networks are more inclusive than common group or ideological identifications, and less purposeful than a desire for public action or to contribute to a common good, which becomes an act of personal expression, recognition or self-validation (#JeNeSuisPasCharlie), accomplished by the sharing of ideas and feelings (justifications for not being Charlie) and the making of a connection (Bennett and Segerber 2012).

Rather than a fragmented society composed of isolated individuals, Bruns has argued that what we see emerging is more "a patchwork of overlapping public spheres centred around specific themes and communities". This 'network of issue publics' replaces the conventional, normative and universal public sphere of the mass media age, which becomes just one among many other such public spheres (Bruns 2008: 69; Ratinaud and Smyrnaios 2015). Normally, issue publics form only *post hoc*: some time after the fact. In contrast to many other such issue publics, however, Twitter hashtag communities can respond with great speed to emerging issues and events, and so issue publics can indeed form virtually *ad hoc* (Bruns and Burgess 2011). Although limited in time and dependent upon the engagement of a transient and ad hoc public (Ratinaud and Smyrnaios 2015), civic engagement through digital media participation is nevertheless a symbolically empowering, legitimising mechanism, which can contribute to the agenda-building process of public issue formation (Bucy and Gregson 2001).

Such ad hoc publics can be said to have emerged in the moments following the January 2015 attacks on the editors of *Charlie Hebdo* (Ratinaud and Smyrnaios 2015). Whereas an initial public (#JeSuisCharlie) developed around an emotive and reactionary defence of free speech, another public (#JeNeSuisPasCharlie) was formed in direct response to the first, and to the dominant media framing of the event in terms of an attack on universal free speech. Far from a rejection of free speech or other 'Republican' values, this equally emotive and reactionary public developed around a debate on the limits of free speech, and, in part, gave expression to a sense of voicelessness for the Muslim community in the French public sphere.

#JeSuisCharlie and #JeNeSuisPasCharlie

In contrast to the initial dismissiveness of some intellectuals towards the 'semantic poverty' and 'political vacuity' of the slogan 'Je Suis Charlie', it responded to, opposed and resisted the violence of the attacks through what was essentially an *emotive* expression (Merzeau 2015). More than just an expression of facile empathy in a victimised register, however, it was also a vector of *identity* construction that was simultaneously individual and collective (Badouard 2016).

The formulation had its precedents, of course, such as 'We are all Khaled Said' (the name of a Facebook page created as a memorial to a man brutally killed in police custody, and which helped incite the Egyptian Revolution of 2011). The popularity in France of the first name Charlie may also have helped encourage an emotional identification (Badouard 2016). According to Roncin himself, the word 'Je' offered a vehicle through which each individual could express themselves in terms of threats to freedom and tolerance (Giglietto and Lee 2015). Others have suggested that the 'Je Suis' element, tapping into a desire for self-reference, encouraged not only the viral sharing but also the memetic appropriation and modification of the slogan (Merzeau 2015).

Enabling users to express emotion in the first person has a transformative dimension on people's perception of their world and of their influence and possibility of action within it (Badouard 2016). The use of the first person corresponds to the way in which opinion movements and collective actions are structured online, presenting individual and collective dimensions simultaneously. By spontaneously adopting the slogan, thousands of people gave body to a collectivity, a mark of recognition and a rallying cry, which developed from pathos to a collective ethos (Merzeau 2015).

In the traditional media, three distinct phases could clearly be discerned: live news for the first few days; national emotion during the weekend of the Republican march; then debate the week after (Badouard 2016). On social media, some diagnosed similarly distinct phases, with initial interventions focused on the real-time description of unfolding events, before successive stages of indignation, homage, commentary, debate and polemic (Ratinaud and Smyrnaios 2015), while others have emphasised how online debate tended to be mixed with news, and how emotional expression tended to be accompanied by the taking of a particular position, and all of this immediately after the attack. This may be partly explained by the tendency for different registers of expression – opinion, analysis and emotion – to be used simultaneously on social media (Badouard 2016).

Contrary to the dominant discourse of identification with Charlie, however, a counter-discourse developed that explicitly countered it (Giglietto and Lee 2015). Among the initial tweets were indeed those celebrating the attacks – #cheh ('well done' in Arab) – and identifying themselves with the assailants rather than with the victims – #JeSuisKouachi, for instance, was used 49,000 times on the day of the attack alone, meaning that it too became a trending topic. However, the majority of these occurrences were not from those expressing a simple and literal message of support, but from those raising attention to the existence of the hashtag in order to condemn it, and by those from the far right manipulating it to strategically exaggerate the level of support for terrorism among the Muslim community in France (Badouard 2016). Of these tweets, a smaller (though significant) number – 3,700 – were identified by police as warranting investigation for 'apology for terrorism'. Other slogans such as '#JeSuisAhmed' (in reference to the police officer killed the same day as the editors) or controversial (and allegedly anti-Semitic) comedian Dieudonné's 'Je me sens comme charliecoulibaly' (juxtaposing the controversial but socially acceptable satire of Charlie with the murder of Jewish people) were also singled out as potentially celebratory of the attacks, although their occurrence alone is perhaps more ambiguous than obviously offensive. Indeed, 76.5 per cent of those tweeting #JeSuisAhmed also mentioned #JeSuisCharlie (An et al. 2016). Similarly, conspiracy theories doubting the official versions of events were also popular, but a mix of seemingly sincere uses and those being apparently ironic makes it again difficult to use the number of tweets as evidence of widespread support for terrorism (Badouard 2016).

Distinct from such counter-discourses, however, were those that included variations of 'Je Ne Suis Pas Charlie' in their tweets, condemning the attacks but distancing themselves from the magazine, and often seeking to justify their reasons for doing so. Among these tweets, Badouard (2016) distinguishes between three main categories. First, and most numerous, were those from a broadly left-wing, critical position. Within this category were criticisms of the façade of national unity and the hypocrisy of those who had never read or supported the magazine before, of the hypocrisy of the march for the presence of controversial world leaders, of the threat of reactionary surveillance and security measures, as well as of the stigmatisation of Muslims in the name of free speech. Secondly, there was a mixture of conservative voices, ranging from Catholic to the far right, and sharing an ideological critique of the magazine for incarnating the 1968 generation of anarchist and libertarian criticisms of traditionally French values, such as family and religion. And thirdly, and least numerous, were those self-identifying as Muslim and criticising Islamophobia in France, the exclusion of Muslims from the public sphere, the selective value of free speech and the double standards applied to Muslims and those criticising Muslims, as well as pleading for the recognition of the right to be offended. Badouard identifies a number of French and Belgian intellectuals (and foreign politicians) speaking on behalf of the Muslim community, but no French politicians.

Because of the inherent risk involved of being viewed as opposing accepted social norms and endorsing violence, many users accompanied the hashtag with a justification for doing so. While the uses of this hashtag also changed over time – from condolences with reservation about the mainstream frame, through resistance against that frame, to proposals for alternative frames (such as hate speech, Eurocentrism or Islamophobia) – they shared in common a desire to debate free speech and its contested limits (Giglietto and Lee 2015). On the '#JeNeSuisPasCharlie' Facebook group (with over 40,000 members joining in the weeks following the attacks), Badouard notes that criticism of the magazine was rare and that most posts were about affirming a Muslim identity suffering from discrimination in the French public sphere, with the 'JeSuisCharlie' slogan seen as exclusionary and as an injunction. Badouard also notes the tone of victimisation, powerlessness and fatalism in the posts: that is, the complete absence of any call for mobilisation or collective action, and merely the intention to socialise around a shared experience, with the expression of mutual suffering constituting the cement that bound the community.

The members of the #JeNeSuisPasCharlie hashtag community did not speak with one voice or one call for action. Rather, participants in the conversation sought to express and formulate their shared reaction to the dominant frame. Some spoke as Muslims, others on behalf of Muslims, and others distanced themselves from the magazine for reasons that had nothing to do with communitarianism, let alone a rejection of Republican values. The hashtag was not about support for terrorism or collective action; rather, its primary goal was for users to form, enhance and declare their self-identity, with the hashtag serving as a vehicle through which a collective identity could be developed by distinction (Giglietto and Lee 2015). It was a discursive device, rather than just a conversation marker, which facilitated the declaration of self-identity and the heterogeneous construction of the collective identities of the hashtag community. Further, through the performance of connective action, and the mixture of emotion and opinion, it helped form an ad hoc issue public around the broad theme of free speech and its limits immediately following the attack on the editors of *Charlie Hebdo*.

The opposition between the #JeSuisCharlie and #JeNeSuisPasCharlie hashtags is, therefore, mostly artificial, illustrating less a polarisation of public debate than the formation of different issue publics, between those arguing for free speech and those offended by the dominant editorial framing of the event (Badouard 2016; Merzeau 2015).

Conclusion

Considering recent analyses of the Twitter data collated post-Charlie in light of the wider literature on ad hoc issue publics and hashtag communities goes some way to help us understand the causes and effects of the viral spread and memetic appropriation of the hashtags. Approaching the #JeSuisCharlie and #JeNeSuisPasCharlie hashtags as discursive devices as well as conversation markers, we can start to make sense of how the large-scale, emotional responses were significant for personal expression, recognition and self-validation, for the sharing of ideas and feelings, and for the collective production of shared values and understandings. And although both hashtags were used emotively and often in a victimised register, they were also significant for self- and collective-identity construction. The socialisation around this shared experience of victimisation demonstrated that users were not just participants in their respective hashtag conversations, but also temporary members of their 'hashtag communities'.

It is also important to note that use of the #JeNeSuisPasCharlie hashtag was in most cases not associated with criticism of the magazine itself, but with criticism of the slogan 'Je Suis Charlie' and, therefore, with the dominant media framing of the event. That the event should have been framed in this way, and that the frame should have generated such a reaction, is symptomatic of both the Republican and laic emphasis adopted by dominant French media, and the perception among some members of the public that this emphasis is exclusionary. Users' justifications for using the hashtag helped to legitimate their dis-identification from Charlie, as well as to empower the community to give voice to that dis-identification and raise attention to their exclusion from the dominant public sphere.

The differences between the mainstream media frame and the debates on social media illustrate the privileging and legitimisation of solidarity with Charlie, and the concomitant marginalisation and de-legitimisation of dis-identification from Charlie. That some of the tweets may have been offensive, and that most were emotive, does nothing to reduce their significance for raising awareness of the stigmatisation of Muslims in the French media and their lack of voice in the public sphere, as well as of the vacuity of the presumption of national unity.

References

An, J., H. Kwak, Y. Mejova, S. A. Saenz de Oger and B. Gomez Fortes (2016) 'Are You Charlie or Ahmed? Cultural Pluralism in Charlie Hebdo Response on Twitter'. Paper presented at the International Association for the Advancement of Artificial Intelligence (AAAI) Conference on Web and Social Media (ICWSM), Cologne, 17–20 May. http://arxiv.org/abs/1603.00646.

Badouard, R. (2016) '"Je ne suis pas Charlie": Pluralité des prises de parole sur le web et les réseaux sociaux' in P. Lefébure and C. Sécail (eds) *Le défi Charlie: Les médias à l'épreuve des attentats*. Paris: Lemieux Éditeur.

Bauman, Z. (2000) *Liquid Modernity*. Cambridge: Polity Press.

Beck, U. and E. Beck-Gernsheim (2002) *Individualization*. London: Sage.

Bennett, W. L. and A. Segerber (2012) 'The Logic of Connective Action', *Information, Communication and Society* 15 (5): 739–68.

boyd, d. and N. B. Ellison (2007) 'Social Network Sites: Definition, History, and Scholarship', *Journal of Computer-Mediated Communication* 13 (2): 210–30.

Bruns, A. (2008) 'Life beyond the Public Sphere: Towards a Networked Model for Political Deliberation', *Information Polity* 13 (1–2): 65–79.

Bruns, A. and J. E. Burgess (2011) 'The Use of Twitter Hashtags in the Formation of ad hoc Publics'. Proceedings of the 6th European Consortium for Political Research (ECPR) General Conference, University of Iceland, Reykjavik.

Bucy, E. P. and K. S. Gregson (2001) 'Media Participation: A Legitimizing Mechanism of Mass Democracy', *New Media and Society* 3 (3): 357–80.

Castells, M. (2000) *The Rise of the Network Society*. Oxford: Blackwell.

Dawes, S. (2015a) '*Charlie Hebdo*: Free Speech, But Not as an Absolute Value', openDemocracy, 9 January. www.opendemocracy.net/can-europe-make-it/simon-dawes/charlie-hebdo-free-speech-but-not-as-absolute-value.

Dawes, S. (2015b) '*Charlie Hebdo* and the Right to Offend', openDemocracy, 21 January. www.opendemocracy.net/can-europe-make-it/simon-dawes/charlie-hebdo-and-right-to-offend.

Dawes, S. (2015c) *'Charlie Hebdo*, Free Speech and Counter-Speech', *Sociological Research Online* 20 (3): 3.

Giglietto, F. and Y. Lee (2015) 'To Be or Not to Be Charlie: Twitter Hashtags as a Discourse and Counterdiscourse in the Aftermath of the 2015 Charlie Hebdo Shooting in France'. Workshop on Making Sense of Microposts at the 24th International World Wide Web Conference.

Granovetter, M. (1973) 'The Strength of Weak Ties', *American Journal of Sociology* 78 (6): 1360–80.

Huntington, H. E. (2013) 'Subversive Memes: Internet Memes as a Form of Visual Rhetoric, *Selected Papers of Internet Research 14*. http://spir.aoir.org/index. php/spir/article/view/785.

Maffesoli, M. (1996) *The Time of the Tribes: The Decline of Individualism in Mass Society*. London: Sage.

Merzeau, L. (2015) '#jesuisCharlie, ou le médium identité', *Médium 43*.

Murthy, D. (2011) 'Twitter: Microphone for the Masses?', *Media, Culture and Society* 33 (5): 779–89.

Murthy, D. (2012) 'Towards a Sociological Understanding of Social Media: Theorizing Twitter', *Sociology* 44 (6): 1059–73.

Ratinaud, P. and N. Smyrnaios (2015) 'Une méthode pour articuler analyse des réseaux et des discours sur Twitter autour des controverses politiques: la web sphère de #CharlieHebdo'. Congrès AFSP Aix 2015, Les appropriations méthodologiques d'internet dans la recherche sur des objets politiques.

Rieder, B. (2012) 'The Refraction Chamber: Twitter as Sphere and Network', *First Monday* 17 (11), 5 November. www.firstmonday.dk/ojs/index. php/fm/article/view/4199/3359.

Shifman, L. (2014) *Memes in Digital Culture*. Cambridge, MA: MIT Press.

Zappavigna, M. (2011) 'Ambient Affiliation: A Linguistic Perspective on Twitter', *New Media & Society* 13 (5): 788–806.

11 | MEDIATED NARRATIVES AS COMPETING HISTORIES OF THE PRESENT

Annabelle Sreberny

Introduction

Historical narratives often congeal into accepted versions of events, especially within specific national contexts. Media play an important role in writing the history of the present, ventriloquising the positions of politicians and commentators as well as setting their own agendas. But global competition for hegemonic dominance in contemporary life means that any version of events often has many interlocutors and contrary expositors. On occasion the media become over-fascinated with specific moments, what media analysts have called 'media events' (see below), that operate along their own distinctive logics.

Both developments risk taking us away from a comprehensive analysis of political representation and into an unhelpful competition over whose historical narrative gains most traction. Analysis of discrete moments actually renders analysis impossible. Singular 'events' exist in a continuous present and have no background, no precursors, no cause or causes, no repercussions. By exploring the example of Charlie Hebdo as a global 'event chain', we can see the manner in which a range of narratives and diverse actors become involved in contemporary historical explanation.[1] Furthermore, by ending with the French panic about the burkini in spring 2016, we can see how the political practice of one nationally dominant narrative becomes perverted into quite its opposite – a classic *enantiodromia*, as Jung via Heraclitus would have it.

It is not only mediated news content that repeats well-worn themes in minor variations, producing a news day that is always different yet somehow the same. Academic research produces long and deep furrows of repeating themes, often until the lifeblood has drained from the initial interesting concern. It is important to maintain a double critique of the 'eventisation' of news by the media *and* the 'media eventisation' discourse of academic labour (ironically, of which this volume is an example?), both of which obscure the processes of narrativising history and the competition for historical hegemony that is now often staged on a global platform. My reading of the 'event chain' that was Charlie Hebdo tries to expand these arguments.

A brief note on the 'media events' discourse

Dayan and Katz (1992) coined the term 'media events' as a way of describing live television coverage of officially planned events (royal weddings, Olympic games, etc.). They suggested that such events provide unifying, celebratory and sometimes even worldwide coverage and thus have an integrative function, binding both national and transnational populations together as a live audience. As more violent, unplanned events such as 9/11 and the Asian tsunami came to dominate television screens, a different discourse grew. Liebes (1998) spoke of mediated 'disaster marathons' and Kellner (2004) argued that 9/11 was a 'terrorist media event'. Katz and Liebes recognised that ceremonial events were challenged by the power of unanticipated negative 'disruptive events' and began to suggest that the disaster marathons of terror, natural disaster and war also meant a loss of control over how these events could be staged, being 'co-productions' between – using their terms – broadcasters and perpetrators, God and the enemy (2007: 164).

More recently, the 'media event' focus has become explicitly internationalised. In their volume on the Danish cartoon controversy, Eide, Kunelius and Phillips (2008) explored further the increasingly 'global' nature of some media events and suggested that "in the case of transnational media events, the national frames of domestication ... are challenged in new and sometimes shocking [*sic*] ways". Hepp and Couldry (2010: 1) want "to establish the basis for researching media events today as an important aspect of power processes in a 'global age'", suggesting that

> media events are certain situated, thickened, centering performances of mediated communication that are focused on a specific thematic core, cross different media products and reach a wide and diverse multiplicity of audiences and participants. (Hepp and Couldry 2010: 12)

Yet if such events are to be seen in the context of 'an increasingly globalized world' (ibid.: 8) of numerous cultural environments, it is frankly impossible to expect there to be shared meaning, and it is naive to be 'shocked' by different responses. Notions of 'thickening' and of 'centring' suggests an agglomerative process towards a core of agreement and shared beliefs and do not leave much room for contestation and disagreement at either national or international levels. And 'reaching' people suggests a rather passive notion of audiences, not fully belied by the invocation of 'participants', while the diffusion of social media to many different geographic regions has radically expanded people's power to create and distribute their own varied visual and aural responses to reported events on a potentially huge scale.

News media are all about 'event-ness', giving some current daily happenings more worth and attention than others. Even the same phenomenon attracts differential attention when it happens in different places. An obvious recent example would be the huge coverage given to Hurricane Sandy when it hit New York in 2012 compared with the limited attention paid to Hurricane Matthew when it devastated Haiti in 2016. For media analysts to fall so readily into the same trap of selective discussion is worrying. History is written backwards; historians working hard to make sense of past 'events' offer a timeline and a suggested analytic, sometimes causal, sequence that links discrete occurrences. In the mix of mediated narratives in which we currently live can be seen the workings of contemporary history, attempts by those with definitional power to claim their narrative, to fix in the present the meaning of events. And we see how these narratives are challenged, rebutted, overturned.

In January 2015, Charlie Hebdo was a massive international media spectacle. It not only exerted a gravitational pull that blacked out other news stories which on another day would have made headlines but also seemed to demand a response from everyone. It is the media that names 'events' as such, elevating them out of the flow of everyday life. Hence, where there is no media there is no event. This bears repeating and reveals the ongoing imbalanced political economy of news-gathering. During those same few days, over 2,000 people were massacred in Baga, Northern Nigeria. But given the absence of both domestic and international journalists, in part due to access and safety issues and because of an endemic shortage of resources to cover and lack of interest in 'developing world' stories, the world did not hear this story. Only when an NGO, Amnesty International, released its own satellite imagery did we have any sense of the scale and horror of this 'event' (Amnesty International 2015).

But beyond this general news imbalance, the claim about the discreteness and singularity of Charlie Hebdo is part of the problem. If negative media events such as terror, natural disasters and wars have "become established genres on mainstream television", as Katz and Liebes suggest (2007: 135), then each moment is itself part of a lineage of similar events covered in a similar manner by big media. That lineage can be quite long or rather short, or probably a mix of both, as I try to explore now.

Charlie Hebdo as part of an 'event chain'

Media studies is implicated in a form of contemporary historical analysis that sees and identifies global linkages between 'moments'. Indeed, on the first page of the first iteration of their argument, Dayan and Katz (1992: vii) ventriloquise the anticipated reaction to their idea:

> The live broadcasting of history? Don't they know that history is process, not events? Certainly not ceremonial events! Don't they know that media events are hegemonic manipulations?

It is a pity that, with the 'media events' approach that subsequently crystallised with its intense focus on discrete and singular 'events', broader ideas about what constitutes history and how historical narratives get written have been lost. The 'media' offer their historical narratives of an event and proffer the narrativisations of others, while inviting responses, indeed challenges, to yet other discourses. The theoretical imperative to understand history as a set of competing narratives that draw events together in chains resonates with Laclau and Mouffe's (1985: 105) account of articulation:

> We will call articulation any practice establishing a relation among elements such that their identity is modified as a result of the articulatory practice. The structured totality resulting from the articulatory practice, we will call discourse. The differential positions, insofar as they appear articulated within a discourse, we will call moments. By contrast, we will call element any difference that is not discursively articulated.

One implication is the need to think about Charlie Hebdo and other such major mediated stories not as a singular event but as a chain of events, the 'event chain'. I will try to distinguish the immediate event chain, since Hebdo was not a singular happening but a set, and a longer event chain, where historical narratives compete for explanation, motivation, rationalisation, justification.

Mid-morning on 7 January 2015, two jihadist terrorists armed with assault rifles and other weapons forced their way into the offices of the French satirical weekly newspaper *Charlie Hebdo* in Paris, firing many shots and initially killing eleven people and injuring eleven others during their attack. This act seems to have been triggered by the publication of a cartoon of the Prophet Mohammed on a recent *Hebdo* cover.[2] The gunmen identified themselves as belonging to Al Qaeda's branch in Yemen, which took responsibility for the attack. Very rapidly indeed, a response of 'Je Suis Charlie' spread across a large swathe of Facebook, colouring it black. French media were rapidly on the scene and actually filmed live the shooting of a French National Police officer as he encountered the gunmen as they left the building.

After the initial attack, France raised its Vigipirate terror alert to its highest level and deployed soldiers in Île-de-France and Picardy. On 9 January 2015, the suspects, brothers Saïd and Chérif Kouachi, who had taken hostages at a signage company in Dammartin-en-Goële, were found by police and were shot and killed when they emerged firing from the building. Coulibaly, another of the gunmen, also shot a police officer on 8 January; the next day he took and killed hostages at a kosher supermarket near the Porte de Vincennes, later being shot himself by police. Both these related 'events' were televised live in France, leading to considerable debate about the purpose and utility of such live coverage. Live-ness is central to the original 'media events' argument that a globalised audience is synchronously constituted through its television watching. In this case, the specifics of live-ness perhaps matter less than the sense of an unfolding event chain that is occurring in real time, even if on 'our' non-French experiential periphery. The terrible refugee crises of the summer of 2015 and 2016 have been presented by the media in a similar interrupted but ongoing manner.

The attacks of the first few days killed a total of seventeen people, in addition to the three perpetrators of the attack, and wounded twenty-two others. A fifth shooting attack did not result in any fatalities. Numerous smaller incidents of Islamophobic attacks, including on mosques, were reported. So even the initial singular 'event' was itself more like a series of events.

Yet after the first few days of the event itself, further events in its event chain developed. On 11 January, about 2 million people, including more than forty world leaders, met in Paris for what was invoked by President Hollande as a French 'rally of national unity'. Another 3.7 million people joined demonstrations across France. The phrase 'Je Suis Charlie' became a common slogan at the rallies and across social media.[3] Numerous world leaders turned up in Paris in support of press freedom, including representatives of nine countries that languish in the bottom third of the World Press Index as compiled by Reporteurs sans Frontières (RSF 2017): Algeria, Mali, Ukraine, Tunisia, Palestine, Jordan, Russia, Turkey and Bahrain.

Other rallies in support of the victims of the Paris killings were held in many diverse geographic locales, including Atlanta, Beirut, Berlin, Cairo, Jerusalem, Johannesburg, Madrid, Montreal, Nicosia, Rio de Janeiro, Rome, Stockholm, Sydney, Thessaloniki and Tokyo. Saudi Arabia called it a "cowardly terrorist attack that was rejected by the true Islamic religion" (Burke 2015: 244). The Arab League and Egypt's Al-Azhar University, the leading theological institution in the Sunni Muslim world, also denounced the incident, while Iran, Jordan, Bahrain, Morocco, Algeria and Qatar all issued similar statements. All this provides some evidence of an internationally shared understanding of and response to the 'event'.

Paris showed the different communities caught up in the Hebdo event-in-itself, with formal funerals for the policemen as well as Muslim and Jewish ceremonies. The hashtags changed to reflect this ethnic diversity: 'Je Suis Ahmed' and 'Je Suis Juif'.[4]

But there were also plenty of contrary and negative responses. Brazilian artist Carlos Latuff tweeted '#JeNeSuisPasCharlie' ('I Am Not Charlie'), accused the magazine of being blasphemous and criticised global reaction as pro-Israel and one-sided. Rallies in Turkey and Indonesia, which enjoys the largest Muslim population in the world, kept the preposition but altered the identification to 'I/we are all Mohammad'. In the Philippines the preposition was altered, suggesting not 'we' but 'you' are Charlie, evidence of the growing international response in the event chain. In some places there were mixed responses. For example, in Turkey, the government condemned the Paris attacks but also warned that rising Islamophobia in Europe risked inflaming unrest. The secular newspaper *Cumhuriyet* actually published translated versions of the *Hebdo* cartoons, which triggered a counter-demonstration in Istanbul, during which protesters burnt copies of the paper and threatened its employees while some support was expressed for the Kouachi brothers who had carried out the original attack.

The critical, contestatory responses continued. On 17 January, there were peaceful demonstrations after Friday prayers in Khartoum, the North Caucasus, Mali, Senegal and Mauritania. In Algiers and Amman, protesters clashed with police and in Pakistan and Niger there was serious violence. Clearly, the 'event' is globalising, travelling further. But I would suggest that these responses are hardly a simple 'thickening' (as Hepp and Couldry (2010) suggest) but a crack in the dominant meaning, a contestation of the narrative, perhaps even a different story altogether.

In writing an event chain, one obvious issue is when to stop: when has the original event ended? What evidence is there for making a connection between 'discrete' events? One answer is that participants are making those connections. On 14 February, there was further violence in Europe with an attack on the Krudttønden Café in Copenhagen where the artist Lars Vilks was discussing Islam and free speech. One person was killed, three police injured; the suspect later went on to shoot a security guard in the great synagogue in the city, but was himself shot by police the next day. In street rallies, Danish was added to French and English in the proliferation of hashtags that explicitly linked the attack to Hebdo: 'Je Suis Danois' and 'Jeg Er Dansk'.

Suddenly, on 18 March, there was a violent attack on the steps of the Bardo Museum in Tunis that killed twenty-two people outright, with another dying later. One could debate whether this was actually a part of the Hebdo event chain, and whether or not it should be included. Its inclusion might require that many other acts of jihadist-inspired violence be attached to Hebdo, an issue that should certainly concern future historians. I include it here because once again the collective response triggered new hashtags – 'Je Suis Tunisie' and 'Je Suis Bardo' – connecting it in representation and memorialisation to Hebdo.

On 26 June, thirty-eight tourists were killed by an armed gunman on a Tunisian beach; this was readily linked by media analysts to the previous Bardo violence, but not to Hebdo. How events form chains or become chained together, what traces link one to another and what discourses claim to make those links is the very stuff of contemporary history-making, in which the media themselves often play immediate and central roles.

On 3 May, gunmen killed a security guard at an event being held in a Dallas, Texas suburb and were subsequently shot and killed by police. The event was the culmination of a contest with a $10,000 prize for the 'best cartoon depiction of Mohammad', staged by the American Freedom Defense Initiative, a group Pamela Geller – the noted US Islamophobe activist – and Robert Spencer had created in 2010. The Southern Poverty Law Center uses the group's other name, Stop Islamization of America, and lists it as a hate group. Again, should we stop and ask about the connection to Hebdo? A competition for cartoons of the Prophet – how can this not be connected in the event chain? Such forms of representation immediately linked Hebdo to the 2005 Danish cartoon controversy. But isn't the Geller event, and Hebdo also, part of a far longer event chain of Islamophobic antagonism inside Western democracies that is often designed to provoke violent responses? And is that not itself part of an even bigger event chain of Western intervention in the Middle East, including the Afghan and Iraq wars and the indifference to Palestinian claims for self-determination? Thus 'an' event is readily seen to compete for inclusion, or not, by the narratives proffered by different political discourses, themselves the very stuff of history. One indication that such Islamophobic events are watched very closely by globalised audiences was the demonstration mounted in Pakistan in direct response to the Geller exhibition.

In May 2015, the PEN America Center announced that it would give the first PEN/Toni and James C. Goodale Freedom of Expression Courage Award to *Charlie Hebdo* at its annual fundraising dinner in New York. Six prominent PEN members – Francine Prose, Peter Carey, Michael Ondaatje, Teju Cole, Rachel Kushner and Taiye Selasi – protested and withdrew from the event. They argued that, while the Hebdo killings were 'sickening and tragic' and that no expression of views should be met with violence, such an award would be "valorizing selectively offensive material: material that intensifies the anti-Islamic, anti-Maghreb, anti-Arab sentiments already prevalent in the Western world" (Weaver 2015). Subsequently, over 200 other PEN members added their names to the protest, while Salman Rushdie among others defended the award.

Also in May 2015, a report by the Committee to Protect Journalists (Crispin 2015) suggested that cartoonists are under particular attack in many countries, including Malaysia and Iran, where its own satirical cartoonists have been imprisoned even as it organised a second Holocaust cartoon competition. Little wonder that in mid-May, Rénald Luzier, the remaining cartoonist at *Charlie Hebdo* magazine and better known as Luz, announced his retirement. Given that this entire event chain all too simply interpellates a 'clash of civilisations' approach, it is interesting to note the not-so-subtle invocation of the policies of Muslim states versus the rights of individual authors; the dominant narrative obscures all issues around 'free speech' within Western countries, a point to which I shall return later.

Other discourses triggered a different trajectory of actions. Ireland initiated a debate about writing new blasphemy laws. In Canada, Prime Minister Harper repealed hate laws in the name of 'liberty' and 'free speech' with Bill C-304. France stepped up its surveillance and arrested the French comedian Dieudonné M'bala M'bala for being an 'apologist for terrorism' after he had posted on Facebook his sympathies with one of the Paris gunmen. The Conservative government in Britain demands greater surveillance of universities while its counter-terrorism Prevent strategy now reaches into primary schools, with a schoolboy's drawing of a cucumber misread as a bomb. Indeed, it is tempting to suggest that such periodic 'terrorist' outrages are necessary precisely in order that governments can tighten their surveillance and control over domestic populations. Outrageous claims by British politicians, such as the one made by UKIP's Nigel Farage that there are no-go zones for non-Muslims in France, get little mainstream rebuttal and the confused rhetoric around immigrants, Muslims and violence played a significant role in the unexpected vote for the UK to leave the European Union. Social media provide sites for ridicule of such statements which otherwise go unchallenged.

Acting as a contemporary cultural historian, the timeline that I present attests to a complex and often antagonistic process of call and response that involved a *range* of audiences and a *range* of participants, developing a media event chain that was precipitated by the shooting. But the second implication, to which I have already alluded, is that an event not only needs to be explored forwards, in terms of the moments that unfolded within 'the' (or is it 'my'?) Hebdo event chain but also needs to work backwards, in a more complex analysis of contemporary cultural politics, to previous moments or discourses to which Hebdo was and could be attached and about which the mainstream media content was regrettably silent.

These include the entire debate about stereotypic and provocative representations of Islam, from Edward Said to the worldwide controversy around *The Satanic Verses* and the Iranian fatwa against its author, Salman Rushdie, at the end of the 1980s to the 'Danish cartoon' controversy of 2005 about the visual representation of the Prophet and on to Hebdo. It should also include the narrative of the 'war on terror' and actual acts of violent terror by various agents, including states, and the media coverage of these versus the lack of mediated coverage of daily car crashes, deaths from alcohol and cancer, and poverty, social forms of structural violence that are not image-rich or media-friendly. And these must include French and other imperialisms and violent wars abroad as well as French (and other) histories of violence on domestic soil including in the *banlieue*, quietly forgotten in the claims to the uniqueness of the Hebdo violence.

Traces of all these discourses and arguments appeared across a range of English-language authors and alternative commentary sites such as openDemocracy, Jacobin, Jadaliyya and Alif, and those pieces were in turn commented upon. Thus, alongside the mediated spectacle, a more measured and analytic exploration of competing historical narratives entwined the event chain as it unfolded. The problem of the sedimentation of historical narrative presumably concerns which of these discourses has sufficient weight and durability to become dominant over time in specific locales. What contemporary analysis can show is the now global competition for that hegemony. What a subtle media studies curriculum could offer is comparative analysis of (all of?) these discourses, their origins, their articulations, their 'stickability'.

Of course, the event chain is also maintained through academic and writerly discussions. In April 2015, a planned academic event, 'Understanding Charlie: New Perspectives on Contemporary Citizenship after Charlie Hebdo', at Queen's University Belfast was cancelled for a 'lack of security assessment', allowing the proposed speakers to have a field day with the irony of the situation. While the Belfast event was cancelled, an academic event was held in Dublin in early May organised by the editors of this volume. Conference papers quickly emerged (my own were given in Doha, London and Montréal), and books and special issues of journals began to be compiled and commissioned. A British television programme, portentously called *3 Days That Shook*

Paris[5] and offering 'the definitive story' of the attacks was shown in September 2015. The *Guardian* keeps adding to its archive, which it claims is displaying 'all content related to the French satirical magazine *Charlie Hebdo*'.[6] And now this book and others!

We begin to see the analytic difficulties in separating out one event from another – or, better, in separating one event chain from another – rather encountering a *range* of historical discourses that national media channels, the commentariat, academics and others attach to 'an' event. Indeed, I would argue that the evidence of such a range of contemporary historical claims and narratives is a useful challenge to the unitary sedimentation of history and a prevalent sense that events are contained by and in a singular narrative. The elaboration of the 'media–events' paradigm has rarely paid attention to the problem of artificially isolating an event, rather than seeing such an event as lying within one or more historical narratives that helped produce its 'event-ness' in the first place. It also becomes clearer that the event chain is itself the object of rival articulations, part of a struggle for hegemonic dominance that is never fully accomplished – although even naming this as 'Charlie Hebdo' suggests the temporary success of a specific articulation.

Perhaps the most dominant narrative that surrounded the Charlie Hebdo event chain was, of course, that about free speech in a modern secular society (discussed in other chapters in this volume). Although little public attention has been paid to the rest of the 110 journalists who were killed in 2015, mostly in 'peaceful' countries (RSF 2016). There have been countless arguments and articles about the right to offend, to challenge traditional mores, religious verities and social shibboleths, which almost turned into a requirement to be offensive. British newspapers were continually provoked as to why they did not reproduce the *Hebdo* cover, as though this was evidence of weakness and capitulation to fanaticism. Subsequent *Hebdo* covers, including one that used the photograph of Alan Kurdi to ask about his future life in Europe, have repeatedly pushed the boundaries of reasonable taste and generated highly negative responses.

Perhaps more interesting, however, is the confused debate and practice around individual freedom that has been unfolding inside France. In summer 2016, both the terrifying Nice attack and the subsequent burkini saga in France captured considerable media attention. In a bizarre twist to the promotion of *liberté, laïcité* and secular values, in August numerous French resort towns banned the wearing of the burkini, a modest one-piece costume used by Muslim women to go swimming. Muslim women at once became the flashpoint of France's war on terror. The weakest, most marginalised and vulnerable social group became the synecdoche for Islamist fanaticism and the great French public seemed to readily submit to its enactment. The burkini episode is the counterpoint to – even the outcome of – the celebration of *Charlie Hebdo*'s 'right to be insulting', of absolute free speech. As a social enantiodromia, the supposed protection of Western democracy and 'secular value' turned into its opposite, to a practice whereby policemen demanded that a Muslim woman take off her shirt (not even a full burkini) on the beach in front of scores of passive French onlookers, a news image reproduced around the world.[7] Thus, a clothing choice made by scores of women became the symbol of the enemy within. Free 'speech' is evidently not available to all.

Conclusion

Historians try to provide post hoc analysis of how events are linked and of actors' motivations, rationalisations and justifications. Media content reveals such claims to us in real time, through raucous, hostile and global dynamics. Different discourses meet and congeal, flare up and down again as events move on.

To seek to separate out events is to render them unknowable, as singular happenings with no past and no future, an endless present of mediated content.

Instead of focusing on 'media events', I have tried to develop the idea of media event chains and to show how the competition for the dominant historical narrative is fought out daily across a range of platforms by a wide array of actors. Hebdo is an excellent example of that.

Journalists might sometimes write the first draft of history but they do not write the last. In Walter Benjamin's terms, we might not be able to recoup the tragedies of the past but we should indeed remember them and understand how even moments from long ago cast a shadow over the present. A deep collective unconscious, not to mention deliberate forgetting, is highly dangerous.

Notes

1 I draw on detail originally published in an article (Sreberny 2016).

2 The magazine's offices had previously been firebombed in 2011 following publication of a cartoon of the Prophet Mohammed on *Charlie Hebdo*'s cover with the caption '100 Lashes of the Whip if You Don't Die Laughing'.

3 The phrase has echoes of 'Ich bin ein Berliner' ('I am a Berliner'), the solidarity phrase used by President Kennedy denouncing the erection of the Berlin Wall. 'Je Suis Baga' was utilised on some critical demonstrations, as was 'Je Suis Nigeria'. 'Je Suis Raif' has been used in support of the Saudi blogger sentenced to 100 lashes by the Saudi authorities; and 'Je Suis Volnovakha' in relation to the 2015 bus attack in Ukraine. During the British election campaign in April 2015, when Labour Party leader Ed Miliband was filmed eating a bacon sandwich rather messily, there were comic photographic responses of people having difficulty eating bacon sandwiches, under the

hashtag 'Je Suis Ed'! Hashtags function as memes, to be used and repurposed endlessly, so a sub-theme that could be developed for analysis would be the history and employment of hashtags such as these.

4 Cartoonists were quick to respond, evoking the destruction of the Twin Towers, turning the Eiffel Tower into a pencil and automatic weapons into pens. There is plenty of focused research to be done on the hashtags, cartoons and memes that were used.

5 The title evokes John Reed's book on the Russian Revolution, *Ten Days that Shook the World*, a far more significant event!

6 Available at www.theguardian.com/media/charlie-hebdo.

7 Image from the *Guardian*, 24 August 2016 (which at least had the decency to pixelate the woman's face). Available at www.theguardian.com/world/2016/aug/24/french-police-make-woman-remove-burkini-on-nice-beach.

References

Amnesty International (2015) 'Boko Haram Baga attacks: satellite images reveal destruction', Amnesty International, 15 January. www.amnesty.org.uk/nigeria-boko-haram-doron-baga-attacks-satellite-images-massacre.

Burke, J. (2015) *The New Threat: The Past, Present, and Future of Islamic Militancy*. New York: The New Press.

Crispin, S. (2015) *Drawing the Line: Cartoonists under Threat*. New York: Committee to Protect Journalists. https://cpj.org/reports/drawing_the_line_cartoonists_under_threat-2015.pdf.

Dayan, D. and E. Katz (1992) *Media Events: The Live Broadcasting of History*. Cambridge, MA: Harvard University Press.

Eide, E., R. Kunelius and A. Phillips (2008) *Transnational Media Events: The Mohammed Cartoons and the Imagined Clash of Civilizations*. Gothenburg: Nordicom, University of Gothenburg.

Hepp, A. and N. Couldry (2010) 'Introduction: Media Events in Globalised Media Cultures' in N. Couldry, A. Hepp and F. Krotz (eds) *Media Events in a Global Age*. London: Routledge.

Katz, E. and T. Liebes (2007) 'No More Peace! How Disaster, Terror and War Have Upstaged Media Events', *International Journal of Communication* 1: 157–66.

Kellner, D. (2004) '9/11, Spectacles of Terror, and Media Manipulation: A

Critique of Jihadist and Bush Media Politics', *Critical Discourse Studies* 1: 41–64.

Laclau, E. and C. Mouffe (1985) *Hegemony and Socialist Strategy*. London: Verso.

Liebes, T. (1998) 'Television's Disaster Marathons: A Danger to Democratic Processes?' in T. Liebes and J. Curran (eds) *Media, Ritual and Identity*. London: Routledge.

RSF (2016) 'RSF Annual Round-up: 110 Journalists Killed in 2015', Reporteurs sans Frontières (RSF), 8 March. https://rsf.org/en/news/rsf-annual-round-110-journalists-killed-2015.

RSF (2017) '2017 World Press Freedom Index', Reporteurs sans Frontières (RSF). https://rsf.org/en/ranking.

Sreberny, A. (2016) 'The 2015 *Charlie Hebdo* Killings, Media Event Chains, and Global Political Responses', *International Journal of Communication* 10: 3485–502. http://ijoc.org/index.php/ijoc/article/view/4814/1725.

Weaver, C. (2015) 'PEN Award for Charlie Hebdo Stirs Controversy', *Voice of America News*, 5 May. www.voanews.com/content/pen-award-charlie-hebdo-stirs-controversy/2750883.html.

Part IV

THE POLITICS OF FREE SPEECH

12 | MEDIA POWER AND THE FRAMING OF THE *CHARLIE HEBDO* ATTACKS

Des Freedman

Introduction

The day after Omar Mateen shot dead fifty people in an Orlando nightclub in June 2016, Dr Sebastian Gorka, a counter-terrorism 'expert', appeared on Fox News in the US to warn viewers of the threat posed by jihadists. "In the past fifteen years, we haven't seen an Episcopalian suicide bomber. We haven't seen Zoroastrian mass murderers. We've seen Muslim extremists. If you deny that, you are in a fantasy land, and you're endangering American citizens." Notwithstanding the murder the year before of nine black churchgoers in Charleston by a man with a Protestant background, the horrific frequency of school shootings carried out by non-Muslims, nor, indeed, the fact that some 3.3 million Muslims in the US are entirely peaceful, Gorka insisted that terror is an Islamic issue: "It's time to wake up, America. The war is here."

Two days after Mohamed Lahouaiej-Bouhlel killed eighty-four people leaving a Bastille Day fireworks display in Nice in July 2016, Gorka was back on Fox News arguing that the attack was "again an instance of the jihadis taking the war to the infidel on their home territory". Another guest, Milwaukee County Sheriff David Clarke, asserted that "I'm through trying to understand the sick ideology of Islamism. Instead of trying to understand it, we just ought to try to kill it."

These three clips from the most influential cable news network in the US epitomise a habitual reaction to 'Islamist' terrorism from major Western media voices: to frame it exclusively in relation to domestic audiences, to largely refuse to consider its roots and finally to declare war on it (even if it is not entirely clear what 'it' refers to). The sickening mass murder of innocent civilians is therefore followed by routine condemnation by commentators not of the range of circumstances that might lead individuals to perpetrate such horror but, more often, simply of the religion that, it is claimed, inevitably leads to acts of terror and that, therefore, justifies punitive action against a minority of the population.

This chapter reflects on the dynamics of mainstream media coverage of recent terror attacks, most notably the murder of *Charlie Hebdo* journalists in January 2015. The events in Paris were overwhelmingly characterised by Western media as an attack on free speech carried out by people with a 'primitive' understanding of liberal speech rights. While such a perspective is obviously understandable given the victims, it allowed key opinion formers to shape an agenda that marginalised other contexts – for example, the impact of Western interventions or the conditions that radicalise Muslim youth in Europe – and naturalised certain tropes about Islam and free expression. The chapter evaluates key framing mechanisms in relation to the *Charlie Hebdo* attack, considers the contributions of some of the most 'muscular' liberal commentators and suggests that there may be a decisive contradiction between free speech advocates and the mechanisms – predominantly corporate media – used to deliver such speech.

Framing terror

Some forty years ago, the American historian Walter Laqueur noted the increasing complexity of terrorism as a *distinct* sphere of political action and insisted that "a comprehensive definition of terrorism ... does not exist nor will it be found in the foreseeable future" (2009 [1977]: 5). Today, despite an industry of academic researchers, military strategists, civil servants and professional commentators, there remains little more than a vague consensus that terrorism involves the use of politically motivated violence imposed on innocent civilians by non-state groups. The definition, however, of what constitutes political motivation and whether only 'subnational' groups can be implicated in terror are highly contested topics. Moreover, given the frequency and scale of such attacks, there remains a very imprecise difference between a 'lone wolf' motivated by mental health issues and a more purposeful assault carried out in the name of a specific ideology or cause. Immediately following an incident, therefore, we wait anxiously for the tweet from the authorities that confirms or denies whether a specific incident is being treated as an 'act of terror' or whether it is simply a 'shooting' or an 'attack'.

In that sense, the meaning of terrorism is far more subjective than scientific and refers to "an interpretation of events and their presumed causes" (Turk 2004: 490). In terms of impact, terror is less an internal property of violent acts than a consequence of the communication of these acts. Little wonder then that terrorism has long been described as a 'symbolic act' (Thornton 1964: 73), because, as horrific as its immediate impact can be, its greater purpose is to produce political reactions and to induce fear among a wider population. Terrorism, therefore, has to be *made to mean*, and who better to 'interpret' these life-changing events – to engage in a hugely important exercise of social construction rather than rigorous classification – than storytellers, mythmakers, media people, journalists? Symbol makers have a unique ability to shape the political agenda by organising the discursive frameworks through which the public comes to understand acts of violence.

Consider the different language used in the Western media to describe the murder of eighty-four people in Nice by Mohamed Lahouaiej-Bouhlel, the shooting of nine young people by a German-Iranian student in Munich and a suicide bombing in Kabul that killed eighty people, all in July 2016. The first was portrayed as an act of terror, the second was the work of a lone 'shooter', while the third was an 'attack' carried out against fellow Muslims. According to the journalist Robert Fisk, what he describes as the 'nonsensical nomenclature' means that "[i]f Muslims attack us, they are terrorists. If non-Muslims attack us, they are shooters. If Muslims attack other Muslims, they are attackers" (Fisk 2016).

These acts of mediated interpretation are generally described in academic literature in relation to theories of framing. Todd Gitlin, for example, borrows from Erving Goffman's account of frame analysis (Goffmann 1974) to argue that frames are crucial ways for journalists to make sense of and to order public life and are based on "principles of selection, emphasis, and presentation composed of little tacit theories about what exists, what happens, and what matters" (Gitlin 1980: 6).

The latter phrase is particularly crucial: framing refers to a process that is an essential part of the journalist's work in helping to assemble a coherent narrative. But it also refers to a process of exclusion: the content that lies 'outside the frame' may be crucial but its invisibility means that audiences are not provided with the opportunity to see this. Downing and Husband argue that framing has been a means by which minority populations have been simultaneously mis-recognised and starved of adequate representations of themselves, with the implication that it will then be harder for majority populations to come to know them. "If tens of millions of people are almost out of frame literally, visually, they are scarcely even dignified with a media stereotype! There is not even an image to contest!" (Downing and Husband 2005: 37).

However, the ability to decide 'what matters' – and, therefore, what does not – is clearly unequally distributed throughout society. Journalists and editors may claim to discriminate between frames mostly on the basis of professional judgement and established cultural norms but there are more deep-rooted influences – such as an ideological sympathy with elite interests and a structural impact of the geography of Western power – that lead to a persistent overvaluing of some perspectives and voices at the expense of others. This power imbalance also relates to the value attributed to human life itself, with Philip Schlesinger's noting of an equivalence in BBC newsroom culture between "one thousand wogs, 50 frogs and one Briton" (1978: 117).

In relation to military conflict, this has led to the regular exclusion of non-Western voices and the belittling of domestic anti-war voices along with the privileging of official military discourse. Gitlin (1980), for example, examined the media's long-standing neglect of the anti-Vietnam War movement in the 1960s, while Entman and Page found that, in the lead-up to the 1991 Gulf War, out of 118 opinion pieces in *The New York Times*, many of which contained limited criticisms of the administration, not a single one actually argued against US involvement in the war (Entman and Page 1994: 96). Criticism, they argue, was 'procedural' rather than 'substantive', accentuated by a routine dependence on official sources and the 'beat' system that "encourages the over-representation of administration views" (ibid.: 96). This is a pattern of coverage that was particularly evident during the 2003 Iraq war. Despite substantial public opposition in early 2003, researchers found evidence in UK broadcast news coverage of a "subtle but clear bias towards ... pro-war assumptions" (Lewis et al. 2006: 126), while, according to Robinson et al. (2010: 104), "British news coverage of the Iraq invasion conformed to the prediction of the elite-driven model. Press and television news relied heavily on coalition sources and supportive battle coverage prevailed even among newspapers that had opted to oppose the war."

Entman argues that, in a less polarised, post-Cold War world framing, what he describes as "highlighting some facets of events or issues ... so as to produce a particular interpretation, evaluation, and/

or solution" (Entman 2004: 5) is the most effective tool with which to explain the elite-dominated nature of media coverage of conflict, rather than what he sees as the ideologically fixed notions of Herman and Chomsky's propaganda model (Herman and Chomsky 1988). The reporting of conflict "does not always fall into the iron grip of hegemonic elite control" (Entman 2004: 147), even though the most powerful actors continue to be better equipped to transmit their frameworks and interpretations through the media and on to publics in what he calls a 'cascading activation' model. While this allows for a certain degree of journalistic autonomy, the news process is still dominated by vested interests to produce, particularly in matters of foreign policy, an "'elite' spiral of silence" together with only very limited contestability (ibid.: 73), a point also made by Schlosberg (2013) in his analysis of the reporting of corruption scandals in the UK.

Framing is certainly a useful way of capturing the dynamics of journalistic practice as they relate to the fraught circumstances of reporting on terrorism, but it has a tendency to privilege the internal mechanisms of newsroom culture more than the broader contexts within which journalists operate. Entman himself acknowledges that he is "more concerned with media interventions in the day-to-day contests to control government power *within* the snug ideological confines of American politics" (Entman 2007: 270) than he is with investigating how these ideological parameters condition the frames and routines of journalists themselves. In order fully to make sense of the coverage of terror, therefore, we need also to highlight the full range of structural constraints that shape contemporary journalism – including the geopolitical contours of the 'war on terror', domestic narratives concerning security and freedom, relationships between media and political elites, and the pressure on news outlets to secure high ratings and exclusives – and that affect the ways in which journalists negotiate their own ideological positions. Crucially, the framing of terror is intimately connected to the operation of media power: the control of material and symbolic resources that are needed to operate inside the media (Freedman 2014). So when mainstream media use language that appears to reproduce dominant definitions of conflict – for example, that 'terrorism' is what others do to us in contrast to 'self-defence', which is what we do to others – this is not a vocabulary designed exclusively in the newsroom, but one that reflects the power interests of the environment in which it is located.

In the UK, we have a situation in which influential tabloid newspapers regularly represent Islam – and therefore Muslims – in terms of a predisposition to violence, while liberal commentators talk of the civilisational shortcomings of Islam in relation to its commitment to democracy and human rights. "The simplistic equation of Islam with barbaric practices," argue Khiabany and Williamson (2012: 135), "is a key aspect of the culturalization of terror and violence. However, this is not confined to the journalism of the tabloid press but spans the British media to include journalism from the liberal media and 'respectable' broadsheet press." They document how significant sections of the media frame Muslims as subjects of terror in such a way as to naturalise anti-Muslim racism within British culture.

This continues a pattern of exclusion *and* misrepresentation that has been prevalent since 9/11. A study commissioned by the Greater London Authority in 2007 into media coverage of Muslims found that 91 per cent of articles in national newspapers in a single week were negative while a mere 4 per cent painted a positive picture of Muslims (Press Association 2007). A survey carried out by researchers at Cardiff University for Channel 4 the following year (Moore et al. 2008) examined 1,000 articles going back to just before 9/11 and concluded that two-thirds focused on terrorism or cultural differences. There was an emphasis on nouns such as 'extremist', 'Islamist', 'suicide bomber' and 'militant' and adjectives such as 'radical', 'fanatical', 'fundamentalist' and 'extremist'. The idea that Islam was dangerous, backward or irrational was present in 26 per cent of the stories assessed while only 2 per cent depicted Muslims as supporting "dominant moral values" (ibid.: 3). Muslims, therefore, appear to feature in the public imagination only in relation to their status as 'problems' and 'terrorists' and by virtue of having a different moral framework to non-Muslim British citizens. This is a type of reporting that helps to legitimise Islamophobia and provides at least part of the backdrop to the rise in attacks on Muslims. For example, the independent reporting service Tell MAMA revealed a 200 per cent increase in anti-Muslim attacks in 2015 and concluded that "anti-Muslim hate is contextualized in broader xenophobic, racist, nationalist and populist discourses and ideologies" (Tell MAMA 2016: 11). Framing is far from a neutral or inconsequential process.

Terrorism is what happens 'here'

One of the central features of the framing of terror by mainstream journalists has been to domesticate it: in other words, to consider its relevance to the home population and its impact on internal politics. This has taken place to the extent that horrible acts of violence that happen 'over there' may still be classified as terrorism – although, as mentioned earlier, Robert Fisk argues that they are more likely to be called 'attacks' – but they are somehow less threatening and more expected because of their distance.

Labour leader Jeremy Corbyn challenged this hierarchy of grieving when he reacted to Islamic State's attack in Paris in November 2015 in which 130 people died by arguing that 'a life is a life' (quoted in Bloom 2015). Reflecting on the disparity between blanket media coverage of the atrocities in Paris and what he perceived as a distinct lack of attention to the loss of life in IS attacks in Beirut and Ankara that had taken place at around the same time, Corbyn insisted that "our media needs to be able to report things that happen outside of Europe as well as inside". This echoed a similar claim (for example, see Alter 2015) that Western media focused on the terror attacks in Paris in January 2015 but paid scant attention to the massacre of many hundreds of people by Boko Haram in Northern Nigeria that took place in the same week. Corbyn's comments were immediately criticised by a number of journalists and commentators who dismissed the idea that they prioritise some lives over others and denied that the media fail adequately to cover events wherever they take place. One *Guardian* journalist claimed that this was "a lie" (Belam 2015) and insisted that there were over a thousand articles – including some in the world's leading news outlets – that reported on the bombings in Beirut even before the attacks took place in Paris.

It is true that the BBC, CNN, *The New York Times*, *Guardian* and the *Daily Mail* did cover the awful events in Beirut. However, none of them led with them; none of them stopped to think that this might be a life-changing event; none of them 'scrambled' to cover the bombings as the *New York Times* admitted it did in relation to Paris (Koblin 2015). Indeed, the major opinion former for the UK, BBC Radio 4's *Today* programme, managed to *completely* neglect what happened in Beirut the morning after the explosions. It found time to talk about foreign affairs – for example the elections in Myanmar, the appeal of Narendra

Modi and the doping of Russian athletes – but Islamic State suicide bombs that killed dozens and injured hundreds beyond the boundaries of Europe did not feature at all on the programme.

Some journalists insist that it isn't the fault of editors but of audiences. "Don't complain that the media didn't tell you about a tragedy on the other side of the world," argued Emma Kelly in the *Huffington Post* (Kelly 2015). "They did. You just didn't click." Readers are apparently interested only in what is 'proximate' and therefore meaningful to us. We can't be bothered with stories about events that happen in 'distant' lands. The number of clicks proves this: "as anyone working in the news will tell you, if you look at your analytics, people don't read them [stories about faraway foreign countries] very much" (Belam 2015).

That is hardly a great character reference for mainstream news: that journalists are reluctant to write about important events in case they bore their readers whose capacity for compassion will travel only very short distances. It is the perfect neoliberal expression of news as a commodity with no value beyond how many hits it can attract.

This patronises ordinary readers who lack the agenda-setting power of large news organisations but it is far from a huge surprise. A Western news media that frames the world in its own image, that is generally very intimate with the powerful (wherever they may live) but that sees the rest of the globe in relation to its own 'sphere of influence' is hardly going to be one that treats every single human life with the dignity it deserves.

You can see this kind of 'selective compassion' (Cook 2015) not simply in tabloid newspapers with more limited foreign coverage but also in titles that do have a commitment to international news. The *Observer*'s Nick Cohen, for example, reacted to the Paris attacks by worrying exclusively about what they might do to European liberalism (Cohen 2015a). The article talks about Europe's "modest response to terrorism" and argues that, despite immense provocation, the continent still remains a beacon of democracy and civil liberties – something that may come as a shock to the victims of extraordinary rendition who didn't quite enjoy the full benefits of the European Convention on Human Rights or to the refugees who have drowned in the Mediterranean Sea because European governments didn't want to spend money either saving them or housing them.

But Cohen's argument also absolves Western powers for any responsibility in unleashing the instability and desperation that might have had an impact on the emergence of the groups from which refugees are now running away – whether in Libya, Syria or Iraq. While faraway countries such as Nigeria and Afghanistan are subject to clerical fascism and civil war, "Europe has been lucky", Cohen writes, because we still have our decency, the rule of law and our quirky sense of humour. It is as if we were never there in those strange foreign lands.

Given that the central aim of Islamic State is to sow division – between Muslims as well as between Muslims and non-Muslims – Cohen's concern that European liberalism might now be under sustained pressure is more than a little short-sighted. After all, it is precisely this history that has been so wrapped up in the colonial and imperial projects that continue to exert their 'blowback'. In these circumstances, we would all benefit from a journalism that takes the lives and histories of non-Europeans just as seriously as those 'lucky' enough to live in Europe – not least if we want to defend civil liberties, defeat terrorism and show solidarity with the lives of others. Reporting terror ought not to be a zero-sum game: there is enough room in a digital age to acknowledge both that the deaths of all innocents are equally worth mourning and that, since January 2015, the Middle East, Africa and Asia have seen nearly fifty times more deaths from terrorism than Europe and the Americas (Gamio and Meko 2016).

The *Charlie Hebdo* frame: free speech under attack

Newspapers around the world reacted to the horrific events in Paris in January 2015 in different ways, with most front pages coalescing around words such as 'massacre' and 'terror' or calling for support for the victims. However, there was another frame that was picked up especially (though not exclusively) in the UK, where the shootings were seen as an attack on democracy and freedom – in particular the freedom of expression that was then celebrated at the huge march the following Sunday which was supported both by journalists' unions *and* by representatives of countries including Turkey, Jordan, Israel, Egypt, Algeria and Russia – countries in which journalists have been jailed or killed by the authorities. As the *Daily Mail* (2015) put it in an editorial the following day, this was a "murderous attack on *Western* freedoms" carried out by people with "mediaeval" motives.

On one level, the framing of the Paris events around free speech is totally understandable. The reality is that the killers *did* single out journalists and that they did time their attack to coincide with the weekly editorial meeting at *Charlie Hebdo* in order to secure maximum impact. The cartoonists therefore joined the growing number of journalists killed 'in the line of duty' that includes not simply the high-profile murders of reporters by IS in Syria but also cases such as the sixteen Palestinian journalists killed by the Israeli army in Gaza together with the sixteen reporters killed by US military fire in Iraq (Tyson 2009) – the latter killings hardly generating the same claims from leading commentators that they constituted a 'murderous attack on Western freedoms'. They are all, nevertheless, indefensible attacks on journalism.

But the framing of the attacks around free speech also served some very useful purposes for UK news organisations. First, it allowed them to marginalise the wider political context as if there were no consequences for the West of interventions in Iraq, Syria, Libya, Afghanistan and Palestine, let alone the consequences for the French given their occupation of Algeria. In their obsession with the sanctity of freedom of expression, they allow no room for the possibility that there might be 'blowback' as a result of Western occupation and intervention along the lines predicted by the former head of MI5, Eliza Manningham-Buller, who described how "our involvement in Iraq radicalised a few among a generation of young people who saw [it] as an attack on Islam" (quoted in Norton-Taylor 2010). This reluctance to examine the impact of Western foreign policy is deeply embedded within dominant journalistic frames of reporting terrorism. Jake Lynch examined three episodes of the agenda-setting BBC *Today* programme immediately after the Paris attacks in November 2015 and found that, out of a total of 12 hours and 45 minutes of broadcasting, just 63 seconds "were allotted for the 'blowback' thesis to be even partially put forward" (Lynch 2016).

Second, it allowed news outlets to continue a particular trope about Islam being a backward religion and Muslims being 'underdeveloped' and in need of civilising and some media literacy lessons. But what they chose not to see is that the attacks were motivated not by a dislike of images per se but by the foreign policy dynamics of France and other Western states. The target, in other words, wasn't an *idea* but, in the eyes of the gunmen, representatives of the forces with whom they are in conflict. So this wasn't about some kind of 'Islamic' opposition to satire or free speech, or evidence of some genetic flaw that results in the lack of a sense of humour, but a violent act designed to spark a reaction – of increased anti-terror laws, of more surveillance, of more anti-Muslim racism – that will fuel the tiny ranks of jihad. It was, as Juan Cole argued (Cole 2015), "a strategic strike, aiming at polarizing the French and European public".

Third, a focus on 'liberty' allowed the media to present themselves as the fearless defenders of free speech – particularly at a time when their role as noble truth-tellers has been subject to increased scrutiny following the events of the phone hacking crisis when public suspicion of the press's abuse of their power reached epidemic proportions (Freedman 2013). Tactically, therefore, it was far more convenient to adopt a 'clash of civilisations' thesis and to shunt aside both uncomfortable geopolitical realities *and* domestic challenges for the more soothing talk of freedom of expression and absolutist speech rights.

For many liberal commentators, free speech has been interpreted as the right to bully, to mock and to stereotype without regard for the consequences. As the *Mail* put it in its leader the day after the *Charlie Hebdo* attacks: "If liberty is to mean anything, it must include the freedom to mock, offend or question the beliefs of others, within the limits of democratically decided law" (*Daily Mail* 2015). Satire – *all* satire, no matter the content or the target – is now to be treated as a basic hallmark of democracy. Indeed, the barometer of freedom of expression for many liberals increasingly seems to be about whether you're 'brave' enough to publish material that you know is offensive to millions of people – like the cartoons of the Prophet Mohammed (discussed by Carolina Sanchez Boe in her chapter) or the notorious cartoon of migrants drowning in the Med by an illustrator who has worked for *Charlie Hebdo* (Meade 2016).

Nick Cohen (2015b), for example, returned from a vigil in Trafalgar Square on the evening of the January attacks not calling for unity and peace but hoping that "tomorrow's papers and news programmes will prove their commitment to freedom by republishing the *Charlie Hebdo* cartoons". David Aaronovitch (2015) then used the freedom afforded by his column in *The Times* to warn those people who don't share his view of 'liberal' tolerance that they should leave the country if they're offended by the publication of the cartoons: "You live here, that's what you agree to. You don't like it, go somewhere else." What kind of freedom is it that is measured by its ability to offend and not to enlighten and that is characterised by an underlying threat that if you don't like 'my kind of freedom' then you're not free to live with me?

It is certainly not the case that the free speech frame was irrelevant to the Paris attacks in January 2015. The issue is that some leading columnists and titles deliberately misused this frame to pursue their own ideological agendas that dovetailed with the central dynamics of a continuing 'war on terror' in which all Muslims are to be positioned either as security problems or cultural misfits. Yet liberal conceptions of free speech weren't originally designed to mean the freedom of the powerful to insult the powerless but precisely the opposite: to make sure that there could be a check on the most powerful groups in society and to protect the speech rights of minorities. Indeed, how wonderful would it be if we actually did have the kind of free speech that protects the vulnerable and scrutinises the powerful – that is, if our speech rights were not curbed either by a panoply of anti-terror laws or more everyday commercial considerations that elevate some forms of speech way above others. Instead, as Onora O'Neill has argued, "we are now perilously close to a world in which media conglomerates act as if they had unrestricted rights of free expression, and therefore a licence to subject positions for which they don't care to caricature and derision, misrepresentation or silence" (O'Neill 2002).

In so much of the media framing of terrorism, horrific crimes are distorted to fit the prism of commentators and politicians who are determined to use these events to further victimise entire communities and to introduce states of emergency. In the case of the *Charlie Hebdo* attacks, journalists who were fixated on a crude and absolutist fetish of free speech chose to ignore the real context of the shootings: of an asymmetrical and violent 'war on terror'. The tragedy is that we need free speech, robust frames and measured reporting more than ever, but that the instruments designed to deliver this kind of journalism are far from its most reliable guarantors.

References

Aaronovitch, D. (2015) 'Our Cowardice Helped to Allow This Attack', *The Times*, 8 January. www.thetimes. co.uk/tto/opinion/columnists/ article4316868.ece.

Alter, C. (2015) 'Why *Charlie Hebdo* Gets More Attention Than Boko Haram', *Time*, 15 January. http://time. com/3666619/why-charlie-hebdo-gets-more-attention-than-boko-haram/.

Belam, M. (2015) '"You Won't Read About This in the Media but ..."', medium. com, 15 November. https://medium. com/@martinbelam/you-won-t-read-about-this-in-the-media-but-b275d46fd51f#.5t2gwrivq.

Bloom, D. (2015) 'Jeremy Corbyn Pleads for More Coverage of Terror Attacks outside Paris Saying "A Life Is a Life"', *Daily Mirror*, 16 November.

www.mirror.co.uk/news/uk-news/jeremy-corbyn-pleads-more-coverage-6841409.

Cohen, N. (2015a) 'After Paris, Europe May Never Feel as Free Again', *Guardian*, 14 November. www.theguardian.com/commentisfree/2015/nov/14/after-paris-attacks-europe-never-same-terrorism.

Cohen, N. (2015b) 'Charlie Hebdo: The Truths that Ought to be Self-evident But Still Aren't', *The Spectator*, 7 January. http://blogs.spectator.co.uk/2015/01/charlie-hebdo-the-truths-that-ought-to-be-self-evident-but-still-arent.

Cole, J. (2015) 'Sharpening Contradictions: Why al-Qaeda Attacked Satirists in Paris', *informed* Comment, 7 January. www.juancole.com/2015/01/sharpening-contradictions-satirists.html.

Cook, J. (2015) 'Outrage at Paris Masks our Racism', Jonathan Cook blog, 14 November. www.jonathan-cook.net/blog/2015-11-14/outrage-at-paris-attacks-masks-our-racism.

Daily Mail (2015) 'Comment: A Murderous Attack on Western Freedoms', *Daily Mail*, 8 January. www.dailymail.co.uk/debate/article-2901368/DAILY-MAIL-COMMENT-murderous-attack-Western-freedoms.html.

Downing, J. and C. Husband (2005) *Representing Race: Racisms, Ethnicity and the Media*. London: Sage.

Entman, R. (2004) *Projections of Power: Framing News, Public Opinion and U.S. Foreign Policy*. Chicago, IL: University of Chicago Press.

Entman, R. (2007) 'Framing Bias: Media in the Distribution of Power', *Journal of Communication* 57: 163–73.

Entman, R. and B. Page (1994) 'The News Before the Storm' in W. L. Bennett and D. Paletz (eds) *Taken By Storm: The Media, Public Opinion, and U.S. Foreign Policy in the Gulf War*.

Chicago, IL: University of Chicago Press, pp. 82–101.

Fisk, J. (2016) 'We Love to Talk of Terror – But after the Munich Shooting, This Hypocritical Catch-all Term Has Finally Caught Us Out', *Independent*, 24 July. www.independent.co.uk/voices/munich-shooting-nice-attack-terrorism-robert-fisk-catch-all-finally-caught-out-a7153176.html.

Freedman, D. (2013) 'Year after Leveson: Has British Press Cleaned up its Act?', *CNN Online*, 29 November. http://edition.cnn.com/2013/11/29/opinion/uk-leveson-press-opinion.

Freedman, D. (2014) *The Contradictions of Media Power*. London: Bloomsbury.

Gamio, L. and T. Meko (2016) 'How Terrorism in the West Compares to Terrorism Everywhere Else', *Washington Post*, 16 July. www.washingtonpost.com/graphics/world/the-scale-of-terrorist-attacks-around-the-world.

Gitlin, T. (1980) *The Whole World Is Watching: Mass Media in the Making & Unmaking of the New Left*. Berkeley, CA: University of California Press.

Goffmann, E. (1974) *Frame Analysis: An Essay on the Organization of Experience*. New York: Harper & Row.

Herman, E. and N. Chomsky (1988) *Manufacturing Consent: The Political Economy of the Mass Media*. New York: Pantheon.

Kelly, E. (2015) 'The Media Did Cover Attacks on *Insert Country Here* – You Just Weren't Reading It', *Huffington Post*, 16 November. www.huffingtonpost.co.uk/emma-kelly-1/the-media-did-cover-attacks-elswhere_b_8574542.html?utm_hp_ref=uk.

Khiabany, G. and M. Williamson (2012) 'Terror, Culture and Anti-Muslim Racism' in D. Freedman and D. Thussu (eds) *Media and Terrorism:*

Global Perspectives. London: Sage, pp. 134–50.

Koblin, J. (2015) 'News Media Scrambles to Cover Paris Shootings', *The New York Times*, 14 November. www.nytimes.com/2015/11/15/business/media/paris-shooting-attacks-news-media-coverage.html?_r=1.

Laqueur, W. (2009 [1977]) *A History of Terrorism*. New Brunswick, NJ: Transaction.

Lewis, J., R. Brookes, N. Mosdell and T. Threadgold (2006) *Shoot First and Ask Questions Later: Media Coverage of the 2003 Iraq War*. New York: Peter Lang.

Lynch, J. (2016) 'The BBC Suppressed a Significant Strand of Thought on Islamic State in a Key Timeframe: The Week after the Paris Attacks', *PeaceWrites*, May. http://sydney.edu.au/arts/peace_conflict/publications/PeaceWrites_May2016.pdf.

Meade, A. (2016) 'Charlie Hebdo Cartoon Depicting Drowned Child Alan Kurdi Sparks Racism Debate', *Guardian*, 14 January. www.theguardian.com/media/2016/jan/14/charlie-hebdo-cartoon-depicting-drowned-child-alan-kurdi-sparks-racism-debate.

Moore, K., P. Mason and J. Lewis (2008) *Images of Islam in the UK: The Representation of British Muslims in the National Print News Media 2000–2008*. Cardiff: Cardiff School of Journalism, Media and Cultural Studies. https://orca.cf.ac.uk/53005/1/08channel4-dispatches.pdf.

Norton-Taylor, R. (2010) 'Former MI5 Chief Delivers Damning Verdict on Iraq Invasion', *Guardian*, 20 July.

www.theguardian.com/uk/2010/jul/20/chilcot-mi5-boss-iraq-war.

O'Neill, O. (2002) 'Shoot the Messenger', *Guardian*, 1 May. www.theguardian.com/comment/story/0,3604,707820,00.html.

Press Association (2007) 'Study Shows "Demonisation" of Muslims', *Guardian*, 14 November. www.theguardian.com/media/2007/nov/14/pressandpublishing.religion.

Robinson, P., P. Goddard, K. Parry, C. Murray and P. M. Taylor (2010) *Pockets of Resistance: British News Media, War and Theory in the 2003 Invasion of Iraq*. Manchester: Manchester University Press.

Schlesinger, P. (1978) *Putting 'Reality' Together*. London: Constable.

Schlosberg, J. (2013) *Power Beyond Scrutiny: Media, Justice and Accountability*. London: Pluto.

Tell MAMA (2016) *The Geography of Anti-Muslim Hatred: Annual Report 2015*. London: Faith Matters. http://tellmamauk.org/wp-content/uploads/pdf/tell_mama_2015_annual_report.pdf.

Thornton, T. P. (1964) 'Terrorism as a Weapon of Political Agitation' in H. Eckstein (ed.) *Internal War: Problems and Approaches*. New York: Free Press.

Turk, A. (2004) 'Sociology of Terrorism', *Annual Review of Sociology* 30: 271–86.

Tyson, A. (2009) 'Military's Killing of 2 Journalists in Iraq Detailed in New Book', *Washington Post*, 15 September. www.washingtonpost.com/wp-dyn/content/article/2009/09/14/AR2009091403262.html.

13 | WE HATE TO QUOTE STANLEY FISH, BUT: "THERE'S NO SUCH THING AS FREE SPEECH, AND IT'S A GOOD THING, TOO." OR IS IT?

Bill Grantham and Toby Miller

In a situation where any allegiance to religion is regarded as odd and to be kept under wraps (like the veil which in France mustn't be worn in public) then what comparable freedom of speech can the 6,000 [*sic*] inhabitants of the *banlieues*[1] in Paris have? They conspicuously lack the money, education, networking skills and expertise realistically to have a voice. Claiming the high moral ground when your opponent can't get a word in edgeways is actually a form of tyranny and not the out-workings of liberty, equality and fraternity. (Watson 2016: 156)

While some were tempted, a year ago, to in effect lay blame on *Charlie Hebdo* for having crossed the boundaries of common decency in publishing cartoons of the Prophet Muhammad, that kind of caveat became impossible to utter after attackers opened fire and detonated explosive belts on just about anyone: people sitting at cafe terraces, spectators at a rock concert, or passers-by near a football stadium. (Nougayrède 2016)

The motive of the attack was mentioned as a revenge against the depiction of Prophet Mohammed (p[eace] b[e] u[nto] h[im]) by the Magazine, hence [the] *Charlie Hebdo* incident then provoked a worldwide shocks [*sic*] against Islam and Muslims which the Observatory would say, was the most significant turbulence since the terrorist attack on 11 September 2001 in the United States. (OIC 2015: 27)

Introduction

The polarities over *Charlie Hebdo*, as exhibited above by a dedicated philosophical religionist, a lapsed *Le Monde* editor, and the organisation of Islamic states, have if anything grown stronger in the period since publication of the satirical magazine's cartoons of Mohammed and subsequent assassinations and reactions: cardiovascular incidents in a

French hospital increased markedly following the attacks, leading to connections being adduced between heightened media coverage and intense illness (Della Rosa et al. 2016), there were riots in Niger because its President supported *Charlie Hebdo*, and massive protests against the magazine were held across much of the Islamic world (Mueller and Matthews 2016; Sreberny 2016).

From François Hollande (2015) marching and militarising to Tariq Ali (2015) marching and moralising, duelling certainties have dominated the discourse. In that context of profound commitment from all sides, this chapter endeavours to do something slightly different. We are not principally concerned with binaristic position-taking, so simply achieved by those blessed with greater certainty about life than are we. Rather, we want to examine the empirical and theoretical questions that both inform and arise from the *Charlie Hebdo* crisis.

We begin with limits to free speech and blasphemy that arise from their very foundational institutions and texts. Then we address some of the literature about the initial cartoons and assassinations, situating the events in debates about speech in the name of liberalism, and violence in the name of Islam.

Free speech

The United States is often represented as the bastion of free speech, and its eighteenth-century Enlightenment project on behalf of white, property-owning men is regularly invoked, both implicitly and explicitly, in cases such as *Charlie Hebdo*. To live in the US, as we both did for more than two decades, is to experience a constantly replenished fantasy of free speech, where competing perspectives forge the truth, unencumbered by censorship. The *locus classicus* is the First Amendment to the US Constitution. The Amendment says the following:

> Congress shall make no law respecting an establishment of religion, or prohibiting the free exercise thereof; or abridging the freedom of speech, or of the press; or the right of the people peaceably to assemble, and to petition the government for a redress of grievances.

Its original six guarantees – against the creation of a state religion and for freedom of worship, speech, the press, assembly, and the right to seek redress from the government – have evolved into more general protections of the right to expression, assembly and activism.

The apparently limiting language of the Amendment – 'Congress shall make no law' – has been taken by successive Supreme Courts[2] to cover the activities of all state and federal governments and agencies. The First Amendment implies that these protections guarantee conduits to power for ordinary people as well as respites from the religious tyranny, sectarianism and warfare of Europe.

In its deliberations on the First Amendment, the Supreme Court has dealt with some complicated issues. Many of them stem from the quandary 'What is speech?' Is burning the national flag a speech act? (Yes.) Is legislation nominating English as the national language unconstitutional? (Yes.) Can governments erect religious statuary? (No.) May a person who peacefully urges citizens to refuse the draft in wartime be treated as a criminal? (Yes, because that is the equivalent of shouting 'Fire!' in a theatre when there is none.)

For critics like our eponym Stanley Fish, limits to speech do not only emerge when governments must deal with the damage that open discourse may cause in extraordinary, limit cases (1994). Rather, the *very idea* relies on limits: the notion that speech is without adverse – or indeed any – material consequences other than the free exchange of views, as per an idealised university seminar, assumes that much speech is not protected, when it promotes and seeks material action, such as harming others. In US jurisprudence, the historical means of regulating expression is to say that a particular form does not constitute speech. Examples have included defamation, blasphemy, sedition, 'fighting words', pornography and motion pictures. Some of these genres have since been re-anointed to fall within the First Amendment's protections. Some have not.

We are suggesting that even in the principal physical and conceptual domicile of free speech, there are limits, at certain times and under certain laws – and especially when one must distinguish between talking and doing. Consider speech-act theory's notions of constative versus performative speech (Austin 1962): 'I thee wed' are not *just* words, because they enact a legal relationship, with lasting implications for the parties concerned, taxation revenue, state expenditure, healthcare, divorce, alimony and inheritance, *inter alia*. The distance between action and speech is compromised.

In the *Areopagitica*, the Anglo world's urtext on these matters, Milton was happy "to suppress the suppressors themselves" – his way of denying Catholics the free-speech rights that he claimed and advocated for his own sect. A less bigoted fellow-traveller, John Stuart Mill, famously put it this way:

> opinions lose their immunity [from sanction], when the circumstances in which they are expressed are such as to constitute their expression a positive instigation to some mischievous act. An opinion that corn-dealers are starvers of the poor, or that private property is robbery, ought to be unmolested when simply circulated through the press, but may justly incur punishment when delivered orally to an excited mob assembled before the house of a corn-dealer, or when handed about among the same mob in the form of a placard. (Mill 1859)

In other words, free-speech supporters confront practical restrictions on speech that are to do with defining it and assessing whether it is in the public interest and how it is phrased – as information and opinion versus demagoguery. This restriction also extends to who owns speech. For instance, the US Copyright Act of 1976 (as subsequently amended) incorporates the doctrine of 'fair use' to manage restrictions on free speech that would otherwise be generated by the concept of intellectual property (17 U.S.C. §§ 107). It grants limited rights, for instance, to comment on and even *through* texts produced by others. Providing the means to speak can also be part of state policy: from the nineteenth century, the US postal service facilitated political conversation by subsidising the transportation of newspapers and magazines. It tried to do the same in the 1980s via the emergent internet, but was blocked by the Republican Party, which favoured granting rights privately to telephone companies (McChesney 2013: 204, 103). So the US once recognised that the state should in fact enable free speech by subsidising it – not just getting out of the way, or regarding it as identical to other commodities.

Beyond the US, the preamble to the United Nations' Universal Declaration of Human Rights calls for "a world in which human beings shall enjoy freedom of speech and belief and freedom from fear and want", describing this as "the highest aspiration of the common people". Article 19 avows that "[e]veryone has the right to freedom of opinion and expression; this right includes freedom to hold opinions without interference and to seek, receive and impart information and ideas through any media and regardless of frontiers".

But even those true believers who style themselves 'Article 19' now offer us *'Hate Speech' Explained: A Toolkit* to guide governments on restricting the very thing their eponym seeks to guarantee. Article 19 (the organisation) favours limits to freedom of speech when applied to individuals' dignity, though not in the name of collective notions, such as national security, morality, or public order. It accepts the category 'hate speech', while noting that this varies in both definition and legal status across jurisdictions and philosophies. For example, YouTube and the South African state both link hate speech to violence, but the European Court of Human Rights does not. Hence Article 19 argues that: "Pluralism is essential, as one person's deeply held religious belief may be offensive to another's deeply held belief and vice versa. By privileging one belief system over another, either in law or in effect, restrictions on blasphemy inevitably discriminate against those with minority religions or beliefs." It insists that human beings have rights, but religious institutions or abstract commitments such as faith do not.

Blasphemy

Blasphemy is currently *the* crucial debating point over free speech. Cartooning in particular seems to rile anxious sacerdotes, notably *Charlie Hebdo*'s caricatures of all three monotheistic religions; it has been unsuccessfully sued for defamation of Catholicism fourteen times (R. Ali 2015). Pope Francis condemned both the 2015 killings and the caricatures: "One cannot provoke, one cannot insult other people's faith, one cannot make fun of faith. There is a limit ... Every religion has its dignity" (quoted in McElwee 2015).

The Organisation of Islamic Cooperation,[3] which represents fifty-seven countries over four continents that define themselves as Muslim, condemned cartoons of Mohammed that appeared in the Danish broadsheet *Jyllands-Posten* in 2005–6. The Organisation subordinates other international protocols to sharia and describes 'Islamophobia' as "the worst form of terrorism". Its members generally walk out of global gatherings that address queer rights (Howden et al. 2006; Wahab 2007; Evans 2012).

The Organisation's Cairo Declaration on Human Rights in Islam (Nineteenth Islamic Conference 1993) avows that in the best world, of which Islam is the sole custodian, "knowledge is combined with faith". Article 16 of the Declaration guarantees moral rights to the creators of texts, provided they do not run counter to sharia. Article 22 (c) reads: "Information is a vital necessity to society. It may not be exploited or misused in such a way as may violate sanctities and the dignity of Prophets, undermine moral and ethical Values or disintegrate, corrupt or harm society or weaken its faith"; and 22 (d): "It is not permitted to excite nationalistic or doctrinal hatred or to do anything that may be an incitement to any form or [sic] racial discrimination."

This logic argues that the *Charlie Hebdo* cartoons may be deemed both blasphemous, because they ridicule a historic leader of a religion, and defamatory, as they also ridicule adherents of that religion. In addition, the way that supporters of the magazine expressed their sentiments is perceived by some as solidarity *against* Islam as much as *for* free speech (Cox 2016).

Emanuel Todd (2015) argues that blasphemy should not be outlawed, but needs self-regulation because of the offence and discord it provokes among the disenfranchised. Advocates for this position also note the ambivalence of existing international accords on the right to mock religions:

> the International Covenant on Civil and Political Rights ... and the European Convention on Human Rights ... quite clearly do allow for the possibility of speech being restricted in the name of public morality, and if and when a religion is inextricably linked with a nation's public morality, then it is difficult to see why this justification for restricting speech could not apply, at least in theory, to irreligious speech. (Cox 2016: 203)

Given that Muslims represent a quarter of the world's population and Islam is the official religion of a quarter of all countries, rejecting their state codes of blasphemy is akin to saying that international law need not be endorsed by vast numbers in order to be sovereign. *Contra* this position, the 2013 Rabat Plan of Action, adopted by the United Nations High Commissioner for Human Rights and many other international authorities, insists that blasphemy should not subvert free speech.[4] As a practical matter, it is clear that countries which favour prohibiting negative representations of religion are most likely to prohibit religious freedom (Henne 2013). Islamic states that prohibit blasphemy are generally authoritarian and experience violent resistance by their subjects. Nilay Saiya's research demonstrates that:

> blasphemy laws encourage terrorism by creating a culture of vigilantism in which terrorists, claiming to be the defenders of Islam,

attack those they believe are guilty of heresy. This study empirically tests this proposition, along with alternative hypotheses, using a time-series, cross[-]national negative binomial analysis of 51 Muslim-majority states from 1991-2013. It finds that states that enforce blasphemy laws are indeed statistically more likely to experience Islamist terrorist attacks than countries where such laws do not exist. (Saiya 2016)

The Qur'an does not prescribe punishments for blasphemy, or prohibit representation of its true believers' favourite prophet (Saiya 2016). There are rather non-specific, albeit vaguely threatening, fates awaiting blasphemers, but no sign of this occurring in the material world. And it is worth noting that #jesuiskouachi was used 49,000 times on the day of the attacks on *Charlie* (Badouard 2016). The hashtag's adherents relished using their right to free speech to support murder. Meanwhile, the mimetic nature of many recent terrorist attacks, combined with the tendency for them to be committed by social outcasts and those imprisoned for petty crime or sectioned for mental health reasons, might make us ponder whether intense ideological force was their sole impetus (Crone 2016).

Besides, not all Muslims are as vulnerable and sanctimonious as their *bien-pensants*. Islamic humourists all over the world routinely engage in religious satire, mocking themselves and others. Their number includes cartoonists subject to fatwas and state harassment, such as Ali Ferzat, Ali Dilem, Zunar and Musa Kart, and authors who specialise in Bakhtinian profanation (Hirzalla and van Zoonen 2016; Salovaara 2015; El Hissy 2013). As blasphemy laws bite, Muslim cartoonists continue to chafe against their governments' pious assaults (Crispin 2015). On the free-speech side of the debate, satirical French Muslim rappers are routinely denied the right to expression by the state (Kleppinger 2016). Both groups of Islamic satirists relish the genre's capacity to cause offence. That is its very point.

So what should we do about the issues raised by *Charlie Hebdo*? To answer that query, we must go back, and back some more.

Diversity and culture

We all know that the history of Europe is chaotic, fraught, global, and forged in relation to bellicose encounters north, south, east and west. This occurred via both Islamic imperialism and the continent's more successful Christian reconquest. The latter regarded religious imperialism abroad as a 'complement' to 'positivist nation-building at home', with bloodletting legitimised by capitalism and nationalism (Asad 2005: 2). But the "history of individual peoples, and indeed of whole continents such as 'Europe', is now being written in terms of a cultural formation defined by something outside, 'the other'" (Halliday 2001: 113). Cultural differences see the colonising nations altered by their migrant populations' languages, religions, cuisines, clothing and senses of self, especially when they come from formerly enslaved/colonised lands; hence the famous slogan from the 1970s popularised by migrant activists in the UK: 'We are here because you were there.'

Debates about religion in Europe were historically about the commensurability of Protestantism and Catholicism within and between states. Today, the issue is Islam, both as a racial referent and a governmental alternative to secularism. Habermas explains that de-territorialised terrorism, by non-state as well as state actors, has been unleashed by a potent mixture of faith, fraud, ethnicity and economics in response to Western violence, taunts and fiefdoms (2006). The reality today is that "[i]ncreasing numbers of *citizens ... do not belong*. This in turn undermines the basis of the nation-state as the central site of democracy" (Castles and Davidson 2000: viii). Working in London or Paris means confronting the endgame of these interactions on a routine basis and encountering vicious reactions from nativists who deny their own bloody past.

That said, one can exaggerate the impact of violent Islamic encounters on European public opinion. According to a 2016 Pew Research Centre attitudinal survey, most people in France, Britain and Germany are positive about Muslims. Spanish views are more ambiguous, while negativity predominates in Poland and Italy. The gap between left and right is relevant: 36 per cent of Germans on the right dislike Islam, but just 15 per cent on the left do so. The situation is similar in Italy and France (Hackett 2016). Across France, Belgium, Germany, Britain and the Netherlands, concerns about Muslim communities have led to calls to restrict migration. Muslims themselves are largely content with a separation of church and state, which finds them delinking faith from fealty (Bertelsmann Stiftung 2015). It is also worth noting that much of this negative public opinion is based on profound ignorance: "European publics wildly overestimate the proportion of their populations that is Muslim ... on average French respondents thought 31% of their compatriots were Muslim, against an actual figure closer to 8%" (*The Economist* 2015).

But regardless of the data, the difficulty of bridging the distance between Europe's dominant groups and its Muslim minorities is very strong, due to a myriad of moral panics, folk devils, incendiary religionists, gullible youth, opportunistic politicians and militarised states. In Jesús Prieto de Pedro's words:

> The European liberal constitutions of the nineteenth century were political constitutions ... The constitutions of the first third of the twentieth century ... were devoted to economic and social issues ... another stage is evidenced in the decade of the 1970s in the eruption of cultural concerns: this generates lexical forms and doctrinal categories such as 'cultural rights' ... the free existence of culture, cultural pluralism, and the access of citizens to culture are guaranteed in intensified forms. (de Pedro 1999: 63)

This raises a series of complex questions, such as whether minority cultures should be protected from external rule when retention of cultural norms may prevent dynamic change and shackle individual autonomy. For example, should members of a culture be protected by the state from internal oppression when their human rights are compromised in the name of religion, or when the well-being of outsiders is threatened? What should be done about host nations' economic and cultural insecurities, which may be projected onto new arrivals? Should liberalism's lofty but contingent sense of tolerance be celebrated or castigated in contrast with religion's pious intolerance? And what is the responsibility of the bourgeois media to cover Islam in ways endorsed by the religion (Johnson 2000: 406, 408; Runnymede Trust 2000: 240; Sian 2015)? Western media representations of Islam continue to stereotype it, emphasising violence and negative storylines (Ahmed and Matthes 2016).

And the response of states confronted by this cultural difference? Driven by a security and financial agenda, European Union cultural policy has focused over the last forty years on the Cold War, terrorism, economic efficiency, Hollywood, and migrant integration. The media are expected at once to inform and represent new arrivals, right the wrongs of stereotypes, encourage identification with Europe, and function as efficient and effective industries. For their part, migrants are dual targets: of the state, to ensure fealty; and of commerce, to ensure consumption (Mattelart and d'Haenens 2014).

There are many complex limit cases – for example, when a British woman rejected her Muslim parents' plans for an arranged marriage, they sought intervention by the state in the name of cultural maintenance, citing the exemption of Sikhs from safety helmet legislation to ensure protection of their headgear culture as a precedent. Here is a case where measures designed to protect minorities from outside harassment may in fact insulate them from internal dissent, with the state ultimately policing religious observance and familial power dynamics. In this instance, the courts found in favour of the woman, citing the priority of protecting individual rights and doubting the representativeness of self-appointed community spokespeople (Benhabib 2002: 19; Kymlicka 1995: 2, 35–6). When such grand narratives of collectivity and individualism collide, liberal states must double-declutch between support for "a community of individuals and a community of communities" (Runnymede Trust 2000: 176–7, 240).

The literature on *Charlie*

The 'Global North' is inclined to explain natural and social phenomena without reference to deities, but equally without reference to the social importance of showing respect for those deities as a means of living together. How does that rate next to the threat and actuality of individual or mass murder (Cliteur 2016)?

Religious philosophy advises that opposing religion and reason amounts to 'intellectual apartheid', arguing that "the anti-religious stance displayed in the cartoons reflects freedom of speech for one set of worldviews but not for others" (Watson 2016). This is a category mistake about cartoons and what they are. Should a sermon, a political column, or a party manifesto include all sides to debates? They are not textbook chapters, mathematical proofs, kinship maps or scientific documentaries, which claim to give unvarnished accounts of fact. There is no reason why a cartoon should enunciate all sides to an issue, or be impartial.

As noted earlier, *Charlie Hebdo* has treated religious icons, figures and beliefs of various kinds with equal contempt across its history. But we are instructed that when it comes to Mohammed, "*Charlie Hebdo* caricatures are an example of ill judged, uncontrolled and limitless freedom of speech and a risky action that may have future consequences that might cause moral harm" (Švana 2016: 67). Again, this is a category mistake. It is ludicrous to place this burden on cartooning as opposed to other genres, such as reportage, religious incantation, or letters to the editor. Balance of this kind should not be expected of particular satirical works of art. Such desires are a philosophical religious indulgence.

More credibly, the Iranian government criticised both the cartoonists and the gunmen (Barry 2016). The eminent Hegelian communitarian and *New Left Review* founder Charles Taylor distanced himself from the murder, but argued that such attacks should surprise no one given the magazine's additions to the social critique and marginalisation already experienced by those it mocked. While opposing limits to free speech, Taylor pointed to the folly of exercising it in such ways (Swan 2015). And Delfeil de Ton (the pen name of *Charlie* co-founder Henri Roussel) denounced his assassinated colleagues for recklessly exposing themselves and others to danger (M.C. 2015).

For Will Self (2015), satire presupposes a shared ethics and sense of justice as its precondition, and the prospect of unsettling power and comforting weakness. The genre relies on social and cultural specificity, not the breadth of interpretation or right and wrong that comes with daily duels between religious and secular governance. So he discerns an error by *Charlie Hebdo*: misreading the nation within which it was nested.

Responses to the attack on Twitter saw #JeSuisCharlie become "a metaphor for organising news flows, opinions, affects and participatory events in the digital media ecosystem". Within an hour of the murders, a dedicated wiki page had emerged (updated and translated into seventy languages), and within a day, over fifty French and international cities featured tributes. A phone application soon emerged to connect supporters wherever they were (Salovaara 2015). "[N]on-Arabs living in Arab countries ... [used] #JeSuisAhmed ('I am Ahmed') five times more often when ... embedded in a mixed Arab/non-Arab ... network. Among Arabs living in the West, we find a great variety of responses, not altogether associated with the size of their expatriate community" (An et al. 2016). The political postures underpinning various hashtags have been clustered to disclose that #CharlieHebdo is linked to sympathy for victims, #JeSuisCharlie with absolutist support for free speech, #JeNeSuisPasCharlie with a cross-sectarian rejection of free speech both *by* Muslims (as offensive) and *for* Muslims (as something they do not warrant), and #JeSuisAhmed with recognition that a

Muslim policeman was among those whose life was taken, and the need for limitations on free speech. Their use maps closely onto regions of linguistic and religious sectarianism, apart from #JeNeSuisPasCharlie, which appealed to right-wing Islamists and Christians alike, for different reasons (ibid.).

Most Parisian marchers supporting the magazine were from the middle and elite classes (Todd 2015). As hundreds of noted writers put it, "'equal opportunity offence' is the aspiration of Charlie Hebdo. But how is such an aspiration to be fulfilled unless the disparate 'targets' of offence occupy an equal position and have an equivalent meaning within the dominant culture?" (quoted in Greenwald 2015). This is the argument in favour of free speech being rooted in respect for differences (Hietalahti et al. 2016).

The 2015 attack and others have unleashed a state response that is unparalleled in the last sixty years, and not just as per the libertarian left's cliché complaints about surveillance. It is much more important and strategic than that logic will admit:

> For the first time since the end of the Second World War, the assumption that France is experiencing a new form of territorial war is explicit in the public debate. It has reinforced the strong conviction among the French politicians and diplomats that security requires close cooperation with the USA and a renouncement of the Gaullist paradigm of exceptionalism. (Lequesne 2016)

The billionaire feminist critic Élisabeth Badinter called for a boycott of stores selling Islamic fashion; Laurence Rossignol, a socialist minister, likened Muslim women in headscarves to African Americans supporting slavery; and Najat Vallaud-Belkacem, the Education Minister, proposed a programme of re-education for pupils who failed to support the magazine.[5] French international broadcasting attributed the attacks to foreigners (Hollis-Touré 2016; Kiwan 2016; Połońska-Kimunguyi and Gillespie 2016). Meanwhile, dissident intellectuals refuse the government's pleas for unity and the call for Islam to denounce the attacks, because this fails to recognise the heterogeneous backgrounds and institutions of Muslims (Kiwan 2016).

Conclusion

Because partially incommensurate world views and ethnicities are now engaged in uncomfortable *frottage*, we need a new *convivencia*

(Veninga 2016). Advocating, protecting and practising free speech is asserted to be socially beneficial, although the claim that a particular text lacks social benefit does not invalidate it. But when the preponderance of discourse is opposed to a religion followed by such vast numbers, something needs to give on all sides. This should be a matter of case-by-case judgement by participants, be they pious or professional. Both doctrinal and public-policy activity must insist on the centrality of living together, with all the contradictions and paradoxes that implies about minority welfare, social peace, and freedom of speech.

Notes

1 The term *banlieues* is not a formal administrative one. No census numbers are kept that would give a clear idea of how many people live in them, but this number appears extremely low. The term is used popularly to describe impoverished areas characterised by housing projects and immigrant populations. France is said to be home to around 6 million Muslims, three-quarters of North African descent (Połońska-Kimunguyi and Gillespie 2016: 570).

2 Interestingly, no free-speech case reached the Court for the first 128 years of the Amendment's life.

3 See www.oicoci.org/oicv3/page/?p_id=52&p_ref=26&lan=en.

4 See www.ohchr.org/Documents/Issues/Opinion/SeminarRabat/Rabat_draft_outcome.pdf.

5 Of the 64,000 French schools, pupils at 200 declined to observe a minute's silence of respect for the deaths at *Charlie Hebdo* (i.e. to agree to have their speech stilled) (Stille 2015).

References

Ahmed, S. and J. Matthes (2016) 'Media Representation of Muslims and Islam from 2000 to 2015: A Meta-Analysis', *International Communication Gazette.* doi: 10.1177/1748048516656305.

Ali, R. (2015) *Blasphemy, Charlie Hebdo, and the Freedom of Belief and Expression: The Paris Attacks and the Reactions.* London: Institute for Strategic Dialogue. www.strategicdialogue. org/wp-content/uploads/2016/02/Freedom_of_expression_02_15_WEB_FINAL_VS3-FINAL.pdf.

Ali, T. (2015) 'Short Cuts', *London Review of Books*, 22 January. www.lrb. co.uk/v37/no2/tariq-ali/short-cuts.

An, J., H. Kwak, Y. Mejova, S. A. Saenz de Oger and B. Gomez

Fortes (2016) 'Are You Charlie or Ahmed? Cultural Pluralism in Charlie Hebdo Response on Twitter'. Paper presented at the International Association for the Advancement of Artificial Intelligence (AAAI) Conference on Web and Social Media (ICWSM), Cologne, 17–20 May. http://arxiv.org/abs/1603.00646.

Article 19 (2015) *'Hate Speech' Explained: A Toolkit.* London: Article 19. www.article19.org/data/files/medialibrary/38231/'Hate-Speech'-Explained---A-Toolkit-(2015-Edition).pdf.

Asad, T. (2005) 'Reflections on Laïcité & the Public Sphere', *Items and Issues* 5 (3): 1–11.

Austin, J. L. (1962) *How to Do Things with Words: The William James Lectures Delivered at Harvard University in 1955*. Oxford: Clarendon Press.

Badouard, R. (2016) '"Je ne suis pas Charlie". Pluralité des prises de parole sur le web et les réseaux sociaux' in P. Lefébure and C. Sécail (eds) *Le Défi Charlie. Les medias à l'épreuve des attentats*. Paris: Lemieux.

Barry, J. (2016) 'Pragmatic Dogma: Understanding the Ideological Continuities in Iran's Response to the Charlie Hebdo Attacks', *Islam and Christian-Muslim Relations* 27 (1): 77–93.

Benhabib, S. (2002) *The Claims of Culture: Equality and Diversity in the Global Era*. Princeton, NJ: Princeton University Press.

Bertelsmann Stiftung (2015) *Religion Monitor: Understanding Common Ground: Special Study of Islam, 2015 – An Overview of the Most Important Findings*. Gütersloh, Germany: Bertelsmann Stiftung. www. bertelsmann-stiftung.de/fileadmin/ files/Projekte/51_Religionsmonitor/ Religionmonitor_Specialstudy_Islam_ 2014_Overview_20150108.pdf.

Castles, S. and A. Davidson (2000) *Citizenship and Migration: Globalization and the Politics of Belonging*. Basingstoke: Macmillan.

Cliteur, P. (2016) 'Taylor and Dummett on the Rushdie Affair', *Journal of Religion and Society* 18: 1–15.

Cox, N. (2016) 'The Freedom to Publish "Irreligious" Cartoons', *Human Rights Law Review* 16: 195–221.

Crispin, S. W. (2015) *Drawing the Line: Cartoonists under Threat*. Committee to Protect Journalists, 19 May. https://cpj.org/reports/2015/05/ drawing-the-line-cartoonists-under- threat-free-expression-zunar-charlie- hebdo.php.

Crone, M. (2016) 'Radicalization Revisited: Violence, Politics and the Skills of the Body', *International Affairs* 92 (3): 587–604.

de Pedro, J. P. (1999) 'Democracy and Cultural Difference in the Spanish Constitution of 1978' in C. J. Greenhouse with R. Kheshti (eds) *Democracy and Ethnography: Constructing Identities in Multicultural Liberal States*. Albany, NY: State University of New York Press, pp. 61–80.

Della Rosa, F., B. Dongay, J. Van Rothem, B. Farah and A. Pathak (2016) 'We Are Charlie: Emotional Stress from "Charlie Hebdo Attack" Extensively Relayed by Media Increases the Risk of Cardiac Events', *Archives of Cardiovascular Diseases Supplements* 8: 2.

El Hissy, M. (2013) 'Veiled Bodies, Vile Speech: Islam, the Carnivalesque and the Politics of Profanation' in F. Peter, S. Dornhof and E. Argita (eds) *Islam and the Politics of Culture in Europe: Memory, Aesthetics, Art*. Beilefeld: Transcript, pp. 127–42.

Evans, R. (2012) 'Islamic States, Africans Walk Out on UN Gay Panel', *Reuters Africa*, 8 March. http://af.reuters. com/article/topNews/idAFJOE82702 T20120308?sp=true.

Fish, S. (1994) *There's No Such Thing as Free Speech, and It's a Good Thing, Too*. New York: Oxford University Press.

Greenwald, G. (2015) 'Read the Letters and Comments of PEN Writers Protesting the Charlie Hebdo Award', *The Intercept*, 27 April. https:// theintercept.com/2015/04/27/read- letters-comments-pen-writers- protesting-charlie-hebdo-award.

Habermas, J. (2006) 'Religion in the Public Sphere', *European Journal of Philosophy* 14 (1): 1–25.

Hackett, C. (2016) '5 Facts about the Muslim Population in Europe',

Pew Research Center, 19 July. www.pewresearch.org/fact-tank/2016/07/19/5-facts-about-the-muslim-population-in-europe.

Halliday, F. (2001) *The World at 2000: Perils and Promises*. Basingstoke: Palgrave.

Henne, P. S. (2013) 'The Domestic Politics of International Religious Defamation', *Politics and Religion* 6 (3): 512–37.

Hietalahti, J., O. Hirvonen, J. Toivanen and T. Vaaja (2016) 'Insults, Humour and Freedom of Speech', *French Cultural Studies* 27 (3): 245–55.

Hirzalla, F. and L. van Zoonen (2016) '"The Muslims are Coming": The Enactment of Morality in Activist Muslim Comedy', *Humor* 29 (2): 261–78.

Hollande, F. (2015) 'Charlie Hebdo – Statements by President Hollande', *France in the United States*, 8 January. www.franceintheus.org/spip.php?article6408.

Hollis-Touré, I. (2016) 'Introduction: Risk Assessing *Charlie Hebdo*', *French Cultural Studies* 27 (3): 219–22.

Howden, D., D. Hardaker and S. Castle (2006) 'How a Meeting of Leaders in Mecca Set off the Cartoon Wars around the World', *Independent*, 10 February. www.independent.co.uk/news/world/middle-east/how-a-meeting-of-leaders-in-mecca-set-off-the-cartoon-wars-around-the-world-6109473.html.

Johnson, J. (2000) 'Why Respect Culture?', *American Journal of Political Science* 4 (3): 405–18.

Kiwan, N. (2016) 'Freedom of Thought in the Aftermath of the *Charlie Hebdo* Attacks', *French Cultural Studies* 27 (3): 233–44.

Kleppinger, K. (2016) 'When Parallels Collide: Social Commentary and Satire in French Rap Before and After *Charlie Hebdo*', *Contemporary French Civilization* 41 (2): 197–216. http://dx.doi.org/10.3828/cfc.2016.10.

Kymlicka, W. (1995) *Multicultural Citizenship: A Liberal Theory of Minority Rights*. Oxford: Oxford University Press.

Lequesne, C. (2016) 'French Foreign and Security Challenges After the Paris Terrorist Attacks', *Contemporary Security Policy* 37 (2): 306–18.

Mattelart, T. and L. d'Haenens (2014) 'Cultural Diversity Policies in Europe: Between Integration and Security', *Global Media and Communication* X (3): 231–45.

M.C. (2015) 'Delfeil de Ton, ancien de "Charlie", accuse Charb d'avoir "entrainé l'équipe dans la surenchère"', *20 Minutes*, 15 January. www.20minutes.fr/medias/1517631-20150115-delfeil-ancien-charlie-accuse-charb-avoir-entraine-equipe-surenchere.

McChesney, R. W. (2013) *Digital Disconnect: How Capitalism is Turning the Internet Against Democracy*. New York: The New Press.

McElwee, J. J. (2015) 'About Paris Attacks, Francis Says Freedom of Expression Has Certain Limits', *National Catholic Reporter*, 15 January. www.ncronline.org/news/global/about-paris-attacks-francis-says-freedom-expression-has-certain-limits.

Mill, J. S. (1859) *On Liberty*. London: Longman, Roberts, & Green Co. www.econlib.org/library/Mill/mlLbty3.html.

Mueller, L. and L. Matthews (2016) 'The National Elections in Niger, February–March 2016', *Electoral Studies* 43: 203–6. doi: 10.1016/j.electstud.2016.06.001.

Nineteenth Islamic Conference of Foreign Ministers (Session of Peace, Interdependence and Development) (1993) 'Cairo Declaration on Human Rights in Islam, Aug. 5, 1990, U.N. GAOR, World Conf. on Hum. Rts., 4th Sess., Agenda Item 5, U.N. Doc.

A/CONF.157/PC/62/Add.18 (1993)'. http://hrlibrary.umn.edu/instree/ cairodeclaration.html.

Nougayrède, N. (2016) 'A Year After the Charlie Hebdo Attack, France is Still in Denial', *Guardian*, 9 January. www.theguardian.com/ commentisfree/2016/jan/09/charlie-hebdo-paris-terror-attacks-france.

OIC (2015) *Eight OIC Observatory Report on Islamophobia May 2014–April 2015*. Jeddah: Organisation of Islamic Cooperation (OIC). www.oic-oci. org/upload/islamophobia/2015/en/ reports/8th_Ob_Rep_Islamophobia_ Final.pdf.

Połońska-Kimunguyi, E. and M. Gillespie (2016) 'Terrorism Discourse on French International Broadcasting: *France 24* and the Case of *Charlie Hebdo* Attacks in Paris', *European Journal of Communication* 31 (5): 568–83.

Runnymede Trust (2000) *The Future of Multi-Ethnic Britain*. London: Profile Books for Commission on the Future of Multi-Ethnic Britain.

Saiya, N. (2016) 'Blasphemy and Terrorism in the Muslim World', *Terrorism and Political Violence*. doi: 10.1080/09546553.2015.1115759.

Salovaara, I. (2015) '#Je Suis Charlie: Networks, Affects and Distributed Agency of Media Assemblage', *Conjunctions: Transdisciplinary Journal of Cultural Participation* 2 (1): 103–15.

Self, W. (2015) 'A Point of View: What's the Point of Satire?', BBC News, 13 February. www.bbc. co.uk/news/magazine-31442441.

Sian, K. (2015) 'How Do You Spot a Student Extremist in a University?', *Guardian*, 21 July. www.theguardian. com/higher-education-network/2015/ jul/21/how-do-you-spot-a-student-extremist-in-a-university.

Sreberny, A. (2016) 'The 2015 *Charlie Hebdo* Killings, Media Event Chains, and Global Political Responses', *International Journal of Communication* 10: 3485–502.

Stille, A. (2015) 'Five Lessons About France After Charlie Hebdo', *The New Yorker*, 28 February. www.newyorker. com/news/daily-comment/five-lessons-france-charlie-hebdo.

Švaňa, L. (2016) '*Charlie Hebdo* Attacks in the Light of Aquinas' Doctrine of Double Effect and Ignatieff's Lesser Evil Theory', *Human Affairs* 26: 63–72.

Swan, M. (2015) 'Charlie Hebdo "Part of the Situation" That Led to Attack, Says Charles Taylor', *Catholic Register*, 12 January. http://catholicregister. org/item/19513-charlie-hebdo-part-of-the-situation-that-led-to-attack-says-charles-taylor.

The Economist (2015) 'Islam in Europe', 7 January. www.economist.com/ blogs/graphicdetail/2015/01/daily-chart-2.

Todd, E. (2015) *Who is Charlie? Xenophobia and the New Middle Class*. Oxford: Polity.

Veninga, J. E. (2016) 'Echoes of the Danish Cartoon Crisis 10 Years Later: Identity, Injury and Intelligibility from Copenhagen to Paris and Texas', *Islam and Christian-Muslim Relations* 27 (1): 25–34.

Wahab, S. (2007) 'Islamophobia Worst Form of Terrorism', *Arab News*, 17 May. www.arabnews. com/node/298472.

Watson, B. (2016) 'Belief and Evidence, and How It May Aid Reflection Concerning Charlie Hebdo', *Think* XV (42): 151–61.

14 | *JOUISSANCE* AND SUBMISSION: 'FREE SPEECH', COLONIAL DIAGNOSTICS AND PSYCHOANALYTIC RESPONSES TO *CHARLIE HEBDO*

Anne Mulhall

What death does one die 'after the colony'? 'There are so many deaths. One no longer knows which one to die.' For there are not only several sorts of deaths. There are also several forms of dying. (Mbembe 2001: 197)

Uncensored speech as guarantor of French liberty and Enlightenment freedoms was emphasised strongly by the psychoanalytic establishment in France during the outpouring of responses to the fatal attack on the offices of *Charlie Hebdo* on 7 January 2015. In a series of issues analysing the event in *Le Point* and *Lacan Quotidien*, Jacques-Alain Miller connected the 'free speech' of the psychoanalytic session to the 'freedom of speech' that *Charlie Hebdo* came to represent, for the 'we' of the Republic that he and others invoked: both insist on the licence to say what is impermissible. In this spirit, in the ambivalent and satirical voice he deploys throughout the series, Miller narrates a history of sorts of what he terms "the adventures of the drive" where *Charlie Hebdo* is installed in the genealogy of European civilisation, beginning with the 'Greco-Roman world', through the 'Christian discourse' and the fusion of these inheritances in the humanism of the Renaissance.

In 'The Return of Blasphemy', Miller (2015a) reflects on the breach in the symbolic that the killing of "Cabu, Charb, Tignoux, Wolinski" (he does not name the eight other people who were killed in the attack) had rent open in 'our world'. Miller articulates this as an eruption of one world into the other in a series of antinomies between two worlds that, "formerly separate and sealed off from each other, now communicate. More than that: they interpenetrate." These two 'discursive universes' constitute separate symbolic orders – that of the French Republic, and that of the 'Islamic tradition', animated by their different modes of *jouissance* – one manifest in the iconoclastic laughter of satire, the other in the cataclysmic violence of terror and annihilation.

While the particular referents of Miller's piece are the slain staff of *Charlie Hebdo* and their killers, the Kouachi brothers, this particularity is assimilated within the 'clash of civilisations' narrative, even while Miller attempts to maintain a certain ambiguity in his own narrativising. Observing that "Nowhere, ever ... has it been permissible to say anything and everything" (a stance that is eroded by his later exchange with Jacques Rancière), Miller nonetheless distinguishes between the 'us' he invokes – undoubtedly what he refers to in that exchange with Rancière as the 'indigenous' population of France (Miller 2015c) – and the 'them' who reside in the same territory but who have not submitted to the values of the Republic. He uses the terms 'Muslims' and 'minority populations' interchangeably as referents for this unassimilated other. How can the sacred and the profane coexist in the state without violence ensuing, Miller asks? Given the impracticality or undesirability (Miller's tone makes it difficult to ascertain which describes his position) of the mass removal of 'minority populations' (a statement that says much about normative attitudes towards both French 'minority' citizens and migrants), Miller suggests that the future direction of the state hinges on asserting with renewed vigour the value of the secular, universalist values of the Republic. Central to this is the right to 'free speech', here articulated as the right to satire and the enjoyment of satire, which is posited as the 'drive' impelling the French secular tradition, as distinct from the drive that animates 'the Islamic tradition':

> Unless we were to turn back time, that of the modern era, and deport all minority populations from the country, the question – a question of life or death – will be to know whether our penchant for satire, for the right to ridicule, to be iconoclast in our disrespect, whether these rights are as essential to our mode of *jouissance* as is the submission to the One of the Islamic tradition. (Miller 2015a)

Miller at least rhetorically finds in satire an origin of sorts for the Enlightenment legacy whose threatened inheritance has been kept alive by *Charlie Hebdo*. "What was the principal lever of the Enlightenment, if not laughter?" he asks. "The doctrines of tradition were not refuted ... but chased away by laughter. *Charlie Hebdo* was, in our world, one of the last visible traces or outcrops of this founding derisive laughter." Miller was not alone in the wake of the attack in positioning *Charlie*

Hebdo within the Enlightenment tradition nor in claiming it a place in the Western satirical canon. Located by several commentators within a French tradition of satire valorised as anti-clerical, iconoclastic and in thrall to no dictates save the exacting rule of truth, *Charlie Hebdo* was positioned as the inheritor of the Enlightenment tradition of Voltaire in a lineage that reached back further still to, as Remi Piet described in his *Al Jazeera* op-ed 'Why Satire is Holy to the French', "the very cradle of European civilisation, from Greece to Rome, from Aristophanes to Seneca" (Piet 2015). The medieval French kings and their buffoons, the plays of Molière, the fables of Jean de la Fontaine, all are cited as precursors to *Charlie Hebdo*'s iconoclastic mocking of the powerful. Writing in *The Wall Street Journal*, L. Gordon Crovitz likewise ventriloquises the indivisibility of the tradition of French satire, the Enlightenment values of the Republic, and the principle of 'free speech', seeing these as intrinsic to 'French identity'. Crovitz cites the example of Voltaire and the moral inviolability of the French satirical tradition:

> Many of us don't share the sensibilities of *Charlie Hebdo*'s leftist politics and sometimes juvenile humor, but the terrorists who massacred its staff attacked a core component of French identity. "Free thought begetting light-hearted satire … is at the root of the French character," observed a 19th-century British history of French literature. French-style caustic satire is less common in the Anglosphere, but the Enlightenment in all forms enrages Islamists. (Crovitz 2015)

A central concern of such genealogical efforts is the assertion on the one hand of freedom of speech as a central French, European and 'Western' value upon which all other freedoms depend, freedoms with which *Charlie Hebdo* courageously and almost uniquely held faith. On the other hand, Islam, 'Islamists' and (whether directly or by implication) other 'unassimilable' populations – people of colour, Muslims, migrants, impoverished suburban youth – are presented as an undifferentiated, inhuman, essentialised enemy, violent, fanatical, alien and hostile to 'the West' even when their birthplace and home place is 'the West'. These genealogies and the strategies of biopolitical management they animate were a more canonical version of an argument broadcast widely and debated ferociously across social media platforms in the weeks following 7 January which advanced an unfeasibly idealised, selective understanding of the objectives and motivations of satire. A certain consensus was apparent in the repetition of clichéd moral aspirations for 'proper' satire: it should "punch up, not down"; it should "afflict the comfortable and comfort the afflicted" (Self 2015).[1]

Bound up with this moral imperative was the appeal to *context*. Specifically, critics of *Charlie Hebdo*'s re-circulation of racist colonial visual tropes of colonised people depicted as primitive, willingly servile and simple-minded were described as ignorant of the French context: both the political contexts addressed in *Charlie Hebdo*'s lampoons, and the tradition of French satire that these continued. Thus in 'On *Charlie Hebdo*: A Letter to my British Friends', Oliver Tonneau defends the publication against charges of Islamophobia from the British left commentariat, who he argues do not understand the complexities of the French political and literary contexts: "Even if their sense of humour was apparently inacceptable to English minds, please take my word for it: it fell well within the French tradition of satire – and after all was only intended for a French audience. It is only by reading or seeing it out of context that some cartoons appear as racist or islamophobic" (Tonneau 2015).[2] In a similar vein, Leigh Phillips impatiently explains to his misguided Anglophone readers that the infamous cartoon of the Minister for Justice Christiane Taubira by Charb, *Charlie Hebdo*'s murdered editor-in-chief, is an anti-racist cartoon satirising the racism of the Front National, despite the cartoon depicting, as he describes it "a black woman's head on a monkey's body above the phrase *Rassemblement Bleu Raciste*" (Phillips 2015). The schooling of the Anglophone anti-racist left is the opening gambit of an article that is primarily concerned to defend the right to free speech as well as define what is and is not to be considered as racialising and racist representation. Here, the defence of free speech is folded into a critique of the 'identitarian left' and the by now galvanised association between 'censorship' and anti-colonial, anti-racist politics. "There is a worrying trend on the left," Phillips frets,

> to dismiss freedom of expression as part of the colonialist project, to repudiate free speech as a meaningless elite piety. In recent years, the liberal-left, particularly in the anglophone world, has taken to demanding the censorship of 'offensive' or 'triggering' speech, and student unions, theatres, universities, schools, municipalities, art galleries and other public venues have increasingly shut down a wide range of speech acts. (Phillips 2015)

In perhaps the most astute and factually accurate description of satire that circulated on social media following the attack, Scott Long (2015) counters its characterisation as the speaking of truth to power. On the contrary: satire is "an exercise in power. It claims superiority, it aspires to win, and hence it always looms over the weak, in judgment." He quotes Adorno: "He who has laughter on his side has no need of proof. Historically, therefore, satire has for thousands of years, up to Voltaire's age, preferred to side with the stronger party which could be relied on: with authority." Irony, he added, "never entirely divested itself of its authoritarian inheritance, its unrebellious malice." These observations recall Freud's brief comments on satire as a form of 'tendentious' joke. The moral impetus of satire is inseparable, in this formulation, from its sadistic impulse. "In satire," Jonathan Greenberg explains in relation to Freud's analysis, "moral outrage and sadistic pleasure *have the same stimulus*; whether a joke appears in good or bad taste depends only on the strength of internal and external inhibition" (Greenberg 2011: 5).

Arguments continue to be made in support of *Charlie Hebdo*'s use of images that remobilise racist colonial stereotypes – hook-nosed Muslims and Arabs, a Black woman with the body of a monkey, undifferentiated masses of African men and women drawn in 'Y'a Bon Banania'-style caricature (Donadey 2000). The apparent disavowal of the connection of such images to what Achille Mbembe has called the 'death worlds' of the colony and the postcolony speaks to the disavowal of race, racism, the colony and its afterlives in a broader French and European context. For instance in his 'Letter', Tonneau feels confident in asserting that in France, "we do not conflate religion and race ... Of course, the day when everybody confuses 'Arab' with 'Muslim' and 'Muslim' with 'fundamentalist', then any criticism of the latter will backfire on the former. That is why we must keep the distinctions clear" (Tonneau 2015). Further, he emphasises the role of 'fundamentalists' in the suffering of the peoples during the Algerian War, decolonisation, the civil war, an emphasis that serves to minimise the role of the French state as a major colonial and postcolonial power: "France is home today to many Arabs, some of them Muslims, who were chased away from their home country by fundamentalists as early as the 1960s" (ibid.).

This disavowal is intrinsic to the imaginary of the French Repub- lic. As Max Silverman notes, "this mythological view of the French republic" simultaneously leans on and energises the dualistic logic that is also intrinsic to the Enlightenment inheritance and its gendered, racialised differentiations between self/other: "the by-now familiar binary oppositions between universalism and particularism, assimilation and difference, citizen and subject, civilization and barbarity, secularism and faith, public and private, individual and collectivity" (Silverman 2007: 631) This Manichean logic undergirds the state, and the emancipatory ideals claimed as its informing ideals serve to both deny and enforce the purposefully racial terms of national belonging, manifest in the regulation of citizenship and what Geoffroy de Laforcade describes as

> a transcendent claim to universalism through which 'assimilation' was conditioned on the unilateral renunciation of one's origins, faith, customs, language and memory; in short, on 'integration' into a preexisting, naturalized community of affinities vigilantly protected by ethnic-neutral republicanism, policed borders and the proclamation of a unitary concept of 'True France'. (de Laforcade 2006: 224)

The imperative to assimilate those paradoxically marked out as unassimilable into a Republic that is likewise imagined as culturally homogeneous also invests psychoanalytic commentary on the atrocities of 2015, and a similar disavowal of the normative racialised assumptions that characteristically subtend psychoanalytic cultural diagnostics is apparent in many of those responses.

Many psychoanalysts have commented extensively on the terrible attacks in France in which so many people lost their lives. The responses and analyses of figures such as Jacques-Alain Miller, Élisabeth Roudinesco, Éric Laurent, Fethi Benslama, Malek Chebel, Gérard Bonnet and Julia Kristeva did not appear out of nowhere; psychoanalytic speculation about the etiology of Islam and 'Islamic fundamentalism' is by now a well-established line of enquiry among psychoanalytic thinkers in France.[3] Nor is such analysis confined to a rarefied specialist milieu. Many of the pre-eminent figures in psychoanalysis in France are also public figures; psychoanalytic discourse is part of a public intellectual discourse, and as a clinical practice psychoanalysis has a strong presence. As Élisabeth Roudinesco notes in *Why Psychoanalysis?*, France has the highest ratio of psychoanalysts per capita in the world – 5,000 analysts, or eighty-six per million of the population. For Roudinesco, this position is the result of conditions created in the first instance by the 1789

Revolution. The Revolution "granted scientific and juridical legitimacy to reason's consideration of madness ... Without the 1789 Revolution, there would not have been a body of psychiatric knowledge in France capable of integrating the universal nature of the Freudian discovery," while the Dreyfus affair, she contends, galvanised "an intellectual avant-garde capable of supporting a subversive representation of the Freudian notion of the unconscious" (Roudinesco 2001: 89–90). In other words, for Roudinesco, psychoanalysis is inextricable from the 'birth' of French modernity. Its trajectory has been coterminous with the Republic, the separation of church and state, and *laïcité*. Psychoanalysis is thus narrativised as an emancipatory practice that uncovers universal truths about the unconscious and the constitution of the subject. Julia Kristeva's writing on religion and Islam over the last ten years has clearly articulated the role of psychoanalysis in the defence of the Republic and its ideals. "The French Republic finds before itself a historical challenge," Kristeva declared in a speech delivered in Stockholm in 2016:

> Are we capable of mobilizing all the means necessary, police forces as well as economic ones – without of course forgetting those that gives [*sic*] us knowledge of the soul – alongside a suitable education program and the generosity required to lend an ear to those we're treating for this poignant ideality disorder that descends upon us with all the atrocities of the radicalized? Interpreted in this way, the barbarity of jihadists prey to the malignance of evil, concerns 'our' fundamental 'values', our humanistic secularized culture and our model of civilization where rationality is not without recourse in the face of radical evil under the cover of divine revelation. (Kristeva 2016)

This symbiotic relationship between psychoanalytic knowledge and the secular Republic underwrites the at times impassioned declarations of allegiance to the values of universalism. In a riposte to an interview with Jacques Rancière in *Nouvelle Observatoire* in April 2015, Miller berates Rancière for his critique of French universalism and *laïcité*. Rancière argues that the meaning and function of universalism and secularism in France have become warped and now operate as explicitly racist techniques of exclusion and punishment, targeted at Muslim and racialised populations who rightly feel that this 'transformed' universalism "is a lie serving only to oppress" (Rancière 2015). The France of Miller's imagination is, as he describes it, a lone bulwark against the economic and cultural violences of global capitalism. In Miller's play on the antinomies of universalism/particularism, the particular 'universalism' of the French Republic takes on a heroic and defiant cast, while Rancière's pretensions to standing with "the most exploited of the exploited" aligns him, in Miller's logic, with the despots of the world (Miller 2015c). "Those who think that 'great universalist values' (your term) are just the 'new look' instruments of Western imperialism are legion ... Putin and his Slavophile philosophers as well as the masters of China, Saudi Arabia, Iran and the new Islamic Caliphate ... are all in agreement on that" (ibid.). Imputations that France is indeed a racist state, where *laïcité* functions as an effective technology of racialised population management, are met with hostility: "in the name of what do you want the indigenous population of France to submit their particularism – which is universalist – to the particularism of the 'particular community in question'?" (ibid.).

In another response piece, this time to an interview with Achille Mbembe in *Libération*, Roudinesco (2016) berates what she frames as Mbembe's unreasonable fixation on colonisation and its consequences. In the interview, Mbembe exposes the central contradiction of a universalism that is focused on maintaining the particularity of French identity through accelerated violence against targeted 'unassimilable' populations whose expulsion from the nation is accomplished through their production as unassimilable foreign bodies by the apparatus of weaponised state secularism. "The problem," Mbembe maintains, "is when universalism is made ethnic. It is when identity is conjugated with racism and culture is made to appear as an immutable essence" (Faure and Daumas 2016).[4] In the French case, Mbembe calls this ethnic universalism *l'universalisme péteux* – a technique whereby the person is clearly marked as 'other', and then held to account for failing to integrate. Roudinesco's response is curt, confined to a complaint that Mbembe "speaks only of French colonialism and not of anti-colonialism at all"[5] – going on to name some French anti-racists of the mid-twentieth century – and, like Miller, asserts her adherence to French secularism and support for the ban on both the headscarf in schools and the niqab in public (Roudinesco 2016).

Responses from psychoanalysts in France to the events of 2015 draw on an established interpretation of Islam as submission to the One that depends for its efficacy on an insistent dualism between Islam as fanatical duty to the absolute, and a Judeo-Christian tradition that encompasses humanism and secularism as part of a Western developmental model of progress. "No religion has magnified the transcendence of the One, its separation, as did the discourse of Muhammad," declares Miller in 'The Lyric Illusion', another of his essays written in response to the *Charlie Hebdo* murders (Miller 2015b). "Faced with the Absolute, neither Judaism, nor Christianity, leave human debility alone. They offer the believer mediation, relief, a people, a church while the Islamic Absolute is not mitigated and remains unbridled" (ibid.). This distinction pivots on the paternal figure and the characteristically ambivalent Oedipal father–son relation. According to Kristeva, for instance, in the Jewish and Christian traditions, God assumes human form as God the Son in the Christian tradition, and is conceived of as the father of his Chosen People in the Jewish faith. She holds that the Judeo-Christian tradition likewise is invested with superior capacities for sublimation due to the patricide at the centre of both and the resulting sublimation of the drive and its channelling into cultural and intellectual production – in an analogous fashion to the Oedipal structure in the Freudian tradition, whereby the son internalises the symbolic father or fear of retribution at the hands of the father, a sublimation that is constitutive of the superego.

Freud's analogising between the psychic development of the individual and what he narrates as the evolutionary trajectory from 'primitive' peoples to civilisation is a touchstone in such analyses, then. The influence of evolutionary science and scientific racism on Freud's thinking is apparent in his application of a universal model of psychic constitution to his anthropological speculations on the evolution of civilisation, and is articulated in some of his more controversial works: *Totem and Taboo*, *The Future of an Illusion*, and *Moses and Monotheism*. It is also apparent in less obviously problematic texts such as 'The Uncanny', where infantile development is nonetheless mapped on to an evolutionary developmental model. Describing the process whereby the primary narcissism of the infant is repressed in the course of socialisation and ego-formation, Freud contends that: "It would seem as though each one of us has been through a phase of individual development corresponding to that animistic stage in primitive men" (Freud 2003: 12). "Civilized people" have "*surmounted*" such "primitive beliefs" (ibid.:16), but, as with the individual, the "repressed desires and archaic forms of thought belonging to the past of the individual and the race" (ibid.:15) are not evacuated once and for all but are retained in the unconscious and persist in the present in more or less evident ways.

In the introduction to *Unconscious Dominions* (Anderson et al. 2011), the editors spell out the connection between Freud's evolutionary model and the continued complicity of psychoanalysis in constructing the colonised as not fully evolved. For early practitioners, even the most 'advanced' of the colonised population had not arrived at civilisation as defined by European norms, which were, of course, deeply invested in and dependent on the positioning of the colonised 'other' in just this way: "Many European analysts implied that native elites were stalled on the road to psychological modernity, requiring continued supervision and discipline" (ibid.: 12). The contemporary manifestations of the inherently racist, racialising construction of a self-legitimating binary between the civilised and uncivilised, coloniser and colonised, self and other are apparent in psychoanalytic constructions of a generalised 'Islam' (and, therefore, of individual Muslims) as 'stuck' in a more primitive stage of psychic and cultural development. In an interview published in *Charlie Hebdo* in February 2015, the first issue following the attack, psychoanalysts Gérard Bonnet and Malek Chebel make manifest in their raw form the essentialist racial norms that can underwrite psychoanalysis in its universalist and culturalist mode. Responding to the question of why some people take offence at representations of the Prophet, Bonnet responds: "They effectively think if you lay into the image of the Prophet you are laying into Mohammed himself. They have remained at an infantile stage which confuses the real and its representation. It is like the primitive who believes that if one takes a photograph of him, one takes his soul. It is an enormous regression" (Bonnet and Chebel 2015: 15).[6]

Seemingly impervious to the imbrications of the religious and the political in the constitution of contemporary France and Europe, Chebel adds that: "In Islam there is no difference between the religious and the political ... In Islam, all the problems comes from the fact that the Prophet got involved in the business of men, and this is what has led to the confusion between the political and the religious" (ibid.: 15). Chebel continues: the Muslim has "no concept of the individual" (ibid.: 16) but instead operates as part of a monolithic, undifferentiated mass. This is a mark of the failure of 'the Muslim' to achieve modernity, which the 'West' has achieved by passing through what we might call the developmental stage of Enlightenment and "the emergence of the notion of the autonomous and responsible individual" (ibid.: 15). Bonnet concurs; further, the "absence of the concept of the autonomous and free subject in the Muslim world" has particular consequences for teenage 'Muslims', who, unlike their 'Western' peers, cannot act out in the family and thus act out instead "in society": "Instead of fighting the ideals of their own society, they fight against the ideals of our own society" (ibid.: 16). It should be noted here that both men are speaking primarily about young people who, for the most part, have been born in and have grown up in France, yet despite the valorisation of universalism, *laïcité* and so forth, these young people – 'Muslims' – are marked out as internal aliens, not of the 'West', not "of our own society". Agreeing with Bonnet's dualistic logic and unsupported speculations, Chebel goes further; the 'problem' afflicts not just "certain teenagers" but that homogeneous racialised figure, "the Muslim", who, he notes, has failed to separate from the mother. As a collective, then, 'the Muslim' "behaves like the child who has not reached the stage of 'I': he is always in a complete fusion with his mother and, thus, with his religion. It is very tribal" (ibid.).

Even while their utterances are saturated with its informing presence, the psychoanalytic commentators dodge around the question of colonisation and its afterlives in the present in the *banlieues* of Paris, in the coercive force and further marginalisations exacted against Muslim women, and in the besieged, harassed encampments on the waste grounds of the nation. The question of what this context of acute intergenerational racialised violence and dereliction at the hands of the Republic might have to do with the vulnerability of disenfranchised young people to 'radicalisation' is rarely the focus of analysis. Instead, defences of French universalism and psychoanalytic interrogations of the Islamic disposition predominate, both in the aftermath of the Paris attacks and in the investigations into the nature of the Islamic subject that began to appear after 9/11. These absorptions are not surprising, given the tensions between (an evasion of) the consequences of social, material conditions for psychic constitution, on the one hand, and the inescapable fact of the interrelation between psychoanalysis and colonialism, particularly evident in France's colonial enterprises in North Africa into the mid-twentieth century, on the other.

The bristling against critiques of universalism and colonial inherit-ances as instanced here in Miller's and Roudinesco's pieces only serves to further destabilise the emancipatory values that the commentators attest as the central cohesive ideals of the Republic. In *Unconscious Dominions*, a collection that interrogates the largely unacknowledged colonial and postcolonial complicities of psychoanalysis, Anderson et al. note that "psychoanalysis and colonialism together forged this conflicted cosmopolitan figure of the universalised, psychoanalysable subject" and call for an examination of "the extent to which the psychoanalytic subject, that figment of European high modernism, is constitutively a colonial creation" (Anderson et al. 2011: 3). In addition to the clearly racially inflected evolutionary models of development that he proposes, Freud's mapping of the unconscious as "a forbidden zone of irrational desire and passionate violence" bears a more than coincidental resemblance to the feverish "imperial imagining" that "structured colonial space in starkly opposing terms" (ibid.). Freud has little to say about Islam, but along with psychology and psychiatry, psychoanalysis played an important role in establishing still-operative racist typologies of 'the Muslim' and 'the Arab' in French-occupied colonial North Africa, and contemporary attempts to psychoanalyse 'the Muslim' and 'Islam' resonate in deeply problematic ways with such typologies and their real and disastrous effects, which I will return to at the end of this chapter. In his excellent critique of contemporary psychoanalytic engagements with Islam, Albert Toscano notes that the consequence of psychoanalytic "defenses of 'our' Western legacy ... is almost invariably 'to enclose the Other in religion all the better to expel him from politics' – turning social struggles and geopolitical strategies into matters of vaguely defined culture and even more vaguely defined mentalities, which no quantity of psychoanalytic sophistication can really sunder from the colonial tradition of inquiry into the native's 'mind'" (Toscano 2009: 114).

In a 2016 keynote speech that responds to the slaughters in France, Julia Kristeva addresses herself to the figure of the psychically sick adolescent. Like Bonnet and Chebel, though far more obliquely, she moves between psychoanalysing the 'problem' of the troubled teenager as a vulnerable subject, at risk of radicalisation, to analysing 'Islam' as, again, stuck in an adolescent phase of development. Kristeva asks how to stop the "unbinding that sets loose the death drive, freewheeling in the adolescent gangster-fundamentalism in our communities", the believer who is "necessarily nihilist because pathetically idealist, the disintegrated adolescent, dissocialized in the ruthless globalized migration imposed by ultra-liberalism, itself ruthless, when it commoditizes and levels out every 'value'" (Kristeva 2016). She has already bracketed off the historical, material and geopolitical violences that have contributed to the rise of fundamentalism. "I won't be able to get into the geopolitical and theological causes of this phenomenon," Kristeva informs her audience, "the responsibility of post-colonialism, the failures of integration and education, the weakness of 'our values' that manage globalization by way of petro-dollars in turn based on surgical strikes, the shrinking of the political in the service of an economy by more or less soft or hard jurisdiction ..." (ibid.).

Recapitulating the call she makes in *This Incredible Need to Believe* for a new 'reformed humanism', Kristeva gives a living example of the salvific effects of the European secular humanist tradition, situating psychoanalysis firmly within that lineage and as perhaps its best hope for survival. Speaking of Souad, an adolescent girl who came to analysis "clinging to barbarity in order to not fall to pieces but to enjoy to death", Kristeva describes how the riches of the French language and the Western cultural tradition (the Western Christian-humanist-secular tradition) gradually brought Souad back to humanity. "Reconnected to the French language, taming through language the drives and sensations of suffering, finding the words to make them exist, to unmake and remake, to share them: language, literature, poetry, theater filled the lack of meaning and undid the nihilism" (Kristeva 2016). The point here is not the efficacy of the treatment for the individual analysed, but the general inference we are to draw from Kristeva's case study: the cure for Islam is immersion in the values of Western civilisation and of the French Republic. The capacity for sublimation that is for Kristeva unique among religions to Christianity is also the foundation of European modernity, connecting Christendom, specifically, to its evolution through Renaissance humanism and the Enlightenment. The reliance of this genealogy of European values on the foil of the Islamic barbarian is starkly apparent when Kristeva makes a similar point in *This Incredible Need to Believe*:

> You see, in trying to plumb the mysteries of Christianity starting from analytical experience, but also starting from philosophy, art, and literature, which very often precede it, it appears, in effect, that Christ leads to Mozart: that Christianity refines suffering into joy. Listen to the Miserere Nobis of the *Mass in C Minor*: the sacrifice resolves itself into serenity, then ecstasy. What an unexpected filiation! Allah's madmen, among others, should give this some thought. (Kristeva 2009: 84)

Toscano's conclusions about the consequences of psychoanalytic thought and practice "taking such a Christian secularism as both historically and psychically normative" are important, and yet the most publicly acknowledged psychoanalytic commentators in France are, it seems, impervious to the implications of their work, and indifferent to the ghosts that haunt their discourse. This investment is disastrous because:

> it ethnicizes and culturalizes the unconscious by presuming that one can gain insight into the psychic disturbances and political difficulties of individual 'Muslims' by postulating fantasies that take place at the level of the religious text itself. This 'textualism' ... is of course one of the primary tropes of the Orientalism explored and dissected by Edward Said. (Toscano 2009: 114–15)

In *The Wretched of the Earth*, Frantz Fanon draws on his experiences working in Algiers and Tunisia to lay bare the racist violence that the 'colonial psychiatry' of Antoine Porot and the Algiers School, most especially, were responsible for propagating in the guise of objective psychiatric knowledge. Fanon's recitation of the typology of the North African and of the Algerian – which were used interchangeably and synonymously with 'The Arab' and 'The Muslim', much like 'Muslim' or 'Migrant or 'Minority Population' are used interchangeably in the contemporary texts considered in this chapter – resonates uncomfortably with Islam and the Muslim as pathologised in those texts. So Fanon tells us that the 'North African' according to Porot lacks reason; is prone to violent outbursts; is incapable of sublimation. "Cartesianism is fundamentally foreign to him," Fanon summarises, "The North African is violent, hereditarily violent. He finds it impossible to discipline himself and channel his instincts. Yes, the Algerian is congenitally impulsive" (Fanon 2004: 223). In relation to the "mental capacity" of the Algerian, Fanon reminds the reader of "the semiology elaborated by the school of Algiers" in a widely used student textbook. Again, these 'characteristics' recall in particular the description of 'the Muslim' and 'Islam' as stuck in various stages of developmental arrest, lacking in properly mature individuation, prone to fanaticism. So the "native" is "highly credulous and suggestible", "doggedly stubborn" and of a "childlike mentality minus the curiosity of the European child" (ibid.: 224) – characteristics that perhaps reverberate still in the many ascriptions of an adolescent or even infantile position to 'Islam' and 'the Muslim' in psychoanalytic enquiries. In his magisterial autobiography of Frantz Fanon, David Macey (2000) demonstrates that Fanon, though interested in psychoanalysis, was not a psychoanalyst. Yet, Fanon's scathing critique of the role that French colonial psychiatry played in the subjection and suffering of North Africans under French occupation and as migrant workers in the *bidonvilles* of metropolitan France speaks across the decades to the psychoanalytic discourse of the present. "If haunting describes how that which appears to be not there is often a seething presence", then Fanon haunts the disavowals, the deflections and the projections that ghost the psychoanalytic engagement with the racialised Other as manifest in responses to the attacks in Paris (Gordon 2009: 7).

In his 2016 interview with *Liberation*, Mbembe speaks to "the rise in Europe of paranoid discourses", framing these as a kind of "witchcraft": "there is always someone who is angry with me because of who I am and not because of what I have done to him". The paranoic needs a scapegoat: "This was the case yesterday with the Negroes and the Jews. If one is not careful, it will soon be the case with Muslims and all kinds of foreigners."[7] If there is to be a psychoanalysis of the catastrophic present, this would perhaps be a more fruitful position to begin from, taking in the first instance the repressed content of psychoanalytic discourse itself as the analytic subject.

Notes

1 Will Self (2015) notes that the much-recycled description of the function of journalism was "coined by the Chicago-based humorist Finley Peter Dunne (1867–1937), who put the words into the mouth of a fictional Irish bartender, Mr Dooley – 'Th' newspaper does ivrything f'r us. It runs th' polis foorce an' th' banks, commands th' milishy, controls th' ligislachure, baptizes th' young, marries th' foolish, comforts th' afflicted, afflicts th' comfortable, buries th' dead an' roasts thim afterward.'"

2 An edited version of Tonneau's article was republished by the *Guardian*'s 'Comment Is Free' on 13 January 2015 (www.theguardian.com/commentisfree/2015/jan/13/charlie-hebdo-solution-muslims-french-arab-descent-newspaper-fight-racism).

3 See, for instance, Bruno Étienne, *Les Combattants Suicidaires* (2005); Julia Kristeva, *Cet incroyable besoin de croire* (2007); Moutapha Safouan, *Why Are the Arabs Not Free* (2007); Joan Copjec et al. (eds) 'Islam and Psychoanalysis', special issue of *Umbr(a): A Journal of the Unconscious* (2009); Benslama, *La guerre des subjectivités en Islam* (2014); Chebel, *L'Inconscient de l'Islam* (2015).

4 "Le problème, c'est quand l'universalisme se fait ethnique. C'est quand l'identité se conjugue avec le racisme et que la culture se présente sous les traits d'une essence immuable."

5 "Mais Achille Mbembe ne parle que

du colonialisme français et pas du tout de l'anticolonialisme."

6 In his editorial comments on this chapter, Gholam Khiabany makes the excellent point that is worth further exploration in specifically psychoanalytic terms that the defenders of *Charlie Hebdo* fail or refuse to see how the conflation of *Hebdo* with the Republic and 'the West' performs a similar 'regression' to the one ascribed to 'Islam' and 'the Muslim': "Perhaps they think 'if you lay into the image of the Republic you are laying into the Republic himself'?"

7 The passage is worth quoting in full in the original: "De tels discours évoquent la sorcellerie: il y a toujours quelqu'un qui m'en veut en raison de qui je suis et non à cause de ce que je lui ai fait. Le discours paranoïaque et le discours sorcier sont tous deux des raisonnements mythologiques. A un moment où la mythologie de la nation est vide de sens, où la politique et la démocratie font de moins en moins sens, où les véritables centres de décision sont dénationalisés, sinon *offshore*, le raisonnement mythologique permet de combler un vide presque métaphysique. Mais il nourrit également des violences potentielles. C'est en effet un type de discours qui a toujours besoin d'un ennemi, peu importe lequel; d'un bouc émissaire ou de quelqu'un contre lequel on peut déployer une violence sans retenue. Ce fut le cas hier avec les Nègres et les Juifs. Si l'on n'y prend garde, ce sera bientôt le cas avec les musulmans et toutes sortes d'étrangers" (Mbembe quoted in Faure and Daumas 2016).

References

Anderson, W. et al. (eds) (2011) *Unconscious Dominions: Psychoanalysis, Trauma, and Global Sovereignties*. Durham, NC, and London: Duke University Press.

Bonnet, G. and M. Chebel (2015) 'Interview: Jihadist and Muslim on the Couch', *Charlie Hebdo* 1179. In *The Libertarian Communist* 29 (2015). https://libcom.org/files/Lib_Com_29.pdf (accessed 1 December 2016).

Crovitz, L. G. (2015) 'Defending Satire to the Death', *The Wall Street Journal*, 11 January. www.wsj.com/articles/gordon-crovitz-defending-satire-to-the-death-1421016982 (accessed 1 December 2016).

de Laforcade, G. (2006) '"Foreigners", Nationalism and the "Colonial Fracture": Stigmatized Subjects of Memory in France', *International Journal of Comparative Sociology* 47 (3/4): 217–33.

Donadey, A. (2000) '"Y'a bon Banania": Ethics and Cultural Criticism in the Colonial Context', *French Cultural Studies* IX: 9–29.

Fanon, F. (2004) *The Wretched of the Earth*. New York: Grove Press.

Faure, S. and C. Daumas (2016) 'Interview – Achille Mbembe: "La France peine à entrer dans le monde qui vient"', *Libération*, 1 June. www.liberation.fr/debats/2016/06/01/achille-mbembe-la-france-peine-a-entrer-dans-le-monde-qui-vient_1456698 (accessed 1 December 2016).

Freud, S. (2003) *The Uncanny*. Harmondsworth: Penguin.

Gordon, A. (2009) *Ghostly Matters: Haunting and the Sociological Imagination*. Minneapolis, MN, and London: University of Minnesota Press.

Greenberg, J. (2011) *Modernism, Satire and the Novel*. Cambridge: Cambridge University Press.

Kristeva, J. (2009) *This Incredible Need to Believe*. New York: Columbia University Press.

Kristeva, J. (2016) 'Interpreting Radical Evil'. Keynote speech, the Kristeva Circle, Stockholm. www.kristeva. fr/interpreting-radical-evil.html (accessed 8 December 2016).

Long, S. (2015) 'Why I Am Not Charlie', *A Paper Bird*, 9 January. https://paper-bird.net/2015/01/09/why-i-am-not-charlie/ (accessed 1 December 2016).

Macey, D. (2000) *Frantz Fanon: A Biography*. London and New York: Verso.

Mbembe, A. (2001) *On the Postcolony*. Berkeley, CA: University of California Press.

Miller, J. A. (2015a) 'The Return of Blasphemy', Lacan.com, 8 January. www.lacan.com/actuality/the-return-of-blasphemy/ (accessed 1 December 2016).

Miller, J. A. (2015b) 'The Lyric Illusion', Lacan.com, 11 January. www.lacan. com/actuality/the-lyric-illusion/ (accessed 1 December 2016).

Miller, J. A. (2015c) 'Response to Rancière', Lacan.com, 7 April. www.lacan. com/actuality/2015/04/response-to-ranciere/ (accessed 1 December 2016).

Phillips, L. (2015) 'Lost in Translation: Charlie Hebdo, Free Speech and the Unilingual Left', *Ricochet*, 14 January. https://ricochet. media/en/292/lost-in-translation-charlie-hebdo-free-speech-and-the-unilingual-left (accessed 1 December 2016).

Piet, R. (2015) 'Why Satire Is Holy to the French', *Al-Jazeera*, 14 January. www.aljazeera.com/indepth/opinion/2015/01/why-satire-holy-french-islam-201511312482960735O. html (accessed 1 December 2016).

Rancière, J. (2015) 'Response to Jacques-Alain Miller', Lacan.com, 10 April. www.lacan.com/actuality/2015/04/jacques-rancieres-response-to-jacques-alain-miller/ (accessed 1 December 2016).

Roudinesco, É. (2001) *Why Psychoanalysis?* New York: Columbia University Press.

Roudinesco, É. (2016) 'Elisabeth Roudinesco historienne de la psychanalyse "Je n'adhère pas à l'idée d'un différentialisme exacerbé"', *Libération*, 1 June. www.liberation. fr/debats/2016/06/01/elisabeth-roudinesco-historienne-de-la-psychanalyse-je-n-adhere-pas-a-l-idee-d-un-differentialisme-e_1456704 (accessed 9 December 2016).

Self, W. (2015) 'A Point of View: What's the Point of Satire?', BBC News, 13 February. www.bbc.com/news/magazine-31442441 (accessed 15 December 2016).

Silverman, M. (2007) 'The French Republic Unveiled', *Ethnic and Racial Studies* 30 (4): 628–42.

Tonneau, O. (2015) 'On *Charlie Hebdo*: A Letter to My British Friends', Mediapart, 11 January. https://blogs. mediapart.fr/olivier-tonneau/blog/110115/charlie-hebdo-letter-my-british-friends (accessed 1 December 2016).

Toscano, A. (2009) 'Fanaticism as Fantasy: Notes on Islam, Psychoanalysis, & Political Philosophy', *Umbr(a): A Journal of the Unconscious*. Special issue: 'Islam and Psychoanalysis' (edited by Joan Copjec and Sigi Jottkandt).

Part V

RACISM AND ANTI-RACISM IN POST-RACIAL TIMES

15 | NOT AFRAID

Ghassan Hage

There is a close relation between satire and secularism as the latter came to emerge in Europe. Secularism, as is well known, gained strength historically as a reaction to an era of European interreligious violence and massacres. It was not only a desire for the separation of church and state, as the classical formula has it. It was also an attempt to keep religious affect out of politics. This was in the belief that religion, because it is faith rather than reasoned thinking, produces too much of a narcissistic affect – that the faithful are unable to 'keep their distance' from what they believe in. It was thought that this narcissism was behind the murderous intensity of religiously driven conflicts. Being able to laugh at yourself literally means being able to not take yourself overly seriously. This, in turn, is crucial for the deintensification of the affects generated by the defence of what one believes in and for the relativisation of one's personal beliefs. Such relativisation, as Claude Lévi-Strauss argued, is crucial for thinking oneself comparatively and in relation to others (the opposite of narcissism).

There is no doubt that the Islamic fundamentalists of today represent the worst of modernity's narcissistic tendencies. They look at the history of colonialism and the relation between the Christian colonial West and the colonised Muslim world and believe, quite rightly, that the colonial world has offered them a rough deal, victimising them and treating them like shit. And, as they see it, this is despite the greatness of their civilisation. So they think they owe the non-Islamic world nothing. They are totally immersed in their Islam, taking it seriously and defending it in precisely the religiously narcissistic way that secularism opposed at the time of its emergence in the West.

So, on the face of it, it appears as if *Charlie Hebdo* and the 'Je Suis Charlie' (I am Charlie) supporters are involved en masse in exactly this kind of secular liberal struggle against Islamic fundamentalists. Unfortunately, this is not the case. And when I say unfortunately, I really mean it. Like many French-schooled people, I grew up with the variety of *bandes dessinées* that made up the field of Franco-Belgian comics: the wit of Jean Cabu and Georges Wolinski was part of the ABCs of my socially acquired sense of humour. So, affectively, part of me 'is Charlie'. The magazine's various cartoonists are like some of my close family members who are infuriatingly Islamophobic, pro-Israeli and to the right. They are part of my history, and regardless of what they politically do or think, I still love them and see myself as a part of them and see them as a part of me. I am seriously devastated by the murders. So part of me wants to believe that to say 'Je Suis Charlie' is not to agree with *Charlie Hebdo* but to defend the space from where it was coming. But – and, once again, unfortunately – I do not believe that space is what it appears to be.

It is worth remembering that if the secularists/satirists were right about the nature of religious political identification and emotions at the time of Europe's religious wars, they were wrong in thinking that those irrational and murderous passions were either essential or specific to religion. As the histories of Western nationalism and colonialism – and particularly the histories of fascism – show, murderous 'over the top' and 'let's take ourselves very seriously' beliefs can easily be generated by all forms of communal identification.

This outcome is true when 'secular democracy' and 'satire' become themselves a 'serious' form of what I see as 'phallic' communal identification. The fact is, as I argue in *Alter-Politics* (Hage 2015), 'democracy', 'tolerance' and 'freedom of speech' all can become – and are increasingly becoming in the Western world – *fin d'empire* colonial, racialised strategies of phallic distinction. They are what Westerners 'flash' to the racialised Muslims to say: "Look what we have and you haven't got. At best, yours is very small compared to ours." And this is at the very same time as Western societies are becoming less democratic, tolerant, and committed to freedom of speech.

The same can be said of satire. Here, paradoxically, satire, which is precisely, as I have argued above, the means of relativising and thinking relationally about oneself, becomes the very means of producing a Western narcissism aimed at making oneself an object of one's own desire in a period of decline. *Charlie Hebdo*'s humour, with its total obliviousness to the colonial histories and relations of power in which it was dispensing its satire, is a prime example of this phallic narcissism: "We're so funny that being 'satirical' and 'funny' is our identity. And you morons who can't take a joke don't even know what being satirical and funny means."

Unfortunately, it is more in this sense that all those valiant defenders of free speech assembling around the Western world and holding their 'I am Charlie' signs are totally correct. Indeed, 'They are all Charlie' in all its colonial narcissistic splendour. They are so oblivious of the reality in which the Muslim 'other' exists today that they even make a point of valiantly declaring that, unlike the Muslim people of Afghanistan, Pakistan, Iraq, Syria and Palestine, who are being murdered by the thousands at varieties of speeds with varieties of techniques, they, the ones attacked by three armed militants, are heroically looking the murderers in the eye and telling it to them straight:

"We are not afraid."

References

Hage, G. (2015) *Alter-Politics: Critical Anthropology and the Radical Imagination.* Melbourne: Melbourne University Press.

16 | 'JE SUIS JUIF': CHARLIE HEBDO AND THE REMAKING OF ANTISEMITISM

Alana Lentin

No, the Inuits, the Dogon people and the Tibetans are not anti-Semitic. (Bouteldja 2016: 55)

The pariah

Enzo Traverso, in the *End of Jewish Modernity*, encapsulates what is captivating about Arendt's use of Bernard Lazare's idea of 'pariah Judaism' (Lazare 1948 in Traverso 2016). Lazare, who defended Alfred Dreyfus, who was exiled from France in the infamous case of political antisemitism, noted: "the pariah was not simply someone who was excluded; he was the proscribed who transforms himself into rebel, who does not accept passively suffering his oppressed condition but makes it the point of departure for political revolt" (Traverso 2016: 64).

Before reading this chapter in Traverso's book, I was reflecting on why I wanted to write about the role of antisemitism in the interpretation of the meaning of race post-*Charlie Hebdo*. Almost two years have passed since the massacre of twelve people at the *Charlie Hebdo* offices and four others at a kosher supermarket, all Jews, a day later. As I was writing these opening paragraphs, Donald Trump's election as President of the US was won by aligning himself with white supremacists, having, in addition to his anti-immigrant and Islamophobic rhetoric, campaigned with overtly antisemitic messages (Pilkington 2016). In a speech hailing Trump's victory on 21 November 2016, the self-professed leader of the 'Alt-Right', Richard Spencer, was met with Nazi salutes by a Washington crowd. In the UK, a row about antisemitism that centred around a Black Jewish woman, Jackie Walker, pitted the supporters of the Labour leader, Jeremy Corbyn, against his detractors in and outside the party (Walker 2016). The results of the EU referendum in the UK laid bare the depth of British xenoracism (Fekete 2001) and the lead-up to it was accompanied by an unabashed use of repurposed antisemitic tropes by the Brexit camp (Brown 2016). Debates about the responses to refugees arriving in Western Europe in unprecedented numbers as a result of war in Syria and the destruction of Libya, Iraq and Afghanistan made continual reference to Jews under Nazism to legitimate arguments on either side (Lentin 2016). Against the backdrop of these events, I began to feel that I was permitted to openly admit antisemitism as a factor that (still) has an impact on how to understand racism, and certainly on how to evaluate anti-racist action.

But while I was observing these developments, I also noticed the ulterior effect this was having on me. I felt more justified as a racialised subject whose legitimation to speak and write about racism has at times been called into question due to my whiteness. And I felt uncomfortable having these thoughts. Then I read Traverso's discussion of the pariah and the remark he cites by Eleni Varikas, who I have long admired, that the pariah's self-presentation as a 'subject in revolt' is "sometimes tinged with narcissism (which Bernard Lazare calls 'the pride of the pariah' and 'the pleasure of being hated')" (Varikas 2007: 76 in Traverso 2016: 67). And there I was back with my discomfort with writing about antisemitism. I was quickly reminded of the fact that there is a Facebook page called 'On the Masada 2000 S.H.I.T List and Lovin' it', whose 'About' section reads:

> We are members of a very special elite group. We are Jews (whether practicing or not) who have been singled out for our work for justice for Palestine, and placed on the Zionist www.masada2000.org hate-site's S.H.I.T. list (acronym for 'self-hating, Israel-threatening Jews').[1]

My own S.H.I.T List entry does not bother with a description but uses a photograph of me standing in front of a Palestinian flag with the caption, 'the Photo says it all!!!' The pride! I am not alone: Google 'Masada 2000 S.H.I.T List' and the third entry is an article by Ami Kaufman with the headline 'Best Day of My Life: Making it into the Jewish S.H.I.T List' (Kaufman 2013). Not wishing to downplay the real threats posed to Jews and Israelis who condemn Zionism, leading even to threats to their career, there is nonetheless a veritable industry around being a 'woke' anti-Zionist Jew.

I feel an undeniable need to justify my right to work in this space, and it appears to me that this is the double bind presented by talking about antisemitism today. The undeniable co-dependency of Zionism and antisemitism (Aminov 2016) carries the consequence that it is no longer possible to discuss antisemitism without discussing complicity in Zionist racism. Many of those who shout loudest about antisemitism do so in the name of a colonialist oppression that reproduces the very crime it decries by associating all Jews, no matter their origins or beliefs, with a murderous regime whose ideological drivers relied on a European supremacism that is dependent to no small extent on the domination of Jewish Blacks and Arabs (Lavie 2012). The route to talking about antisemitism is necessarily paved with caveats: both the impossibility of decoupling from actions carried out in the name of all Jews[2] and the relative inconsequentiality of antisemitism when confronted with the unbearable magnitude of racism faced by Black people, Muslims, migrants and refugees in the societies I have lived in and studied.

Nevertheless, the problem of antisemitism – and here I mean not just as a problem for Jews but for others as a result of its mobilisation as a comparator, a benchmark, an endpoint (Lentin 2016) – cannot be denied. This is particularly so when turning to France and discussing the ramifications of how Islam and those who Mayanthi Fernando (2015) calls the 'Muslim French' have been made to over-signify in the French context, and how the event of *Charlie Hebdo* brought that signification to bear in a transnational dimension like no other event before it. For, in France, as Houria Bouteldja (2016) impresses upon us from the very title of her book, *Les Blancs, les Juifs et nous*, there is no extracting the discussion of race, coloniality and immigration from the status of Jews, and consequentially antisemitism. And in these times, with the Holocaust just edging out of living memory, this appears increasingly to be true.

The aftermath

Freeze the frame in the forty-third second of an RT 'Ruptly' video of Israeli Prime Minister, Binyamin Netanyahu, arriving to pay his respects at the Hyper Cacher supermarket, the site of the siege that ended in the deaths of four Jewish people on 9 January 2015.[3] In the forefront there is Netanyahu surrounded by armed guards. Behind him are several placards. One displays the names of the victims: Yaron Cohen, Yohav Hattab, Philippe Braham, François Michel Saada. To the right is another that reads:

Je Suis
Charlie
Policier
Juif.

Each word, on a separate line, is in a different colour: grey, blue, white, red. The words '*Charlie*', '*Policier*' and '*Juif*' are each given one of the colours of the *Tricolore*. Differentially punctuated, the placard could read, 'I am Charlie, a Jewish Police(man)'; French does not demand the word 'a' (un) in order to be read in this way. Of course, the intention of the authors of this placard was to underscore the martyrdom of the victims, grouped here as 'Charlie', 'Police' and 'Jew'.

These placards allow us think for a moment about what is allowed and what is not to be revealed; what can be made visible and what must remain hidden. It is a glimpse into the particular ways in which racial codes are arranged according to a post-racial logic. What do the three words '*Charlie*', '*Policier*', '*Juif*' (re)present and what do they conceal? I like the French formulation 'de quoi X est-il le nom?', as Alain Badiou uses it in his 2007 book on French President Nicolas Sarkozy, *De Quoi Sarkozy est-il le nom?* It was translated into English as 'The Meaning of Sarkozy'. However, this misses the contribution made by the word '*nom*'. A literal translation would be 'What is Sarkozy the name of?' So, what are *Charlie*, *Policier* and *Juif* the names of?

The person

Charlie *is* a name.

Twelve people were killed at *Charlie Hebdo*, only seven of whom were contributors to the magazine. Yet, apart from the police officer ('*policier*'), Franck Brinsolaro, they collectively became 'Charlie'. De-individualised on one level, they were also personified, given a name, a friendly, diminutive one at that. Charlie and the invocation to *be* Charlie – which was not a request but a requirement – named (*était le nom de*) the purported sanctity of liberty of expression and Enlightenment values that *Charlie Hebdo* was resurrected to represent. Never mind that the compulsion to 'be Charlie' contradicts the fundaments of individual freedom. Under the guise of 'muscular liberalism', the freedom to self-identify is far less protected than the freedom to question another's right to do so.[4] But, more than that, the truncated renaming of both the magazine and its dead as just Charlie personified them in a way not granted to either '*Policier*' or '*Juif*'. Charlie was de-titled, de-italicised, taken out of inverted commas and brought to life.

Twelve people became one. Three police officers became 'The Police' and four Jews banally buying kosher groceries became (one) 'Jew'.

I recall Fanon's conclusion to *Black Skin, White Masks* that, having examined the potential avenues of negritude in Chapter 5, issues a forward-looking call to arms for an anti-essentialist commitment to struggle for the "open door of every consciousness" (Fanon 2008 [1952]: 181).[5] In it, he remarks: "There is no white world, there is no white ethic, any more than there is a white intelligence" (ibid.: 179). He is of course right. But as per his discussion of recognition in the penultimate chapter of the book, it was unavoidable in the context of places colonised by France, such as his native Martinique, that "the Martinican … compares himself with his fellow against the pattern of the white man" (ibid.: 167). As he explains, this is not due to any intrinsic fault in the colonised, but to the fact that the terms of comparison had been set to whiteness. So, he remarks, "the Negro knows nothing of the cost of freedom, for he has not fought for it. From time to time he has fought for Liberty and Justice, but these were always white liberty and white justice; that is, values secreted by his masters" (ibid.: 172).

Thus, freedom is not Liberty, a fact we should bear in mind when considering the question: 'What is Charlie the name of?' Charlie is whiteness. And just as Fanon understood that the Black man, the colonised, was asked – no, expected – to identify with his coloniser to the extent that only recognition by him or her accorded him "consciousness in-itself-for-itself" (ibid.: 173), so too identifying with Charlie was the only way that those who were not white could be thought of as fully human in France after January 2015. What else can explain the fact that an eight-year-old was taken to court accused of 'apology for terrorism' following his claim during a class debate that he was "not Charlie. I am with the terrorists"?[6] The terms of reference are set within a context where white supremacy, Frenchness, Europeanness and all they stand for continue to dominate, long after Fanon more optimistically observed: "The Negro is not. Any more than the white man" (ibid.: 180).

This division between the "disaster of the man of colour" and that of the white man, which Fanon associates with his (*sic*) 'inhumanity' is that which permits the personification of Charlie. The opportunity to claim to be Charlie was offered as a route to whiteness, which, *contra* Fanon, who designates it inhuman, is made synonymous with a humanity that recognises individuals, and so names them. But this opening will always be accompanied by the bitter aftertaste of white self-congratulation, as Fanon also knew when he wrote:

> On the field of battle, its four corners marked by the scores of Negroes hanged by their testicles, a monument is slowly being built that promises to be majestic. And, at the top of this monument, I can already see a white man and a black man hand in hand. (Fanon 2008 [1952]: 173)

This realisation did not deter Fanon from refusing to reify himself or the history of those with whom race arbitrarily associated him. But it did mean "he must forever absorb himself in uncovering resistance, opposition, challenge" (ibid.). So many words written about liberty, about the pen being mightier than the sword. And yet what the naming of Charlie reveals is the extent to which a simple symbol – a pen – not only mocks that 'resistance, opposition, challenge', even when the racialised play by the rules of non-violence; it also hides a million crimes of a much less literary nature.

The state

When I think about the word '*policier*', I think about Paris, 17 October 1961.

This morning I listened to the radio. It happened to be a year since the terrorist attack on Paris, larger and more murderous than the day that became synonymous with *Charlie Hebdo*; the assault on the Bataclan, the Stade de France and various cafés and bars on 13 November 2015. The announcer named the event the largest loss of civilian life in Paris since the Second World War. I remembered that an acquaintance in Paris, an educated woman, had never heard of the massacre of up to 300 people marching for Algerian liberation on 17 October 1961. Their bodies were thrown into the Seine by the officers of the Paris Prefect, Maurice Papon. Papon had previously been responsible, first, for the deportation of Jews from Bordeaux under Vichy, and later for the torture of countless Algerians in the late 1950s. In 1998, he was convicted of crimes against humanity, for the deportations. Not the torture and not the drownings. Then again, it was only in 1995 that President Jacques Chirac officially recognised France's role in the deportations. France's loss of 'its Algeria' is at least one reason for the lack of a similar stance on this equally damning episode, in many ways foundational to the particular constellation of the formation of race in France.

One of the three '*policiers*' killed was Ahmed Merabet, a forty-year-old police officer patrolling the streets near the *Charlie Hebdo* offices while the attack took place. It did not go unnoticed that he, like the assailants, was the son of North African migrants, in his case Algerian, earning him his own '#JeSuis': #JeSuisAhmed. But while this placard was carried by friends and family accompanying Merabet's coffin to the mosque at Bobigny (Willsher 2015), and later adopted by social media users, it was the deracialised '*Policier*' that accompanied the words '*Charlie*' and '*Juif*' on the wall behind Netanyahu outside the Hyper Cacher. It is feasible that for some it was only through his de-identified designation as '*policier*' that Ahmed Merabet could be uncoupled from the Kouachi brothers.

The potential for ideological alignment with French Republicanism, or the spirit of Charlie – even in death – framed and thus redeemed Merabet. The discussion of Merabet's significance seems to end with Dyab Abou Jahjah's endlessly shared tweet:

> I am not Charlie, I am Ahmed the dead cop. Charlie ridiculed my faith and culture and I died defending his right to do so. #JesuisAhmed.[7]

Abou Jahjah's critique of *Charlie Hebdo* cannot exist on its own; it is only described as 'moving' because it relies on the trope of tolerance, meme'd out of all recognition in the days and weeks after January 2015 (Chandler 2015). And although Adam Chandler claims that the tweet "prods at that French universalism", it reminds us that there are only two routes open to the racialised, both of which end in abjection, as Fanon's evocation of the monument to the end of slavery prophesises: full acceptance of the language of secular humanism that masks the crimes on which its ascendance relied, or its full-scale rejection. This is what the spokesperson for the 'Party of the Indigenous of the Republic', Houria Bouteldja, also knows when she addresses '*Nous les indigènes*' in the penultimate chapter of her book. Recalling that "a handful of us take up arms to kill people on café terraces", she claims:

> Larvae or monsters, knaves or slaughterers, sycophants or suicide bombers. Here is the alternative offered to us. We have fulfilled the white prophecy: become nonentities or barbarians. (Bouteldja 2016: 101)[8]

Just over a month before the November attacks on Paris, the March for Dignity, led by the MAFED women's collective[9] assembled "the descendants of postcolonial immigrants and people from the popular suburbs [*les banlieues populaires*]" for a march against police violence and crime, systematic discrimination, humiliation and organised precarity.[10] Police violence and police murder such as that which befell Zyed Benna et Bouna Traoré in 2005 – the teenagers whose electrocution unleashed the infamous *Intifada des banlieues* (Lentin 2005) – was decried by speaker after speaker. "Our neighbourhoods are not shooting ranges".[11]

The marchers' call for "justice, reparations, unity" replicated those of countless times before, when they left from the '*Sonacotra*' hostels, the *bidonvilles* (shanty towns), the outer-outer suburbs and, as Bouteldja recalls, in 1983, marched on Paris for equality and against racism. But then as now, this alternative route, a route that across Europe and the settler colonies is taken by the descendants of Fanon's 'wretched', is met with a mix of exasperation, derision, anger and fear. An interview with a French 'anti-racist' organisation I conducted in June 2015 revealed the depth of its revulsion for activists, such as those around the Party of the Indigenous of the Republic, an autonomous decolonial movement that insists on the continuous nature of French coloniality. According to my respondent, the *Indigènes de la République* is a "racist antiracist movement" (Lentin and Humphry 2017: 7). Racist for rejecting the Republic's false offering of inclusion in return for an assimilation that, despite years of commitment – even by becoming its '*policiers*' – it fails to deliver on. Bouteldja recalls her father's gratitude to a France that had been "our salvation and that of the family in Algeria who he had fed for three decades on his miserable salary ... I cannot contradict my father" (Bouteldja 2016: 109).

The parvenu

Returning to the alternative reading of the placard that framed Netanyahu's head – 'I am Charlie, a Jewish Police(man)' – the role of the Jews between '*nous*' and '*les blancs*' addressed by Bouteldja becomes an uncomfortable one (and so it must be). The Jews are not synonymous with the police, of course. But in that the police represent the state, the Jews of France, if we follow Bouteldja, have been elected to legitimate it in the face of those it continues to reject as it once did the Jews.

Enzo Traverso puts the emancipation of the Jews of France into perspective. He reminds us that, for the Orthodox Ashkenazi Jews of Northern France, revolutionary emancipation did not equate with freedom; the Jews were the objects, not the subjects, of their emancipation. Forced assimilation as the condition of emancipation meant that, for these eighteenth-century Jews, the granting of rights was a "revolution from above" (Traverso 1996: 24). Traverso may just as well have been speaking in Fanon's voice. After all, they both deal with the particularity of racial formation in France. Fanon notes that once the end of slavery was decided, not by the enslaved but by their masters, "the black man was acted upon ... The upheaval did not make a difference in the Negro. He went from one way of life to another, but not from one life to another" (Fanon 2008 [1952]: 171). Even when Black people did act – in Haiti, as Maroons (Roberts 2015), as the subverters of enslavement through the sheer determination to survive (Weheliye 2014) – they could not be recognised for doing so. This leads Fanon to say that "the black man has no ontological resistance in the eyes of the white man" (Fanon 2008 [1952]: 83).

What changes for the Jews? At what point do we diverge from our points in common with Blacks and Arabs? It was Fanon who remarked that "the anti-Semite is inevitably a negrophobe", a fact echoed by bell hooks when she said that "white supremacy relies on the maintenance of anti-black racism and antisemitism" (hooks 1996). But this does not mean that the racism experienced by Blacks and Jews is the same.

Enzo Traverso argues that the era of Jewish modernity has come to a close because "anti-Semitism had completely lost any respectability" (Traverso 2016: 82). Islamophobia, on the other hand, "plays the role for the new racism that anti-Semitism had in the past" (ibid.: 94), even as far as the portrait of the Arab or the Muslim as a fundamentally menacing and foreign *Jud Süss*.

"By a strange coincidence," Traverso writes, the marginalisation of "minorities with Arabic, Asiatic or African sound" has occurred "in parallel with the acquisition of a new respectability by Jews" (ibid.: 89). 'Coincidence' is a strange word to choose for a writer who recognises the significance of Palestine and the wilful confounding of antisemitism and anti-Zionism in contributing to 'left antisemitism'. He also, misguidedly to my mind, makes reference to the 'new Judeophobia'.[12] Indeed, while insisting that antisemitism among racialised minorities should not be justified, Traverso recognises that the misplaced targeting of Jews in sporadic attacks on synagogues, schools and most recently at the Hyper Cacher is not incidental to the French state's incessant memorialisation and exceptionalisation of the *Shoah*. Why is this crime held above all crimes? Neither Traverso nor I are the first to ask this question.

I employ the term 'frozen racism' to explain why racisms past are used to perversely legitimise racism 'post-race' (Lentin 2016). The tendency to locate the genealogy of race in Europe in the nineteenth and twentieth centuries denies its older foundations, beginning with the invasion of the Americas through the spread of European colonialism, the expropriation of lands and resources and the genocides of indigenous peoples, the institution of slavery and later indentured servitude (Hesse 2007, 2014; Goldberg 2006). What we are left with is the moment of the *Shoah* that is presented Eurocentrically as both the start and the endpoint of racism.

Racism, as Hesse shows, is a European neologism invented in the inter-war years to contend with the rise of fascism and political antisemitism but which neglects the conterminous existence of colonialism and the crimes committed in its name, some of them, most notably the concentration and death camps of Namibia and elsewhere, replicated on European soil mere decades later (Hesse 2007). So the calls of 'never again' and the commemoration of Jewish deaths by a state that refuses to discuss reparation for slavery or torture while proclaiming itself the birthplace of human rights stick in the throat. Leaders of European states in general – in particular Germany, France and the UK – use the fact of the Holocaust both as evidence of their non-racism, and even their anti-racism, but also as the standard by which to measure all racisms. In that it is vital to separate Zionism and the actions of the Israeli state from Jews, it is nonetheless impossible to ignore Jewish complicity in the creation of this situation.

Back again to '*Je Suis Charlie, Policier, Juif*'. I can't help but hear the '*Je suis*' as a plea for demarcation. The lack of symmetry does not go un-noted. For the forebears of the 'Muslim French' (Fernando 2015) of North African origin this imbalance did not begin with the Holocaust, because that history did not concern them. Houria Bouteldja quotes her '*cousin du bled*'[13] who asks, "But who is Hitler?" She asks us not to be shocked. Her cousin's words are precious to her, not so much because she wants to "keep this history at a distance as long as the history and the life of the wretched of the earth also remain but 'a detail'" (Bouteldja 2016: 55). No. The real reason she thanks her cousin for his ignorance of the *Shoah* is because, *contra* the 'New Judeophobia' argument, which attributes contemporary antisemitism to Arabs and Muslims (Taguieff 2002), his words remind her that "antisemitism is European" (Bouteldja 2016: 55).

But European antisemitism cannot exist without its mirror: philosemitism. Arendt knew this about the last two centuries as much as Bouteldja knows it today (Bouteldja 2015). And so it is not with the purpose of mounting a real fight against antisemitism that her thoughts on philosemitism were viciously attacked across the political spectrum in France. For example, one author deplored her use of the term 'state philosemitism', as the antidote to this, she proposes, "would be none other than ... state antisemitism (e.g. Vichy) or, worse still, mass antisemitism (e.g. pogroms)" (Kandel 2015). But Bouteldja's logic is clear. Despite official state philosemitism and the special status accorded to the Holocaust, there is always a separation made between French citizens and Jews in official discourse that ultimately demonstrates that "'Jews' as a category are still not a fully legitimate part of the nation and its identity" (Bouteldja 2015).

This is why Bouteldja's manifesto of 'revolutionary love' extends a hand to Jews who, she writes, are "our veritable cousins" (Bouteldja 2016). This relationship is founded not on common ancient ancestry but on a shared rapport with whiteness. The sole difference between the Jews and the Arabs of France – one created by the Crémieux Decree, when 35,000 Algerian Jews were granted French citizenship, well before the consequences of the *Shoah* were revealed – is the possibility the former has to 'melt into whiteness' in a way desired by the *indigènes* but still out of reach for them (ibid.: 49). The Jews of Algeria lost their "*arabo-berbérité*. Dare I say it, your Islamicness" when they were granted French citizenship in 1870. But Algerians too, Bouteldja says, lost "our Jewishness ... you have left a hole that we can no longer fill and about which I am inconsolable" (ibid.: 56).

In addition to accusing Bouteldja of condoning antisemitism by critiquing philosemitism, Kandel also accuses her of '*Shoah* hatred', or "more exactly, [of hatred] of its historical and philosophical significance in the memory and collective European conscience" (Kandel 2015). But on this, too, Bouteldja is clear. The manipulation of this memory has the sole aim of "sharing the Shoah, diluting it, deracinating Hitler, shifting it to the colonised people, and finally whitening the Whites"

(Bouteldja 2016: 57). It is not, as Kandel would have it, that Bouteldja wishes to diminish the significance of the Holocaust by placing it among 'all racisms'. Her wish is to historicise it so as to imbue the cry of 'never again' with real meaning. For "if white ferocity beat down on you with such savagery, it is because the European people closed their eyes to the 'tropical genocides'" (ibid.: 59). Colonialism was a warning that went unheeded by those who said it could not happen to us.

Conclusion

Given the mobilisation of antisemitism as an unparalleled offence and the dangers for anti-racist resistance to which this gives rise, it is insufficient to remark that past antisemitism segues into current-day Islamophobia. It is politically useful perhaps to point out that Muslims are discursively and materially targeted in similar ways to the scapegoating and violence against Jews in Europe during what Arendt calls the times of "social antisemitism" (Arendt 1966). But this should be accompanied by an explanation of the type offered by Gil Anidjar in his analysis of the relationship to both Jews and Arabs (which includes Muslims) as a constitutive one for Europe (Anidjar 2003).

When the racial classification 'Semite' was invented, Anidjar argues, it indicated "an almost *absolute* identity shared between Jew and Arab, so that whatever is said about one could equally be said about the other".[14] What happens after the Second World War, he explains, is that, because race becomes unmentionable in relation to Jews, they are deracialised, effectively becoming a religion again. Furthermore, Judaism is rewritten as conjoined with Christianity following the Cold War invention of the 'Judeo-Christian tradition'. Non-existent before the mid-twentieth century, 'Judeo-Christianity' is often used interchangeably with 'Western'; it is "an ideological construction, not a historical one" that obscures Christianity's long history of antisemitism (Burrows 2015). The only remaining Semites are thus the Arabs, who remain racialised. This is despite the fact that, in Europe at least, it is Arab Muslims who are, and are perceived to be, more 'religious' than Jews. In allowing Jews to become a (mere) religion rather than a race, they become secularised while religious practice itself is considered in racialised terms.[15]

The seeds were sown with the *Décret Crémieux*. The possibility for citizenship to trump race was opened to Algerian Jews and not to Muslims. This was a decisive step towards the deracialisation of the

Sephardi Jews, who, Bouteldja reminds us, are also Arabs, but whose Arabness has been purposefully negated, a trade-off in return for acceptance and accession to whiteness (Bouteldja 2016). Antisemitism is then rendered useless as a tool of critique. It can but function as a means to rupture the potential that Anidjar identifies in the past unicity of Semitic identity. There is then no way for the attack on the Hyper Cacher to be read in any other way than through the lens of the 'New Judeophobia'. The term Judeophobia denotes the rupturing of Semitism. Antisemitism can now be frozen in the past where racism generally and purportedly is located. In a post-racial era during which racism is rewritten as multipolar, Arabs – now recast exclusively as Muslims – are seen in France as its principal perpetrators (Lentin and Titley 2011). The shrillness with which antisemitism is decried by French officials depends on the coterminous denial of racism against Arabs, Muslims, as well as the Black people with whom they are associated – those who reclaim the name *indigènes*.[16] Antisemitism and anti-white racism thus become co-dependent, the latter requiring the former for legitimacy. If Jews are now folded into secularism – and are often its principal defendants, for example in the Republican anti-racism of organisations such as the *Licra* or the *Ligue des droits de l'homme*[17] – the racism they experience can only be external, the deed of those whose Semitism remains intact: Arabs, Muslims.

The attacks of January 2015 on *Charlie Hebdo* and the Hyper Cacher were a critical moment. The ways in which they were made to mean from a hegemonic liberal perspective had little to do with any real attempt to unpick the colonial routes that brought the perpetrators to their murderous endpoint. While the backlash has much longer antecedents, there is no way to understand this event without setting it in the context of the backlash against multiculturalism that has framed politics in Europe since the beginning of the twenty-first century (Lentin and Titley 2011). Jewish condoning of Zionism – or, at the other end of the spectrum, self-critique of our comfortable accession to whiteness – while vital, has largely obscured the role of antisemitism in the construction of anti-multiculturalism, which is now, with the election of Donald Trump, a globally hegemonic world view. There is a clear thread that connects the attacks on multiculturalism that came thick and fast in the wake of the 'war on terror' to the white identity politics that framed the advent of Trumpism. It was close to unimaginable until extremely recently to consider antisemitism as a tangible threat to all but a tiny, visible minority. It is now time to assess the conjunction between the onslaught on multiculturalism – code for an anti-immigration, anti-Black, anti-queer of colour, anti-Roma, and Islamophobic politics – and social antisemitism as code for the mistrust of cosmopolitanism, and build new pathways of solidarity.

Notes

1 www.facebook.com/groups/187037802706/ (accessed 11 November 2016).

2 After his return from Paris in the days following the *Charlie Hebdo* and Hyper Cacher massacres, Israeli Prime Minister Binyamin Netanyahu remarked: "I went to Paris not just as the Prime Minister of Israel but as a representative of the entire Jewish people." While visiting a synagogue in Paris, Netanyahu addressed the congregation saying, "God willing they will come and many of you will arrive in the home which belongs to us all. Am Yisrael Chai." The crowd responded by singing the *Marseillaise*. Anshel Pfeffer, 'The Jews Who Said "No, Thank You" to Netanyahu', *Haaretz*, 14 January 2016. www.haaretz.com/israel-news/.premium-1.697066 (accessed 11 November 2016).

3 www.youtube.com/watch?v=TKEs2HJlpKs.

4 As an example of this, in his failed pitch to be selected as the candidate in the upcoming French presidential elections, Nicolas Sarkozy claimed: "We can no longer tolerate the right to be different."

5 As an aside, I wonder if Fanon would have been as committed today to a refusal to seeking 'retroactive reparations' given the persistent injustices that imbue our current racial landscape (Fanon 2008 [1952]: 180).

6 'Entendu à 8 ans pour apologie du terrorisme: que s'est-il vraiment passé?' *L'Obs Société*, 29 January 2015. http://tempsreel.nouvelobs.com/charlie-hebdo/20150129.OBS1220/entendu-a-8-ans-pour-apologie-du-terrorisme-que-s-est-il-vraiment-passe.html (accessed 17 February 2017).

7 https://twitter.com/Aboujahjah/status/553169081424420864?ref_src=twsrc%5Etfw.

8 All translations from the French are my own.

9 MAFED stands for the Women's March for Dignity.

10 'Meeting: Marche de la Dignité', 1 October 2015. http://indigenes-republique.fr/meeting-marche-de-la-dignite.

11 www.liberation.fr/france/2015/10/31/des-milliers-de-manifestants-marchent-pour-la-dignite-a-paris_1410317.

12 The so-called 'new Judeophobia', a neologism introduced by Pierre-André Taguieff (2002), contends that French North Africans are uniquely responsible for antisemitism in the twenty-first century.

13 Loosely translatable as 'my cousin from the old country'.

14 'The Jew, the Arab: An Interview with Gil Anidjar', http://asiasociety.org/jew-arab-interview-gil-anidjar (accessed 20 November 2016).

15 This is why Anidjar believes that it is problematic that race studies do not take religion into account to a great enough extent. While this may be somewhat rectified in the more than a decade since Anidjar published *The Jew, the Arab* with the arrival on the scene of critical Muslim studies in particular

(cf. Sayyid 2015; Grosfoguel 2010; Morsi 2015), there is still room for further historicisation of the ways in which race and religion are made to interrelate.

16 'L'Appel des indigènes de la République'. http://indigenes-republique.fr/le-p-i-r/appel-des-indigenes-de-la-republique.

17 These historical French anti-racism organisations are well known for their secularist discourse, which warns of the danger of what they call 'communitarianism', and they are especially wary of accepting the realities of Islamophobia (Lentin 2008).

References

Aminov, E. (2016) 'The Mutual Dependency of Zionism and Anti-Semitism', *Alternet*, 28 May. www.alternet.org/grayzone-project/mutual-dependency-zionism-and-anti-semitism (accessed 15 November 2016).

Anidjar, G. (2003) *The Jew, the Arab*. Stanford, CA: Stanford University Press.

Arendt, H. (1966) *The Origins of Totalitarianism*. New York and London: Harcourt Brace Jovanovich.

Badiou, A. (2007) *De Quoi Sarkozy est-il le nom?* Paris: Éditions Lignes.

Bouteldja, H. (2015) 'Racisme(s) et philosémitisme d'État ou comment politiser l'antiracisme en France?', *Parti des indigènes de la république*, 11 March. http://indigenes-republique.fr/racisme-s-et-philosemitisme-detat-ou-comment-politiser-lantiracisme-en-france-3/ (accessed 21 November 2016).

Bouteldja, H. (2016) *Les Blancs, les Juifs et nous*. Paris: La Fabrique.

Brown, A. 'Leave.eu's Cartoon is Not Just Racist – It's Worse Than That', *Guardian* 15 June 2016. www.theguardian.com/commentisfree/2016/jun/14/leave-eu-cartoon-racist-nazi-brexit-antisemitism-1945?utm_source=esp&utm_medium=Email&utm_campaign=The+Best+of+CiF+base&utm_term=177297&subid=10139402&CMP=ema_1364 (accessed 10 November 2016).

Burrows, D. M. (2015) 'There Is No "Judeo-Christian Tradition"', *Patheos*, 20 November. www.patheos.com/blogs/unfundamentalistchristians/2015/11/there-is-no-judeo-christian-tradition/ (accessed 21 November 2016).

Chandler, A. (2015) '#JeSuisAhmed: The Muslim Victim in the Paris Massacre', *The Atlantic*, 8 January. www.theatlantic.com/international/archive/2015/01/Ahmed-Merabet-police-officer-killed-charlie-hebdo/384331/ (accessed 15 November 2016).

Fanon, F. (2008 [1952]) *Black Skin, White Masks*. London: Pluto Press.

Fekete, L. (2001) 'The Emergence of Xeno-Racism', *Race and Class* 43 (2): 23–40.

Fernando, M. (2015) *The Republic Unsettled: Muslim French and the Contradictions of Secularism*. Durham, NC: Duke University Press.

Goldberg, D. T. (2006) 'Racial Europeanization', *Ethnic and Racial Studies* 29 (2): 331–64.

Grosfoguel, R. (2010) 'Epistemic Islamophobia and Colonial Social Sciences', *Human Architecture: Journal of the Sociology of Self-Knowledge* 8 (2): 29–38.

Hesse, B. (2007) 'Racialized Modernity. An Analytics of White Mythologies', *Ethnic and Racial Studies* 30 (4): 643–63.

Hesse, B. (2014) 'Racism's Alterity: The After-Life of Black Sociology' in W. D. Hund and A. Lentin (eds) *Racism and*

Sociology. Berlin: Lit Verlag, pp. 141–74.

hooks, b. (1996) *Killing Rage, Ending Racism*. London: Penguin.

Kandel, L. (2015) 'Le contraire du "philosémitisme"', *Huffington Post*, 7 May. www.huffingtonpost.fr/liliane-kandel/le-contraire-du-philosemitisme.

Kaufman, A. (2013) 'Best Day of My Life: Making it into the Jewish S.H.I.T List', *972 Mag*, 4 July. http://972mag.com/best-day-of-my-life-making-it-into-the-jewish-s-h-i-t-list/75150/ (accessed 11 November 2016).

Lavie, S. (2012) 'Writing Against Identity Politics: An Essay on Gender, Race, and Bureaucratic Pain', *American Ethnologist* 39 (4): 779–803.

Lazare, B. (1948) *Job's Dungheap*. New York: Schocken.

Lentin, A. (2005) 'The Intifada of the Banlieues', *openDemocracy*, 17 October. www.opendemocracy.net/globalization-institutions_government/intifada_3037.jsp.

Lentin, A. (2008) 'Racism, Anti-racism and the Western State' in G. Delanty, R. Wodak and P. Jones (eds) *Identity, Belonging and Migration*. Liverpool: Liverpool University Press, pp. 101–19.

Lentin, A. (2016) 'The Lure of "Frozen" Racism', *The Occupied Times*, 31 March.

Lentin, A. and J. Humphry (2017) 'Antiracism Apps: Framing Understandings and Approaches to Antiracism Education and Intervention', *Information, Communication and Society* 20 (10) 1539–53.

Lentin, A. and G. Titley (2011) *The Crises of Multiculturalism: Racism in a Neoliberal Age*. London: Zed Books.

Morsi, Y. (2015) 'Melbourne's Islamic Museum of Australia: The "White-Washed 'I'" as an Apollonian Celebration of Liberal Myths', *Journal of Muslim Minority Affairs* 35 (2): 203–14.

Pilkington, E. (2016) 'Senator Al Franken Accuses Donald Trump of Launching Antisemitic TV Ad', *Guardian*, 7 November 2016. www.theguardian.com/us-news/2016/nov/06/senator-al-franken-accuses-donald-trump-of-launching-antisemitic-tv-ad (accessed 10 November 2016).

Roberts, N. (2015) *Freedom as Marronage*. Chicago, IL: University of Chicago Press.

Sayyid, S. (2015) *Recalling the Caliphate*. London: Hurst Publishers.

Taguieff, P.-A. (2002) *La nouvelle judéophobie*. Paris: Milles et une nuits.

Traverso, E. (1996) *Pour une critique de la barbarie moderne: Écrits sur l'histoire des Juifs et de l'antisémitisme*. Lausanne: Éditions Page Deux.

Traverso, E. (2016) *The End of Jewish Modernity*. Chicago, IL: University of Chicago Press.

Varikas, E. (2007) *Les rebuts du monde. Figures du paria*. Paris: Stock.

Walker, P. 'Jackie Walker Stripped of Momentum Post in Antisemitism Row', *Guardian*, 4 October 2016. www.theguardian.com/politics/2016/oct/03/momentums-vice-chair-removed-antisemitism-row-jackie-walker (accessed 10 November 2016).

Weheliye, A. (2014) *Habeas Viscus: Racializing Assemblages, Biopolitics, and Black Feminist Theories of the Human*. Durham, NC: Duke University Press.

Willsher, K. (2015) 'Charlie Hebdo Attack: Fallen Policeman Ahmed Merabet Buried in Bobigny', *Guardian*, 14 January. www.theguardian.com/world/2015/jan/13/charlie-hebdo-attack-ahmed-merabet-buried-bobigny (accessed 14 November 2016).

17 | RACE, CASTE AND GENDER IN FRANCE[1]

Christine Delphy

The subject of this text is the situation of the descendants of ex-colonized North African immigrants in contemporary France – a condition that everyone admits is 'problematic'. My hypothesis, which I already put forward in 2001, is that today in France we are witnessing the creation of a system of racial castes. Sociologists and political scientists in France do not use the concept of 'castes', whether they are Marxists or otherwise (Delphy 1998). However, in my view this concept is of some use for explaining the specific place of racial oppression within the class system: for which the concept of racism is insufficient. Indeed, while the concept of racism lays emphasis on process, 'caste' instead stresses the results of this process, in terms of the social structure. It struck me that the situation of the descendants of these immigrants has not followed the same processes as other immigrant groups' descendants, and that they have 'inherited' their parents' social inferiority.

I will try to demonstrate this social 'immobility' of the so-called 'Maghrebian' (North African) group, and identify some of its mechanisms, including the aggravation of the racism against them. I will also examine the way in which the social construct 'race' is articulated with that other social construct known as 'sex'. These social constructs are built in the same way, through domination and for the purposes of domination, though they obviously take distinct forms. The debate on the Islamic headscarf does play some role in this interaction and interlinking of sexism and racism, but mostly as a telling moment of crisis.

Indeed, this situation is not a static one, and the crisis over the headscarf is typical of the dynamic of oppression in general, and thus also of 'racial' oppression. We can see it as a repressive response to a rebellion. But this rebellion itself followed a period of oppression. This sequence – oppression, rebellion, repression – explains the dynamic behind the treatment of 'immigrants and their descendants'. I also see this sequence as a French tragedy, since the rebellion should have led to liberation, and not the increased oppression that resulted from its repression.

In each of these phases, the thing that interests me is the way in which gender – a caste system based on the invention of different sexes – is used to construct a caste system based on the invention of different races.

Act I: oppression

The first act, oppression, dates back to conquest and the colonization of Algeria, now more than a hundred and fifty years ago, and then that of the other countries of North Africa a century ago. Unlike what happened in Indochina, religion was the basis of the differential treatment expressed in the *'indigénat'* status imposed on the colonized peoples. In 1945 the status of *indigénat* was dismantled. In theory all men (for women it came only years later) were citizens. But after negotiations with white settlers, the population of Algeria was divided into two categories of citizens: 'French men of European stock' (whites) and 'Muslim Frenchmen', voting in different 'colleges'. The end result was that the vote of one Frenchman of European stock was worth the vote of five Muslim Frenchmen.

Since the beginning of colonization, the question of sex, or gender, set the dividing line between the two 'communities' that were thus created. According to the colonial power's racist stereotype, the indigenous North African men 'treated women badly'. Polygamy in particular was considered a sign, or even the sign, of indigenous men's 'backwardness', even though it was in fact an uncommon practice (Clancy-Smith 1996).

'Muslim French' status had the effect of subjecting the women of this community to a civil code for marriage, parentage and inheritance called 'personal status', which was considered to be 'trailing behind' the French code. Nonetheless, we should emphasize here that apart from the question of polygamy the French civil code of that era – between 1830 and 1962 – was hardly any less detrimental to women than the Muslim French one was, especially before the Second World War. Allowing mass exemption from the civil code in one French *département* certainly did have deleterious effects on indigenous women, who like women of French stock were not considered citizens until the end of the Second World War. But it also allowed for a continued denigration of Islam. In truth, this was nothing new: maligning Islam has a long tradition in

Europe, stretching back to the age of the Spanish Reconquista and the Crusades (Daniel 1993; Geisser 2003).

Thus gender – which establishes a hierarchical division splitting the human species into two opposed categories, men and women – served as the dividing line for a further separation, between two 'ethnicities'. And these, too, were fabricated by domination – in this case, colonial domination.

In occupied Algeria, 'natives' of male sex could escape their status as sub-citizens, but only on condition that they renounced their religion, culture, beliefs, family and neighbours. As such, on the ideological and legal plane, Islam became the reason that was given for their inferior status as *indigènes*. This allowed for the principal, objective reason – occupation and colonization – to be obscured.

Following the conquest of Algeria, the denigration of Islam became centered on the classically colonial opposition between the 'civilized' and the 'barbaric'. And no less classically, this counter-position also concerned the relations between the sexes. When the colonizers spoke of indigenous women – ignoring their own patriarchy, which they doubtless considered normal, just like today – it was always with tears in their eyes. They only referred to the differences between these two patriarchal regimes – the French one and the Algerian one – at the cost of any mention of their far more considerable commonalities.

Indeed, one central point is systematically passed over in silence in studies on colonization and in today's studies on racism or discrimination. Namely, that the relations between the colonizing society and the colonized society are also the relations between two patriarchies. The protagonists of the colonial conflict on both sides were men. In each of the two societies, only men had the status of subjects; women were objects, property. It is logical enough that the colonizer wanted to dispossess the indigenous men of their most precious possession, indeed the last one that was left to them: women. A nineteenth-century French official cited by Frantz Fanon said, "If we are to strike against Algerian society's capacity to resist, then we must first of all conquer their women," adding, "We have to go and find these women, under the veils they hide behind" (Fanon 1967: 14).

In fact, the French did nothing to help North African women. But they did carry out a few 'un-veiling' campaigns during the Algerian war, already back then under the pretext of 'liberating women'. In reality, the purpose of these campaigns – like the rapes committed by soldiers or the use of 'lascivious' native women in brothels – was to demoralize the Algerian men by 'stealing' their last bit of property: women. And since the colonizer blared the trumpets of women's liberation in the interest of destroying the autochthonous identity, those fighting for independence logically enough rejected it, presenting the maintenance and strengthening of the hierarchy between the sexes as a constituent part of their national project (Gadant 1995).

Let's jump forward a few decades. Now the North African countries are independent. The former colonial subjects were already present in the metropolis before independence, and they came in even greater numbers afterwards.

Three historical events created a problem for the so-called 'people of European stock' – which means whites – and there is one that they have still not managed to resolve. This immigration was long purely masculine, comprising men only. But the immigrants who wanted to go back often found that they couldn't; then, in 1974, the law on family reunion allowed them to bring their wives to France. Finally, the French nationality law, despite the changes made to it, kept the element of jus soli, and their children became French. French society had not foreseen this series of events. It did not see that the combination of family reunion and jus soli would place it in a situation where the children of former colonial subjects theoretically have exactly the same rights as any other French citizen.

French society only offers them the same status as their parents had, while these children of the Republic, sure of their rights, demand their due as French citizens – and they insist on this ever more noisily and ever more 'arrogantly', as the minister Xavier Darcos put it. This is what Farad Khosrokhavar (1997) called the 'misunderstanding' between French society and the descendants of immigrants; I would call it France's dilemma. France does not want to accept them, but nor can it send them 'back home', because they have no home other than France. Having to find a third way – obstinately refusing to accept them, but unable to kick them out – it has tried to uphold and strengthen a caste system. And one of the ways of doing so is to criminalize Islam.

After the war, immigrants were treated more or less as they had been when they were colonized. But as guest workers they made few demands (though an 'Arab Workers' Movement' existed between 1945 and the beginning of the Algerian war). They accepted the hardest jobs, the lowest salaries and being penned into the *bidonville* slums.

Their only goal was to be able to send money back home and build a house there. Keeping their heads down and putting up with racism was just the price they had to pay for the eventual recompense of being able to return to Algeria. This light at the end of the tunnel kept them going, even if they didn't all get there. This explains their patience, their humility and their resignation to practising their religion in cellars rather than mosques. Today French people are nostalgic for this Islam – of which they were ignorant when it did exist – honouring it with the label 'traditional', as if it were a Camembert AOC. Except that here 'traditional' doesn't mean ladle-moulded, but invisible. The best Islam, in a way: in any case the only suitable one, i.e. the only one that suits us. But the hope of recompense that allowed the immigrant parents to put up with this situation does not exist for their descendants. Yet it seems that the immigrant status of the parents of Maghrebians and Africans has been passed down across the generations, both materially and in terms of other people's perceptions. That is, they still imagine that these people are destined to one day leave French territory. And when people inherit exactly the same status that their parents had, with no probability or even possibility of social mobility, then what we're dealing with is a caste situation, not a class situation. That's what's now being created in France. We even see it in language: when we speak of 'second-' or even 'third-generation immigrants', we transform the immigrant condition – which is, by definition, temporary – into a hereditary and almost biological trait.

This racism has long been made light of, understood as a matter of certain people's overtly racist attitudes and not in terms of the objective treatment of the population concerned (Simon 1997; Tripier 1999). But we do know that this population suffers enormous discrimination, whether in housing, education, or employment or in terms of judicial repression (Beaud and Pialoux 2003; Tribablat 1995).

Hardly ever studied, however, is the mental suffering that racism induces in its victims. This was very clear during the debate 'on the veil'. Discrimination was only mentioned as an afterthought to the discussion, in the euphemized form of references to 'failed integration'. Moreover, such 'failures' were attributed to the discriminated-against population itself, allegedly having chosen to live 'among themselves' twenty miles from the city centre and refusing to mix in with 'people of French stock', seemingly out of snobbery. This common-sense point of view was also the official stance of the Interior Ministry (Tissot 2004).

As for those concerned, they know well enough that society excludes them. In the 1980s they organized an imposing 'march for equality' across the whole country. But the movement was recuperated by the Parti Socialiste, which created SOS-Racisme for the purposes of neutralizing these protests ... and succeeded in doing so. This respectful, 'properly French' revolt – with its secular, Republican protests – failed lamentably (Bouamama 1994).

Act II: rebellion

Thus the bitterness caused by this failure compounded this population's bitter everyday experience of racism. They played the game, and it didn't work.

As for the Franco-French, they are no longer concerned with discrimination or ghettos. Rather, they're preoccupied by the integration or non-integration of youths of North African origin. But the meaning they attribute to the word 'integration' is biased: in TV reports and political statements, this always refers to how much effort the children of Maghrebians are making to fully resemble the children of Bretons or Auvergnats. Sometimes they manage without too much trouble; at other times, they have to renounce their own identity. For example, talking about your childhood is an important part of sociability. In the case of Bretons and Auvergnats it is allowed or even encouraged, with people from rural areas and city-dwellers marvelling at the similarities and differences between their respective experiences. But no one's interested in your Arab parents: you'd best not mention them. This population is thus caught in a formidable double bind: they are called on to show that they're 'the same' but they are perceived and labelled as 'different'. Whatever they do, in the end they always fail the exam, and they will never manage to satisfy the criteria of Frenchness. The unspoken reality is that these criteria exclude anyone of Maghrebian or African origin by definition.

Several generations obeyed these contradictory racist and sexist injunctions, which exhort the dominated to erase and yet simultaneously be comfortable with their 'difference'. But that changed when some of them understood that this whole game deliberately sets out to exhaust them physically and mentally; that the 'difference' they're labelled with is nothing other than an inferior status; and that they cannot be at ease with this difference unless they accept their own inferiority, which they can't shake off because – according to racism's essentialist thinking – it is indelibly inscribed on their bodies. Ultimately, they discover that there is a hidden clause: inclusion has a racial condition that they could never satisfy, because they aren't of the right race.

What can the people and groups caught in this kind of double bind do about it? What do you do when you are attacked for your appearance, your parents, and your origins: all the things for which you aren't responsible and cannot change? Well, you can either live in shame, or else revolt against this injustice. You can either kneel down and accept defeat, or else turn around and face your aggressors. Facing up to them means asserting what you are attacked for, refusing to be ashamed. And this is what French society terms 'communitarian' reactions, which supposedly deserve condemnation. Why? Because when the dominant assigned these identities to the dominated, they did so in order to make them accept their inferior status; and not so that the dominated could make use of these identities in order to rebuild their self-esteem destroyed by racism or sexism.

For a decade now the descendants of immigrants have been rejecting the idea that their origins are a source of shame; they assert an 'Arabness' and an Islam 'made in France', created as a response to exclusion. Some might call this 'identitarian', or a mark of pride, or anti-racism; but certainly it does not stand in contradiction with their rights and demands as citizens. If the dominant society sees this self-assertion as subversive, that's because it's a means by which the dominated resist internalizing an inferior status, and repair what Goffman called a 'damaged identity' (Goffman 1964). But the dominant society wants the dominated to hold onto a damaged identity; this being one of the conditions of perpetuating their exploitation.

The Franco-French thought that the descendants of immigrants would simply accept stepping into their parents' shoes: they were shocked when the children of immigrants took seriously the paperwork telling them they were French.

What is the role of gender in this caste system? After all, the hostility of this discourse is mainly directed against those perceived as the only subjects: men. Women are exempt from the worst stereotypes. The *beurettes* (female, 'second generation immigrants') are pleasant enough (Guénif-Souilamas 2000), unlike their brothers, the bad boys (or Arab boys – it's the same difference, as Nacira Guénif-Souilamas and Éric Macé (2004) tell us). That explains why they face an even more difficult dilemma than men do. Subjected to the double bind of integration, a test they cannot pass, women are also the target of a subliminal injunction. Indeed, these kindly *beurettes* are more pitied than blamed – that is, pitied for belonging to these men, these Arab fathers and Arab boys. And they're told to abandon them. Some obey, leaving their families and neighbourhoods, only to find themselves isolated. After all, here, too, Franco-French society imposes the same double bind we saw earlier: it seeks and finds in these women the difference – in their names, their facial features or their accents – that marks them as essential inferiority, their 'human stain'. So as Christelle Hamel (2003a) explains, these women are caught between the very real sexism of their own surroundings – a sexism exacerbated by counter-racism: that is, men taking pride in the machismo that they're reproached for – and the dominant society's desire to capture them from the men it still sees as its enemies. This was the context for the 'headscarf controversies' of 1989, 1994 (Gaspard and Khosrokhavar 1995) and 2003, this latter case ultimately culminating in the 'anti-veil law' (Bouamama 2004). We cannot understand these controversies, nor the reasons underlying the persecution of schoolchildren who posed no problem to their teachers, unless we understand the prominent role of gender in this caste system.

We've seen that colonial ideology characterizes Maghrebian, Arab and African men in terms of their relation to women; and the colonial strategy consists of condemning this culture as particularly sexist. At the same time, following a fine patriarchal logic, it tries to capture the women from these same backgrounds, symbolically, at least.

A good measure of this unspoken desire is the national joy whenever *beurettes* denounce Arab men, for example when gang rapes come to light. Collective rapes, which have always existed, have never captured public attention and we never hear them mentioned, any more than discussion of rape in general (Hamel 2003b). But when this is going on among the North Africans in the *banlieues*, all France pretends to have discovered a phenomenon that was hitherto unknown in the Hexagon.[2] And it exploits the differentness imposed on Arabs in order to crush in the womb any attempt to recognize and combat its own, purely autochthonous sexist barbarism. It uses circular reasoning to arrive at this conclusion: if they, who are different from us, are getting up to all this, then that's evidence enough that it isn't happening among our own kind. This sophism allows France to kill two birds with one stone: not only can it use it to condemn the 'others', but above all it can absolve itself of the sin now being 'exposed' (Delphy 2004).

Here I ought to speak of what I think are the reasons why the sight of a few headscarves has plunged France into what Emmanuel Terray has called 'political hysteria' (Terray 2004).

The colonized deserved to be colonized because they were uncivilized and had a barbarous culture based on a barbarous religion; and their treatment of their women was proof of this barbarism. The colonized women, the victims of their men – unlike civilized men, who only kill six of their women a month (at least) – were thus the colonizers' natural allies, if only they would rally to the cause. If they did, then the colonized men would be deprived of their greatest support, and it would also prove how barbaric their treatment of women was. This hope still exists among the French, who treat immigrants like colonial subjects and the children of the colonized as immigrants. In reality, the women are racialized just as much as the men: discriminated against and humiliated every day.

When women wearing the headscarf appeared, the French were shocked – politicians, journalists and secular activists repeated ad infinitum – because they are so attached to equality between men and women. One reader of the LDH (Human Rights League) bulletin even wrote that "the headscarf tears a hole in equality between the sexes". It was here that I first learned that women in France are men's equals. But enough pleasantries. I don't believe that the French are shocked by the absence of something that doesn't exist, and which they don't really want to exist. Yes, they were 'assaulted', as Chirac put it: the appearance of these women in headscarves upset their unspoken, irrational hopes.

Effectively, they refused to live with the descendants of Arabs, but also couldn't just drive them into the sea. My hypothesis is that faced with this unanswerable dilemma they hatched a plan: if they took these women, even taking them as their wives – as Emmanuel Todd (1997) predicted a decade ago – then given that women are nothing more than receptacles for men's semen, this 'race' would soon disappear. This plan – which in France is unconscious rather than explicit – has been the basis of government policies enacted in other racist countries. For example, in the 1950s Brazil had an explicit policy of encouraging mixed marriages in order to 'whiten' the population.

But the headscarf told the Franco-French that their dream of dividing the descendants of immigrants along gender lines was finished. These women would not reject their fathers, brothers and husbands. They did not believe in the image of the triumphant, emancipated *beurette*; they knew they were subject to the same racism as the men. If the headscarf provoked such strong, apparently disproportionate reactions, it was because it was itself such a strong message, a nightmare called 'the return of the repressed'.

Such were the boomerang effects of French society's blatant discrimination against these women. The headscarf tells this society: 'You have marginalized us and penned us in, you tell us we're different, well, look: now we are different.' The 'veiled' woman is the alien landing in our midst. But this alien does not only challenge the 'French integration model'. This alien causes such malaise because her mere presence suddenly makes us see so-called 'sexual liberation' for what it is: the obligation for every woman to be 'desirable' at each and every moment. And women wearing the headscarf contravene this obligation. As Samira Bellil remarked in an interview a few months before her death, some men's obsession with veiling us is only equalled by other men's obsession with stripping us naked. These two obsessions are two symmetrical forms of one and the same negation of women: one wants women to arouse men's desires all the time, while the other forbids them from doing so. But in both cases the reference point for women's thinking and bodies is men's desire. The headscarf unveils the fact that in our supposedly liberated epoch, a woman's body is still not hers and hers alone.

Moreover, this alien makes Islam visible. Which the Franco-French can't stand. Islam has only ever been tolerated in France on condition that it is discreet, preferably underground. And now these people are proud of it! There's something that defies sense here – the dominant common sense, anyway. We saw the same incredulous outraged reactions over gay pride.

Domination is based on tolerance, which is the opposite of acceptance: that is, it rests on the idea that the practices or the very existence – or both – of the dominated, of the gay and lesbian, of the Muslim, are bad. But we let them exist all the same, so long as they admit that they're in the wrong. And the proof that they admit it is that they're ashamed. And the proof that they're ashamed is that they hide. So when the dominated no longer hide, asserting that their existence or their practices are the equal of anyone else's, they are trashing the rules of the game, breaking the contract that allows them to exist in the shadow of the dominant. So these latter have no other choice but to pull them back into line, putting them back in their place and showing them who's boss. That's what France did with the headscarf law.

However, the headscarf is just one skirmish in the war against Arabs, Africans and Muslims. The local system of domination – France's caste system – is now compounded by its participation in a global project: the 'war on terror', which is in fact a war against the Arab and Muslim world. The partisans of the anti-headscarf law deftly linked the question of adolescents wearing the veil to the threat of al-Qaeda terrorism. French racism, without which these castes could not work, was thus strengthened by the myth of the dangers that the Muslim world posed. These attacks on the Arab and Muslim world are not new: for a long time Western essayists have been denouncing it as intrinsically incompatible with democracy, human rights, modernity, etc. In the 1970s, Bernard Lewis presented his theory of a clash of civilizations, though only with Samuel Huntington's version did it really 'take off' (Gresh 2004).

In continuity with its support for the State of Israel's policy of expansion, from the 1990s onward the United States launched a series of attacks: the first Gulf War, Afghanistan, Iraq again, and so on.

France did participate, whatever its assertions to the contrary, in this enterprise of destruction and large-scale massacres of civilians. And domestically it benefited from its rhetoric. After all, there were plenty of advantages to be had from creating a climate in France where every Arab is seen as a Muslim, every Muslim as a fundamentalist and every Arab as a potential terrorist. Indeed, when Arabs are accused of being the fifth column in an international plot, and when they are attacked all day long for supposedly planning to replace Western civil codes with sharia (Lepage 2004), it becomes almost impossible to recognize them as victims of racism. We can't treat them as a domestic enemy and at the same time carry out positive actions to their benefit. France thus has some more breathing space to not put an end to its caste system, for the moment at least.

Act III: repression

Thus the veil affair opened the third act of this French tragedy: after the first act (oppression) came the second act (rebellion); and the third act is the repression of this rebellion.

There is a striking parallel between this repression of protests against injustice in France and the United States' war without end after 9/11.

Never asking itself any questions about its own responsibilities and the wrongs it has itself perpetrated, the West everywhere reacts to protests against the injustice it causes by aggravating the situation. It rejects dialogue and negotiation, always instead choosing intimidation and exemplary punishment. However, we could have imagined the third act turning out differently, very differently. We could have hoped that France would regain control of its senses, recognizing its past and present wrongs against immigrants and their children, starting to redress these wrongs and deciding to eliminate racial discrimination; we could have hoped that it would finally get down to dismantling the patriarchal system rather than denying its existence; that it would put its own house in order rather than preaching to others; that it would stop setting women against the children of immigrants, and vice versa; in short, that it would finally adopt the path of equality, having already proclaimed it on the frontispieces of its town halls for some two hundred years. Can we still hope for or even imagine this happening? That's the key question. Even if the third act is off to a bad start, the play is still not over yet. The future will tell us if we are headed toward the consolidation of the caste system or its disappearance.

But this question will not be resolved on French territory alone; for it is connected to the US war against the Arab and Muslim world. And we shouldn't neglect the irrational or affective elements of France's little war against the headscarf, nor of America's big war: we are Westerners, and as Sophie Bessis (2003) tells us, the West's culture is a "culture of supremacy". This culture is reminiscent of the madness that the Greek gods inflicted on those they wanted to destroy. It is the origin of the double standards that the rest of the world criticizes the West for, and it is the reason why rather than righting this wrong the West stubbornly presses on, aggravating its own situation. The spiral of oppression, revolt and repression is constantly accelerating and taking on ever-larger dimensions.

Faced with this whirlwind, for the moment at least the oppressed's capacity to resist is weakened. One may fear that their patience is at an end, and that they will lose hope in the effectiveness of peaceful and legal protests when they see the barrier represented by the West's combination of immoderation, irresponsibility, arrogance and the desire to dominate – in short, its hubris – in its current relations with the rest of the world.

Notes

1 This chapter is extracted from *Separate and Dominate: Feminism and Racism after the War on Terror*. Translated by D. Broder. London: Verso, 2015.

2 Translator's note: *L'Hexagone* is metropolitan France, as distinct from the French Republic including its various non-European *départements* and territories.

References

Beaud, S. and M. Pialoux (2003) *Violences urbaines, violences sociales*. Paris: Fayard.

Bessis, S. (2003) *L'Occident et les autres*. Paris: La Découverte.

Bouamama, S. (1994) *Dix ans de marche des Beurs: Chronique d'un mouvement avorté*. Paris: Desclée de Brouwer.

Bouamama, S. (2004) *L'Affaire du foulard islamique: la production d'un racisme respectable*. Paris: Le Geai bleu.

Clancy-Smith, J. (1996) 'La femme arabe: Women and Sexuality in France's North African Empire' in *Women, the Family and Divorce Laws in Islamic History*. Syracuse, NY: Syracuse University Press.

Daniel, N. (1993) *Islam et Occident*. Paris: Éditions du Cerf.

Delphy, C. (1998) 'La transmission héréditaire' in *L'Ennemi principal*, Vol. I. Paris: Syllepse.

Delphy, C. (2004) 'Une affaire française' in C. Nordmann (ed.) *Le Foulard islamique en question*. Paris: Amsterdam.

Fanon, F. (1967) *A Dying Colonialism*. New York: Grove Press.

Gadant, M. (1995) *Le Nationalisme algérien et les femmes*. Paris: L'Harmattan.

Gaspard, F. and F. Khosrokhavar (1995) *Le Foulard et la République*. Paris: Éditions la Découverte.

Geisser, V. (2003) *La nouvelle islamophobie*. Paris: Éditions la Découverte.

Goffmann, E. (1964) *Stigma: Notes on the Management of Spoiled Identity*. Englewood Cliffs, NJ: Prentice-Hall.

Gresh, A. (2004) *L'Islam, la République et le monde*. Paris: Fayard.

Guénif-Souilamas, N. (2000) *Des beurettes*. Paris: Grasset.

Guénif-Souilamas, N. and E. Macé (2004) *Les Féministes et le garçon arabe*. Paris: L'Aube.

Hamel, C. (2003a) 'L'intrication des rapports sociaux de sexe, de "race", d'âge et de classe: ses effets sur la gestion des risques d'infection par le VIH chez les Français descendant de migrants du Maghreb'. Thesis, EHESS, Paris.

Hamel, C. (2003b) '"Faire tourner les meufs": les viols collectifs dans les discours des médias et des agresseurs', *Gradiva* 33: 85–92.

Khosrokhavar, F. (1997) *L'Islam des jeunes*. Paris: Flammarion.

Lepage, C. (2004) 'Retrouver les valeurs républicaines', ResPublica.org.uk.

Simon, P. (1997) 'La statistique des origines: l'ethnicité et la "race" dans les recensements aux États-Unis, Canada et Grande-Bretagne', *Sociétés Contemporaines* 26: 11–44.

Terray, E. (2004) 'Une hystérie politique' in C. Nordmann (ed.) *Le Foulard islamique en question*. Paris: Amsterdam.

Tissot, S. (2004) 'Le "repli communautaire": un concept policier. Analyse d'un rapport des Renseignements généraux sur les "quartiers sensibles"', LMSI.net, 29 October. http://lmsi.net/Le-repli-communautaire-un-concept.

Todd, E. (1997) *Le Destin des immigrés*. Paris: Seuil.

Tribalat, M. (1995) *Faire France. Une enquête sur les immigrés et leurs enfants*. Paris: La Découverte.

Tripier, M. (1999) 'De l'enjeu des statistiques "ethniques"', *Hommes et Migrations* 1219: 27–31.

18 | THE IDEOLOGY OF THE HOLY REPUBLIC AS PART OF THE COLONIAL COUNTER-REVOLUTION

Selim Nadi

But what, concretely, is this uncriticized ideology if not simply the 'familiar', 'well known', transparent myths in which a society or an age can recognize itself (but not know itself), the mirror it looks into for self-recognition, precisely the mirror it must break if it is to know itself? What is the ideology of a society or a period if it is not that society's or period's consciousness of itself, that is, an immediate material which spontaneously implies, looks for and naturally finds its forms in the image of a consciousness of self-living the totality of its world in the transparency of its own myths? (Louis Althusser – 'The "Piccolo Teatro": Bertolazzi and Brecht Notes on a Materialist Theatre')

The aim of this chapter is to examine the role Republicanism plays as an largely uncriticised ideology in the French colonial counter-revolution. Republicanism is a concept widely used across the French political spectrum: from the far right to some sections of the radical left. However, this chapter does not seek to offer a 'real progressive Republicanism' in opposition to a 'false reactionary' one, but rather aims at analysing the way in which Republicanism pre-empts any possibility of a materialistic analysis of racism *as a system*. Hence, a materialistic anti-racism must leave the 'Republicanist political sphere' in order to build an anti-racism based on what French society really is, and not on a Republican mythology widely used in order to shut down any analysis of social antagonisms – and thus, of racial antagonisms.

In his classic work 'Ideology and Ideological State Apparatuses' (1971), Louis Althusser stressed the difference between state power (which is the objective of the political struggle) and state apparatuses. For Althusser, the evolution of state power does not necessitate an evolution in state apparatuses:

We know that the State Apparatus may survive, as is proved by bourgeois 'revolutions' in nineteenth-century France (1830, 1848), by coups d'état (2 December, May 1958), by collapses of the State (the fall of the Empire in 1870, of the Third Republic in 1940), or by the political rise of the petty bourgeoisie (1890–95 in France), etc., without the State Apparatus being affected or modified: it may survive political events which affect the possession of State power. (Althusser 1971: 141)

But within the state apparatuses, Althusser accentuates the difference between repressive state apparatuses and ideological ones. Of course, the French philosopher does not describe repression only through physical violence, recognising that repression can also be administrative. According to Althusser, the main difference between repressive state apparatuses (RSAs) and ideological state apparatuses (ISAs) is that the first subsist mainly in the public sphere, with the latter part of the private sphere (political parties, trade unions, churches, schools, etc.). But, how can a private institution play a role in state ideology? Quoting Gramsci, he stresses the fact that this distinction between the 'public' and the 'private' is primarily a distinction "internal to the bourgeois law":

It is unimportant whether the institutions in which they are realized are 'public' or 'private'. What matters is how they function. Private institutions can perfectly well 'function' as Ideological State Apparatuses. A reasonably thorough analysis of any one of the ISAs proves it. (Althusser 1971: 145)

In France, the values linked to Republicanism are embodied in almost all institutions and in particular in the educational system. As Ian Birchall pointed out regarding *laïcité* (one of the so called 'values' of French Republicanism):

the significance of *laïcité* is that it is not just a 'value' washing around inside people's skulls; it has a very concrete material embodiment in the French educational system. And since in France today around a quarter of the population (24.7%) are involved in the education system, either as employees or as students, it is central to the social and economic structures of the French nation. (Birchall 2015)

Indeed, *laïcité* is probably the most abstract and empty value within the Republican framework – becoming a kind of secular religion, used from the far right (even if, historically, the right and the far right were opposed to the 1905 law on the separation of the church and state) to some parts of the radical left – but given reality through its institutional embodiment. *Laïcité* today is often quoted as a justification for excluding girls wearing the veil from public schools or forcing Muslim pupils to eat pork, but it plays a larger role in the hegemony and security of the French state. In the case of the colonial counter-revolution, the ideological state apparatus operates hand in hand with the repressive one to exclude Muslim people as racialised outsiders.

After the *Charlie Hebdo* attacks, this collaboration between the apparatuses became more obvious; any non-white child as young as eight *who was not Charlie* could be sent by their own school to the police station, as was the case for Ahmed in Nice.[1] Not being *Charlie* could lead to arrests and unemployment, under charges of being an 'apologist for terrorism' or the implication of every single person who was not *Charlie*.[2] Thus, Arab children who refused to remain silent during the official minute's silence or who supported the attacks did not just get in trouble in their schools, but were often sent to the police station. State racism has a very strong class basis, exemplified in the fact that the only families who can manage school exclusion and discrimination are those whose children can go home for lunch or who can afford a private school. Thus one of the many contradictions of French Republicanism is that it asks non-white people – even if they are French, for as long as they are not from a white Christian background they need to prove that they can be part of the French Republic – to 'integrate' themselves, but at the same time the French state creates the conditions of their exclusion from the 'Republican ideal'. This contradiction was highlighted by the political consequences of the *Charlie Hebdo* attack.

As we have seen, Republicanism displaces the political analysis of racism onto the terrain of 'moral values', which sees racism as something happening in the sphere of ideas. This focus on abstract values obscures the reality of social relations. These 'values' are not just part of the Republican rhetoric; they have an embodiment in institutions – as we have seen – and more broadly in the social and political system. In the second chapter of his book *La contre-révolution coloniale en France* – entitled 'The Republic is a Liar' (*'La République est une menteuse'*) – Sadri Khiari writes that:

The Republican pact 'as it really exists' is produced by the combination of institutional, political and ideological State devices that create 'consent' (Gramsci), which 'morally' bind those who are defined as citizens. (Khiari 2009: 45)

The conclusion of this idea is that Republicanism is both produced and used by the state, especially in times of political or economic crisis. Thus, it was not particularly surprising that in the days after the *Charlie Hebdo* attacks the dominant political rhetoric was full of prayer for the holy ideology: the Republic. However, criticism of the mainstream political uses of 'Republicanism' quickly began to appear – mainly through the work of academics such as Abdellali Hajjat (see Hajjat 2013) and Marwan Mohammed, or by left-wing intellectuals including Jacques Rancière and Alain Badiou. In France, the concept of 'Republicanism' is often mobilised in order to justify racism, and racism is thus justified as a result of Republican ideas. But if racism is obviously related to Republicanism in France, one cannot explain French racism only through this concept. Criticising 'ideological content' – like Republicanism – is not enough if one wants to produce a materialist analysis of racism and thus develop a consequent political strategy. Rather, the ideological forms – Republicanism, Universalism, *laïcité*, etc. – used by the French state in order to legitimise its racism are part of the wider strategy of the colonial counter-revolution, in that the denunciation of ideological content, even if a necessary step of political analysis, does not provide a convincing explanation of the material basis of racism.

Following Sadri Khiari, we could define racism as the "ideological modality of the race struggle" (Khiari 2009: 21). Hence, it is necessary to focus on the link between this 'ideological modality' and the material structure which produces the social race struggle. Thus, in order to combat postcolonial racism, especially after the *Charlie Hebdo* attacks, it is necessary to go further than a 'simple' critique of Republicanism. Hence, the role Republicanism has played in France should be integrated into the material roots of French racism. The aim of this chapter is to try to demonstrate how Republicanism works as an ideology that is strongly linked to state racism in France, but which also secures the interests of the ruling class and plays an important role in the defeat of the French working class.

Racism is not a 'magical phenomenon'

In France, racism has too often been analysed as either 'a bad idea' or as a simple obstacle against the unity of workers, as a kind of false consciousness. Thus, it has eluded explanation; it has been understood as a kind of magical phenomenon. The only proposed solution – by a certain 'moralistic left' – was to influence the consciousness of the people, especially through education. This understanding of racism through a moral lens began to be hegemonic in France in the 1980s, after the abandonment of Socialist Party President François Mitterrand's socialistic promises and the turn to budgetary rigour, which dealt a blow to the radical left. The decline of Marxist paradigms opened space for the ideologies of 'human rights' and 'societal progress' to become dominant in the French political field. The right in general dominated politically, while the far-right Front National achieved its first electoral successes, leading many on the left to start to fear a fascist backlash in France. For many activists, however, moral anti-racism became the weapon of anti-fascism; a good example of this kind of anti-racism is the organisation S.O.S. Racism, which condemns racism from an abstract point of view, seeing it as an individual intolerance, without analysing its social and political core. Thus, it is this abstract vision of racism that became hegemonic in France during the 1990s.

Since the late 2000s, the critique of radical left and anti-racist activists such as the Mouvement des Indigènes de la République (see Lentin's chapter) has been bolstered by some activists or theorists from the Ligue communiste révolutionnaire (LCR)/Nouveau parti anticapitaliste (NPA) and Ensemble – Mouvement pour Alternative de Gauche, Ecologique et Solidaire distancing themselves from this Republican/moral anti-racism and openly criticising the French tradition of Republicanism – especially regarding its mobilisation during French colonisation. This critical stance has been a very important step in the fight against racism. However, today it appears that anti-racist activists are not willing to go further than maintaining a simple criticism of Republican discourse, which, from a methodological point of view, replicates the problem with the moral anti-racism of the 1980s and the 1990s. That is, by approaching Republicanism as belonging to the realm of 'ideas', rather than as an ideology proper with material roots, it fails to produce an efficient political strategy beyond the focus on the fight against ideas and rhetoric.

This analysis of Republicanism is obviously linked to the French left's frequent problem with the concept of 'race'. Before developing this point, it should be noted that the concept has garnered interest of late in the French leftist political field, being used not only by radical anti-racist activists and/or theorists such as Sadri Khiari, but also in some feminist groups and academic publications, such as Elsa Dorlin's work (Dorlin 2006), and, more recently, in the work of Matthieu Renault, who published the first French intellectual biography of C. L. R. James (Renault 2016). However, the term has often remained depoliticised, an abstract concept that is used without consideration of its effects in reality. Speaking about 'race' in the singular has no political sense, as racism is the ideological reflection of the balance of forces between two racial 'poles'. Thus, racism is a political and social relationship and not an abstract sociological object or a fixed category. The inability to grasp what racism is and how Republicanism works through it is part of the wider problem in France with abstract thinking across the whole political sphere, including by some leftist activists and organisations. It is precisely that ideology of abstraction – especially, but not only, through Republicanism – that the colonial counter-revolution uses in order to secure its hegemony. It is therefore necessary to work on the building of a real counter-hegemonic political force, something that a large part of the French left fails to do.

The conceptual and strategic blind spots in the French left

Traditionally, the left has tried to position itself on the side of the oppressed and exploited. However, French Republicanism has played a key part in perverting such goals under a veneer of progressivism. One good example is a comparison of UK Labour leader Jeremy Corbyn and Front de Gauche presidential candidate Jean-Luc Mélenchon. Both Corbyn and Mélenchon are contemporary faces of left reformism. Yet the difference between them is striking when one looks at their political positions regarding Islamophobia. While Corbyn condemned the "general [Islamophobic] narrative in our society and in our media",[3] Mélenchon blamed Muslim women who wore the veil for being responsible for their own exclusion and discrimination. Despite an apparent evolution in his approach to Islamophobia through more recent acknowledgements of the racism faced by Muslim people in France, Mélenchon has continued to exhibit the racial blindness central to the Republican framework.

When Nadine Morano – a member of the conservative party Les Républicains – declared publicly that "France is a country of white race" ("*La France est un pays de race blanche*"), Mélenchon forcefully condemned her words, but based his rebuttal on skewed reasoning, stating that "not all French people are white, and in any case, race does not exist" (Mélenchon 2015a). Using the idea that the French Republic is 'indivisible', that it cannot be divided by class or race, Mélenchon made use of the racist framework promoted by the Republican ideology, one that holds much ground within part of the left in France. This stance may have originated from his background as an activist in the student movement in 1968 and his participation in a Trotskyist sect (the *lambertistes*), while Corbyn campaigned for Irish unification and against apartheid in South Africa. Of course, this does not mean in any way that the students' or workers' movements should not play a role in the fight against racism, but that anti-racist and decolonial struggles were never really political priorities for the French left that Mélenchon stands for.

It was thus not surprising that, after the attacks against *Charlie Hebdo*, Mélenchon called for a "mass popular Republican response" (Mélenchon 2015b) to terrorism. He also stressed, with a French flag flying in the background, that the victims of such events are always those "most persistent activists of *laïcité*" (ibid.). In his use of Republicanism and *laïcité*, Mélenchon acted as a social-chauvinistic political leader. While this does not make him a conservative or extreme right politician, it demonstrates the inability of the social-democratic left (and of some parts of the radical left) in France to grasp the political and social roots of racism, and the key role Republicanism plays to secure it. In his famous book on Europe and the French Revolution, the historian Albert Sorel (1842–1906) – neither a radical nor a leftist – wrote that French Republicans identify humanity with their own homeland, and their own national cause with the cause of every nation. As such, they confuse "the emancipation of humanity with the greatness of the Republic" (Sorel quoted in Deutscher 1953: 17). Therefore, Republicanism is not an abstract ideological framework but deeply rooted in the French tradition of chauvinism and, of course, colonialism.

Terrorist attacks like those against *Charlie Hebdo* or the horrific attacks in Paris on 13 November 2015 can therefore be used by the French state to articulate more explicitly the ISA and RSA. Throughout French history, there have been six instances of a state of emergency: three times during the Algerian Revolution (1955, 1958 and 1961), during political unrest in the 'overseas territory' of New Caledonia (1984), when French working-class suburbs were rioting (2005), and after the attacks in Paris (2015). Colonial subjects have thus always been the targets and victims of the state of emergency (*état d'urgence*), and the present situation is no exception. While the left – from the reformist left of the Front de Gauche to the radical left of the NPA and Lutte Ouvrière – always condemns the use of such methods, convincing anti-racist strategies have so far failed to be developed in tandem. A successful anti-racist strategy would not only see the left condemn the use of a state of emergency, but also make a break from French Republicanism as it is inherently linked to colonial legacies. Such a strategy must be at the core of a left-wing approach to social change, as it is an essential part of anti-capitalist and anti-imperialist struggles.

Indeed, the 'classical' anti-imperialism of the radical left – which considers imperialism as "the export of capital by monopoly firms, the coalescence of industry and banking in the form of 'finance capital', the competition between monopoly firms and their respective States, and the turn to Colonialism and warfare by European powers" (Serfati 2015) – must be linked to French racism. However, analysing imperialism through monopoly capital and competition between European nations, while essential, does not grasp the specificity of this French phenomenon. As Giovanni Arrighi wrote in *The Geometry of Imperialism*, Lenin "first asserts that the definition of imperialism must be historically determinate if it is not to fall into the 'Greater Rome and Greater Britain' type of banality" (Arrighi 1983). It is therefore obvious that one cannot analyse French imperialism in the 1920s, the 1960s and today in the same way. An understanding of Lenin's analysis should also remind the reader not to confuse imperialism with colonialism, but, as Claude Serfati wrote:

> In the case of France, only an extreme form of economic reductionism and a deep misunderstanding of the role of Africa ... in the history of French capitalism would deny the importance of colonies in French imperialism. (Serfati 2015)

Serfati stressed several aspects of French colonialism. First, a moral project of civilising the colonies, which signifies a whole ideology underlying French colonialism and thus motivates and justifies French expansionism. Serfati also outlined the political factors, such as preventing other colonial powers from accruing more territory, and also that:

> After 1870, the French military viewed colonial conquest in a positive light after Germany seized Alsace and Lorraine and the Paris Commune challenged the bourgeoisie's power. In this context, the outward migration of people from Alsace and Lorraine, especially to the Maghreb, spurred French colonialism as a means of exporting and managing social unrest at home, a process similar to the British colonisation of the Americas. (Serfati 2015)

Here, I mainly focus on the ideology that underlies French colonialism and, thus, plays a major role in French imperialism and the Republican construction of colonial subjects. The 'civilising mission' of the French state emerged from the Republican framework through which French expansionism itself developed. French colonialism found its support in two sources: a conservative and a humanist one. Conservative supporters of colonialism believed that people from colonised areas should be transformed into colonised subjects. Hence, for conservatives, people from colonised areas should be treated as inferior to white colonisers. This was clear in Ernest Renan's famous 1871 *La réforme intellectuelle et morale*, where he developed the idea that France's aim was not to bring equality but to impose its domination so that inequality would become a social law in colonised countries. In contrast, as the historian Francis Arzalier (2007) wrote, French colonialism was often presented by part of the left as an exception within European colonial projects precisely because of its Republican 'humanism'. Whereas Jules Ferry justified colonialism by the right of 'superior races' over 'inferior races', Jean Jaurès condemned the excesses of colonialism, but justified the French colonial project through the 'civilising mission' of the Third Republic. This colonial ideology became widespread in schools and the press, with Jules Ferry playing a key part in the 'democratisation' of the school system. Arzalier wrote that, in 1932, during a conference in Vichy entitled 'Colonialism and Human Rights', the sociologist Albert Bayet had declared that colonialism should be purified if one wanted it to become beneficial, and that modern France represented an ideal that should be spread across the world (Arzalier 2007). Such discourses were not just rhetorical battles but underpinned the French regimes in Africa and Asia. Thus, if French Republican idealism was not real, its effects on colonised subjects were very much so.

Today's French imperialism and neo-colonialism are different from their manifestations in the first half of the twentieth century, but it is important to grasp the ongoing link between imperialism and French racism. The '*Union sacrée*' desired by French President François Hollande was not just an internal union, but also an alliance between Western countries in order to fight against the enemy from both the inside and outside. The enemy from the outside is easy to define: Daesh is the main target, and civilian casualties from the coalition bombing campaigns across the Middle East are considered a price necessary to pay to protect the Republic. The 'enemy from the inside' is more difficult to grasp. With Daesh claiming to be an international organisation with 'soldiers' spread across the globe, including France, every Arab or Black becomes the potential suspect, at least on an ideological level, of terrorist sympathy. As it does against the enemy from the outside, the French state uses both the ideological and repressive state apparatus against this 'fifth column'. It is therefore not enough for an Arab or Black person in France not to pledge allegiance to Daesh; one must pledge allegiance to the Republic if one hopes to be cleared of suspicion. Thus, a football player who does not sing the *Marseillaise*, an eight-year-old child who is not Charlie, anti-racist organisations that point to the rise of Islamophobia, all become part of this fifth column – the enemy from within – as they distance themselves from the Republican framework by denouncing its very links to racism in France. Republicanism is one of the key producers of the French 'imagined community' (Anderson 1983) and Republicanism is used to give this nation, particularly when on a 'war footing', a certain coherence by excluding those who do not assume its values. As Neal Wood writes, "the coercive power of the State is not enough to maintain the solidarity, allegiance, and support of citizens" (Wood 2002: 23). In the French case, this is the role played by Republicanism, by creating a new kind of enemy.

To conclude, one can say that the expression of Republicanism after the *Charlie Hebdo* attacks and those of 13 November shows the aggressive face of the French state, but also – in a very obvious way – the role played by Republican ideology in state racism in France. Yet it would be a mistake to see Republicanism only through the role it played after the *Charlie Hebdo* events or as a producer of state racism. Republicanism is a strong ideology in France, and it can be found across the political spectrum, from the far right to some factions of the far left. Above all, it is an ideology that has played an important role in the defeat of the French working class in its struggles since the 1980s, as well as the growing proletarianisation of Muslim people in France. The positioning of non-white people in the relations of production (or their exclusion from such relations) is, in France, largely justified by Republicanism. A good example of this is the witch hunt that took place in the aftermath of the *Charlie Hebdo* and 13 November attacks, during which many people lost their jobs. Anecdotally, my position as a history teacher in a high school, in Alsace, during the attacks on *Charlie Hebdo*, was threatened when I did not take the time to speak about the events to my students and thus appeared suspicious to some parents (and especially to a local right-wing politician).

This kind of threat to the jobs or private lives of French colonial subjects is justified by Republicanism, by a political discourse of non-compatibility of some ideas, clothes, diets and so forth with the French Republic – a discourse exemplified by the ridiculous 'burkini debate' and municipal bans in the summer of 2016. Hence, one of the strengths of Republicanism is that it does not look like an ideology, which, according to Althusser, is one of the main defining characteristics of an ideology:

> what ... seems to take place outside ideology (to be precise, in the street), in reality takes place in ideology. What really takes place in ideology seems therefore to take place outside it. That is why those who are in ideology believe themselves by definition outside ideology: one of the effects of ideology is the practical denegation of the ideological character of ideology by ideology. (Althusser 1971: 176)

At the very beginning of his book *The Ideologies of Theory*, Fredric Jameson notes that:

> Ideology is the mediatory concept par excellence, bridging gaps between the individual and the social, between fantasy and cognition, between economics and aesthetics, objectivity and the subject, reason and the unconscious, the private and the public. This is to say that ideology is not an achieved concept at all, but rather a problematic, itself subject to profound historical change and upheaval on both slopes of its mediatory function. (Jameson 2008: ix)

One could easily define Republicanism as a 'total ideology', permeating every aspect of society and of individual life. After the terrorist attacks in France, the most visible part of this ideology became explicit and was criticised by a small part of the political sphere, such as Nouveau Parti Anticapitaliste or some members of the Green Party, for example. Yet the more insidious part of the ideology used by the state and the ruling class to justify everyday racism and secure their hegemony has remained unchallenged. Indeed, Republicanism is needed by the French state in order to enforce the idea of its legitimacy and to give more and more power to its repressive state apparatuses, in particular the police, who began by killing non-white people and who now participate in the repression – and even killing, as in the case of the ecologist and activist Rémi Fraisse – of social movements.

An affinity with Republicanism is also widespread among the working class, with non-white people or associations, and in popular culture. One should not forget that a subject can share an ideology even if this ideology is part of the repression of this subject. Thus, the first French President to promote non-white ministers was Nicolas Sarkozy, in using Fadela Amara (former member of the racist and anti-feminist organisation 'Ni putes, ni soumises') and Rachida Dati in order to legitimate the racist policies of his successive government. This is another aspect of racism that should push us not to forget the material roots of ideology, and that criticising Republicanism as a discourse is not enough if one wants an efficient anti-racist grass-roots strategy in order to pass from the clouds to the resistance. Today, Republican ideologists are the monks of the bourgeois state. But they are monks playing a crucial role in the reproduction of the relations of production in France as well as in the colonial counter-revolution. Thus, our role, as anti-racist activists, should be to leave the monastery of 'pure' ideological critique in order to work on a concrete analysis of the concrete situation in which we are living.

Notes

1 See 'French Police Question 8-year-old on Suspicion of "Defending Terrorism"', *The Electronic Intifada*, 28 January 2015. https://electronicintifada.net/blogs/ali-abunimah/french-police-question-8-year-old-suspicion-defending-terrorism.

2 See, for example, '"Non, je ne suis pas Charlie": là où s'arrête la liberté d'expression', France 3 Corse, 16 January 2015. http://france3-regions.francetvinfo.fr/corse/2015/01/16/non-je-ne-suis-pas-charlie-la-ou-s-

arrete-la-liberte-d-expression-634010.
html.

3 See Corbyn's 2014 parliamentary
question on Islamophobia. http://

jeremycorbyn.org.uk/articles/jeremy-
corbyn-prime-ministers-questions/
(accessed July 2016).

References

Althusser, L. (1971) 'Ideology and
Ideological State Apparatuses (Notes
towards an Investigation)' in L.
Althusser, *Lenin and Philosophy and
Other Essays*. New York and London:
Monthly Review Press.

Anderson, B. (1983) *Imagined
Communities: Reflections on the
Origin and Spread of Nationalism*.
London: Verso.

Arrighi, G. (1983) *The Geometry of
Imperialism*. London: Verso.

Arzalier, F. (2007) 'Colonialisme et
impérialisme: "L'exception française"
ou le mythe humaniste' in G.
Labica, F. Arzalier, O. Le Cour
Grandmaison, P. Tevanian and S.
Bouamama (2007) *Une mauvaise
décolonisation. La France: de
l'Empire aux émeutes des quartiers
populaires*. Pantin and Naples: Le
Temps des Cerises/La Città del Sole,
pp. 15–43.

Birchall, I. (2015) 'From the Schoolroom
to the Trenches: Laïcité and its
Critics'. Paper given at the London
Historical Materialism Conference,
November. http://grimanddim.
org/historical-writings/2015-from-
the-schoolroom-to-the-trenches/
(accessed September 2016).

Deutscher, I. (1953) *Stalin*. Paris:
Gallimard.

Dorlin, E. (2006) *La matrice de la race*.
Paris: La Découverte.

Hajjat, A. (2013) *La Marche pour l'égalité
et contre le racism*. Paris: Éditions
Amsterdam.

Jameson, F. (2008) *The Ideologies of
Theory*. London and New York: Verso.

Khiari, S. (2009) *La contre-révolution
coloniale en France. De de Gaulle à
Sarkozy*. Paris: La Fabrique.

Mélenchon, J. L. (2015a) 'La France est une
nation universaliste – Réaction aux
propos de Nadine Morano', October.
http://melenchon.fr/2015/10/02/la-
france-est-une-nation-universaliste-
reaction-aux-propos-de-nadine-
morano/ (accessed June 2016).

Mélenchon, J. L. (2015b) 'Charlie Hebdo:
Conférence de presse', January.
www.alexis-corbiere.com/index.
php/post/2015/01/08/Charlie-Hebdo-
%3A-Conf%C3%A9rence-de-presse-
de-Jean-Luc-M%C3%A9lenchon
(accessed June 2016).

Renault, M. (2016) *C. L. R. James. La vie
révolutionnaire d'un "Platon noir"*.
Paris: La Découverte.

Serfati, C. (2015) 'Imperialism in Context.
The Case of France', *Historical
Materialism* 23 (2): 52–93.

Wood, N. (2002) *Reflections on Political
Theory. A Voice of Reason from the
Past*. New York: Palgrave.

ABOUT THE CONTRIBUTORS

Valérie Amiraux is Professor of Sociology at the Université de Montréal and Canada Research Chair in Religious Pluralism and Ethnicity.

Carolina Sanchez Boe is a post-doctoral researcher at SERR, Aalborg University, and teaches sociology at Université Paris V and at Columbia University Global Center in Paris. Her current research project compares the measures taken in Denmark and France to define and counter the problem of 'prison radicalisation' in the aftermath of the Paris and Copenhagen attacks. She is the author of *The Undeported: The Making of a Floating Population of Exiles in France and Europe* (forthcoming).

Simon Dawes is Maître de Conférences at the Université de Versailles Saint-Quentin-en-Yvelines (UVSQ), France. He teaches courses on cultural industries and the UK, and writes about media theory, regulation and history. He is the author of *British Broadcasting and the Public–Private Dichotomy: Neoliberalism, Citizenship and the Public Sphere* (forthcoming).

Nicholas De Genova (www.nicholasdegenova.com) has held academic appointments at King's College London, Goldsmiths, Columbia and Stanford, as well as visiting research positions at the universities of Chicago, Amsterdam, Bern and Warwick. He is the author of *Working the Boundaries: Race, Space, and 'Illegality' in Mexican Chicago* (2005), co-author of *Latino Crossings: Mexicans, Puerto Ricans, and the Politics of Race and Citizenship* (2003), editor of *Racial Transformations: Latinos and Asians Remaking the United States* (2006), and co-editor of *The Deportation Regime: Sovereignty, Space, and the Freedom of Movement* (2010) and *The Borders of 'Europe': Autonomy of Migration, Tactics of Bordering* (2017).

Christine Delphy is a sociologist, feminist, writer and theorist, a co-founder of the Mouvement de Libération des Femmes in France, and of the journal *Nouvelles Questions Féministes* (with Simone de Beauvoir). Among her many books is *Separate and Dominate: Feminism and Racism after the War on Terror* (2015).

Arber Fetiu is a doctoral student in the Department of Sociology, Université de Montréal.

Des Freedman is Professor of Media and Communications at Goldsmiths, University of London. He is the author of *The Contradiction of Media Power* (2014), *The Politics of Media Power* (2008) and *Misunderstanding the Internet* (with James Curran and Natalie Fenton, 2nd edition, 2016), and he has edited several books including *Media and Terrorism: Global Perspectives* (2012) and *War and the Media: Reporting Conflict 24/7* (2003) (both with Daya Thussu). He is the former chair of the Media Reform Coalition and was project lead for the recent Inquiry into the Future of Public Service Television.

Bill Grantham is Visiting Professor of Media Law and Policy at the Institute for Media and Creative Industries at Loughborough University London and a partner in the law firm Rufus-Isaacs, Acland & Grantham, LLP of Beverly Hills, California, USA. He has been a sporadic reader of *Charlie Hebdo* since the 1970s, at which he occasionally laughs out loud, but his native squeamishness means he usually prefers the staider, more square *Le Canard Enchaîné*, to which he has a subscription.

Ghassan Hage is the inaugural Future Generation Professor of Anthropology and Social Theory at the University of Melbourne. His most recent books are *Alter-Politics: Critical Anthropology and the Radical Imagination* (2015) and *Is Racism an Environmental Threat?* (2017).

Abdellali Hajjat is Assistant Professor of Political Science at the University of Paris Nanterre, and researcher at the Institute for Political Social Sciences. His books include *Islamophobia: How the French Elites Forged the 'Muslim Problem'* (with Marwan Mohammed, 2013), *The March for Equality and Against Racism* (2013) and *The Boundaries of 'National Identity': The Injunction to Assimilate in Metropolitan and Colonial France* (2012).

Gholam Khiabany teaches in the Department of Media and Communications at Goldsmiths, University of London.

Arun Kundnani is a scholar-in-residence at the Schomburg Center for Research in Black Culture at the New York Public Library and a former editor of the journal *Race & Class*. He is the author of *The Muslims are Coming! Islamophobia, Extremism, and the Domestic War on Terror* (2014) and *The End of Tolerance: Racism in 21st Century Britain* (2007).

Alana Lentin is Associate Professor in Cultural and Social Analysis at the University of Western Sydney, and in 2017 the visiting Hans Speier Professor at the New School for Social Research. Her publications include *The Crises of Multiculturalism: Racism in a Digital Age* (with Gavan Titley, 2011), *Racism and Anti-racism in Europe* (2004) and *Racism* (2008).

Philippe Marlière is Professor of French and European Politics at University College London. He was educated in France and was awarded a PhD in Social and Political Sciences at the European University Institute (Florence) in 2000. He was a researcher for the Centre de la Recherche Scientifique (CNRS) in France between 1989 and 1994. He is the author of multiple publications on European social democracy and Islamophobia in France, and is currently writing a book on identity politics and the Republican ideology in France today.

Toby Miller (www.tobymiller.org) is Emeritus Distinguished Professor, University of California, Riverside; Sir Walter Murdoch Professor of Cultural Policy Studies, Murdoch University; *Profesor Invitado*, Escuela de Comunicación Social, Universidad del Norte; Professor of Journalism, Media and Cultural Studies, Cardiff University/Prifysgol Caerdydd; and Director of the Institute for Media and Creative Industries, Loughborough University London. His most recent volumes are *The Sage Companion to Television Studies* (with M. Alvarado, M. Buonanno and H. Gray, 2015), *The Routledge Companion to Global Popular Culture* (editor, 2015), *Greening the Media* (with R. Maxwell, 2012) and *Blow Up the Humanities* (2012).

Aurélien Mondon is a Senior Lecturer in French and Comparative Politics at the University of Bath. His first monograph, *A Populist Hegemony?:The Mainstreaming of the Extreme Right in France and Australia*, was published in 2013. He is a regular contributor to the mainstream media and has written for CNN, *Newsweek*, openDemocracy and the *Independent*, amongst others.

Anne Mulhall teaches queer, gender and feminist issues in literature, culture and theory in the School of English, Drama and Film at University

College Dublin, where she also co-directs the UCD Centre for Gender, Feminisms and Sexualities.

Selim Nadi is a French PhD candidate at the Centre for History at Sciences Po Paris and at the University of Bielefeld. He is a regular contributor to the French journal *ContreTemps* (www.contretemps.eu/) and a member of the board of the French marxist online journal *Période* (http://revueperiode.net/). He is also an anti-racist activist and a member of the Parti des Indigènes de la République.

Annabelle Sreberny is Emeritus Professor of the Centre for Media Studies at SOAS, University of London. She was President of IAMCR from 2008 to 2012 and the first elected Director of the Centre for Iranian Studies, SOAS, 2010–11. For almost forty years, her work on Iran has examined the nexus of politics and communications, including *Small Media, Big Revolution* (1994), *Blogistan* (with Gholam Khiabany, 2010), *Cultural Revolution in Iran* (2013) and *Persian Service* (2014).

Gavan Titley is a Senior Lecturer in Media Studies in Maynooth University, and a Docent in the Swedish School of Social Science, Helsinki University. He is the author of *The Crises of Multiculturalism: Racism in a Neoliberal Age* (with Alana Lentin, 2011) and *Racism and Media* (forthcoming, 2018) and his most recent edited book is *National Conversations? Public Service Media and Cultural Diversity* (2013). He is a co-editor of the book series *Challenging Migration Studies*.

Markha Valenta is an interdisciplinary scholar in the Netherlands, working at the interstices of historical anthropology, geopolitics, and political philosophy. Core themes include the globalisation of diversity politics, religion, urbanity and agonistic democracy. Valenta lives in Amsterdam, teaches in Nijmegen and is a regular participant in Dutch public debates.

Aaron Winter is Senior Lecturer in Criminology at the University of East London. He is co-editor of *Discourses and Practices of Terrorism: Interrogating Terror* (2010) and *Researching the Far Right: Theory, Method and Practice* (forthcoming), and a contributor to *Extremism in America* (2013) and the *Handbook of Terrorism and Counterterrorism* (forthcoming).

INDEX